THE LIFE OF
J. A. ALEXANDER

PROFESSOR IN THE THEOLOGICAL SEMINARY AT PRINCETON, NEW JERSEY

by Henry Carrington Alexander

Volume 1

AUDUBON PRESS
2601 Audubon Drive
P.O. Box 8055
Laurel, MS 39441-8000 USA

Orders: 800-405-3788
Inquiries: 601-649-8572
Voice: 601-649-8570 / Fax: 601-649-8571
E-mail: buybooks@audubonpress.com
Web Page: www.audubonpress.com

© 2008 Audubon Press edition
All rights reserved.
Printed in the United States
Cover design by Crisp Graphics

ISBN # 978-09820731-1-7

Original Publication:

In Two Volumes

Volume 1

New York:
Charles Scribner & Co., 124 Grand Street
1870

PREFACE.

I SHALL make no apology for writing the LIFE OF JOSEPH ADDISON ALEXANDER. If the facts recorded in these volumes be not a sufficient justification, there could be no other. Why the duty has been devolved on his nephew rather than upon some one else, is a question which need not be discussed here. It is enough to say that the work was undertaken not at his own instance but in compliance with the wishes of the surviving members of the family.

The task, though a grateful, has been an arduous one. The thing aimed at has been not so much any mere literary excellence as an array of competent and incontrovertible testimony. The career of a quiet student affords small material in the way of biographic incident, but it is hoped that the remarkable private and domestic character, and personal traits and idiosyncrasies, of the subject of these memoirs, have not been lost sight of in the attempt to portray his life as a recluse scholar, as a teacher, as a minister of the Word, and as an author.

The present biographer is indebted to so many sources, and especially to so many individual friends, for much of the substance of his narrative as well as for much that is valuable and entertaining in the way of criticism, description, and illustrative remark and anecdote, that he finds himself unable to make particular acknowledgments to them all, or even to cite every one of his authorities by name. In most cases he has done so, in the body of the two volumes which are now respectfully offered to the candid judgment of his readers. Where nothing is said to the contrary, it will be right to infer that any matter incorporated in the words of another was contributed originally to this work. Sometimes the language is much stronger than he should have dared to use himself, but is retained as showing his uncle's rare gift of inspiring his pupils with enthusiastic, if extravagant, admiration.

To the rule of making no specific acknowledgments of personal obligation in the Preface, there must, however, be one signal exception; and that is in the case of a surviving brother of the deceased, and the editor of several of his posthumous volumes, the Rev. Samuel D. Alexander, D. D., of New York. Indeed so large and important has been Dr. Alexander's share in these labours, that it is only because of his earnest protestation, and inflexible purpose to the contrary, that his name is not associated with that of the nominal author upon the title-page. The first rough draught of the narrative was prepared by him, from the journals of his lamented brother, and his subsequent toils and efforts bearing in one way or other upon the book as it is now presented, have been excessive and invaluable. I may add that the reader will not stray far from the truth, if he will bear in mind that while we have both worked in the quarry and upon the block, the work of my relative and coadjutor has been mainly though by no means exclusively in the quarry, and my own principally upon the block, though also very extensively in the quarry. Each of us has exercised the powers of the veto and of elimination, though the present writer has reserved to himself the power of decisive choice in the few cases where there has been a fixed difference of opinion between us. Where the opinions of the subject of this memoir are given without comment, it is not to be taken for granted that they are also those of his biographer.

We have discovered with regret that many errors have

crept into the printing that could not be indicated within the ordinary limits of a table of errata. Some of these are trivial or will at once be detected as typographical mistakes, but others for which we equally repudiate the responsibility are more serious, or of such a nature as to baffle all curiosity as to their precise extent and origin. Under these circumstances we throw ourselves upon the mercy of those of our readers who, having suffered themselves in like manner and from the same cause, will, we trust, regard our frailty and unavoidable misfortune with indulgence. The writing of this work was not commenced until after the late war; and though the printing began as far back as November 1868, the publication has been delayed until the present moment for reasons which we the editors could neither remove nor modify. Some of these reasons might also be pleaded in extenuation of the manner in which the volumes are now put before the public. It is true the copy as furnished to the printer was in a state not at all unlike that of the leaves of the Delphic sibyl. But, to borrow a caveat from the Preface of "Alexander on Isaiah," "instead of resorting to the usual apologies of distance from the press and inexperience in the business, or appealing to the fact that the sheets could be subjected only once" to our revision, we prefer to commit ourselves to the generosity of those who are willing to believe that in spite of present appearances we have made every reasonable effort to secure accuracy. For the foot notes that are given without signature, I am, except in one * instance, myself responsible.

May the Lord make this account of the life of one of his devoted servants, instrumental to the promotion of his own glory!

H. C. A.

---

* The foot-note at the bottom of p. 45, should have been under the signature, "R. B."

CONTENTS.

CHAPTER I.

Parentage.—The Mother.—The Father.—The Old Pine Street Church.—James Alexander.—Lombard Street.—Old Philadelphians.—Germantown.—James Ross.—Anecdotes of Addison.—Princeton.—The College.—Nassau Hall.—Revolutionary Incidents.—Thirst for Knowledge.—Love of Books.—Rapid Growth.—Beginnings in Latin.—Introduction to Hebrew.—Other Oriental Languages.—Princeton under Dr. Green.—Passion for Music.—European and American Choirs.—Influence of this Taste on his Sermons.—Imagination and Fancy.—Intellectual Amusements.—The Boyish Orator.—Facetious Turn.—First Efforts at Verse.—Early Poetical Ventures.—Early Attempts at Rhyming.—Poetical Talents.—Early Teachers.—Jemmy Hamilton.—Salmon Strong.—Horace S. Pratt.—Classical School.—Robert Baird.—Talent for Writing.—Great Industry.—Facsimile of Arabic.—At School.—Trenton Reminiscences.—Traits of Character.—Personal Appearance.—Mr. King's Recollections.—Humorous Writing.—"The Medley."—Original Composition.—Stony Brook.—Mr. Baird.—Edward Irving.—James.—Appointed Tutor.—Characteristics.—Visits Philadelphia............ Page 1

CHAPTER II.

Dr. Lindsley.—His Pupils.—Power of Memory.—Princeton of 1824.—College Curriculum.—Old Commencement.—Princeton Society and Celebrities.—Mr. Janvier.—The McCarriers.—Jemmy McCarrier.—Mr. Alexander in College.—His Speeches.—At College.—Habits and Appearance.—Quickness of Parts.—Many-sided Character.—Judge Napton.—Early Taste for Literature.—Moral Habits.—Highly Gifted.—Character of his Mind.—Equality of his Faculties.—College Club.—G. W. Bolling.—Valedictory.—Clerk of Common Council.—First Letter.—Letters Received.—Visits Long Branch.—Letter of Mrs. Graham.—Mr. McCall.—His Scholarship............ 61

CHAPTER III.

Declines the Tutorship.—Charles Campbell.—Testimony of Professor Hart.—Philological Society.—Love for English Classics.—The Patriot.—Persian Poets.—Oriental Scenes.—Persian Legends.—Persian Mind.—Persian Mythology.—Poet's Paradise.—Literary Caprices.—Imitation of Johnson.—

Arabian Nights.—Articles signed Trochilus.—Commencement, 1827.—Alumni Association.—Foreign News.—" The Sea."—Critique on Shelley.—Party Politics.—Puzzling Leader of August, 1827.—Writing of Fiction.—Jewess of Damascus.—The Emporium.—Estimate of Time.—Reading Homer.—Early Letter.—When Written.—Admiration of Hebrew.—Italian and Spanish Studies.—Tears of Esau.—Monthly Magazine.—Writing Verses.—Dr. Snowden.—His Letters.—Monthly Magazine.—Persia and the East.—Fall of Ispahan.—A Vision of Greece.—English Poets.—Change of Studies .... Page 96

CHAPTER IV.

Journal.—Daily Studies.—English Reading.—Early Criticism.—Studies for the Month.—Studies for the Week.—Quarterly Retrospect.—Varied Reading.—Philological Society formed.—Scenery of Princeton.—Devoted to his Books.—Nucleus of a Library.—Begins Chinese.—Retrospect of the Year.—Memoranda of Dr. Rice.—Old Black and Peter Arun.—Their Characteristics.—Johnson, Crow, Lane.—Reading for the Day.—Aristophanes and Shakespeare.—English Metaphysics.—Brown's Lectures.—Dante and Spenser.—Scott's Napoleon.—Scott's Style.—Persian New Testament.—Greek Writers.—Letter from his Brother.—Scott's Napoleon.—Estimate of Xenophon.—Hearing Sermons.—Joseph Sandford.—Recollections of Dr. Rice.—Visit to New York 146

CHAPTER V.

Rezeau Brown.—Visits New Haven.—Seeking the Ministry.—In Philadelphia.—Failing Health.—His Death.—Traits of Character.—Lines on his Death.—Their Character.—About the Geography.—Daily Study.—Pope.—Biblical Repertory.—The Repertory.—Change of Plan.—Its Writers.—The Druses.—Extracts.—Study of Arabic.—An Old Tradition.—Study of Arabic.—Robert Walsh.—Opinions of him.—Walsh in Paris.—Recollections of Dr. Jones.—An Incident.—Contributions.—Letter to Dr. Hall.—Article on Coffee 182

CHAPTER VI.

Becomes a Teacher.—The East.—Early Dreams.—Study of Greek.—Remarkable Letter.—Greek Grammar.—Hellenistic Studies.—Purity of Life.—Conversion.—Diary of Experience.—Comfort in the Bible.—Light in Darkness.—Confessions.—Experimental Journal 212

CHAPTER VII.

Entrance upon his Professorship.—Progress in Studies.—Subjects of Study.—Pursuing Hebrew.—Leading Characteristics.—In the Class.—Mr. George

Leyburn.—Articles Written.—Parke Godwin, Esq.—Studies of the Year.—Turkish Language. — Burlesque Writing. — Metaphysics. — Grammatical Studies.—Journal.—Religious Experience.—The Two Brothers.—His Reading.—He Loves the Bible.—Temptation.—Daily Reading.—Letter to Mr. Hall.................. . ... Page 242

CHAPTER VIII.

Oriental Preferences.—The Koran.—Mohammedanism.—The False Prophet.—The Perspicuous Book.—The Study of Arabic.—Foreign Grammars.—Familiarity with Current Arabic.—Henry Vethake.—College Manners.—Anecdotes.—Public Prayers.—Modesty and Skill as a Teacher.—The Trenton Pastor.—Newspaper Scribblings.—Progress in Studies.............. 265

CHAPTER IX.

Sails from New York.—Ship Samson.—English Stage Coach.—Portsmouth to London.—House of Commons.—Edward Irving.—His Church.—" Tongues." —Coach-ride from Oxford.—Dashing Coachman.—Visits Prof. Lee.—Lafayette.—A Visit.—Religious Service.—Travelling Companions.—Letter.—Singing School.—Swiss Songs.—Visits Merle.—Letter Finished.—Verses Written at Turin.—Poem.—Travelling Companions.—Journey.—On to Rome.—Via Cassia.—Thoughts of Home.—Leaves Rome.—New Chair in the College.—Tholuck.—Von Gerlach.—Daily Life in Germany.—Professor Pott.—Contribution of Professor Sears.—Walk with Tholuck.—Anecdotes. —Tholuck's Estimate of Alexander.—Anecdote of Louis von Gerlach.—Karl Ritter and Hengstenberg.—Neander and Schleiermacher.—Visits Neander.—Bopp, Rheinwald and Nitzsch.—Reminiscences by Dr. Samuel Miller.—Paris and Princeton Habits Contrasted...................... 283

CHAPTER X.

The New Professor.—Severity in the Class-room.—Growth in Gentleness.—Dr. Lyon's Recollections.—Manners in his Study.—Power of Sarcasm.—Literary Recreations.—Knowledge of European Politics.—The Literary Association.—Repertory Articles.—Evening Diversions.—Colloquy with Three Bishops.—Remarks of Dr. Scott.—Dr. Hilyer.—Studies of the Brothers.—Bearing in his Private Classes.—Testimony of Professor Hart.—Tribute by Dr. Wilson.—Biblical and Oriental Labours.—Plan of Study.—His New Chair.—Messianic Interpretation.—English Reviews.—Miscellaneous Reading.—Bible Study.. 332

CHAPTER XI.

Old and New School.—Scripture Reading.—Professorship Declined.—Dean Swift.—Mr. James Alexander.—Dr. Archibald Alexander.—His Preaching.

—Private Classes.—Personal Traits.—Bearing towards his Class.—Sharp Censure.—Conversation.—Observer of Men.—Dr. Hall.—Correspondence.—Arabic Letter.—Prayers.—A Specimen.—Resolutions.—Estimate of his Prayers.—Prayers before Lecture..................... .. Page 358

CHAPTER XII.

Discursive Reading.—Quarterly Review.—Dr. Ramsey.—Abhorrence of Drones.—Gentleness.—Interest in his Class.—Oral Expositions.—Massive Intellect.—Impetuous Feelings.—Current Stories.—Offensive Manners.—Effects of the Weather.—Art Napoleon.—Private Pupils.—Rhyming Letter.—Travelling.—Teaching under Difficulties.—Writing Letters.—Alphabets.—Correspondence.—Seeking Books..380

CHAPTER XIII.

Personal Appearance.—Social Intercourse.—High Pressure Teaching.—Hard Study.—Stolid Students.—Assembly of 1837.—A Latin Tense.—Picture of Princeton.—Contributions to the Papers.—Letters to a Pupil.—True Happiness.—Isaiah begun.—The Doomed Man.—When Written.—Parallel Bible.—Letters to Dr. Hall.—First Efforts in Pulpit.—Experiments with his Class.—Questions in the Class.—Methods of Study.—With his Private Class.—Bible Studies.—A Poem Suggested.—A Sermon.—Princeton Review.—A Letter.—Philosophical Club.—Curious Incident.—Missionary Herald.—Diary.—A Sermon.—Exegetical Study.—A Candidate.—Beggars.—Growth in Grace.—Scripture Reading 402

CHAPTER XIV.

As a Preacher.—Dr. Ramsey's Estimate.—First Sermon.—Diversity of Methods.—True Eloquence.—Travelling.—Preaching.—Views of the Disruption.—In Boston.—Dr. Hodge's Estimate.—Letters to a Boy.—Day-Book.—Writing Sermons.—Journal.—An Elocutionist.—Dr. Abel Stevens.—Style of Preaching.—Invitations to Preach.—Installation.—Inaugural.—A Sermon.—Manner of Preaching.—Writing Sermons.—Not dependent on Notes.—Scripture Study.—Cicero.—Talk of the Brothers.—His Ordination.............439

CHAPTER XV.

Presbyterial Examination.—Joseph John Gurney.—Little George.—Dr. Jacobus.—Power over the Class.—First Thoughts of Isaiah.—Isaiah.—Hebrew Text.—Princeton.—Preaching.—As a Teacher.—His Audience Moved......468

THE LIFE

OF THE

REV. JOSEPH ADDISON ALEXANDER, D. D.

CHAPTER I.

JOSEPH ADDISON ALEXANDER, the subject of this memoir, was the third son of the late Archibald Alexander, D. D., of Princeton, and was born in the city of Philadelphia, on the 24th day of April, 1809. Of his father I need not speak. His mother was the daughter of the Rev. James Waddel, of Louisa and of Hanover Presbytery, who is still spoken of in Virginia and elsewhere as the "Blind Preacher," and whose name is preserved in the well-known essay of Mr. Wirt in the British Spy. The late Governor Barbour was wont to speak of him as the most eloquent man he ever heard, with the single exception of Patrick Henry. Mrs. Alexander was a beautiful and lovely girl, and was comely and fascinating almost to the day of her death. The portrait by Mooney, which is in the possession of the family, is very like her. She had dark liquid eyes, and her face wore a look of repose, benevolence, good sense, and sometimes, when animated in conversation, of gentle raillery and humour. Her sensibility was extreme and tremulous. She had a sweet gayety of spirits, shaded at times by a pensive melancholy. She was, in every acceptation of the word, devotedly pious. Her laborious readings to her aged and sightless father had injured her own vision. She loved her Saviour, and the house, people, works, and word of her God. She was fond of religious books. No one could take a more unaffected pleasure in the writings of Flavel, Bates, and other non-conformists. It was her study to do good, and to make her home and the home of her husband and children cheerful and happy; nor did any one ever succeed better in such an attempt. Though naturally diffident and very sensitive, she loved company, and when she pleased was one of the most entertaining persons in the world. Her children were all proudly attached to her, and her son Addison not only loved but admired her above all living women.* There was an indescribable charm

---

* The testimony of one of Addison's teachers on this point is exceedingly just and valuable. It is contained in a letter from the Rev. Dr. R. Baird to the Presbyterian, which he wrote at Yonkers, N. Y., May 12, 1860.

"I may remark, in passing, that few men in our country or any other, had greater advantages for the acquisition of knowledge and the formation of well-developed characters, than the sons of the late Dr. Archibald Alexander. Their mother was a daughter of the celebrated Dr. Waddel of Virginia, of whose eloquence William Wirt has given such a glowing description in his British Spy, and possessed much of her father's character and strength of mind. She was a woman of excellent judgment, well-cultivated intellect, most amiable disposition, much decision of character, sincere piety, and even in old age retained much of the beauty of her youth, and of those pleasant and winning manners which are better than beauty. Well qualified as she was to adorn any circle of society in which she might have moved, she devoted herself with most unremitting care to the training of her children, rightly believing that this was the first and great duty which she owed to the Saviour and to them. Her delightful influence greatly contributed to make home the most pleasant place in the world to them. The company, too, of an accomplished and affectionate sister, and often that of most agreeable female relatives from the Old Dominion, as well as of friends from Philadelphia, where their father had been pastor of a church during several years, contributed to make the house of their parents all that could be desired. I have sometimes thought that it was almost too pleasant; on any other principle it is hard to account for the fact that so many of them have remained unmarried.

"The influence of their father was not less happy and effective than that of their excellent mother on all these sons. Dr. Alexander was a kind father, but not too indulgent. At all times he lived on terms of great intimacy with them, and sometimes, especially in his younger life, would take part in their youthful

about her voice and manner, and she had a fine and cultivated understanding.

It is impossible to exaggerate the influence of such a mother upon the mind and character of her children. In appearance, and many habits and traits of character and intellect, Addison was like the Alexanders, and especially like his father; but in many particulars of mind and disposition he was, to use the language of another who is not a resident of Staunton and not related to the family, " his grandfather's son (James Waddel)." He was still more his mother's son; though in after years he grew to be more and more in person, if not in temperament, like his father and one or two of his father's sisters.

The commentator on Isaiah had the most exalted notion of his mother's rare powers as an interpreter of Scripture. He preferred her plain, unaided judgments to the opinions of all the Fathers and Councils. It would be hard to find a more passionately devoted son. He has been heard to expatiate with delight on the soft attractions and ingratiating charm of her society. His eye would sometimes kindle, and his voice become tender, when he was on this theme. She was equally wrapt up in her famous son. But if she indulged him it was in reason, and with a wise consideration of the future. The truth was, from the very beginning the boy needed little guidance and little correction. Even his profound, sagacious father, that thoughtful and patient student of mental and

---

sports with evident gratification to himself as well as to them. I often had occasion to call upon him in his study at night, and frequently found some of the smaller boys about him, reading or amusing themselves; and he told me that it never interfered with his studies. They had free access to his library, which was large, and, as they grew up, to the libraries of the Institutions in Princeton. And as all the sons received a classical education, and graduated at the College of that place, they had abundant advantages for becoming well-instructed men. The daily converse with their parents did much to create and increase the love of knowledge for which they became so much distinguished. I have been told by the late James W. Alexander, that he had heard at his father's table very many of the most important things which he ever learned. The advantages of growing up under such an influence, and in the midst of so many incentives to the acquisition of knowledge, cannot be overrated."

spiritual phenomena, though ever on the alert as regarded acts of disobedience, like the father of Pascal left his son pretty much to his own bent. His discipline was suggestive, rather than strictly coercive. He saw clearly from the first that Addison was to be his own master. The fruits of this training are now evident in the life and fame of the great Biblical scholar. We cannot but rejoice that his powers were not too much restrained in infancy and youth, but were allowed to develop themselves in the natural ways. There are few cases in which such a course would be wise; but this was one of them.

His ancestry was Scotch-Irish, and as much of the manly and racy vigour of his mind, and bold intrepidity as well as honest frankness of his temper, are traceable to this sturdy stock, I think it well to say a word or two about the emigration to this country from the North of Ireland.* Many of these stout Presbyterians went to the Great Valley, and laid the foundations of civil and religious liberty in Virginia. These reputable settlers had been taught to thirst for the best literature of the age. Their earliest predilections were for the union of regulated freedom and sound learning. Their descendants followed in their footsteps. "Reasons might be given why the sons of Scottish settlers in Ulster, more than any others of the British isles, should come to this country; impelled by the same causes which drove the Huguenot and the Palatine. During their sojourn in Ireland, they had never lost one Scottish peculiarity of mind or dialect. They came ready to coalesce with the Puritan sons of men who had sometimes fought, and sometimes suffered with their fathers. A common creed and common purpose knit them together in asserting the consecration of science and letters to the church." † The catalogue of Princeton College shows that no other race added so many to the names of her alumni. With some ex-

---

* See the account by Dr. A. Alexander, in his biography by his son, p. 2.

† Address at Centennial Celebration of the College by Rev. J. W. Alexander, D.D. This address has never been published.

ceptions, the founders of the college were of this stock, and mingled cordially with their brethren of English descent. "Carolina, East Jersey and Maryland received these exiles, panting from persecution, as early as 1679. They spread themselves over the Great Valley, a hardy, athletic, shrewd, inquisitive, and remarkably persistent race." * This was the stock from which Archibald, and James, and Addison Alexander sprung.

Dr. Alexander removed to Philadelphia in the winter of 1806–1807, and became the pastor of the Third Presbyterian Church, now known as the old Pine street Church. His eldest son speaks of having had a few dim recollections of Prince Edward, and clearly remembered the old prayer-room of Hampden Sidney College. He also had some faint remembrance of the journey to Philadelphia. His first bright reminiscences were connected with a house in Pine street, just opposite St. Peter's churchyard. This was the first house occupied by his father. He calls to mind his surprise at the burial of several persons with military honours, and wondered, as children will, why they should fire guns over the grave. He says that in the spring the rank grass, interspersed with buttercups and dandelions, made the churchyard a delightful spot. He was afterwards told by his mother that he was a stubborn and ungovernable child. He was once taken home by her and corrected for playing with a little girl in church—he never repeated the offence. An old Bible lay in the pastor's pew, which the little urchins used to tear up and twist into "ear-ticklers," which they profanely used during prayers. He well remembered the singing of James McGathery, who was precentor, and the acerbity of David Allen, the old Scotch sexton, and the goats which used to browse in the churchyard. A very excellent Quaker lady named Price lived next to them in Pine street, who was very kind to James and used to encourage him to get upon a table and preach, which he was accustomed to do with much applause. An old family servant

* Ibid.

named Daphne, once a slave in Virginia, who returned to the Valley after receiving her freedom, and who lived to a great age, was full of anecdotes relating to these juvenile exploits. She could tell them long after she had forgotten nearly every thing else. Mrs. Price was still living in 1829, and spoke of James as "a very pious child." He was however too much given to imitate the clerical actions of his father, and was once chastised for solemnly pouring water on a little chair and uttering the formula of baptism. Once during the prevalence of a thunder-storm, he said to his brother or his nurse that it was "God talking," and even undertook to tell what He was saying; for which he afterwards had some twinges.

The cries of the man who sold clams and oysters were matters of deep interest in those days. Even Addison could also recall the song of the little chimney sweeps. The nurse used to take the older boys to a cake shop in the vicinity, and the eldest of them in his simplicity thought that what they got upon trust they got for nothing.

The next house in which they lived was on the south side of Lombard street, between Second and Third streets. It was used in 1828 as a "finding store" for shoemakers. One of the boys remembered being taken thither in a coach, but none of the circumstances attending the removal. This must have been in 1808, and consequently before the birth of Addison, which occurred the following spring. This event was distinctly remembered by his brother James, who was moved by it to tears. He says it gave him much pain, and in the tenderness of his heart he wept to think that he should be supplanted in the affections of his parents. Little did he know the joy he was to take in his new brother.

The late Dr. Addison Waddel, afterwards of Staunton, Virginia, his mother's brother, was at that time living with Dr. Alexander. Here it was that James began to study the Latin grammar, reciting it to his father, and he long afterwards regretted his "wicked craft" in peeping over his shoulder at the book. The study fronted the street, on the first floor, with a little window opening upon the stairway, through which the boys used to look in upon marriages which sometimes took place there. These were the days of the first stir in America about Bible Societies, and the Philadelphia pastor used to give Bibles to poor people. In the little court behind the house was an arbour covered with a grape-vine, and some little beds of flowers. Long afterwards Dr. James W. Alexander could scarcely ever see a *pink* without thinking of Lombard street. It was, he says, with an indescribable pensive satisfaction that he looked back upon those days of comparative innocence. He scarcely ever went to bed without talking to his mother about the unpardonable sin; which he stood in daily fear of committing. There were no Sunday Schools then, but he remembered going every Saturday afternoon to Pine street Church to be catechised. Almost every day he went to Second street, to the house of Mr. John Steele, who having no children of his own was very kind to him. He was an Irishman, and a brother of the Rev. Robert Steele of Abingdon, Pa., and the Rev. Samuel Steele of Kentucky. Here the little visitor used to read the Pilgrim's Progress, and the Olney Hymns, which he always held in high affection. On his seventh birthday his father presented him with Day's Sanford and Merton, telling him that he was " now a *youth*, and must begin to prepare for manhood." This somewhat singular advice was heeded. The lad was fond of reading, and used to pace the floor for hours. He fairly gorged the English classics, and in course of time not a few of the Latin ones, especially the poets. He used to say that he had read the whole college course in Latin, and possibly in Greek, before he was matriculated. He recollected well that Dr. James P. Wilson of the First Church, told him that he was "a little *peripatetic* philosopher." This habit of pacing his study floor he kept up through life. He went to his first school about 1810–1811. It was under the charge of Madam Thomson, as the scholars called her, on the north side of Lombard street, below Third. He never could remember learning to read and write, nor did he ever have any distinct impressions about beginning Latin. About the time of the birth of his brother Addison, *i. e.*, in

April, 1809, he began to go to the school of a Mr. Littell, and retained a disagreeable remembrance of "the squalid and dark appearance of the room," and the tricks which the rude boys used to play upon him, who, taking advantage of his smallness and timidity, appear to have fagged him dreadfully. His principal reminiscences of Lombard street were the marriages which took place in his father's study, his frequent visits to the market, the book-binder's, and the flour shop, the song of the oysterman, which I have often heard him sing, and the books given him by his friends.

The family next removed to Fourth street below Lombard, west side, next door but one to Gaskill street. "And here," he records, "a crowd of early impressions contend for precedence." There he began to remember his father's preaching, the people that used to visit them, and the tradesmen with whom they had dealings. The house was occupied at a later day by a Major Linnard. In the neighbourhood was a chocolate factory in which James took much interest, and a gilder's shop, out of the windows of which were thrown the little red books in which gold-foil is kept. The little fragments of the precious metal he accounted a great prize. The *coup d'œil* of a print-shop two doors off from his father's house remained in his memory. Near them on Gaskill street was a mustard factory. His father's study was here the front room on the second story, and in it were spent some of his son's happiest hours. His father used to give him, on slips of paper, a text for every day; and these, when a certain number had been learned, he would redeem with small gifts of money. Dr. Alexander, with several others of the city clergy, took lessons in Hebrew about this time from one *Horwitz*, a Jew, who afterwards fell into some degree of disrepute.

The family commonly spent their summers at Germantown, six or seven miles out of town, where they hired a small house for the season. This captivating region, as it is now, of suburban drives and cottages, of green and shadowed lawns, and clambering exotics, was already beautiful, though plain and little celebrated. Old Dr. Blair was then alive, and

James Alexander was often at his house. The Rev. Mr. Dunn was the Presbyterian minister, and his son James's intimate friend. One of his little Philadelphia comrades was Silas, a brother of the late George Potts, D.D., of New York. One day an English missionary was addressing a large number of children, of whom he would collect hundreds, upon the journeys of St. Paul, and particularly his imprisonment at Antioch. Having finished his "preachment," he began to catechise the boys and girls on what they had heard. Among other questions, he proposed this, "Who was Silas's companion?" George Potts answered with a very loud voice—"James Alexander, sir,"—to the great amusement of the congregation.

During all the time of their living in Philadelphia, so far as he can recollect, he was constant in the performance of the duty of secret prayer, had a very tender conscience, and was often exercised about the concerns of his soul. He was pleased at the thought that he should one day be a preacher, and once wrote a sermon, part of which was recovered and held in trust for him by one of his aunts.

He went to school, while they lived in Fourth street, to a Mr. McCleese, who had nearly 100 pupils, and used the ferule in Lombard street, the north side. Here he was taught reading, writing, &c. In Germantown he was put under the care of a Miss Hotchkiss, and all that he could remember was that he once was made to wear the fool's cap, with bells, and that he used to write in Carver's copy-books.

His first Latin teacher was the Rev. Samuel B. Hare, in after days his predecessor in Trenton, and then President of Dickinson College. He next went to the noted James Ross, author of the Latin grammar, whom he pronounced "an Orbilius in severity, but a most accurate scholar of the old British school." The famous pedagogue was wont to call his little pupil, "Alexander Magnus," in allusion to his diminutive size. Ross scourged the elder scholars unmercifully, but James must have pleased him, either by his deportment or his recitations, for the crabbed master always treated him with positive affection. Years after, he sent his old pupil, who was by this time a well-known clergyman, Stockius's Greek Lexicon, with a kind inscription, which was doubtless not in the vulgar tongue.

Dr. James Alexander had no recollection of the sermons he heard in Philadelphia, except one from his father in commemoration of the burning of the theatre in Richmond, which was printed, and from which extracts were taken by his biographer. Once, indeed, he went with Martha Jones, a negro servant, to St. Thomas's African Episcopal Church; where, and, as I believe, for the only time in his life, he saw the rite of confirmation solemnized by Bishop White. His father, he says, sometimes took him (I presume on week days) to the Romish chapels; and he retained a lively impression of the music, vestments, incense, holy water,* &c.

It is now high time we were inquiring about the early life of Addison, who at the latest date involved in the preceding narrative was little more than a mere babe.

Addison was a little Hercules, even in his cradle. There was never a moment's doubt as to the boy's capacity, and it was always evident that he was destined, if he lived, for something great. He was regarded as a prodigy before he left his nurse's arms; but the accounts of his very early days are, as usual in such cases, provokingly slight and fragmentary. When but a few months old, at a time when infants of the common order manifest scarcely any signs of intelligence, I am informed his perceptions were singularly quick, and his evident appreciation of what was said to him was truly wonderful. The materials out of which the story of his childhood will have to be made up are too meagre to afford much satisfaction to those who are curious in such matters, and may perhaps not be thought to bear out the impression produced upon the minds of all who came in contact with this remarkable boy, that he was gifted from the first with faculties of the highest

---

* These particulars of the Philadelphia life are for the most part abridged from a manuscript by Dr. James W. Alexander, entitled "Recollections of my Early Life." The language is largely though not exclusively his own.

order, and that those faculties were already well developed at an astonishingly early period. Whatever may be the judgment of the reader as to the inferences to be drawn from the particular facts about to be recited, there can be no question in any reasonable mind that considers the unanimity of the witnesses who speak of this period, or that duly reflects upon the degree of mental advancement implied in the diaries of a somewhat later period, that the boy Addison was worthy of being mentioned among *les enfans celèbres*.

The few anecdotes which are preserved of this period will doubtless interest some on account of their unquestioned authenticity. They also shed some light on the character and disposition of the man, which were in many respects, and more than is usually the case, the same with those of the boy.

When he was still in the arms of his nurse, his mother was in the habit of saying to him, "Addison, say your prayers:" upon which he would shut his eyes, place the palms of his hands together, and look up with an appearance of solemn reverence.

When he was about two years old, his father read one morning, at the daily worship of the family, the eleventh chapter of the Evangelist John, in which the account is given of the raising of Lazarus. Addison seemed to have listened attentively to the narrative, and in the course of the morning, when but one person was in the room, was observed to take a small book from the table and place it in a corner on the floor, and after standing over it for a short time, was heard to say in a loud voice, "Lazarus, come forth:" immediately after which he placed the book on end.

On one occasion he was sent by his mother to carry to his father's study a manuscript in which she had been placing a stitch. On leaving the study he turned round to make a bow (which was an accomplishment that had been lately taught him), but stepped too far back and fell a short distance down the staircase, which was immediately at the study door, and fractured his collar-bone. His brother James, who was then a little boy of seven, was immediately despatched for the late

Dr. John Dorsey, at that time rising into eminence as a surgeon, who promptly repaired to his assistance, reduced the fracture, and secured the arm to the breast in many folds of linen, *secundum artem*. While his arm was thus confined, Addison indulged in much of that playful humour which in after life so distinguished him in the family.

At the age of four years he removed with his father's family to Princeton, which was destined to be the spot of his life-long residence, the place of his early education, the field, more than any other, upon which, in after years, he was to deploy his splendid abilities, and which was to be the theatre of his extraordinary labours and hard-earned unregarded fame. It was here too that his body was to rest in hope.

He was at this time a gentle, retiring, observing, thoughtful child—full of animal spirits and genuine humour; the delight of the household, the astonishment and despair of his little school-fellows; invariably attracting the notice of every visitor by the sparkle of his wit, and the originality of his remarks.

There is to some minds a strange beguiling pleasure in the attempt to trace out the localities which have been the home of men of worth or talents. Princeton is ten miles from the State capital, in Mercer county, and lies embosomed in a very lovely region, of late years made more pleasing and fragrant than ever before. It is the centre of a wide circumference of champaign country, broken in the rear of the town by abrupt rocky barriers, and terminated in the extreme distance on several sides by a faint wavy line of blue hills, which sometimes shine with a light as soft as that of Pentelicus, but are often nearly invisible. The level fields and graceful laps of tilled surface composing this fine prospect show every token of thrift, plenty, and the most careful husbandry. The whole is dotted over with snug homesteads and orchards, and intersected with neat fences. Red and white cattle are everywhere to be seen browsing upon the close-cut pastures. Through the midst of plain, grove, green protuberance and meadow, the landscape is streaked by the sinuous current of Stony Brook, or as it is known at one romantic spot, Pretty Brook, a stream of pellucid brightness when not troubled by rains, and that, as it glides within its tortuous avenue of tall trees, whispers to itself legends of Revolutionary battle.

From the heart of the town itself there are a number of inviting views commanded by those buildings which are favourably situated. One of the best of these cheered the eyes of Dr. Archibald Alexander for forty years, as he sat in his study wrapt in thought but now and then darted glances of admiration through his south window. Another broad and grateful prospect enlivens both sides of the main thoroughfare where, after penetrating the town, it goes on easterly towards Kingston.

Still another of these refreshing pastoral landscapes, though in some particulars the same with one of those just mentioned, is thus described by Professor James Alexander in his unpublished journal for Saturday the 19th of May, 1838. Alluding to his keen enjoyment that year of "the placid rapture of spring," he writes as follows: "From my south study window the prospect is delightful; hill, forest, field and orchard—it only lacks mountain and water. In the background, Rocky Hill begins to show a feathery green upon its thickest forest. On this side and next to it stripes of green grainfields; and still farther hitherward, as the ground slopes down toward the large and lovely orchard just in the richest bloom!"

The street which passes in front of the College branches some hundreds of yards beyond it to the west into two beautiful village roads, which for years have been studded with dwellings and gardens. On one of these is Morven, the seat of the Stocktons, adorned with the oldest of elms, catalpas, and walnuts, and on the other, under its own ample summer shade, is the Theological Seminary. Between the two lie the Lenox Library, the beautified grounds of the late John R. Thomson, Esq., and the green turf and trim hemlock hedges of Professor Wm. Henry Green; while far to the west and some distance beyond the borough limits are the delightful groves, parterres, and winding walks and drives of Judge Richard S. Field.

Of course this description belongs to the town and its environs of to-day, not in all the particulars mentioned, to the surroundings of President Green.

If Princeton cannot lay claim to the rows of mighty elms which have thrown their immemorial charm over New Haven, it has nevertheless an abundant shadow not only from the elm but from the maple, the sugar maple, the paper mulberry, the buttonwood, and the weeping-willow, with here and there a forlorn relic in the shape of a half-extinct Lombardy poplar. In June and July the place is now fairly embowered in foliage. Its College lawns are not greatly surpassed in New England. Its public buildings are picturesque, and on every account well deserving of attention at the hands of the antiquary and the scholar. Its libraries are important and costly. Its literary and theological name has long been honoured on both sides of the Atlantic. It can show an imposing catalogue of Alumni, and can count among its nursing fathers not only men like Dickinson, Burr, Davies, Finley, and Green, grave masters as these were of the old-time piety, learning and eloquence, but "that prodigy of metaphysical acumen, Jonathan Edwards,"* that intellectual giant and almost universal genius, Witherspoon, and that scholar of magnificent and princely gentlemanhood, Samuel Stanhope Smith.†

The town of Princeton is intimately connected with the Revolutionary Annals. The President, Dr. Witherspoon, who for obvious reasons was regarded with a peculiar enmity by the Royal army, fled from his country home at Tusculum,

---

* Robert Hall in the Sermon on Modern Infidelity.

† SAMUEL STANHOPE SMITH.—" A little later, we who first saw these shades in 1812, recall the venerable form of the President, as he laid aside his symbols of learned rule; beautiful and lordly in his decay, unsurpassed in our [memory] for perfect gracefulness and a stateliness which had lost all that was once [considered] as pomp. He crept to the retirement where he renewed his [early love] of classical [studies] with two beloved grandsons, one of whom has been for twenty years in Peru. And we, my beloved coevals, of 1819, joined in the concourse which followed the remains to the cemetery, where you have seen his tomb which you have visited."—Centennial Address, 1847.

"taking only a wagon-load of his effects, and driving his stock before him." On the 22d of July, of the same year, two stories of the college were full of Hessian soldiers. On the 1st of Jan., 1777, Mawhood's brigade were quartered in Nassau Hall,* and made their barracks in the dormitories, using the basement for their stables. Nor is this believed to be the first instance of such outrages. The college lawn is said to have been covered with their crimson uniforms. Washington, as all the world knows, retreated from Trenton, on January the 2d. A little after sunrise, he exposed himself before the lines at Stony Brook. This was the commencement of the battle of Princeton. The Hessians in the college building ran out tumultuously at the front doorways, on the approach of the American troops, and fell back to New Brunswick. The mark of a ball from one of the American cannon was at one time to be seen 'near the projection of the old Hall.' Another cannon ball entered a window, and struck the portrait of

---

* *Nassau Hall.* This was the name suggested for the old college building by Governor Belcher, under whose fostering care it was erected. His words are still preserved. The original thought was to call it Belcher Hall. The worthy Governor seems to have been also the first to suggest, and in this very letter to the trustees, in 1756, the motto of the Cliosophic Society. "I take a particular grateful notice of the respect and honour you are desirous of doing me and my family, in calling the edifice lately erected in Princeton by the name of Belcher-Hall; but you will be so good as to excuse me, while I absolutely decline such an honour, for I have always been very fond of the motto of a late great personage, *Prodesse quam conspici.* But I must not leave this head without asking the favour of your naming the present building *Nassau Hall ;* and this I hope you will take as a further instance of my real regard to the future welfare and interest of the college, as it will express the honour we retain, in this remote part of the globe, to the immortal memory of the glorious king *William* the Third, who was a branch of the illustrious house of NASSAU. * * * * And who, for the better establishment of the true religion and English liberty, brought forward an act in the British Parliament, for securing the Crown of Great Britain to the present royal family, whereby we now become happy under the best of kings, in the full enjoyment of English liberty and prosperity. And God Almighty grant, we may never want a sovereign from his loins to sway the British sceptre in righteousness."—Extracted from a slip of an old newspaper, which is made use of in the Centennial Address.

George II., tearing it from the frame, which has since been graced by Peale's full-length of Washington, and the death of Mercer. A mess of the 40th regiment of British had ordered a breakfast in the President's house, and were just sitting down to it when the firing began. That breakfast was eaten with appetite by the American officers. The college became a hospital for the wounded, and so continued to be for six or eight months. During these bewildering changes, the old Hall was sadly knocked to pieces. Every perishable part of the structure was destroyed. "The wood-work was used for fuel, and the apparatus, including Rittenhouse's orrery, was demolished or injured." There is still in the space to the rear of the old college, and in the very centre of the enclosure formed by the ancient edifice and the new buildings, a thirty-two pounder left by the British in their fright, which was abandoned by Washington "on account of its carriage being broken." There is, of course, a legend connected with this old piece.

The Continental troops occupied the college as barracks till about the fifteenth of June of the same year, and as an hospital, from the first of October till the twenty-third of November of the year following. The church was repeatedly desecrated, being occupied continually "by every party passing."

After this, Dr. Witherspoon granted two rooms to the tailors of the Jersey Brigade. The grant expired, or the tailors yielded their claim, some time in April, 1780. "The college was entirely disbanded, and all regular business was interrupted for two or three years."* The Congress met in Princeton in 1783. A letter from the Rev. Ashbel Green, D. D. (afterwards President of the College), to his father, dated Nassau Hall, 5th of July, 1783, gives a bright and cheerful glimpse of the place as it was at that day. "The face of things is inconceivably altered in Princeton within a fortnight. From a little obscure village we have become the capital of

* In the above narrative I have made free use of the Centennial Address, and other sources of information.

America. Instead of almost total silence in the town, nothing is to be seen or heard but the passing and rattling of wagons, coaches, and chairs, the crying about of pine-apples, oranges, lemons, and every luxurious article both foreign and domestic." The Congress papers, which had all been lodged in college, amounted to about five or seven wagon-load. The members sat from 11 to 3. The day before, he had had "the honour of delivering a declamation before them on the dangers and advantages of Republican government." After which he received an invitation to dine with them. "Dinner began about 6 o'clock. It was a public occasion—all the Congress, foreign ministers, and gentlemen, with the faculty of the college, and some gentlemen of the town, to the amount of 70 or 80, were present." In the evening sky-rockets and a variety of fireworks were displayed, and were repeated on the evening of the day on which he wrote. At one o'clock a salute of thirteen guns was fired in the front Campus. After dinner the President gave out as many toasts, each of which was accompanied by a discharge of artillery. "I retired to my chamber about 9 o'clock."*

One of the matters that was engaging the attention of this important body, was a proposal from a gentleman of Virginia to exhibit "a method of working a boat of twenty tons burden by the force of machines, with only one man, without sails, against the tide, so that it shall run eight miles in an hour; with the tide twelve miles in an hour."

Princeton, on account of its salubrious air, has been happily styled the Montpellier of America.† It is the seat of one of the oldest institutions of academic learning in the country, and also of the most celebrated of the distinctively Presbyterian schools of theology. In addition to the charm of the landscape gardening, and of the surrounding scenery of nature, it could always boast a considerable number of highly cultivated

---

* Culled from a slip of the "Daily News," which is given entire in the Centennial Address.

† By Dr. Witherspoon. See Life of Dr. Archibald Alexander, p. 385.

men and women and attractive households. But the noblest part of Princeton, after all, as many love to think, lies sleeping in its venerable graveyard, where, enclosed within massive walls and shadowed by giant trees, repose the ashes of nearly all the former college Presidents, and of Dod and other college professors; as well as Samuel Miller, Archibald Alexander, James Waddel Alexander, and now, amidst the verdure of nine years, of Joseph Addison Alexander, of the Theological Seminary. Whatever may happen to the rest of Princeton, it may be safely said of the old cemetery on Witherspoon street, that it will continue to grow green with precious and hallowed remembrances, even as now, "incontaminatis honoribus refulget."

After the removal to Princeton, Addison made brave advances. His proficiency in study, and the ease and exactness with which he mastered the elements of knowledge, were almost incredible. It is impossible to point to the time when he did not know his letters. He soon learned to read, under the tuition of a young lady then resident in the family, who has since that time been made a widow, and is believed to be now living in Texas. Once possessed of this delightful and invaluable art, his appetite for books became perfectly insatiable. He was never at rest. His thirst for knowledge was unquenchable and constant. He hungered after his intellectual pabulum as a carnivorous animal hungers after his prey. His eyes never wearied in the attempt to decypher unaccustomed characters. The strangeness of a foreign language was no invincible obstacle in his path. He would get hold of an old grammar, or part of a grammar, or else make one for himself that would answer for the nonce; he would disinter from a heap of waste paper and forgotten volumes some venerable dictionary, with the back gone and many of the leaves torn out or hopelessly defaced, or in lieu of that he would store his mind with the new vocabulary as he went along. In this way he soon learned to knock a language to pieces, resolve it into its structural parts, and examine its hidden machinery; and all this he did with a vehemence of impulse and a rapidity of work that must have been very startling to the other boys, and was sufficiently surprising to all who were in any measure acquainted with his habits. But most of these efforts were put forth in solitude, and he did not care to speak of them to a living soul. Some of the facts here mentioned did not come to light till long afterwards.

He was at this time, in all strictness of speech, what is called an omnivorous reader. He read literally every thing that fell in his way. This was one of his characteristics in after-life. Though he often checked himself in the indulgence of a taste for general literature, the propensity was always strong. Though he had habituated himself to the most severe and rigid courses of study, he did not disdain to read the smallest newspaper, or even the almanac. I have often heard him say, in response to a question about some particular book of travels, then just out, that "*all* books of travel were interesting to him." Though at all times a recluse, supposed to be conversant only with what was in books, the saying of Terence was applicable to him, and not only in regard to books, but in reference to every thing else, *humani nihil alienum*. He would look out of his open window, as he gaily turned the huge leaves of his folios at Princeton, and see more of human nature in an hour than some men would see in a twelvemonth. But I am anticipating.

At the time I speak of, there were in the garret in his father's house certain old worthless books, that had been thrown away with other rubbish, and had many of them passed entirely out of recollection. There the boyish scholar would sit for hours together devouring the contents of these volumes. Among the works thus read was an old romance called "The Midnight Bell," a book full of horrors and mysteries. He used often to speak with zest in after years, of the terror with which he gloated over the dark and bloody revelations of this story, in the silence, solitude, and gloom of that unfinished and unfurnished attic.

There was an odd mingling in him of the solitary and social tendencies. From early childhood he showed a disposition to communicate his stores of knowledge to others. When about six years old, it was his daily custom to repair after the evening meal to the kitchen, and read aloud to an aged black woman who was cook in the family, from Bunyan's Pilgrim's Progress, stopping every now and then to explain and comment as he went along. This may be said to have been his first exegetical exercise, as well as his *coup d'essai* as an extemporaneous orator; and visitors were sometimes taken to the door which separated the kitchen from the apartments of the family, and would stand there, as if riveted to the spot, listening to the boy-interpreter, amazed at the display of so wonderful a talent for language and exposition in a mere child.

At a period somewhat later he became possessed of a copy of Miss Edgeworth's Tales of Fashionable Life, and growing deeply interested in them, he was not satisfied until he had read them aloud to another old black woman, who had succeeded his first pupil in the culinary department of the household.

His advancement in learning was now progressively rapid. It seems to have resembled the quick but regular and healthy budding-out of vernal plants during a favourable season. It was no hot-house vegetation that was thus maturing. There was no forcing of the natural processes. The ripening change that was going on was normal—spontaneous—joyous—and at the same time uninterrupted and sure. The growth of the human mind is always a surprising and edifying study. The process is carried on while men sleep. There is something apparently automatic about it. The seed cometh up of itself, the observer knoweth not how. The movement is conducted through a variety of stages, "first the blade—then the ear—after that the full corn in the ear." Great geniuses do not seem to be exempt from this universal law. The mightiest scholars have had to begin with the alphabet. Pascal rediscovers without assistance, and in childhood, the mysteries of geometry, but he has to proceed like other mortals, step by step from the definitions; and his attainments are successive, and in the order prescribed by the experience of ages as a necessity of the human intellect. But in the case of these penetrating and comprehensive minds the *rate* of progress is increased indefinitely, and the results are sometimes so marvellous as to appear incredible. Such an one was Joseph Addison Alexander. As soon as he was able to understand the meaning of English words his father began to teach him Latin. His habit was to write out for him each day a number of Latin words on a slip of paper, with the meanings in English, and make him commit them to memory. The same plan was pursued with his other sons, and subsequently with his grandsons. It was not long before Addison had thus committed *a thousand* of these Latin vocables. In due course of time the number had amounted to many thousands. This was the foundation of that enormous vocabulary which was afterwards to be of such incalculable service to the commentator on Isaiah, on the Psalms, on the Acts, on Mark, and on Matthew, and the remote origin of that classical scholarship which shines with no dim or uncertain lustre in every page of his somewhat voluminous writings. It is instructive to notice here that the same method precisely of commencing the acquisition of a new language was followed by the polyglot-Cardinal Mezzofanti,* who afterwards so much excited his marvelling curiosity.†

The chosen playmate and most intimate friend of James Alexander, was Edward Kirk, now the Rev. Edward N. Kirk, D. D., of Boston. Dr. Kirk has "no distinct recollections of Addison beyond some very minor points." His shyness and quietness, his studiousness and gentleness, embrace the substance of his image as it hangs on the walls of his fancy. "The only external fact I can recall, is his walking about while James and I were playing; he with a little card in his hand, on which his father had printed a list of Latin words with their English equivalents, to be committed to memory." Thus it was that the happy linguist began to train that quick

---

* See his Life, by President Russell, of Maynooth.

† In one of his later letters to his brother James, he pronounces the Italian linguist "a marvel."

and retentive faculty, which in later life enabled him to call up at will almost any thing he had ever treasured in his mind. It is easy to picture the stout little fellow, with his bright affectionate face, and cheeks like lady-apples, and his alternate fits of studious abstraction and uncontrollable liveliness. He was the delight and pride of the house.

But the young scholar was now to enter a new and boundless field for his exertions. He was to break the lock from the Semitic tongues, and to obtain an easy mastery over several of the languages of the Orient. As soon as he was six years old, or thereabouts, his father wrote out for him in the same manner as before, the Hebrew alphabet, of which the little philologist soon possessed himself, and thus laid the groundwork of his subsequent proficiency in that and kindred languages. At a somewhat later period, the same kind and capable hand prepared for him a Hebrew grammar, adapted to his years, which manuscript was carefully preserved by the youthful Hebraist, and was in his possession at the time of his death. That old manuscript Hebrew grammar, in the well-known handwriting of Dr. Archibald Alexander, is now one of the family treasures. The title-page of that grammar is now before me, and reads as follows:

"HEBREW GRAMMAR,

WITH THE POINTS,

Translated from Leusden's

Compend of Buxtorf,

FOR JOSEPH ADDISON ALEXANDER.

Princeton, New Jersey,

A. D. 1819."

This date furnishes us with pretty exact information as to the time when he commenced the regular study of Hebrew. It was when he was just ten years old. He could read the letters almost as soon as he could read English. What extraordinary advances he afterwards made, in this and cognate languages, we shall presently have occasion to notice.

Little Addison taught himself to write, and was able to do so before the family were aware of it. He soon acquired that firm, beautiful hand, with which his friends are so familiar.

An extract from a letter from his father, to his aunt, Mrs. Graham, dated July 22, 1817, gives an exact view of what he was at this time:

"Addison is also learning Latin, and greatly exceeds all our other children in capacity. He does not equal James in quickness, nor William in memory; but in the clearness of his ideas, and his steady attention to whatever he undertakes to study, he is greatly superior to them both. He has written several poems, but they are not worth sending so far."

The following account*by one who was the teacher who prepared him for college, is almost literally correct, but Addison began Hebrew and Arabic, and perhaps Persian and Syriac, at least two years before the date of his connection with that gentleman as a pupil:

"Whilst pursuing his studies with me, Addison (or 'Addy,' as the boys called him) commenced studying by himself the Hebrew language, and had made considerable progress in the Arabic before he entered College. I am not aware that he had at that early period of his life done much with the modern languages. In after years his acquisitions of both ancient and modern languages included nearly every one that is really worth learning. The Hebrew, with the cognate languages and dialects, he mastered when he was quite a young man. French, German, Italian, and other modern languages he next learned, including even the Turkish. The last languages which he acquired were the Danish and Coptic. What is wonderful about his linguistic attainments, they were in many cases made purely for the sake of the *literature*, (poetry, &c.,) which they contained."

This is an anticipation of disclosures that will be more fully made in the sequel.

For the sake of giving a glimpse of what was going on at Princeton about this time, I insert here the following extracts of a letter from Dr. Archibald Alexander to one of his wife's relatives in Virginia, which was written when Addison was

---

* In the Presbyterian of November 5th, 1853.

ten years and one month old, and which has never before been published. The whole letter exhibits much of the shrewd discernment of human nature, and knowledge of what was passing around him, which so distinguished this venerable man, and contributed so much to his character for wisdom. We may also see in this simple and homely letter the traces of his amiable feeling towards all, and of his affectionate disposition towards those with whom he was nearly connected.

"PRINCETON, *May 26th*, 1819.

" Dear ——

"Yours was received the day before yesterday. Since I wrote before, nothing worthy of notice has occurred among us. Mr. Menteith arrived here last evening, on his way home from a long Southern tour, which he took to solicit money for building a church in Detroit. Mr. Rice and his wife are in Philadelphia, but I have not been there, nor do I expect to go there, as I understand that they will not extend their visit to this place. Mr. Rice is the Moderator of the General Assembly, and preached an admired Missionary sermon last Sunday evening. Dr. Hill and Mr. Wilson of Fredericksburg were also there.

"I have this morning seen a letter from Armstrong. He appears much engaged in his work, and very much pleased. He says he would not exchange his situation as a poor missionary at present, for the best congregation in the land. Peters has gone to the Northeast. Hunter is licensed and preaching in this State, under the commission of the Female Missionary Society of this town.

"The Seminary, for the last week, has been nearly deserted. Pierce, Wisner, and Davies were the only persons seen about it. Wisner is a fine fellow.

"William * has entered the Sophomore class half advanced. I had no idea that he would be admitted, but he insisted on trying, and waited nearly three days to be examined. I neither went with him nor sent note or message to the faculty; but when he was introduced he acquitted himself in a way so masterly that Dr. Green was delighted, and told him he had never admitted any one with more pleasure in his life, and spoke of his elegant examination to the gentlemen who were in his house."

Addison's early education was almost entirely domestic,

* His second son.

for though before entering college he attended a variety of schools, in which all the usual branches were taught, he was up to the time of his entering these schools under the sole tuition of his father, to whom he owed more, even in the way of mere learning, than to any other living man. Nor is it too much to say, that at the time he entered the first of these schools, Addison if judged by the ordinary standard had already " received his education." This is a somewhat precarious assertion, but I hope to be able to show in the sequel, that at the time Addison entered school he was in point of scholarship in advance of many when they leave college, and are said to be " educated men."

It is difficult to say, we can only reasonably conjecture, in what relative order his remarkable powers first gave evidence of their existence, or what was the secret history of their successive or simultaneous appearances and steady and symmetrical development. He early showed a love of, and a taste and talent for music, and had he devoted himself to the cultivation of this gift, it is the opinion of one who was fully acquainted with the facts at the time, a contemporary and chosen play-mate, and who is himself by no means insensible to the "concord of sweet sounds," that he would have become as eminent in this department as he was in that to which he applied himself. This is saying a great deal. The expert commentator had certainly a fine ear for music.

There had long been lying about his father's house an old bamboo cane or staff. This staff was hollow, and had been perforated with holes as a flute. It also had a coarse common key. When about ten years old he took up this old cane flute, and upon it began to play. He studied and copied music, and learned it systematically. After practising for some time in this way, he was presented with a small octave flute, which after a few years was succeeded by a large one.

He became a proficient on the instrument, and for many years the use of the flute was his favourite recreation.

One of my first recollections is seeing him with a yellow flute in his hand or at his lips. He often played in my hearing, during my early boyhood, but it was for his own amusement, not mine. He preferred being alone on these occasions, and then I dare say his delectation was often great. He rendered simple and melodious airs with what afterwards struck me as perfect accuracy and much sweetness. I never heard him attempt any thing *hard*, but on the other hand I never heard him attempt any thing which he did not execute with consummate ease. His brother James was himself a delightful amateur flute-player. I never heard the two brothers playing in the same room.

Among the pieces thus melodiously rendered by the younger brother, was an affecting air which I shall always associate with an Arabic song, about a rose, which he was accustomed to sing to it. His voice was a high tenor, and plaintively sweet without being strong. He was fond of singing hymns, understood the mystery of "notes," and once pointed out to me a new tune, which has rung in my ears ever since. I also remember his song of the scales* and one of the tunes sung by his ghosts.† His European journals are full of allusions to the chants and chorals and masses he went to hear, but in these foreign diaries (which were designed to be a mere record of facts) he has, for the most part, sedulously suppressed all outbursts of feeling. When he was in the mood for it, he would talk with enthusiasm of music he had listened to with rapture in London, in the chapels of the English Universities, in Strasbourg, in Berlin, in Rome. He heard a boy at Cambridge who " had a voice like an an angel." But of all he ever heard he spoke with greatest admiration of the effect of a great number of priests' voices, accompanied by the organ, that on one occasion almost overpowered him, if I mistake not, at Rome. He sometimes affected to know nothing, and care nothing about music. This was his humour. He despised the poor American imitations of the Old-World ritualism. He had a certain æsthetic sympathy with the gorgeous cathedral service of the Old World. For the florid

---

* A pretty tune bringing in the eight notes.
† These ghosts were characters in some of his stories.

and effeminate church music of the New World he had none. He loved the plain old tunes, and regarded the old-fashioned congregational psalm-singing as the true way to worship God. He was sometimes irritated by the fastidious pertinacity of choirs, and never could understand the importance of "having the hymns." Yet he never failed in courtesy towards the musical gentlemen who solicited this slight but sometimes annoying compliance. He would say goodnaturedly enough that the choristers who were most particular about "having the hymns" could do best without them, and that he had noticed that the singing was always better where the hymns were not given. He probably meant in this delicate way to express a preference for the time-honoured tunes which are so apt to be lost sight of in the prevailing lust for novelty and for music such as is heard on week-days in the theatre or at the opera-house.

Some of the most impassioned pages in his printed sermons are strongly coloured by his native fondness for sweet voices and majestic harmonies. His unprinted sermons contain, perhaps, an equal quantity of this sort of writing, in which (especially near the close of the discourse), as by an accumulation of all his gifts and attainments toward a common centre, he makes painting, architecture, music, poetry, learning, genius—all he knew, all he imagined, all he felt, all he was, do tribute to the cross of Christ, or else shed a blaze of light on the joys or sorrows, the terrors or the glories of the eternal world. He exulted in the deep, mysterious, yet glorious organ-tones of the Revelation, reverberating as from afar with the roll of tumultuous waters. He actually seemed to have caught the sound of the "harpers harping with their harps," and the swelling cadence of that song, which peals like successive strokes of thunder through the Apocalypse, "Alleluia, for the Lord, God, omnipotent reigneth."

His imagination was from the first rich and vivid, and it is hardly a figure of speech to say that in his solitary hours he erected many an airy castle in the clouds, fought many a visionary fight, and attended many an illustrious but unreal audience on cloth-of-gold. There can be no doubt whatever, from the weight of authentic tradition on this subject, that as a boy Addison was a true child of genius, a dreamer of chivalrous and stately dreams, a hearer of voices and a beholder of faces and actions such as can be conjured up by no sorcery of earthly enchantment. He thus created for himself an imaginary world in whose fantastic but exquisite and varied enjoyments he continually revelled. The love of the preternatural and the intellectual exerted a joint sovereignty over his childish feelings. He could say with Shelley*:

> "While yet a boy, I sought for ghosts, and sped
> Through many a listening chamber, cave and ruin,
> And starlit wood, with fearful steps pursuing
> Hopes of high talk with the departed dead."

But in all this there does not seem to have been a particle of what is called absence of mind.† These reveries, if such they could be called, were indulged in solitude—never in the company of others. Moreover, during their continuance, the mind was ever present and intensely active. Sometimes, especially as he grew older, the imaginary scene merely afforded field and play to his common sense—his ingenuity—his laughing wit and humour—the heartiness and vivacity of his animal spirits. This was his sport—his recreation. For he too had his hours of mental relaxation, though he spent them very differently from his fellows of his own age. It was characteristic of him that he found pleasure in what would have been to others nothing but toil. With him duty and satisfaction ran in couples. As a lad at school, he seems to have been nearly always in good spirits. He made every thing around him conducive to his enjoyment, and while unremittingly engaged in the pursuit of knowledge, was as bright, joyous, and perfectly happy a boy as the sun ever shone on.

* Hymn to Intellectual Beauty.
† This is in some measure an inference from his later life. He was the least absent-minded man I ever knew, and has scourged this infirmity in his discourse on the text, "Watch."

Solomon tells the sluggard to go to the ant, for a lesson in diligence, and the improvident man to go to the bee for a lesson in wisdom. This wonderful boy probably stood in little need of instruction from these sources, but there was another species of animals, the fowls, to which he loved to repair for his diversion. A large number of chickens on the place were called into requisition to minister to his enjoyment. He gave to each a name, and organized them into a "chicken-college."* He arranged them in classes, and printed in his fair round hand a catalogue of the matriculates. He also devised, and issued in the same way, a curriculum of study which they were supposed to be pursuing. He conducted imaginary examinations, and published the names of those who were proficient in each department. He would announce public exercises—oratorical exhibitions, &c., prepare bills of the same, and publish accounts of the performances. He would announce annual commencements, put forth programmes, and give reports of what occurred on these festive occasions. In all this there was the same completeness of plan and the same scrupulous nicety and finish of detail, which marked every thing he ever did. In this innocent way would he spend hours of leisure which most boys would have devoted to pure idleness or even mischief. In company with the brother immediately older than himself, he would on holidays or when not engaged in study, go to a room where they would not be interrupted, or to a secluded part of the grounds, and would there organize with him a sort of moot-court, (the two acting alternately as judge and advocate,) and would imagine causes, civil and criminal, argue cases, harangue and charge unseen juries, and render verdicts, or give judicial opinions. A favourite amusement was indicting and trying a black boy named Ned, a servant in the family. Sometimes they would erect themselves into a congress and declaim on topics of public interest, and in this way entire mornings and afternoons were not unfrequently consumed, the sessions sometimes

* He afterwards amused some of his little friends among the children in the same way.

lasting uninterruptedly for many successive hours. The usual arena for these intellectual contests was a chosen place at the back of the garden. Here they would resort and "speechify" till the sun had visibly and greatly changed its place in the heavens. These legal and senatorial efforts were no ignoble training for a life of oratory. The brother * who shared with the *soi-disant* advocate and politician in these entertainments, testifies that any readiness in public speaking, any knack of prompt reply, any appearance of self-possession in embarrassing circumstances, and any facility in adapting words, acts, and circumstances to the occasion, and pressing them into his service, which have stood him in stead during a long and active professional and public life, he ascribes to these early intellectual and forensic efforts, taken up, as they were, at the time as a mere matter of amusement. Sometimes the two boys, both of them being gifted with remarkable powers of memory and fluency, would personate the different professions and callings in life; they would be lawyers, doctors, merchants, mechanics, officers civil and military, etc., etc., and would carry on dialogues, sometimes grave, sometimes gay, for hours.

It was to be expected that one so richly endowed with poetic faculties, and poetic tastes and sympathies, and so richly stored with the proper material for poetic composition, should turn his attention to the subject of verse and rhythm, and even put forth early essays in this style. Such we find to be the case. His earliest effort in metre is a piece composed in 1816, when he was about seven years old. It is an imaginative flourish on "the Seasons," and is not devoid of a certain excellence. The melody is perfect, and some of the epithets are happy. This was immediately followed by one on *the Yellow Fever*, and is marked by the same well-defined rhythmical structure which is conspicuous in his later effusions, and in some degree the same masterly command of language which could at all times bend the simplest words to the exigencies of the most measured cadence. This trait is singularly exemplified in some powerful lines entitled "Monosyllabics."

* The Hon. W. C. Alexander.

Yet he now and then indulged in children's games, perhaps for the amusement of others, though they were never of the ordinary kind, and always gave evidence of humour and originality. Mrs. Alexander, one day hearing a noise made by some children up stairs, as if applauding or laughing obstreperously, went up to see what it was. "She found in the room Addison and a parcel of children. In one corner of the room a counterpane suspended, formed a curtain. Mrs. A. peeping behind the curtain, discovered a small boy dressed up in red flannel, monkey-fashion, and seated. It thus proved to be a monkey-show, and Addison was the showman." *

But in general it was true that he found his chief pleasure in pursuing mental or manual diversions, and none at all in the favourite sports of boys, in which a good deal of exciting bodily exercise is called into play. He dwelt alone. He looked out of his studious window with a kind of speculative interest upon the green where the lads of his own age and "set" were hard at work flying the kite or scampering after the ball; but he was not of them. His joys were of another realm.

Mr. Alexander, through life, took a strange pleasure in noticing people that had any laughable peculiarities, whether of looks or manner, or as evinced by some absurd remark. He would bring up these things years after, and would turn their comical speeches into household proverbs, or would bring the tears into his eyes as he rehearsed their little adventures.

Mr. Charles Campbell apprises me of the fact that a lady of Staunton, Virginia, now deceased, once gave his mother, Mrs. Campbell, an account of a very odd-looking and pompous little preacher, before unknown, who in these days visited Dr. Alexander and staid all night. "He was of an outré appearance, looking like some kind of queer bird, *rara avis in terrâ*. He was quite conceited withal, and had a way of asserting trite truth in a very emphatic tone, e. g. straightening himself

---

* This incident has been preserved by the venerable Mrs. Campbell, of Petersburg, Virginia.

up he would exclaim *ore rotundo,* 'Dr. Alexander, I am firmly of the opinion that mankind by nature are totally depraved.' This eccentric little minister had the manner of a bantam cock. Towards bed-time, becoming uneasy lest the stranger should tarry all night, one of the boys inquired whether if he did, he would sleep in *his* bed? to which Addison replied, 'No, he will roost on the tester.' At prayers the stranger officiated, and happened to read the CII. Psalm: 'By reason of the voice of my groaning, my bones cleave to my skin. I am like a pelican of the wilderness: I am like an owl of the desert. I watch, and am as a sparrow alone upon the house-top.' When he read these ornithological verses, it was with difficulty that the ladies could repress their risibilities."

I give below extracts from another piece which he wrote about the same time. It is certainly good, to be the production of a very little boy:

"THE PARRICIDE.

"Ah! who is that with glittering blade,
Standing beneath the elm-tree shade,
The tear-drop glistening in his eye,
His bosom heaving with a sigh.
Why does he turn and fearful start,
And lay his hand upon his heart;
Why does he start with conscious guilt,
And grasp his sabre's shining hilt?
He turns and rushes to the tide,
And cries—'I am a parricide!'
* * * * * *
* * * * * *
But who comes there? 'Tis Osman dire,
His bosom burns with generous ire,
* * * * * *
* * * * * *
Juan to desperation driven,
One poisoned arrow from the seven,
His quiver held one poisoned dart,
Drew forth and hurled at Osman's heart.
False to its aim the arrow fell,

>   But human tongue can never tell
>   The rage that flashed from Juan's eyes
>   When he perceived he'd lost his prize.
>   Another dart to end the strife
>   He hurled ;—it took brave Osman's life."
>   * * * * * * *

The two following pieces were written in his eleventh year. They both exhibit a marked increase in the poetic power, but are chiefly interesting as shedding a curious light on the character and extent of his childish studies. The first is entitled—

"SOLITUDE.

>   " Now in the eastern sky the cheering light
>   Dispels the dark and gloomy shades of night;
>   And while the lowing of the kine is heard,
>   And the sweet warbling of the songster bird;
>   Where from afar the stately river flows,
>   In whose bright stream the sportive goldfish goes;
>   Where the thick trees afford a safe retreat,
>   From public eye and summer's scorching heat;
>   There let me sit and sweetly meditate,
>   Far from the gleam of wealth and pomp of state.
>   And while I listen to that murmuring rill
>   Which pours its waters down the neighbouring hill,
>   I can despise the pride and pomp of kings,
>   And all the glory wealth or power brings.
>   Here in deep solitude remote from noise,
>   From the world's bustle, idleness and toys,
>   Here I can look upon the world's vast plain,
>   And all her domes and citadels disdain."

The next, which was was written in the same year, affords us a pleasing glimpse of the boyish student and a charming picture of his early recreations. It is entitled—

"THE PLEASURES OF STUDY.

>   " The setting sun's resplendent shining ray
>   Illumes the West and brings the end of day;
>   And now across the mirthful village green,
>   Returning school-boys with their books are seen;
>   Who, wearied with the duties of the school,
>   Rejoice to enjoy the summer evening cool.

The beggars also wander thro' the street,
Entreating charity of all they meet;
Now learned men, philosophers profound,
In gloomy silence meditate around;
* * * * * * *
* * * * * * *
Now the poor peasant with his little store,
Returns with pleasure to his cottage door,
The rich upon their couches slothful roll,
With ease of limb, but restlessness of soul;
They still are restless when the glorious sun
His daily course through the broad heavens has run;
No rankling care afflicts the poor man's breast,
Who with a conscience light retires to rest.
Now o'er his books the studious scholar pores,
Nor hears the creaking of the opening doors;
Nor sees the visitors until they place
Their unwelcome forms before his studious face.
By him the wars of ancient Greece are seen,
While others sport upon the village green;
And while he dwells on Plato's flowing words,
He knows the pleasure study deep affords;
The Spartan chiefs and Athens' mighty son,
Who conquered on the plains of Marathon,
Pharsalia slow now rises to his view,
And all the millions Julius Cæsar slew;
Nor sleeps great Pompey nor Mark Antony's shade,
Who on the field of battle dead were laid.
He sees them all in fancy and he knows
When brave Camillus into splendour rose;
He feels the terrours of the Trojan crew,
Whom on the waves relentless Juno threw;
He hears the clamour rising to the skies
When haughty Taurus from the battle flies;
Loud cries of victory he hears,
And clamour bursts upon his startled ears;
He sees the young Julius clad in arms,
Resolved t' avenge his country's woeful harms;
He sees the place where noble Paris lies,
And hears the groans with which that hero dies;
And when from these reluctantly he goes,
To enjoy the time allotted for repose,
The shade of many a mighty hero seems,
To speak and hover round him in his dreams."

Some of these youthful attempts were copied into a little book in a fair copper-plate hand, by one of his instructors, and carefully preserved by his mother. This book I have seen. The pieces which I have inserted are not given so much for their intrinsic value, as to show the versatility of his parts and his early taste for versification, as well as to exhibit the maturity of his thoughts, his correct view of human life, and his ardent but already ripe and discriminating love for books, and what books contain. Literature was even at this early date beginning to afford a field for his indefatigable intellect and boundless ambition. It is not to be denied that his scholarship and general intelligence were at this time far in advance of his poetical talents. Many bright boys, such as Chatterton, Pope, and Kirk White, may have excelled these efforts in rhyme and metre at the same tender age. But these precocious versifiers were much inferior to the boy Addison Alexander in several other and more important particulars. Junctures, however, were to arise; themes were to be presented; culture of a special kind was to be gained; that were soon to lead to results even in the domain of poetry that could not have been anticipated from these first crude attempts. Qualities as yet almost unsuspected in this boy were presently to spring into existence, or burst into exuberance, that were one day to astonish and delight the admirers of prodigal genius.

It would certainly require sharp penetration to detect the author of the "Doomed Man," the noble lines on the Rhine, and on the Mediterranean, the sweet verses on the "Fatherless Girl," the powerful stanzas entitled "Be still, and know that I am God," and the exquisite fragment on the theme "He is Arisen from the Dead, He is not Here"—in "The Parricide" or even in the "Pleasures of Study."

He never referred himself to these boyish efforts except with a sort of good-natured, laughing malice. He always spoke contemptuously of immature essays of this kind, and I have heard him say that in his opinion one secret of Cowper's extraordinary success as a poet was that he never let the world see any of his "juvenile poems." One reason, perhaps, why these boyish effusions in verse fail to show Addison Alexander in his strength, is that after his very first ventures in this line he threw himself with his whole soul into the pursuit of classical and oriental learning; which for many years afterwards was to engage his highest powers, and to take up almost his whole time.

And yet if, when we compare him with his own later self, and with a few surprising genuises, his talent at this time for making verses may not strike one as very singular or wonderful; if we compare him with the majority of clever boys, it will appear to have been by no means inconsiderable. There is certainly promise in some of these nervous and sonorous couplets of greater things to come. If, as Wordsworth says, "the boy is father of the man," we may hope for fine poems from this sagacious judgment and glowing fancy when they shall have become matured and chastened. Nor shall we be disappointed in this expectation. Though the cloud is as yet no bigger than a man's hand, a storm of verse is brewing: " poetica surgit tempestas."

From this point onward, there are few traces of that imperfection or crudity which is naturally associated with the period of youth. His mental development was now so rapid that in a very short time from the date of these little juvenile poems, Addison, though in years still almost a child, was in power of thought and range of information a full-grown man; and in some respects a man, too, of extraordinary ability.

We have seen that he began the study of Latin at a very early age, and had even commenced the study of Hebrew. He had also entered upon a course in Greek. Exactly when he began Greek I have been unable to find out. It remains to be said, however, that he had been some time *reading* Latin and even Hebrew before he ever began to go to school. His first teacher out of the family was named James Hamilton, and was known generally as Jemmy Hamilton.

The Rev. George Burrowes, D. D., now professor at Easton, tells me he has often heard Mr. Hamilton " speak with pride of his connection with Dr. Addison Alexander, as his teacher in the early stage of the Latin; and mention that with such facility did he even then—a small, chubby, rosy-cheeked boy, pick up the language, that the perfect mastery of the lessons of his class in Historia Sacra, seemed to him a mere childish diversion."

Hamilton was a man of no ordinary ability; a ripe scholar, and a teacher of great merit. He was a native of Princeton, and was graduated at the College of New Jersey in 1814. After his graduation, he became an assistant teacher in the Princeton Academy, of which his brother-in-law, the Rev. Jared L. Fyler, was the principal. On the removal of Mr. Fyler from Princeton, Mr. Hamilton established a school there, which he conducted with distinguished success for many years. Among his pupils were the three oldest sons of Dr. Alexander, and the Rev. Edward N. Kirk, D. D., of Boston.

Mr. Tyler having opened a private school at Trenton, Mr. Hamilton joined him there as an assistant, and succeeded to the management and control of the school, on the removal of Mr. Fyler to Mississippi.

On the appointment of the Rev. Philip Lindsley, D. D., to the presidency of the University of Nashville, he took Mr. Hamilton with him as a Professor of Mathamatics. This position he is said to have filled with signal ability. After a few years he resigned his chair, returned to New Jersey, and reopened his school in Trenton; but after a time he gave it up and resumed his professorship at Nashville, where he died of cholera during the epidemic of 1849. Mr. Hamilton was, according to the standard of that day, a scholar of rare and varied attainments, and while thoroughly grounded in the languages, was eminently distinguished as a mathematician. He was by nature exceedingly diffident and retiring, and this prevented his filling that space in the public eye which was occupied by men of humbler talents and more slender acquirements.

It was under Hamilton that Addison probably received his best schooling in the mathematics. This and the kindred sciences was one of the few branches of study which he did not continue to prosecute with avidity in after life. There is no conclusive evidence, however, that his powers were not equally adapted to the class, or rather classes of studies he actually pursued, and to the regular demonstrations of geometry, or even the refined methods of the modern analysis. He was always quick at figures, and was in the habit, at least when travelling, of keeping accurate accounts. I have never detected any error in any of his calculations. He divided (as we shall presently see) the first honours of his class in college, and mathematics, though not carried to the lengths that are now familiar to our American students, yet formed an essential part of the course. There can be little doubt that his superb analytical discussions, his rare faculty of generalization, his exact habits as an observer, and his prodigious memory, might have placed him in the front rank of physicists or astronomers, had he chosen to devote himself heart and soul to these pursuits. It was his tastes rather than his abilities that pointed in another direction. Aside, moreover, from his natural turn or inclination for the study of languages, and the burning zeal with which he loved to ransack the treasures of ancient and modern—of oriental and occidental literature, the time was now at hand when a figure typical of the ignorance and sin that are in the world, and of the struggles of mankind after light, and hope and consolation that are only to be found in the Bible, was to stand before him in his dreams, and cry " Come over into Macedonia and help us."

I cannot fix the date precisely, but about the year 1817 or 1818, the Rev. Dr. Lindsley, then Vice-President and Professor of Languages in the College of New Jersey, opened in Princeton a select classical school for the preparation of young men for college. At the head of this school was placed Mr. Salmon Strong, of New York, and the school was visited, and the classes were examined once a week by Dr. Lindsley. Mr. Strong had been a student of the Theological Seminary, and was a graduate of Hamilton College. He had the reputation of being a good scholar and an experienced and successful teacher, a reputation which he fully sustained while in connection with Dr. Lindsley. He afterwards became the principal of an academy at Aurora, New York.

This school was attended by Addison and one of his brothers, as long as it was kept up. His next instructor was Horace S. Pratt, of Connecticut. Mr. Pratt, like Mr. Strong, was a student of the Seminary, and was a graduate of Yale College. He taught privately a few boys, and among them the subject of this Memoir. This was in 1818 and 1819. Mr. Pratt was settled as a pastor at St. Mary's, Georgia, and afterwards, I think, became a Professor in the University of Alabama at Tuscaloosa. The tuition under Hamilton was in 1816 and 1817. Addison, therefore, must have studied under Hamilton, when a boy of seven or eight, and under Strong and Pratt, when a boy of nine or ten years old. It was partly under the stimulus of these studies that he wrote the verses which have already been given.

His mind was now daily expanding to the sun and breeze of ancient learning; and he was soon to make his first acquaintance with the tongues of modern Europe, for which he continued through life to entertain an extraordinary fondness.

In the autumn of 1819, there came to Princeton as a theological student, a gentleman by the name of Robert Baird. At the instance of one of the professors, he spent some time daily in giving instruction to the young. He first taught in a private family in or near the village, and then in his room in the Seminary. Some time during the summer of 1821, Mr. Baird formed an acquaintance and pretty close intimacy with the eldest son of Dr. Archibald Alexander, who read French for a while with the ardent divinity student. How it was at this time, I do not know, but in after life French was to Mr. Baird as familiar and as easy as his mother tongue. At the same time he had an hour in the afternoon every day in Greek with the brothers William and Addison, at his own room in the seminary building, the former of the two boys being at the time in question twelve, and the latter fourteen. In the autumn of 1821, Mr. Baird succeeded Mr. Breckinridge as tutor in the college, and saw the older of the two boys enter as a sophomore. The younger joined a class of private scholars formed by Mr. Baird, but taught by two other theological students.

In the autumn of the year 1822, a new academy was established in Princeton of which the now celebrated Robert Baird became the principal. Mr. Baird was from Pennsylvania, and a graduate of Jefferson College. He had been, as we have seen, a student of the Theological Seminary at Princeton, and also a tutor in the College of New Jersey. Mr. Baird was already somewhat famous for the accuracy and extent of his scholarship, and for his success as a teacher, and in this new undertaking, succeeded in imparting an extraordinary degree of ardour to his pupils. Among his first scholars was Addison Alexander. In addition to his regular lessons, which were always perfectly prepared, Addison here devoted himself with renewed assiduity to general literature. He established and edited a newspaper, which was beautifully printed* with a pen, and of which, I am assured, the contents would have done no discredit to his mature manhood. He united with several others in founding a literary society in the Academy, and devoted himself to it with wonderful relish and enthusiasm.

In conjunction with the Hon. William Barclay Napton, the late Chief-Justice of the State of Missouri, he opened a moot-court in which causes were argued with technical propriety and elaborate skill. Minutes of this court were regularly kept, in which the arguments and decisions were duly recorded.

Among the other pupils of Mr. Baird at this time, were Mr. William King, of Savannah, now of Marietta, Georgia, an intimate friend both of Mr. Alexander and Judge Napton, and Mr. David Comfort, formerly of New Jersey, and now of Charlotte County Virginia.

* Dr. Alexander had much of Porson's love for calligraphy, and often amused himself with what might have seemed to some a frivolous eye to the appearance of his manuscript. We shall have abundant testimonies as we go on to his success in this particular. Even in these small matters, it might be said of him that he touched nothing that he did not adorn.

The circumstances under which Mr. Baird came to be one of Addison's teachers are recounted in an obituary notice of the latter, in the Presbyterian, in which Mr. Baird says:

"When I entered the Theological Seminary at Princeton, in the autumn of 1819, I was encouraged by the late Dr. Archibald Alexander to devote two or three hours daily to giving instruction; and this I did throughout the entire course; first in a private family, then for a year and a half in my room in the Seminary to a son and nephew of the late Dr. Green, then President of the College, and lastly as a tutor in the College. In the summer of the second year [1821] I became somewhat intimately acquainted with the late Rev. Dr. James W. Alexander, who, having graduated the autumn previous, was devoting himself to historical and general studies, under his honoured father's direction. He came often to see me, for the purpose of reading French, to which language I had given some attention. During that summer, at the request of their father, I undertook to give some lessons in Greek to Addison and William Alexander, and for that purpose they came every afternoon to my room for an hour. The former was then twelve years old, the latter fourteen.

"In the autumn of 1821 I took the place of the late Dr. John Breckinridge as a tutor in Princeton College; William entered the Sophomore class that autumn, and was no more under my instruction; but Addison joined a class of boys which I formed, but not being able to teach them on account of the tutorship, I committed them to two fellow-students in the Theological Seminary. In the autumn of 1822, leaving the tutorship, and having completed the course of studies in the Seminary, I took charge of a classical school in Princeton, which I conducted till the spring of 1828, when, for want of sufficient health, I gave it up for an active course of life, which, under one form or other, I have pursued ever since. Addison entered the school at the outset, and continued in it till the age of fifteen, when he entered (in the autumn of 1824) the junior class in the college. His brother Archibald entered the school at a later day, and remained in it till he entered College."

Never was a sensitive and bashful man more misjudged than was Addison Alexander. From the first he was shy reserved and diffident; not diffident perhaps of his abilities or acquirements, but unwilling and almost incapable of showing them off. It is interesting to know that his early efforts in declamation, like those of Demosthenes and Webster, were failures. Yet he afterwards excelled most of his mates in the gift and art of oratory. On these points his preceptor continues:

"When Addison came under my instruction he was a short and stout boy, possessing fine health and a fine flow of spirits, but exceedingly diffident. His first attempts at speaking before the school were about as unpromising as can well be imagined. He was so diffident that he could scarcely get on at all; and yet when he left the school to enter the College, at the age of little more than fifteen, he had grown very much, and was a graceful and effective speaker. And when he graduated, two years later, he was a very fine speaker—finer, I think, than he was in the later periods of his life. I do not believe that he ever got rid of the extreme diffidence which characterized his youth. It was, undoubtedly, the principal cause of his strong repugnance to going freely into society. It combined with his delight in study to make him more of a recluse than his friends desired him to be."*

Perhaps no one was more struck with his cleverness and versatility than the head of the Academy himself. The "compositions" of his round-faced little scholar greatly and especially attracted him. On this point he says:

"At that early period he displayed much talent for writing. At twelve o'clock every day it was my custom to require two of the boys to read each a sketch of one of the deities of the Roman and Greek mythology, or of some of the heroes or authors of ancient or modern times, or of some country, or of some portion of history. The epitomes which he produced were always excellent. Even then, I may add, he had a great fondness for writing stories for the small boys, in which he displayed great tact as well as taste. A fondness for this sort of amusement he retained, I believe, to his dying day—passing from the gravest and severest studies with the most extraordinary ease to the writing of pleasant and interesting stories, and pieces of poetry for youthful minds. He began also at that time to be an editor. He established a weekly journal, writing every word in such a way as wonderfully to resemble printing. I have forgotten the name of his periodical; but I remember that an opposition paper soon appeared, and as might be expected, it was not very long before I had

---

* Dr. Baird, in the Presbyterian.

to *suppress* both—the first and second '*warning*' which I gave only provoking both editors to say some very bold things, things which encroached too much on my magisterial prerogatives."*

In a letter to Mrs. Graham, dated July 22, 1823, Dr. Alexander refers to Addison's extraordinary industry, his Homeric studies, his penchant for the law, his aversion to teaching, his joy at finding some Persian manuscript, and his admiration for Sir William Jones. The greatness and goodness of Jones always seemed to exert an influence on him whenever he had occasion to go to him for pleasure or instruction. "Addison is at home, not loitering, but engaged fourteen hours of the day in hard study. He read five books of Homer in one week, and is going through the Odyssey as well as the Iliad. Unless the grace of God should prevent, the law will probably be his profession. He is fond of legal disquisitions. But I never heard him express an opinion on the subject of a profession. To teaching he has a strong aversion, which is the case with all my children. Addison has found two old Persian manuscripts in the College Library, and the very sight of them gives him pleasure. I can see very plainly that his admiration of Sir William Jones influences him in all his literary pursuits."

An interesting relic of this period is given below, which bears this inscription:

"An Arabic translation of the title-page of 'Waverley,' by Jos. A. Alexander.

"Princeton, August 20, 1822."

The facsimile of a page of original Arabic, composed and written by a boy of thirteen, will be regarded as a literary curiosity.

There is another specimen of this kind of the same date, and his journals of subsequent years are full of this flexible but difficult character. There are also letters of his extant

---

* The reader will be amused by comparing this account of the suppression of the weekly paper with that given in these pages by Mr. King.

written partly in this tongue. But the fragment here given is, not only from its early origin and its occasion, but also from its subject, probably the most singular memorial of his oriental studies.

كتاب

واوردلي او

ستون السنة قبل

اسغلً الاليك بروتيان قل او قتنله
الوي رابع

ثلاثة كتاب في احد كتاب

كتاب اول

نو يورك
ياكوب يسنبورن وكن
ذ لونع ربستر

الب ثمان مايت عشرون اثنان

His old teacher, Dr. Baird, has put his hand to the discriminating judgment of his early powers as a linguist, which I give below:

"I cannot say that he was remarkably accurate in his knowledge of the Latin and Greek languages when he first came to me, although he had read nearly every author that was required for entrance into the Freshman class. But such was his progress in two or three years that he became a remarkably fine scholar, entered the College with high reputation, and took the first honours of the Institution.* I have never seen a better classical scholar at the age of fifteen than he was. Nor was his knowledge of mathematics much inferior to that of the Latin and Greek languages. He wrote Latin, both in prose and verse, with great ease and purity. Many of his imitations of the Odes of Horace were admirable. Towards the end of his course in the Academy he could read with ease several pages of Herodotus or Thucydides, or two hundred lines of Homer in an hour.

"During almost all his course with me he taught for nearly an hour every morning and afternoon one of the lower classes, and he did it well. He was a great favorite with the boys. He was sure to have a crowd around him, if he came half an hour or more before the school opened. On these occasions his diffidence always left him. He was the master-spirit in the Literary Society of the Academy, as well as in the Moot-Court, which the boys held once a week, where he was sure to be eminent, whether he acted the part of the judge or that of the advocate."

As to his disposition to stick to his books, and his geniality of feeling, he adds the following handsome testimony:

"For reasons which I have stated, Dr. Joseph Addison Alexander was never fond of going into society; but he was far from being of a morose disposition. On the contrary, his feelings were genial, and his attachments were sincere and enduring. His delight was in his books, and in the society of his intimate friends. But he had neither time nor inclination to go into company."

* Several of those who were fellow-students of Addison in the Academy have become men of more than ordinary usefulness and distinction. One of them, who is now Judge Napton, of the Supreme Court of Missouri, was his classmate both in the Academy and the College, and shared with him the highest honours of the class in both. It was impossible to determine which of them was the better scholar. Judge Napton may have his equal in the knowledge of law, but I am sure that he has no superior, either in legal or classical attainments, in all the West.

I might add almost indefinitely to the testimonies already given. A few more may be appended here. Dr. George M. Maclean, the brother of the President, and, as I have reason to remember, a skillful and accomplished physician, writes as follows:

"I remember him as a boy of unusually great promise, one far in advance of those of his years in attainments. He associated but little with other boys."

This was when he was a school-boy, say of ten or twelve. I also feel at liberty to mention the name of James Ewing, Esq., of Trenton, who carried off the highest honours of the class of 1823, and who does not hesitate to express himself in similar terms. He has told me that though he saw little of Addison in those days, he remembers distinctly that his extraordinary promise as a scholar was matter of general talk in Princeton. He says he was exceedingly fleshy, with a face that bloomed with health and high spirits. A venerable lady living in the same town (Trenton), who is now upwards of eighty, and long a valued friend of the family, confirms both of these statements, and adds that she recollects one occasion in particular, on which his father called Addison up to his knee and made him recite Latin words to her. This was when he was a very little boy. The same lady also recalls to mind a meal that she once took in his house after his father's death, and how singularly charming and entertaining he was.

Mr. Comfort, who is himself a teacher of many years standing, has informed me that Addison's recitations at this time were faultless, and that his manner of making them was very similar to his manner in after life when lecturing or preaching without notes. He says that his fluency of speech, and unerring accuracy of expression, were quite as remarkable at this, as at any later period. He would pour out his words with vehemence and rapidity, in a sort of clear, steady, and voluble torrent. He always got a perfect mark. His habits of solitary study and segregation from the mass of his fellows, were already formed. His gentleness, liveliness, and sparkling wit and humour, when in a happy frame of mind and in society he loved, were just as conspicuous as afterwards. He also occasionally exhibited the same high-toned firmness and frankness of character which, in some of its manifestations, always excited wonder if not resentment among those who did not know him thoroughly. Just here I will say, that in my opinion he was one of the most intrepidly honest, as well as, when so disposed, one of the most open-hearted and generous-hearted of men. The brother who sat by his side at Mr. Baird's school, testifies that Addison was then, as he was always, noted for his singular *truthfulness.* This was a remarkable trait in his disposition. The brother to whom I refer never knew him flinch from telling the plain truth about any thing. This peculiarity characterized him throughout life, and was one cause of his giving offence sometimes. He "came right out with a thing," as we say, where many would have smoothed or softened a little, at the expense of strict veracity. He seems to have held to the opinion once advanced by John Randolph of Roanoke (but now not much in vogue), that candour is as great an ornament in a man, as modesty is in a woman. He never learned, and certainly never practised the wiles of small dissimulation which, though undoubtedly repugnant to the strict Bible standard, are not flatly condemned, but are rather tolerated, if they are not expressly sanctioned by the canons of the world. He was indeed a stranger to many of the arts of society which are unquestionably innocent; but there was a fount of native politeness in his heart, and no high-bred courtier ever knew better how to charm. His eye had a merry twinkle that is indescribable, and that resembled bright sunshine glancing over blue seas. His cheek was fair and rosy; his head was too broad and massive for the impression of simple elegance, but his features were delicately regular, and his face was round and decidedly comely. His hair was dark brown — chestnut brown, and thin; his lip was chiselled like a piece of statuary, and expressed decision and resolve; it was like the lip of Bonaparte. His head was large and broad, beyond almost any thing I ever saw in a person of his height; and yet it was not at all too large for his body, and was perfectly well balanced. His brow would have served a sculptor for a model of Jupiter. I doubt whether Webster or Cuvier had a much larger brain. His stature was below rather than above the medium, yet his bulk would always impress one as being very great. His tendency was always to corpulency. His figure and head have reminded many of Napoleon. His face was certainly like the Napoleon at Fontainebleau of Paul de la Roche. It had the same air of concentrated passion in repose, though it had nothing of that look of fiery and intrepid gloom. His countenance was like a clear sky that might one day rock with whirlwind. When he laughed, there was a fine union in his face of masculine genius and child-like mirth. This picture is of course taken at a later period, but it corresponds in general with the accounts of his boyhood.

One of his school-fellows says he distinctly remembers how " Addison " looked as he sat in the school-room wrapt up in his cloak, and mentions his fleshy person, ruddy cheek, and twinkling eye. The brother who studied with him says that, as when he had his father for a master, Addison while under these new preceptors never engaged in ordinary boys' sports. Even his plays partook of an intellectual character; they were, for the most part, legal, forensic, or political combats, such as holding courts, having mock trials, editing newspapers, etc.

It gives me pleasure to insert here several large extracts from a letter I have lately received from his school-mate and early friend, Mr. King. Mr. King, writing from Marietta, Georgia, says:

"You have greatly contributed to my gratification, in putting upon me the task of communicating to you my recollections of the youthful days of my highly esteemed friend, the late Rev. J. Addison Alexander; thus bringing afresh to my memory the pleasures of my boyish days, and my intimate associations with one so much beloved; but a lapse of over forty years has damped the ardor of youth, and put memory at fault. None however of my early friends have left more durable and pleasant impressions upon my memory, or which I have cherished with more care.

"My acquaintance with Addison was formed early in the year 1823, when I attended the Princeton Academy, then in the charge of Mr. Robert Baird; and I continued in personal intimate association with him until the fall of the year 1824, when these relations were interrupted by my return to the South. I never saw him but once afterwards. We regularly corresponded for many years. His last letter to me was written about two years before his death. He was near two years my junior, but was then well grown, having indeed nearly attained his full height, with an excess of flesh; weighing, I think, over a hundred and fifty pounds. Though very fleshy, he was always quick and sprightly. He had at this time a round red face, with brilliant and mischievous eyes, that were nearly always full of fun. Among strangers (whose presence he avoided as much as possible) he was very quiet and reserved, but so observing that their peculiarities supplied him with a stock of amusing comments for the gratification of his friends. With his intimate friends (very few in number) he was a most incessant talker, and so abounding in life, wit, and humour, that he was generally allowed to occupy as much of the time as he desired. His sarcasm was often of the most caustic nature; kind-hearted as he was, his best friends were often made to feel the severity of his wit. His life and buoyancy when in the society of his chosen companions was extraordinary; but the sudden appearance of a stranger as suddenly transformed him into a serious, silent boy, exhibiting all the modesty of a girl, but giving full employment to his eyes and ears. He realized, in a certain sense, the old figment of the duality of the soul. He seemed to possess two different natures. To one person, he appeared a boy of unbounded life and conversational powers, to another his character seemed thoughtful and silent. He never betrayed any malicious feelings nor immoral tendencies. As a boy, his disposition for placing persons and things in a ridiculous attitude was extreme, and his powers in this direction were seldom equalled. His most valued associates enjoyed no privilege in this respect; yet this strange treatment of those he really loved sprung from pure vivacity of mind, untinctured with any bitterness of feeling. He was a hard student then, as in after life, seldom wasting any time." Mr. King says that Addison "was fond of long walks in the country with one companion, and that *he* was generally the one to enjoy the pleasant walks with him, often to a distance of two or three miles from the town." He adds that "during those long walks his tongue was kept as active as his body. He had acquired a large stock of knowledge even in those early years of his life. He was then considered a fine Arabic scholar, and perfectly at home in the Latin and Greek languages. His general reading was extensive, and he seldom forgot any thing he read, heard, or saw, and was very quick in bringing into use the stock he had thus stored in his remarkable memory. His compositions for school were written in the finest style, and were remarkably interesting." Many of these, says Mr. King, "I had taken possession of, and retained to read and re-read in my after-years for the gratification of myself and my friends. So valued were these remains of his boyish effusions, that they, with his many letters written in his early and later years, were carefully preserved by me; and they would now be a treasure to you. But they are all gone; not a single one is left to me. His piece for a school exercise, on the 'Wandering Baboon,' an extravaganza founded on the supposed escape of such an animal from a menagerie in Princeton, exhibited the greatest talent as a descriptive writer, and the greatest powers of wit and satire. The young humourist represented the creature as roving over the Rocky hills lying north of the town, much to the dismay of the honest country folk who inhabit that serrated ridge. Another piece in which he had collected together to convey his ideas all the difficult and unused words in our language, was a model of his skill, although each word was properly used and carefully read.* From his hearers generally, his ideas, as expressed in this remarkable effort, were as

* These feats in English composition were always favourite diversions with Dr. Addison Alexander. The Princeton Magazine is full of his Essays of this character, but some of the most astonishing among them have never seen the light. This periodical also contains specimens of his humourous pieces in other styles. The ingenuity, scholarship, and wit that were put to the stretch in these amusing exercises seemed to be inexhaustible. The variety of styles in which this comic humour was indulged was without known limit. Scarcely two of these pieces are composed on the same principle. I shall have occasion to refer to this subject again in other connections. I need only point now to such articles in the Princeton Magazine as the one on "Economy of Thought," the one on "Economy of Words," those on "Freedom of Speech," and those entitled "Correspondence of the Princeton Magazine," "Counsellor Phillips," "Gentlemanly," "Ham and Eggs: A Plea for Silent Legislation," "Mother Country and Father-Land: A Dialogue," "Nil Admirari," "Westminster and Washington," "School of Legislation," "Some People," "Something New," "Utilitarian Poetry," "The Tailors' Strike: An Humble Attempt at The Newest French Style of Romantic Fiction," "The King's English," by "Miss Mary," and "The Riches of the English Language." These are some of the most striking. The last contains a composition that almost meets the conditions of Mr. King's description of the one which excited the laughter of the boys at Princeton. It is made up of words all of which are (or were) to be found in Webster's Dictionary; "although," observes the writer, "some, I regret to say, are marked as obsolete."

"During a short outlope, which I took one rafty morning, in my olitory fell, to discover the ublcation of a vespiary which annoyed me, I saw a tall, wandy, losel lungis, in a leasy roquelaur, thridding my gate, and knabbing a jannock which I had just before inchested in my pantry. From his xanthic colour I took him for a Zambo poller who had sometimes shaved me. As it was gang week, I thought he might be maunding, and would willingly have given him a manchet; but I was not such a hoddy-doddy as to suffer every patibulary querry to go digitigrade about my house and grounds. I mounted my horse, which I had left to gise on a seavy eyot in the neighboring beck during my grassation, and pursued him, but he seized a clevy and tried to blench the horse's chaufin and to hase him back into the fell. Failing in this, he began to accoy me, and begged me to employ him as an abacist, pretending he had served as a lancepesade of infantry in Hayti. But I snebbed and gouged him, and not wishing the affair to be known to the neighbouring clerisy, who were already not a little roiled by some things I had said too overlashingly, I let the lown go shot-free, and went home rather lateward, feeling very hebete

much concealed as if it had been written in an unknown tongue; still its reading afforded an immense amount of mirth to his hearers, ignorant as they were from the beginning to the end of the novel recitation as to the meaning embodied in the rapidly uttered and enigmatical syllables that saluted their ears.

"His chief, if not his only intimate companions of that time were Judge Napton and myself, boys of near the same age, and having much congeniality of feeling and opinions. For a long time the three issued from the Academy a weekly manuscript paper entitled the 'Medley,' which received an extensive circulation, being often carried over into New York and Philadelphia. This paper afforded much entertainment to the readers, and much intellectual profit to the editors. This journal was suppressed by Mr. Baird, the Principal of the Academy, whose order conveying the injunction was the occasion of serious murmurs and discontent among his pupils. He was willing that the good should be lost rather than hazard an apprehended evil. Sometimes the wit and satire were too scathing; the students of the academy, the community, and sometimes the opinions and doings of our highly-esteemed teacher, though the names of the parties satirized were never mentioned, were the subject of that paper's comments. Addison was the chief contributor to its columns. In the debating Society of the Academy he took little interest. He performed his part, but more as a duty than a pleasure. He manifested very little desire for argument or discus-

---

and curst; but after eating a chewet and drinking a few mozers of perkin, I slumped into the quag and slept till morning."

The "Fandango of Osiris," "An Oriental Tale," &c., are in the same general character, though each of these absurd effusions is marked by its own native and incomparable peculiarities. A friend has called my attention to the striking resemblance of some of these to some of Swift's humourous pieces. The point is well taken. The likeness in some respects is apparent; yet in others the spontaneous effusions of which I have been speaking are without a parallel in the whole range of English Literature. One is a little reminded at times of Rabelais or Le Sage.

sion, but generally he brought into exercise his masterly power of destroying the force of his opponent's argument by wit and burlesque. Young Napton's talent was of a different order. Although a hard student and good scholar, his general reading was less, and his memory more like that of other men." Mr. King, however, was under the impression that Judge Napton's thinking powers and argumentative skill were superior at that time to those of his friend. This, if true, would be no derogation from his talents.

Mr. King concludes his interesting letter as follows : " In the days of Addison's boyhood, his subsequent greatness was shadowed forth; he was as remarkable as a boy as he afterwards became remarkable as a man. God in his wisdom has cut him down in the prime of life, and in the midst of usefulness; but he had even then attained in knowledge, the position of old age in other learned men."

Whenever any thing was to be done in the way of rapid original composition, and the dull or lazy fellow on whom the task had been imposed could not or would not do it; whenever a boy wanted to astonish his teacher and companions with an uncommonly humourous or florid oration—something quite out of the usual line—recourse was had at once to Addison. He was easy and accommodating in his disposition, and always willing to help a classmate out of the slough. One of his school-fellows has told me that from the very beginning, the precocious linguist and satirist gave him the sense of inexhaustible capacity for every species of writing. He said the quick and exact mathematician, the young master of Latin and Greek, and English, the blue-eyed lover of the Arabic and Persian, seemed to be up to any thing, and always ready for a good practical joke. He was a round-bodied, merry, rather silent, shrewd, accurate, kind-hearted, startling, comical lad. His complexion was white and red, and his plump figure threatened trouble on the score of too much flesh.

"Did I ever mention to you," asks a friend, " having heard of Addison's writing speeches for older boys, while he was quite a junior pupil in the old Princeton Academy on the hill, near Mr. John Potter's? The older boys were required, on set occasions, perhaps at the close of the sessions, to deliver *original* speeches before public audiences. While Addison was a mere boy, I think not more than thirteen years old, he would write speeches for his seniors which would 'bring down the house.' You and I can understand how he would appreciate such a joke; and how much better than most boys, or men either, he could keep such a secret."

He always entertained an affection for the umbrageous solitudes of Stony Brook. The memory of green woods and silver streams as a part, and a most delightful one, of the scenery of his school-boy recreations, was always cherished by him. O that I knew how to tell how he wandered in the summer afternoons under the spreading branches of the elm and the chestnut; and how, perhaps, like his brother James, he cut letters in the beech or aspen!

One day long afterwards he wrote in his journal, " walked to Stony Brook," and then appended the lines given below, and which were " composed while walking, Nov. 5, 1853."

They may chance to strike some as being pretty, and are undoubtedly of biographical interest. They throw an additional ray here and there upon his boyish fancies and ambition, and the mental struggle it must have cost him, with his sense of rare powers and precocious acquisitions, to give up his early dreams of fame in the world of letters, and perhaps of active exploit. They also show how much he loved the place and associations of his childhood.

"Dear Princeton! What a volume is contained
In that one word! How many memories,
Both sweet and sad, come pouring out of it,
As from an ancient spring, long choked or dry,
But now reopened with a sudden burst
And gush of waters. Oh beloved home
Of my long lost, irrevocable youth!
Even in sleep, when I revisit thee,
I cease to be my present self—I grow
Preposterously young—I am a boy,
A wild, ambitious, visionary boy,

> Dreaming the old dreams all alive with hopes
> Long dead and buried, till I start awake
> And know them to be phantoms. How much more
> When in reality I travel back
> To these familiar places, does my life
> Go backwards too!"

After finally establishing the academy and bringing it to a high state of prosperity, Mr. Baird, in the spring of 1828, gave it up and sought a renewal of health in the more active pursuits in which he spent the remainder of his life. Mr. Baird was in many and perhaps all respects the best of Addison's teachers before he entered college.* This estimable gentleman afterwards married a Miss Dubuchin, the daughter of a French *emigrée*, and French and perhaps one or more of the modern languages were spoken freely in his family. Two of his sons, when many years had rolled by, became pupils of Dr. Addison Alexander, then professor in the Theological Seminary, and it was evident that the kindly and admiring feeling with which he regarded them, was not due alone to their acknowledged excellence as men and students, but in part also to old recollections. Dr. Baird was a frequent guest of Dr. Archibald Alexander, and the master and pupil of former days spent many a long hour together conversing upon topics of common interest.

For several weeks in the month of February, 1824, the elder brother was engaged in the study of German, with Mr. Zadig, a native of Silesia, who had relinquished the Jewish religion, and been baptized. This was the beginning of an acquaintance with the language, which was afterwards a great delight to the American student, and enabled him to read, write, sing, and speak it admirably. At this time he paid little attention to French, though acquainted with it. The Christian Advocate about this date published a communication upon the Praise of God, from the pen of the same young scholar writing under the signature of Cyprian. He also contributed for the January number of the American Monthly

---

* At a later date he prepared another of Dr. Alexander's sons for Nassau Hall.

Magazine, a poetical address to the New Year, under the same *nom de plume*. He was much interested in current literature, and suffered nothing of value to escape his eye or comment. The winter was the most extraordinary for mildness of temperature that had ever been experienced in Princeton. Every thing was sheeted in ice. This did not prevent his fancy from roaming in the fields of English poetry and over the objects of the American landscape. " Our forests and mountains," he writes to Dr. Hall, " and waters, surely furnish scenes second to none that European poets and romancers have hackneyed, and our mighty works of nature might, I should suppose, inspire a feeling as ethereal as ever prompted the Theban Pindar."*

Edward Irving, whom Addison was presently to see and hear in his own chapel, was now just rising into fame in Scotland. At the close of a warm but careful panegyric of his ability as a writer, the eldest of the Alexander brothers remarked in his adversaria, " One cannot help regretting that a man who possesses so great a share of originality and poetic inspiration, and who might be so powerful in a natural path of composition, should wander off into this uncouth, untrodden region, and put on the manacles of an abolished style. Eloquence, and power, and imaginative soaring are compatible with the simplest, chastest style, and the most strict obeisance to the canons of right criticism, as may be seen in the single instance of Robert Hall."

The vernal season was not much advanced before the writer of this critique, disgusted with the results of a mere discursive reading of the classics, had resolved to enter upon the regular perusal of the principal Greek and Latin writers of antiquity, pursuing the method laid down by Le Clerc, of taking them in chronological order. In the course of time he thus accomplished all of the principal Latin writers of the classic eras and many of the Church fathers. He also read many of the Greek writers. He at first did not scrutinize the text with the eye of a critical grammarian, but read as he would English, for

* Fam. Letters I., p. 36.

recreation, and improvement in taste. He was already an exact linguist. His task for March 3d was in Homer and Plautus.

A few days after I find this entry: "Spent last evening at Dr. Lindsley's, where as usual I was very kindly and agreeably entertained. The Professor, as he is wont to do, descanted upon the superiority of the ancients to the moderns, and urged many weighty arguments to prove that literature was more generally diffused among the Greeks than among any modern people. Gained much useful information." Every glimpse of this great and good man ought to be prized by the men of this day, who owe so much to his labors.

Mr. James Alexander (whose brother Addison was now a lad of not quite fifteen, and on the verge of college) wrote frequently at this period for Walsh's Gazette and the American Monthly Magazine, and he was in no lack of letters containing flattering allusions to these articles. He was much given to visiting the theological students at their rooms, and found himself constrained to adopt a resolution of greater temperance if not of total abstinence in this respect. The social tendencies of Addison were not so overbearing. It required no formal regulation or conscious purpose, to cause him to keep his room. In after days the elder brother was constantly making and breaking resolutions to "go abroad." He found that in his case solitude tended to produce hypochondria. I find him engaged during these days on Plautus, Terence, Homer, certain works in French, Turretin, Pictet, Hodgson's Travels, Marcus Antoninus, Leighton, etc. He wrote at the time, that he never expected to find studies more congenial to his taste and inclinations than those in which the Seminary students were then engaged, especially that of Didactic Theology.

On the night of the 11th of April, he had the pleasure of hearing Mr. George Bush, afterwards so famous first as a Scripture Commentator and then as a writer upon Swedenborg. Mr. Bush had not very long before left the Seminary, where up to that time he had been pursuing his theological studies. The sermon was an admirable one, "rich in original and important matter, adorned with striking illustrations, and remarkable for the uncommon force of language." Mr. Bush sometimes reminded his friend of *Chalmers* in the novelty of his thoughts, and the powerful mode he had of expressing them. The next morning he woke up to find himself appointed tutor in the College of New Jersey, by the Board of Trustees, who were then sitting. This excited his wonder, and aroused some apprehension; but he accepted the proffered chair (or footstool), and on the twenty-first of May sat down where he had never expected to be situated in that capacity, a tutor of the college, and occupant *ex officio* of No. 25 Nassau Hall. His first care was mathematics; afterwards he was placed over the Latin and Greek classes.

James was young, and exceedingly sensitive, and at this time a little shamefaced. He was one of the most mercurial of men. He was often deeply despondent, but just as often carried away with high spirits. He was prepared for many mortifications and trials. He dreaded among other things having to confront the whole body of students upon the stage, and to pass through their ranks, and head them in entering the Refectory. "My youth," he writes, "is likely to call forth the disrespect and presumption of some, and the exercise of that authority which I am called upon to assume must gain me the ill-will and ill offices of those who are its objects. Yet this is the tax which every man must pay, who is so happy as to aim at the welfare of his fellow-creatures." He found his position an easier one than he supposed. A fellow-student of his brother Addison, and pupil of the young-looking, but extremely dignified mathematical tutor, tells me that he vividly remembers Mr. James Alexander's spare person and deep black eye, and how he would draw himself up and place a visible constraint upon his mobile features when any thing of a laughable nature occurred. His hair and his complexion were both uncommonly dark. His head was high, and somewhat narrow, and his face long and oval. His temples were finely moulded, and were unusually bare. The expression of his countenance was frank, noble, generous, intellectual, and in a singular degree captivating and engaging. It was forever changing with his changing feelings. He always stood upon his native dignity, and seldom or never had cause to administer a reproof for misconduct. The classical felicity of his taste and of his diction were subjects of marvel. His piety was as evident as it was unobtrusive. He was eminently popular, without once letting down the bars of discipline. By many, he was beloved with an extraordinary affection; by some with an almost passionate devotion. These remarks apply particularly to the time during which he occupied the chair of a professor, but are not false in their reference to the period of his tutorship. On May 22d he writes, "Made my first attempt to-day at hearing a recitation. The Sophomores recited to me in Algebra. Was astonished at nothing so much to-day, as the self-possession which I was enabled to exercise $A\pi o\ \tau o\upsilon\ \theta\epsilon o\upsilon$. My room is an agreeable one; my accommodations delightful; the fare in the Refectory excellent; the students, hitherto, complying, and all things ordered in a way to suit my wishes."

He resolves about this time to give one-tenth of his salary ($300) for charitable institutions. He was always open-handed in his expenditures of every sort for the poor, and for sufferers of every description. It was never hard to persuade him that the money solicited was needed, and would be well bestowed.

The text-book in college was Bonnycastle's Algebra. His taste for this study had been marked, and obtained public notice when he was a student. His enthusiasm on the subject is very much in character.

"That the pursuit is delightful I have the experience of this day to prove: amid all the difficulties of this morning's toil, the delight occasioned by the sudden flashing of the truth or relation anxiously sought is transporting. The ecstacies of Pythagoras and the abstraction of Archimedes excite my wonder no longer."

During one of his vacations he visited Philadelphia, in hopes of invigorating his health; and there partook of the delightful hospitality of Mrs. Hall, the mother of the friend whom he had known from boyhood and with whom he continued to correspond for forty years. While in the city he yielded himself up too much, he thought, to the attractions of gay company and of seductive letters. He frequented the shops of the booksellers; saw all the new prints; gazed with delight upon the clean and lively streets and the decorated windows; listened to much good music from sweet instruments and yet sweeter voices; tasted all the joy of friendship, and felt the glow of what is judged to be innocent hilarity. He returned to his quiet room in college to experience a painful reaction in his sensibilities. His conscience smote him on the score of worldly conformity. He became greatly revived in his religious ardour, and much exercised for the spiritual welfare of the students. On one occasion at a prayer-meeting his feelings overcame him, and he "burst into a profusion of tears."

A severe attack of sickness, which befell the older brother in this year, occasioned a letter of mock condolence from Addison in Latin hexameters, four verses of which are here given, which breathe an affectionate spirit and shed a twinkle of humour.

> "Crede mihi, juvenis docilis, me maxime tædet
> Audire ægrotum esse virum, tam longe celebrem.
> Pulveribus (quid tu Anglice vocas?) te cumulârint,
> Et medicus, veneranda materque, AnEliza, niger Ned."

The piece will be found complete in the Familiar Letters. These comic effusions were often made the channel of true and even tender regard, as any one can see was the case in the present instance. The two boys were attached to one another with a devotion that is rare even among brothers, and that continued through life. There is a sense in which it might be said that Addison had *no* friend but James. When James died, Addison was restless and inconsolable, and soon after followed him to heaven.

CHAPTER II.

The College of New Jersey was at this time under the Presidency of Dr. Carnahan, during whose administration it enjoyed a high measure of prosperity. Dr. Ashbel Green had but lately retired from the post. As a President he had been both feared and honoured. In the instructions of his department, Dr. Green had succeeded in reviving the traditions of a Witherspoon and a Smith. None could question his attainments in theology and the kindred sciences, and all without exception acknowledged and venerated his exalted character. He was moreover the master of a grave and sonorous eloquence. Dr. Green was the last of the old school of Presidents, of whom Burr, Davies, Finley, Witherspoon and Smith had been, with Dickinson, the first of the series, the models in a former generation. The lamented Carnahan was the connecting link between the old school and the new. The recent retirement of President Maclean marks another era like that of the retirement of Finley. The Vice-President and Professor of Languages was the Rev. Philip Lindsley, D.D., whose collected works have recently been published;* a man of rare scholarship and of the ripest classical culture. It may be safely averred, that this country has not often seen the equal of Dr. Lindsley as a student and teacher of the Greek and Latin tongues, and as a man imbued with the living spirit of antiquity. He was a suggestive scholar rather than a mere drillmaster, and was one of those instructors whose main forte

---

* "The Works of Philip Lindsley, D. D., formerly Vice-President and President Elect of the College of New Jersey, Princeton; and late President of the University of Nashville, Tennessee. Edited by LeRoy J. Halsey, D. D., Professor in the Theological Seminary of the Northwest. 3 volumes. Philadelphia: J. P. Lippincott & Co., 1866."

seemed to lie in bringing out what is in the best men. A greatly honoured clergyman of the Episcopal Church in Virginia is my authority for saying that, while he was at Princeton, Dr. Lindsley was of invaluable aid to those students who knew how to use him. He distrusted his own administrative talents, which were not believed by the young men to be very considerable. In this impression the young men were probably mistaken. Dr. Lindsley was sensitively modest, and at that time had not been tried. He also laboured under the delusion that he could not preach. In both capacities, that of a teacher and that of a minister of the word, he afterwards showed himself to be a master.

His life, as one of his most accomplished pupils and most ardent and grateful admirers has said, was preëminently that of an instructor and educator of youth. He set about the work of self-culture before he was thirteen, and left the College of New Jersey as a graduate before he was nineteen. He began the work of teacher as an humble usher in an academy, and then filled successively the posts of tutor, professor, vice-president, and president of a college. All his writings and most of his discourses have a bearing on the work of education. This was his meat and drink. The University of Nashville is his noble monument; but nobler than all is the long race of his pupils who have risen to eminence through his instrumentality. The range of his reading was so great, that there was scarcely a topic of interest on which he was not extensively and even profoundly informed. He was an accomplished theoretical statesman, versed in the sciences of government, finance and political economy, and in all questions touching public morals, the administration of justice, and civil or religious liberty. His knowledge of the classics was almost unequalled in his day. His acquaintance with the Belles Lettres of various languages seemed unlimited, and his love of literature was a passion. His administrative and executive ability is thought by those who knew him in the West, to have been of the highest order. He distrusted himself in the pulpit, and preferred the position of a hearer; yet his biographer, Dr.

Halsey, does not doubt that "the grand element of his power and of his success was his magnificent preaching."

He has left important monuments in his published writings, but, as one of his pupils,* who seems animated by a spirit of filial enthusiasm, well says, while these "show the brilliancy of his genius, the peculiarities of his mind, the ardour of his nature, and the depth and earnestness of his spirit, his nobler works,—'living epistles, known and read of all men,' are his two-thousand pupils, who, in all spheres of active usefulness, have been perpetuating his influence; and having received from his generous hand the lighted torch of knowledge, they have handed it to the generation now succeeding, and thus the blazing link, growing brighter as years pass, shall continue to descend as an heirloom of priceless value." * * * Among these pupils were the Alexander brothers, who never ceased to speak of their old preceptor in terms of cordial regard and sincere veneration. Such men as Dr. Philip Lindsley are blessings to the church and to the world. They can never be forgotten by those who prize the fruits of piety and sound learning. Their jewels they have left as a legacy behind them, in the persons of those who have received their impress, and are animated by their unearthly sentiments. By these their living memorials they will be remembered and honoured by children's children, when the titled desolators of history shall be mentioned only to be execrated. It is pleasant to know that Princeton was graced at this particular epoch with several literary clubs or debating societies, the meetings of which proved highly interesting to the youthful contestants. Chief among these, in the estimation of the young people generally, were the Round Table and the Chironomian. The question before the Round Table one night was, "Ought religion to be supported by law?" Mr. James Alexander advocated the affirmative, and was gratified to find that he had more freedom than formerly in speaking extempore. The question before the Theological Society of the Seminary, the week previous,

---

* Chancellor Waddel, in the Southern Presbyterian Review.

was upon the propriety of instrumental music in churches. Mr. James Alexander defended the negative.

The elder brother of the two Alexanders was still in the seminary, and refers in his diary about this time to "my friend Bethune," who seems to have been a fellow-student. They were fast friends through life. This was the celebrated orator, debater, poet, rhetorician, lecturer, preacher, the Rev. George W. Bethune, D. D., afterwards of Brooklyn, N. Y.

The name of this genial clergyman brings up an anecdote, which I may as well tell here. The minute history of these past times soon fades out, and the old inscriptions on the palimpsest are not often restored. Sometimes, it is true, the labours of some Pepys, or Evelyn, are brought to light, and the magical hieroglyphics start out once more before us in all their former significance. Dr. Archibald Alexander was always himself a firm believer in the doctrine, and was accustomed to impress it upon the minds of his classes at Princeton, which has since been illustrated in so solemn a manner by De Quincey and Coleridge, that *we never forget any thing:* in other words, that there is an important sense in which there is *no such thing as forgetting.* The word forget, as has so often been said before, is obviously ambiguous, being the opposite of remember as well as of recollect. The doctrine in question is that though we fail to *recollect* many things, and though there is the greatest diversity among different minds as regards the power of recollection, we never forget in the sense of failing to *remember* or *hold in memory.* The hidden tablets still retain the traces that have been originally imprinted on them; and in the moments that precede death (or what would have proved to be death but for the interposition of Providence) these traces have been known to flash out upon the startled conscience with instantaneous rapidity, and with the most perfect and terrible distinctness, so as apparently to afford to the soul a sudden and comprehensive view of all that it had ever known. Dr. Alexander had been lecturing on this subject one day to his theological pupils, and the young men had repaired to the Seminary Refectory to get dinner, when the conversation at table fell upon the topic that had been presented to them in the class-room that morning. One of the students was noted for a disposition to call in question the conclusions of his preceptor, and on the occasion to which I now refer boldly proclaimed his dissent from the position that had been cautiously taken by his venerable instructor. "I *know*," said he, "there are some things *I* have totally forgotten, and shall *never* be able to recall!" Dr. Bethune, who was a student at Princeton at the time, and who was also boarding at the Refectory, a man through life distinguished for his sparkling wit and repartee, immediately threw the table into roars of laughter by crying out in his comical way, "*Name* one of them, Sir!" I give this anecdote on the authority of the Rev. James W. Alexander, from whose lips I heard it.

The Princeton of 1824 contained a number of well-known families and many interesting people, besides one or two justly distinguished public men. Dr. Carnahan, as I have stated, was President of the College when Addison Alexander entered it as a student. The Rev. Luther Halsey was Professor of Chemistry and Natural Philosophy; Dr. Maclean of Mathematics, and my informant * thinks of Latin (temporarily supplying the vacancy occasioned by the removal of Lindsley to Nashville); and Robert B. Patton of Greek and Belles Lettres. The latter is considered to have been a fine Greek scholar, and a gentleman of cultivated taste and manners, though in wretched health. The tutors were, Messrs. Lowry, Talmadge and Aikman; but with these neither Mr. Alexander nor any of his classmates had any thing to do; he and Mr. Napton having entered Juniors. The standard of scholarship in the ancient languages (at least before Mr. Patton's advent) was greatly below that which my informant found subsequently at the University of Virginia; and none of the modern languages were taught. "The old routine," he says, "or curriculum then prevailing in the Northern Colleges was not designed for

* Judge Napton.

the attainment of the abstruse or profound depths or heights of science, or for its application to practical use, nor even for a scholastic and critical knowledge of Latin and Greek.* Grammars and dictionaries, those helps to the youthful traveller up the steep," were very imperfect, he thinks, as compared with the Zumpts, Madvigs, Buttmanns, Matthiaes, etc., since introduced; "and the classics were still read in the old Delphine editions with side-notes and ordo in Latin, and foot-notes to point out the most attractive passages." He is not clear, however, that any greater proficiency is attained under the new system of adjuncts than under the old, rugged and rough as it was. The inquisitive and ambitious student will, he thinks, attain his end under either—perhaps more thoroughly under the first, " as people learn more of a country over which they travel on foot, than those who pass through it in railroad cars."

The following picture of the old Commencements cannot be spared : " *Commencement* was a great day in Princeton in old times—it may be yet—but my conjecture is, that along with

---

* The Centennial Address has this allusion to the same subject: "The curriculum has been perpetually enlarged, with the increase of knowledge in the world. . . . The earliest period of our history was before the very *rise* of certain great sciences in their present form." . . . And a little before this occurs the following : " Sound methods of instruction, rather old than new, have continued through every stage." The earlier Presidents had all been learned men, in the most exact as well as the most enlarged sense. Their scholarship, though it could not boast the exquisite finish of Oxford or Cambridge, was of the type then prevailing in the great universities of England. None of the first batch of Presidents occupied the seat long. But Dr. Witherspoon in his twenty-six years of administration stamped a new character on the instructions of the college. To him must be ascribed the introduction of the Edinburgh course. Much of this influence had worn out at the period during which Mr. Alexander was a student, and had again and yet again to be renewed and extended. The genuine learning of Dr. Lindsley was of the old school, and his removal from Princeton was a misfortune that for the time seemed irreparable. Nor were there wanting other men of commanding talents in the faculty at this period. But it cannot be asserted with too much emphasis that the future interpreter owed little to his professional teachers. He was an original genius and " a self-made man."

other old-fashioned institutions and customs, it has gone to the 'tomb of the Capulets.' On this day, during my time, all the surrounding country was (as Mr. C. J. Ingersoll would have said) *ejaculated* into the village, and such rows of wagons, booths, stalls, tents; such huge piles of melons (out of season); such barrels of cider (a choice beverage in New Jersey); and such a concourse of people of every variety of shade and conformation, physically, morally and intellectually, could be seen nowhere else." He remembers especially the brilliancy of the fire-works and the illuminated College edifice at night, which were the admiration of the youthful spectators. "Then there was the regular anniversary ball at Joline's tavern, who was successor to and perhaps once the rival of the famous English publican, George Folct, whose sign of the Red Lion was still swinging between two posts in my days, though probably of ante-Revolutionary origin. This ball attracted all the élite of the village, and some additions from the fashionable circles of the two great cities lying on either side of it; and the music was by the famous Philadelphia band of Johnson."

In regard to Princeton society, male and female, outside of the two great schools of theology and literature, the same writer says, "The Stocktons were the leading family of the place. At their head, in '24, was Richard Stockton,* a great

---

* Whose father, *Richard Stockton* (the grandfather of the Commodore), was a Judge of the Supreme Court, a member of the Continental Congress, "an ardent defender of liberty," and a signer of the Declaration of Independence. In this cause he suffered the loss of his estate and library, and personal imprisonment in New York. He died at Morven, at the age of fifty. This was in 1781. He had been a trustee and warm friend of the college as well as of its great founders. Of *Richard Stockton* (the father of the Commodore) "it is enough to say that, among the members of a bar which holds its place with any in America, he maintained by common consent the unrivalled precedence." "He was long the honour of Princeton, and a guardian of the college. His voice of eloquent argument and lofty invective was heard in Congress; and he sent five sons to the college, of whom one is now in a distant ocean on the service of his country."—Centennial Address, 1847. Richard Stockton, the father of the late Commodore Robert F. Stockton of the Old Navy, died in 1779, the same year

lawyer, as I have heard and do not doubt; having read his argument in a celebrated and very important case that went up from New Jersey to the Supreme Court of the United States, involving the title of one Love to a large landed estate abandoned by him when the secession of the Colonies from Great Britain occurred. Mr. S.'s practice was chiefly in Trenton and Philadelphia. He was a large man, of rather unwieldly dimensions, bordering on extreme obesity, incapable of much locomotion on foot, and therefore I presume, was seldom seen in the village adjoining which was his residence." He does not remember to have seen Mr. Stockton more than once or twice, and one of these occasions was indelibly impressed on his recollection by an interview which he witnessed between Mr. Stockton and Charles Fenton Mercer of Virginia, who had been appointed to deliver a discourse before the two literary Societies of the College. There was a mixture of the grand and grotesque about the scene. "They met in the Hall, where the Trustees, Professors, students and other spectators had previously assembled, and it was rather ludicrous to observe the extreme difficulty which Mr. Stockton had in responding with corresponding civilities to the multiplied bows with which Mercer greeted him—the latter being a small and flexible person, of rather French manners, and both gentlemen of the old school, which exacted more ceremony than modern times tolerate."

The writer, after speaking of Mr. Stockton's gallant son, the Commodore, goes on to mention the Craigs and Potters, Thomsons and Fields, families which still have their representatives in Princeton, "and the Bayards, a family of historic fame both in Delaware and New Jersey." "Mrs. Maclean, the mother of the late President,* and sister of Commodore

---

with President Witherspoon, who had shortly before given up his house on the College grounds to his son-in-law Dr. S. Stanhope Smith, and removed to the place still known as Tusculum.

* Of John Maclean, the father of the President, the Centennial Address says, " A name beloved in the recollections of every student, during the 17 years of his residence; a scholar, a benignant friend, a wise preceptor; one of the earli-

Bainbridge, a naval officer of great distinction in the war of 1812, was also there receiving friends and strangers with indiscriminate hospitality, and with her lived her daughter, Mary, the gentlest of her sex, a model of every female excellence, and esteemed by rich and poor, high and low."

My informant * then goes on to say that "near by lived the two daughters of Dr. Samuel Stanhope Smith, *ci-devant* President of the College, Mrs. Salomans and Mrs. Pintard, the former with two attractive daughters, one of whom married my friend and school-fellow, Alfred A. Woodhull. Conspicuous among the fashionable ladies of the place were the Passages (of French extraction, as I infer from the name); the Thomases, one of whom married Mr. Alston of South Carolina, and the other Gen. Lytle of Cincinnati, at one time a prominent Congressman from that district; the Whites; the Renshaws, daughters of Commodore Renshaw; the Morfords, daughters of an old Revolutionary soldier who was postmaster, one of whom married a McCormick of Winchester, Va.; and I may add, a daughter of President Carnahan who married Mr. McDonald."

Among the professional characters of the day, besides some that have been named, he remembers "the three lawyers, Green, Bayard, and Hamilton; a younger lawyer of ability, but indolent, named Walter Skelton; the Van Cleves, the father an eminent physician,—one of the sons, Horatio, now in the U. S. army; the Woodhulls, the father being minister of the parish, and the oldest son, John, becoming distinguished

est to explode the Priestleyan bubble of phlogiston, and to introduce the new chemical revelations of Lavoisier." Dr. Ashbel Green, the former President, was also living, though he had perhaps already removed to Philadelphia. Dr. Carnahan succeeded him before the time of Addison's entrance as a student. "The time has not come to write of living greatness and goodness. Otherwise we might dwell on the ten years' toil of President Green, whom we hoped to meet, but whom the weight of six and eighty years presses so heavily that he cannot revisit the spot where, years ago, he pronounced the valedictory in the presence of Washington, and received his personal applause."—Dr. J. W. Alexander, Centennial Address, 1847.

* I have made free use of Judge Napton's own words.

in his profession of medicine; the Wilsons, Jolines, &c. *Voilà tout!*"*

* One of the most remarkable men in Princeton at the time was undoubtedly a coach-painter named Francis D. Janvier, who is fully described in the fifteenth chapter of the American Mechanic (see pp. 80, 85), under the style of August. This admirable person deserves mention by the side of such men as Pendrill, Bloomfield, and Ferguson. The author introduces his description with the following lines from Wordsworth.

> * * * "Strongest minds
> Are often those of whom the noisy world
> Hears least; else surely this man had not left
> His graces unrevealed and unproclaimed.
> But as the mind was filled with inward light,
> So not without distinction had he lived,
> Beloved and honoured—far as he was known.
> And something that may serve to set in view
> The feeling pleasures of his loneliness,
> His observations, and the thoughts his mind
> Had dealt with—I will here record."

After a little further prefacing, the account runs on thus: "It is now more than twenty-three years since I became acquainted with a coach-painter in a village of New Jersey. At that time he occupied a very small shop adjacent to a large building which was used by the coach-maker. Even in early youth I was led to observe something in the manner and countenance of this man, indicative of superior reflection. I shall conceal his name under that of AUGUST, which will point him out to many who knew him. As I advanced in life, I gained access to his painting-room and his dwelling; and as he was particularly kind to young persons, I passed in his company some of the pleasantest hours which it is my fortune to remember. August was then in the prime of life, and his character and habits were fully unfolded. In looking back upon the acquaintances of many years, I can declare with sincerity, that I have never known a more accomplished man. In his trade he was exemplary and approved. His taste led him to make excursions beyond the sphere of his daily work; and I call to mind a number of portraits and fancy-pieces which ornamented his own house and the apartments of his friends. I am not prepared to say, however, that he was eminent as an artist. But there were various other walks of life in which he was a master. He was fond of reading to a degree which wholly interfered with the care of his business and his health. Indeed he was a devourer of books. Attached to his easel one was sure to find an open volume; and sometimes he caused a favourite boy to read aloud while he was grinding his colours. I well remember that, on a certain day when he had to walk five miles to do a piece of work, he travelled the whole distance book in hand; it was a quarto volume of Hobhouse's Travels. There was nothing in the whole circle of English literature, so far as it is traversed by most professed scholars, with

Among the oddities of the place were the brothers Jemmy which August was not familiar. He had made himself master of the French language, spoke it with some facility, and had perused its chief treasures. Among other evidences of his application, he put into my hand a laborious translation from the French, of a work by Leatude detailing the events of his long and cruel imprisonment ; a narrative not unlike that of Baron Trenck."
* * * "I have vividly before my mind the scene when August was busy with his palette, in a rude loft, and a litttle boy seated on a work-bench was pouring into his delighted ear the early fictions of the author of Waverley. Sir Walter himself would have been repaid by the spectacle.

"Such tastes and habits gave a richness to his mind, and a refinement to his manners. August was fully suited to mingle with any group of scientific or literary men. His love of talk was unbounded, and his hilarity most genial. I remember no acquaintance whose discourse was so stimulating or instructive. Many an hour of summer days I whiled away in his shop, listening to the sentiment, humour, and wit, which would have graced any company I ever met. All this was without a trace of self-conceit or arrogance. His conversation was the easy overflowing of a full mind. It was always animated, and always arch: there was a twinkle of unutterable mirth in his expressive eye, which won regard and awakened expectation.

"August was a musician. This delightful art had been his solace from childhood. He played on several instruments, but the clarionet was that of which he had the greatest mastery. Often have I heard its clear melodious tones for successive hours on a summer evening. He seemed to use it as the outlet for those musings which found no vent among his ordinary associations; for most of his performances were voluntaries and fitful *capriccios*. Yet he was a sight-singer, and read even intricate music with ease. It was one of his whims to have a number of flageolets, lessening by degrees until the smallest was a mere bird-pipe, with the ventages almost too near together for adult fingers. Such is the power of association, that to this day I sometimes amuse myself with that feeblest of all instruments, a French flageolet, in affectionate recollection of poor August.

"I have heard that he sometimes wrote verses, but have never been so fortunate as to alight on any specimen. August was a man of poetic tendencies, living habitually above the influences of a sordid world, and seeking his pleasures in a region beyond the visible horizon of daily scenes. In this connexion, I ought with great seriousness to mention, that during the years of my acquaintance with him, he was an open professor of Christian faith, which he exemplified by a life of purity, patience, and benevolence. His family was a religious household. When he came to enter the valley of poignant trial with which his life terminated, he is said to have evinced great joyfulness of confidence in the propitiation and grace of our Lord Jesus Christ."

and Joe McCarrier,* the college servants. The subjoined account of Jemmy is from the pen of Dr. James W. Alexander, and was written while he was himself a tutor, and living in Nassau Hall. Addison had not then entered the institution, but soon came into close and amusing relations with the generous but testy Irishman and his brother Joe.† "It may not

* Or McCarryher.

† One of the earliest of Addison's extant compositions of the facetious order is one he wrote probably when a Junior, that is at sixteen, and is a broad parody on the well-known verses of Campbell. Its connection with the matter now in hand is, that it brings in an allusion to the brothers Jemmy and Joe McCarrier. I give as much of it as now exists, or perhaps was ever written. It is only necessary to say in explanation for the benefit of persons who did not study at Princeton, that it contains references to the final examination of the Senior class for degrees, to Cavallo's Natural Philosophy, then a text-book at college, and to the horn by which the students were summoned to their meals in the old refectory adjoining the college; and that "stumping" and "rowling" are the slang terms respectively for the failure to recite when called on, and brilliant success in recitation or speaking; while the first-honour man of course obtains "first grade," and the good for nothing idler is sent off on "probation." The laughing good-nature of the writer is apparent.

AIR: "*The Exile of Erin.*"

"There came to the door a poor student of college,
The coat on his shoulders was ragged and thin;
He sighed and he wept from the exquisite knowledge
That the final so soon was about to begin :
But a figure attracted the glance of his eye,
As it rushed with a horn from an edifice nigh,
Where oft in the moments of hours gone by,
He had sung the bold anthem of Dinner Hurrah.

"'Oh sad is my fate,' said the heart-broken fellow,
'The Juniors, Sophs., Freshmen may walk, run, or sleep,
But I,' he exclaimed, with a soul-touching bellow,
'To my Euclid, my room, and Cavallo must keep.
Where is my Euclid, bought new the last session ?
Jemmy and Joe, for the dear creature call !
Where is Cavallo, my dearest possession ?
Ah no! for Longinus is dearer than all.

"'But hunger [at last] these sad fears moderating,
One darling wish from my bosom would draw:
Jemmy, Oh Jemmy, do blow without waiting;
Comfort of nature, dear dinner Hurrah!
Stumping or rowling, first grade or probation,
Thy memory shall hold in my heart the first station,

be uninteresting at some future day to recall to mind my servant Jemmy McCarrier. He has been for many years head servant in the College, and has fulfilled his duties with a zeal and fidelity which are seldom witnessed. His greatest delight is to serve; no office is too menial or too laborious for him; he insists on doing favours, and with the true Irish spirit is offended if you decline to receive them. It is amusing to see him pacing about the College on a dog-trot, which his continual errands, for many years performed always in haste, have made a habit characteristic of him. He seems always to be in the greatest possible hurry, and yet is punctual to the moment, and most minute in his business. His affection for friends and his gratitude to benefactors are fervent, and expressed with all the native eloquence of an Irishman. Rage too burns in him with sudden impetuosity, that while it lasts is furious, but soon dies away. If I wished a friend who would flinch from no danger and draw back from no sacrifices or privations for my sake, I would lay my hand on Jemmy." *

Mr. Alexander, the subject of this biography, was matriculated as a student of the College of New Jersey, and entered

> And never, I vow, till the examination,
> Will I cease the bold anthem of Dinner Hurrah!'"

The four last lines of the first stanza seem to be erased, but are obviously requisite to finish both the sense and the melody. What adds to the fun is that the fare at the refectory in those days was plain and bad enough for an anchorite.

* The father of the McCarryhers came over with three sons from "the ould counthry," and is remembered by a Princetonian of the former days as a shrivelled up old little Irishman, who lived at different times in two miserable houses in the environs of the college. When the parent died, Dr. Archibald Alexander preached his funeral sermon, and thus made a deep and lasting impression on the intelligence and feelings of the son, who was taught in this way to look up to him with unmeasured regard and reverence. Before the Seminary building was put up and the oratory used, and of course long before the erection of the Seminary chapel, the families of the theological professors used to worship in the old college chapel, and my informant vividly remembers how every Sunday morning, in cold weather, McCarryher *fils* used to place a covered pan of hot coals at Mrs. Alexander's feet as she sat in chapel.

one of its advanced classes, at an age when the majority of boys are still at school. He was only fifteen. He might easily have entered the Sophomore at fourteen, or the Freshman at thirteen, or even twelve, had he been so disposed, or had his parents thought it wise. He was judiciously kept back, not eagerly pushed forward. No one ever had more prudent counsellors. He connected himself with the Junior class in the autumn of the year 1824, and at once took his stand among the first scholars of his class. This position he maintained during the whole college course. Nothing is known positively as to his examination on entrance, but it may be safely inferred that it was entirely satisfactory. His scholarship was never known, either before or afterwards, to fail to come up to the most stringent tests which could be applied to it. The boys at the academy thought he knew as much Greek as Mr. Baird, and that it was impossible for him to be entangled amidst the intricacies of mathematics; and some of his associates of the college fancied that he was superior on the score of his attainments to most of his instructors of the college faculty. This was not only the enthusiastic estimate of youth, but the deliberate and mature judgment of riper years. But whatever may be the impartial decision upon this point, it is certain that he had no superior among his fellow-students in the branches embraced in the usual curriculum; and in the various branches of learning outside of that curriculum, it was cheerfully conceded that he distanced the others so far, as to put all ideas of competition out of the question. But no one regretted this state of things. He bore his honours meekly, and was universally regarded as the prodigy of Nassau Hall. The men were proud of him. They regarded him as one of the bright ornaments of the institution. His standing as a scholar was equal and uniform, being the same at the end of his final term as it was at the beginning of his course. There was nothing in his progress through college to arrest attention, except his assiduity, his punctuality, his accurate and eminent scholarship, and his scrupulous fidelity in the performance of every duty.

In the autumn of 1825 he was one of the four selected by the American Whig Society to represent that society on the night before Commencement, in its annual oratorical contest with its Cliosophic rival. His subject on this occasion was "*Monachism*," and it was treated in such a manner as to draw many discerning eyes upon the young orator.* The speech attracted marked notice on account of its style, and the evidence that it gave of mental power and mature culture.

During the ensuing winter he appeared again before a public audience, at the performance of one of the divisions of the Senior class; the class being distributed by lot into four "divisions," as they were called, which appeared successively, at intervals of a few weeks, during the winter. His subject this time was "*the Fire Worshippers*," a theme which gave full scope for the exercise of his rich and exuberant imagination, and the gorgeous drapery in which he clothed his ideas on this occasion, was a topic of general remark, and was much admired.

At the summer exhibition of the Senior class he again appeared before the public, and again made the pillars of the old chapel shake with applause. His attention, as we know, had long before this been directed to the languages, literature, and history of the East, and he now looked once more in that quarter for a theme for his discourse. The thing he seemed to have in view was a defence or eulogy of the Mohammedan race. He spoke (says the brother from whom I have derived these particulars) in glowing terms of "that race which in former days had passed the Pillars of Hercules in the face of the Spanish chivalry, had built the mosque of Cordova,† the palace at Seville, and beautified and adorned Castile and Aragon with those delicious gardens and fountains which made Spain the paradise of the world." He

---

* Another of his college efforts was on "Russia," and some of its brilliant sentences are still in preservation.

† ———" the regal seat
Of Abdaldzis, ancient Cordoba."
———" till they saw

pictured with graphic power the arrival of the day "when the magnanimous Arab shall with his own hand plant the Cross upon his own mountains; when the Christian anthem shall be echoed and reëchoed from the opposite shores of the Adriatic, and the Christian's hymn of praise once more resound within the dome of St. Sophia."

The following extracts of a letter from Thomas Flournoy, Esq., of Bentfield, Brunswick County, Virginia, give an excellent picture of the young scholar at this time.

He says Addison "was a very remarkable boy, as he was universally conceded to be a most remarkable man. The impression with most of his compeers doubtless was, that he was naturally unsociable and taciturn. Such I consider a misapprehension. We were classmates; he was my junior by, I suppose, four or five years. I always found him very accessible. He enjoyed a good joke and laugh, within reasonable bounds. He was a purely modest youth; but his vast resources, even at the tender age I knew him, precluded every thing like diffidence, as I understand the purport of that word." He used frequently to meet with him on his longest walks from his father's house to the recitation rooms in College. "He was always pleasant and communicative, and always kind and polite. I have seen him very much bored by his brethren of the Whig Society, in their zeal for the first distinction, by urging him to give more undivided attention to college studies. I will not say he never thought about college honours; but I am certain he never expressed or manifested any concern on the subject." If he put forth any effort in that direction, Mr. Flournoy verily believes it was wholly to gratify the ambition of the Whigs. "I believe he could have graduated with distinction the day he was matriculated. It was

> The temples and the towers of Cordoba
> Shining majestic in the light of eve."
> *Southey, Roderick*, Book V.

> "And strangers were received by thee
> Of Cordova the chivalry."
> *Byron.*

quite farcical for him to be reciting to professors whom he could have taught. I suppose it was altogether a formal requisition that influenced him in regarding a college curriculum as imperative." The writer was much taken with his friend's drollery and good-humour, as evinced in his college exercises. "He always manifested genuine wit, humour, and good feelings, in his pointed criticisms on compositions and declamations and debates. He never evinced selfishness, vain-glorying, or the least pride of superiority over his fellows, though acknowledged head, neck, and shoulders over all, by all. I don't believe he had an enemy on the earth. His high attainments for one so young and unpresuming, commanded the admiration of all without exciting the envy or jealousy of any."

His general appearance, Mr. Flournoy says, was sedate and sober-minded; but when in conversation, animated and sprightly. "I considered him blessed with a cheerful and happy temperament." His looks were prepossessing. "He was very handsome, rather under the medium height, but stoutly formed, and with proper exercise would have been very muscular. He had a fair, ruddy, almost transparent complexion. His dress was of the most tasteful description, exciting no attention whatever. I looked upon him as one of the cleanest and purest persons I have ever known. His general walk and deportment was that of a consistent Christian, though I am unable to say whether he was a professor." The first trip he ever made from home, Mr. Flournoy thinks, was with his father to New York City. "I heard Dr. Alexander say, laughingly, he never saw Addison but at meal-times and at night; and supposed 'he was on the pad' all the time, looking after the lions of the city; but he ascertained the extent of his peregrinations was from the hotel to a large book-establishment, where he regaled himself during the days they were in the city." He never knew one so young take so little bodily exercise and keep so perfectly healthy; for he never heard of his being sick.

The youthful intercourse between the two friends can

scarcely be said to have been renewed. Mr. Flournoy returned to Virginia and lost sight of Addison. "I never had the pleasure of meeting with him but once after our boyhood days. I heard him preach in Dr. Boardman's church in '48, and then had only a brief interview in the church." It must have been on this occasion (as he tells me himself) that Mr. Flournoy could not resist the temptation of going up into the pulpit and shaking him by the hand.* He adds, in closing, "You will doubtless be surprised that I am able to furnish so few striking incidents in relation to Dr. Alexander; but his was a quiet, gentle, and unobtrusive course to eminence."

The account given in this letter of Mr. Flournoy is a true sequel to the statements of Mr. King. It is evidently the same person that these two gentlemen describe; showing himself more completely and unreservedly, however, to the one with whom he was more familiarly associated in the careless freedom of a village school, and with whom he was more nearly connected in point of age, than with the other, who was also several years his senior, and who was his fellow only in his collegiate studies. We may also, perhaps, discover some signs of growth in character, manners, etc., since the playful satirist excited the mirth and aroused the admiration of Mr. Baird's academy by his scintillations of fancy, and wild bursts of fun at the expense of every body and every thing. He was now, according to all accounts, a short, stout, striking-looking, rosy-faced, marvellous-minded youth of seventeen, with a remarkable head, that was stored with unknown treasures of strange learning, and possessing a quickness and versatility of parts that could not easily be matched. If he was reserved towards strangers, he on some points opened his heart to his nearest friends with the confidence and simplicity of a little child. To them, and to his juniors in years, he was almost uniformly gracious and affable, if not demon-

---

* He remembered his friend "Tom Flournoy's" shake of the hand, and referred to it when in Europe in 1833, in connection with what he says of the proverbial coldness of English manners.

stratively affectionate: nay, there were times when he abounded in exuberant and effervescent hilarity and pleasant mischief.

A gentleman now residing in Charlotte, Virginia, who visited Princeton in 1828, with a letter to Dr. Alexander, tells me that Addison, who was some years older than himself, at once became his chaperon, and with the greatest kindness showed him the various objects of interest connected with the seminary, and among them the fine prospect which is commanded by the cupola. This gentleman represents him as being at that time "the *wildest* boy he ever saw," explaining himself to mean the most talkative, sprightly, humorous, witty, gaily enthusiastic, and intrepidly frolicsome and mischievous. He says that his comical guide fired his shots at every body and every thing, but that the flame was of the most lambent character and hurt nothing. My informant adds, that Addison convulsed the little satellites by whom he was attended, and that he himself nearly died laughing. And yet this was the same person of whom Mr. Flournoy truly says, that ".his general appearance was sedate and sober-minded;" though in conversation he considered him "animated and sprightly." The truth is, the boy, like the man, had almost as many sides to his character and genius as there were persons to look at them. He was different to different people, and different on different days. He was like a kaleidescope in this, that you could never touch him without producing in your mind a new impression of his boundless variety.

The destruction of the papers in the hands of Mr. King will always be a subject of regret to the admirers of Dr. Alexander, and to those who are inquisitive about the events of his early life. In the absence of these interesting manuscripts, I give a few extracts from a letter of Judge Napton to William C. Alexander, Esq., of New York, bearing upon the same period:

"You are right in supposing that no one could appreciate the genius and worth of your brother, Addison, more than myself, or had better opportunities of understanding his peculiarities when we were both young. It would be difficult for me to express the great respect and veneration I had for your father—*clarum et venerabile nomen*—and the great obligations I owed him for kindness to me in boyhood, and for wholesome advice (I have his letter yet) which was *not* thrown away, as advice usually is.

"As to Addison, I looked upon him as one of extraordinary mind, and gifted with a superiority of the *imaginative faculty* which was never developed, but which might have placed him among the Irvings, Coopers, and Pauldings of his and our day. Whether he acted wisely in devoting himself to other branches of literature, more congenial to his profession, I cannot say; but I confess that I regretted he did not enter into a more popular department of literature, where he was certain of success." * * *

I am also indebted to Judge Napton for the following particulars. It will be remembered that these reminiscences and criticisms are from the pen of the man who was one of his best friends, and without qualification almost his only rival of those days as a student.

"Our acquaintance began at a very early period of our lives, and ceased before either of us could be said to have reached manhood. I can only speak in general terms of impressions and convictions then formed of the peculiar intellectual and moral traits exhibited by my friend. My acquaintance with Addison Alexander commenced, I believe, on my leaving the school at Lawrenceville, then under charge of the Rev. I. V. Brown, and joining the academy at Princeton—a sort of preparatory school then just established by the Rev. Robert Baird, a gentleman subsequently well-known for his labors in Europe and his valuable sketches of them. Addison and I must have been at this time about fourteen years old, and our intimacy, which then sprang up, probably from some congeniality of tastes and studies, continued till the close of our college career, which was when we were each eighteen."*

The most prominent and striking characteristic of Addison Alexander at this period—at all events, the one which impressed itself with the greatest force on his young com-

---

* Addison, as we have seen, was a year or two younger.

panion, was "the extent and power of his creative and imaginative faculties, which, combined as they were with good judgment and discriminating taste, a remarkably retentive memory, and a facility of expression in language chaste, smooth, and elegant, fitted him, as I thought, for ultimate distinction as a great writer in the field of popular literature." His peculiar talent in this line exhibited itself at a very early period of their acquaintance, upon their publishing, or rather circulating in conjunction, "a sort of literary hebdomadal for the amusement of the school and for the young people of the town, to which he was the principal contributor. For this sheet he wrote tales after the manner of the 'Rambler' and 'Spectator' (in those days we read Johnson and Addison); poetical effusions after the style of Swift, though by no means partaking of his uncleanness; sketches of scenes and characters of a humorous sort; with an occasional dash of satire, in the shape of advertisements or announcements of passing events, and all kinds of puerile badinage. He had a peculiar fancy and talent for imitations of the florid style of Eastern tales, and took great delight in perplexing the *savans* of the village with imaginary translations from the Persian, Arabic, Hindostanee, or Sanscrit, etc., to all of which languages he was, of course, at this time a perfect stranger. His skill in the invention of names for his characters, appropriate to the country and time, was remarkable, and reminded me of a similar capacity so memorably displayed by the great Scotch novelist."

He was, the writer remembers, fond of paradox: "Nothing delighted him more, when his school task was to read an essay, than to present views and advocate opinions at variance with those generally received, and probably at variance with his own. I remember an essay of his, read at the academy, setting forth the great superiority of a monarchical over a republican form of government—a position *then* regarded as totally heterodox." Neither then nor afterwards, during his acquaintance with him, was he fond of metaphysical studies; "though before the close of his college career he doubtless was familiar with the views of Locke and the Scotch metaphysicians." He often wrote at this time for the newspapers.

"During our college life he occasionally contributed articles to the political newspapers, discussing with great apparent zeal the merits of the then Presidential aspirants—a subject however in which he took no real interest, but in which he entered the lists *en masque* purely for amusement.

"Besides the regular routine of collegiate studies, he explored every by-path of literature, however unfrequented, and there were probably very few books, on any branch of science, or in any department of learning, which he had not looked into and formed some estimate of.

"His facility in acquiring languages, both ancient and modern, is well known."

His conduct was irreproachable.

"In reference to his morals or moral habits at this period, it is impossible to speak in terms which could be regarded as exaggerated commendation. He was, or seemed to be, purity itself; he appeared to hold in complete subjection all those passions and appetites which so often lead youth astray.* His intellectual faculties had the entire predominance, and their cultivation and improvement was his sole care. He neither used tobacco in any form, or stimulating drinks of any kind; he never uttered an oath nor engaged in any kind of games, noxious or harmless.

"On the subject of religion I never heard him speak; nor did he, during my acquaintance with him, attach himself to any religious denomination.

"In one respect his habits were singular, and perhaps not so commendable. I mean his almost total isolation—his aversion not only to crowds, but to all social intercourse, except of course with his father's family and a few, very few friends. And this seemed the more remarkable, as nature had given him a robust constitution of body, a rather large and imposing person for his years, inclining even in youth to corpulency, a most cheerful, nay, quite hilarious temperament, and withal a considerable propensity and talent for satire. These natural gifts, with acquisitions in learning so much in advance of his fellows,

---

* Mr. Vandyke Joline of Trenton, formerly of Princeton, another classmate at Mr. Baird's school, bears the same testimony.

united with uncommon conversational powers and a keen appreciation of the ludicrous, would seem to have fitted him for general society. But his aversion to it was insuperable, and, I have understood, was never in after life greatly changed.

"I do not think it necessary to refer particularly to his scholarship. That he possessed higher natural gifts and far greater attainments than any of his age, both at school and college, was conceded by all who knew him; and in all branches of learning embraced in the college course, and in general literature outside of it, among hundreds of students of varied talent and industry, he was confessedly *primus inter pares*. In a word, nature and education had fitted him for almost any sphere of life he might select. Had he chosen that occupied by Scott and Irving at the beginning of the century, and more recently by Thackeray and Dickens, I am persuaded he would have delighted the world by his imaginative creations and his charming, easy and attractive style. But he selected a more narrow, laborious, and perhaps useful path, of his success in which I am not competent to speak."

There is much in this letter to set the mind to thinking, and to shed light on the inner history of our wonderful boy-student. It will be noticed that it is written in a very grave and cautious style, that every word is well-weighed, and that every influence that could prejudice the feelings of the critic seems to have been sedulously repressed. It was written, too, by one of the very few persons who really know any thing about the boyhood and youth of Addison Alexander from actual experience, and by one who was not only then abreast of the young genius in his collegiate studies, and therefore capable of appreciating his unusual attainments, but who by the natural bent of his tastes, and by the cast given his reflections by his professional education and habits, and experience on the bench, was singularly well fitted to pronounce an intelligent and accurate opinion in the premises. The judgment here expressed may therefore be regarded as almost judicial. And what is that judgment? That he was by far the most highly and variously gifted of his coevals of the school and college, and that his learning extended indefinitely beyond the usual boundaries. It is certainly a remarkable statement of Judge Napton's, that "there were probably very few books, on any branch of science, or in any department of learning, which he had not looked into and formed some estimate of." Addison's most extraordinary gift, he thinks, was " the extent and power of his creative and imaginative faculties," and he almost regrets that his friend " had not turned his attention more seriously to the department of elegant letters, and especially of romantic fiction." It does not appear that he thought him particularly distinguished at this time for powers of intellectual analysis. It is somewhat odd that a friend and pupil of Dr. Alexander, who however knew him at a much later period, after presenting (in a letter which will be given in the sequel) a masterly view of his preceptor's fondness for, and success in, the analytical processes as contrasted with the synthetic, leans to the opinion that he did not possess in any uncommon degree the faculty of construction; in other words, that his mind was essentially and exclusively an analytical one. These opposite statements must be combined and reconciled, before we can obtain a true conception of Dr. Alexander's real intellectual greatness. One of the most striking peculiarities of the case, to those who knew him long and intimately, was the regular and equal development of all his powers. He had the same turn for science and for art. Each one of the faculties of his mind seemed to be *what it ought to be*, without reference to any of the others. We shall have abundant occasion to show that he was as remarkable for analysis when a boy as when a man, and as remarkable for synthesis when a man as when a boy. The exegetical and critical exercises of his school days are as much marked by sagacious discrimination and acute, analyzing logic, as his later commentaries; and the sermons and poems which were composed when he was at his meridian show full as much of "creative imagination" and marvellous constructive skill, as the grave or more fantastic effusions of his prodigal humour, which put all "the savans of Princeton" at fault during the time that "the sun shone fair" on Dr. Baird's academy. But the surprising thing is, that his school-fellows did not more generally or more fully suspect at the time, not only the exceeding brilliancy, but the extreme versatility of his mental powers, and the immense range of his scholarship. The truth was, Addison kept his own secrets. On certain subjects, or when for a purpose it pleased him to be so, he was as silent as the grave. He took few into his confidence at all, and fewer still into the inner sanctuary of his feelings. To a very select circle he revealed something of his hidden life, but he always kept back a part. The half was not told them. No one of his young companions seems to have comprehended him thoroughly, or to have known precisely how he employed his leisure hours. At the very time he was supposed by one of the most congenial spirits he had in the academy to be writing *imitations* of oriental tales and poems, he was filling column after column of Walsh's Quarterly with elaborate criticisms upon the Persian and Arabic texts. Another[*] of his schoolfellows, who had also the opportunity of observing his career in after life, seems to have been impressed just as I am with the uniform equality of his faculties, and the rounded completeness of his mental culture. He says his conviction was that Addison could do any intellectual thing he pleased. I may add on my own responsibility that he was emphatically, and beyond all men I have ever known, so far as regards the character of his mind, *totus teres atque rotundus*. His genius was, as regards its symmetrical form and finish, as smooth and circular as a polished ivory sphere. He could turn his mind to any thing, from a comic almanac or a child's dialogue, to bursts of eloquence in the pulpit, or a gush of impassioned and imaginative song, or to a prodigious refutation, or rather extermination, of the neological interpreters of Germany.[†]

The writer from whom I have been chiefly quoting looks back with lively pleasure on the newspaper venture in which he and Addison were interested, and towards which, he says, Addison was the principal contributor. There can be no doubt whatever that the latter loved to change his hand, write

---

[*] David Comfort, Esq.

[†] I feel that I am justified in the use of this language, by the example of others in this volume.

in different styles, occupy unwonted positions, and make inroads upon untrodden ground, and thus mystify the citizens of Princeton and even his most intimate acquaintances. This was perhaps the diversion in which, of all others, he most delighted. The friend from whose letter I have been making such large extracts, adds, in a postscript,

"These labours, or rather amusements of his continued long after the cessation of our puerile 'weekly' at the Academy, and were subsequently, during the entire period of our acquaintance, published from time to time in a newspaper in Trenton, called *the Emporium*. Some of them may yet be extant."*

I now cite as a witness of this time Mr. Charles Campbell, the author of the History of Virginia, who, though not a classmate, was a contemporary and friend. He says, among other things, that

"Addison Alexander entered the College of New Jersey during the time when I was there, about 1824 or '5. I occasionally met with him in the College, and remember his communicating to me a scheme which he proposed, of forming a debating society among the students. Why he should propose this, when there were two well-established literary societies connected with the College, I do not remember. I attended a preliminary meeting, and I believe the scheme was carried into effect, and that Addison was the secretary of the society and kept a record of the proceedings."

All such clubs and meetings, when well managed, gave him pleasure. He cared little for oral debate himself, but liked to listen and take notes. As a young man at least, he thirsted for this sort of social companionship, and his reputed *mauvaise honte* did not embarrass him or others on the occasions of these literary hobnobbings. He was as free, gay, and cheerful as he was learned.

Dr. John Maclean, so long the honoured president of the college, and one of its instructors when Addison was the ornament of the classes, writes that he has a distinct recollection

---

* They are not, or at least are not recognizable.

of him from his early childhood. "While yet a child," as he remembers, he gave promise of becoming an eminently learned man. At school and college he was distinguished for his devotion to study and his attainments in learning; not that he was equally fond of all the different branches to which his attention was directed by his several teachers, or that he was equally proficient in them. From the first he manifested a peculiar fondness for the study of languages, and an uncommon aptness in acquiring a thorough knowledge of them. He also devoted himself to the use of his pen, on a great variety of subjects, both mirthful and serious; and his style was as varied as the matters concerning which he wrote. The training which he may be said to have given himself in these departments of learning, was adapted, in connection with his great intellectual vigour, to make him the eminent scholar and writer which he became.

A gentleman of Petersburg, Va.,* has favoured me with the following valuable and interesting statements:

"The Rev. Joseph Addison Alexander was a classmate of mine at Princeton for certainly two years, perhaps also one session of another year; then he was very young, not more than nineteen to twenty-one years old; but even at that age, as when a man, he was distinguished for dignity, circumspection, and sterling integrity—polite, but very bashful, social with familiar friends, but averse to mingling in society generally. In this disposition he was peculiar." Mr. Alexander did not commonly visit the rooms of the students, but Mr. Bolling's was an exception. "He was a frequent visitor at my room, and would make himself always agreeable and instructive, provided you let him alone and did not show him attention by introducing him to others, and avoided all formalities towards him. He graduated with distinguished honour. He was even at that early day a ripe scholar, and in after life in a most remarkable manner verified the correctness of the impress he then gave of his great talents and scholarship. I often desired to hear him preach, but such good fortune was not allowed me, nor had I, since we parted at the Commencement when we graduated, the opportunity to see and associate with one for whom I entertained such high regard as a friend and admiration as a great and good man. For the

---

* G. W. Bolling, Esq.

want of associating with him in after years, I am only able to furnish you this meagre statement of his distinguished virtues. But meagre as it is, I regard it a privilege to have an opportunity to bear my testimony to his worth."

His last public appearance as a student was on Commencement day, 1826, when he proceeded Bachelor of Arts.

At that day the first honour was usually divided among several. Mr. Alexander shared it with the Hon. Peter McCall, who has long been a distinguished lawyer of Philadelphia, and the Hon. William B. Napton, the late Chief-Justice of Missouri. The valedictory was then given to the best speaker taking the first honour, but in this case the faculty found themselves unable to decide between Alexander and McCall, and it had to be determined by lot. Mr. McCall pronounced the Latin salutatory, Mr. Napton the English; the valedictory oration falling to the lot of Mr. Alexander. His subject, in this his last college effort, was, "The Pains and Pleasures of a College Life."

The oration was finished in style, and the addresses to the trustees, the president, the faculty, and his classmates were touching and impressive.

Many distinguished men attending the Commencement were greatly attracted by this performance, and the late Hon. Richard Stockton (who was one of the trustees) at the close predicted with emphasis the future eminence of the youthful graduate, and not content with this, stepped out and congratulated his father Dr. Alexander on the stage. A near relative of the young man who received such marks of consideration, remembers being put up on the seat at church, when but a little child, to get a sight of him when he was speaking; but thinks this must have been his Junior speech, as the impression remains strong on the mind of my informant that it was at night.

Mr. Alexander took his diploma at Princeton on the last Wednesday of September, 1826; which would put him in his eighteenth year. His seventeenth birthday occurred in April, when he was a Senior looking forward to graduation the ensuing autumn. It would be pleasant to know precisely what were his feelings in that prospect, but this is more than can be determined. It is enough to say that they seem to have been comfortable and buoyant, though as yet he had no settled plans for life.

One of his brothers who had been graduated two years before, then a student of law, was at this time the clerk of the borough of Princeton. In the month of October, 1826, being the month succeeding Commencement, that brother left for Virginia, and the Common Council of the borough appointed the renowned young scholar in his place. This position he held for some time, and discharged its duties, so far as I am aware, to the satisfaction of the body appointing him.

About the same time, also, his eldest brother* removed permanently to Virginia, to take charge of the village church at Charlotte Court House, of which he became the first settled pastor. The father of the young pastor just referred to, had preached to another generation at the same spot many years before, and the memory of Drs. Archibald and James Alexander is still as ointment poured forth over that whole region.

The following lively epistle to his brother James will be found to be copious, playful, affectionate, and learned, and to mirror the writer's habits of life at this time. It is chiefly interesting, however, as being the first of his letters that is now extant. It implies a certain degree of knowledge of Latin, Greek, Italian, Arabic, and Persian, but might not indicate that the writer was a prodigy.

The queer names of his fowls arose from his strange way of determining upon them. He would open a book at random, and the first word that struck his eye was to be the *nomen*, and the first on the next opening of the book, the *cognomen*.

---

* A full account of these matters will be found in the Memoir of Dr. A. Alexander, and in the Forty-Years' Familiar Letters.

PRINCETON, NEW JERSEY, U. S. OF N. AM.,
Friday, 21*st of April*, 1826.

CHARISSIME VOADELI,

I had intended to indite you an epistle in classical and Ciceronian Latin, but the thought that you have probably dropt the acquaintance of Greek and Roman sages, since your departure from this celebrated seat of the Muses, has induced me to " effere vernaculé "—as we used to say in the garret when you were a schoolmaster. As letter-writing is a species of composition in which I have had little practice, I find it necessary in digesting my epistles to adopt the same rules by which I am guided in writing an essay for the ears of our illustrious President, whose logical exactness of thought and nicety of expression render it *nessy* in stringing our *pairls* to be very methodical. I shall therefore consider my subject under three heads, 1. the news; 2. replies to your inquiries; 3. original messages and remarks, which I am directed to communicate by my constituents (for in writing this letter, I stand in a federal capacity, being the representative of the household). First, then, the news,—which is very scanty—nor should you lament this if you are endued with reason, for " βουλεις, ειπε μοι, περιιων, πυνθανεσθαι λεγεται τι καινον;" it cannot be supposed that any man who has taken the oaths of allegiance in Henrico County, Virginia, and received the power of marrying and giving in marriage throughout the Old Dominion, can care for intelligence from the Jerseys. Be that as it may, I shall proceed to communicate the facts with which I have been supplied. Imprimis—we are all well (you know with what limitations to understand this statement). Item, Mr. Woodhull is not very well, but on the contrary, is very ill, and it is expected that he will "go into a consumption." Item, Dr. Miller has been confined to his bed for some time. Item, a Cherokee Indian, by the name of Chew, was buried here to-day—the obsequies being conducted by Dr. A. Item, Green was here last night and went off at five o'clock this morning. Item, Mrs. Field has bought Mr. Baird's house and will enter it next Spring. Item, Dr. Carnahan is going to Washington. Item, Mr. Patton is going to deliver expository lectures on the "'Επτα επι Θηβας" of Æschylus. Item, Mr. David Minge, of emancipating celebrity, has pitched his tent among us, and intends to pursue his studies under the care of Luther Halsey, Jr. Item, Hatching Harpoon has hatched six chickens—to wit—Ruby Cobweb, John Peaseblossom, Cheerfulness Plenty, Egg Sacrifice, Corpulent Ostrich, and Grapevine Moth. Two of these are dead, the rest are in very good health. The Chicken College is in a flourishing condition. Pompey Jack has resigned the presidency, and is engaged in writing a work with the following title—"Istoria del collegio dei Pollastri, nella Universita di Grattocane pollastr'anitra, del anno 1820, al anno presente. Per Pompeio Giacco, Dottore di Penne è di mustacchi e ultimo Presidente del collegio."* Item, Capt. Renshaw is appointed Commander of the Navy Yard in Philadelphia, vice Biddle.

II. In your letter by J. F. Caruthers, you earnestly desire to be informed what letters have been received from you—I therefore subjoin as perfect a list as I could obtain:

No. 1. To Mrs. Janetta Alexander, dated Baltimore, Nov. 3, 1825.
2. " Miss Ann H. Waddell, " Petersburg, Dec. 18, "
3. " Mrs. Janetta Alexander, " Petersburg, Jan. 5, 1826.
4. " do. do. do. " do. Jan. 26, "
5. " Mr. Joseph A. Alexander, " do. Feb. 13, "
6. " Rev. Dr. A. Alexander, " do. March 3, "
7. " Miss Ann H. Waddell, " Richmond, March 8, "
8. " Mrs. Janetta Alexander, " Petersburg, March 16, "
9. " Rev. Dr. A. Alexander, " Richmond, April 1, "

Add to these a letter to Wm. from Washington—another by Mr. Nisbet, a third by Jno. F. Caruthers, and a fourth received to-day, and I believe you have the whole of your epistles before you. I can hardly imagine your motive for requesting such information as this.

III. Mrs. Alexander asks you whether the accounts of Virginia, once given you by herself and Miss W., appear to you now as the offspring of wild enthusiasm.

(Then follows a line in Arabic character.)

سلام عميكم صن أل واهر

Salamu alaikum miu ali wa ahli.
i. e., You are saluted by kith and kin.
Scritto per il tuo fratello,
J. ADDISON ALEXANDER.

During the summer of 1826 Addison, it seems, took a trip to the sea-shore at Long Branch, and had his first view of the

---

* "History of the Chicken College, in the Cat-Dog-Chicken-Duck University, in the year 1820, the present year. By Pompey Jack, Professor of Feathers and Whiskers, and late President of the College."

ocean. Dr. Archibald Alexander drove the Jersey wagon in which were Mrs. Campbell, Mrs. Alexander, Addison, Mr. (now Doctor) Alfred Leyburn of Lexington, and perhaps Miss Ann Eliza Caruthers (afterwards Mrs. Leyburn), and Mr. Charles Campbell of Petersburg, and one or two others. The last named is the *raconteur*.

"My mother and myself once accompanied Dr. Alexander with his wife and daughter and some of his sons, including Addison, to Long Branch, the watering-place on the Jersey coast. Dr. Alfred Leyburn was also in company and I believe Ann Eliza Caruthers, whom he afterwards married. The greater part of these rode in a Jersey wagon, Dr. Alexander driving. Addison sat in the seat before my mother. For some time he was engaged in writing, and at length his mother inquired of him what he was writing, when he handed her the manuscript, which she read aloud. It proved to be a report of what each one had said during the ride. His mother once remarked to mine, that she never had seen Addison angry and that she had one day asked him how he managed to keep his temper so quiet? He replied, that he should have gotten angry just like others, but that he had never met with any provocation which he thought it worth his while to get angry about. This is something like the reply of the Earl of Peterborough, who, when asked how it was that, in all the dangers of a recent campaign, he had never exhibited any fear, answered, 'I should have been as much frightened as any body, but I never saw any good reason to apprehend danger.' Addison's sedate face denoted the equanimity for which he was distinguished. To borrow an expression, he moved about 'with all the concentrated energy of a young monk.'

"My brother Alexander, who is younger than myself, was some years after I left Princeton with my mother at Dr. Alexander's. Addison wrote his biography for him in some little volumes the pages of which were about the size of those of a thumb-bible. One of Dr. ———'s sons, it appeared, had poked a stick through the fence and hurt Aleck in the eye. The first chapter of the biography dilated upon 'the operation performed on his eye.' These little volumes were preserved for many years but are now lost."

That ride may not have made any great impression on a mind that was perhaps meditating on the college honours or the fragrance of roses sung by Hafiz and Sadi; but the sight of the sea as it rolls in upon the crushed sands, and elevated green fields and bare levels, of the Jersey coast was one of the things that, as Keats says, are a joy forever, and was on this occasion a memorable joy to him. If he did not himself write the powerful description of the mighty element which soon after appeared in the columns of the Patriot while he was its editor, he undoubtedly inserted it with approbation of its sentiments and with the warmest recollections of the great original.

A letter from his father to Mrs. Graham gives a picture in masterly outlines of the young graduate and valedictorian, and touches upon his rare attainments in general literature, his reception of the President's medal for best composition, his promise as an eloquent speaker, his taste for law and politics, his regularity and quietness of deportment, his reserve, and his blameless manners.

"Addison has just passed through his final examination in college. He stands at the very head of his class in scholarship. Two others however were put with him *in the first honour*, as it is called, one of whom is fully equal to him in the studies of the college, but in general knowledge is a child to him. For without any partiality to him because he is my son (to which I believe I am very little prone) he is very far superior to any one of his age I ever saw in literary attainments. The Senior class, to which he belongs, were called upon a few days ago to decide by ballot to whom the President's premium should be given for excelling in composition, and Addison obtained the first place by a large majority. His ability to speak in public is also uncommonly good; and he has been appointed to deliver the valedictory on the day of Commencement. But to what use he will apply his learning and eloquence I know not. Probably he will be a lawyer and politician. His views and feelings on the subject of religion are known only to himself. He is so reserved that nobody attempts to draw him out; but his whole deportment is as correct as it easily could be. Nobody ever expects to see anything in him but regularity and equanimity."

The expectation as regards his following the profession of the law was not fulfilled; but we shall soon hear him crying out to God for mercy through Christ Jesus, and in thanks for the infinite favours already bestowed on him. It is by no means unlikely that his thoughts were often turned to this great subject at this grave juncture in his life.

It is a little remarkable that so many distinguished men who were his classmates still survive, and these still retain a pleasing and vivid memory of their college friend and rival. I shall now present the reminiscences of Mr. McCall of Philadelphia (who drew lots with him for the valedictory), which cannot fail to be read with gratification.

Mr. McCall writes:

"Addison Alexander was rather reserved and retiring in his disposition, and residing at home, he did not mingle with the students as much as he otherwise would have done. It was only towards the close of our college career that I saw him quite frequently, and had the pleasure of a somewhat intimate fellowship with him. I was then struck with the vein of rich humour and pleasantry that played under his quiet exterior.

"His brilliant talents and fine attainments were appreciated by all of us. He was without doubt the first scholar in the class. Napton came nearest to him, but I think Alexander, take him all in all, had the pre-eminence. An excellent mathematician, a first-rate linguist, an accomplished writer—he failed in nothing and was the object of general admiration.

"I had the unmerited honour of drawing lots with him for the Valedictory and the Latin Salutatory. He drew the former, and I well remember that his performance was distinguished for its excellence.

"I have always felt proud of being his classmate, and although I saw him very rarely after leaving college, I never ceased to entertain for him an admiration which increased year by year with his expanding fame.

"The traits of his character and the leading incidents in his career, alas! too short, well deserve to be preserved in a biographical memoir. I am delighted to learn that you have undertaken it, and I only regret that I am not able to furnish you any material worthy of being introduced into your work."

I have it on the best authority that Mr. McCall was himself in the judgment of the faculty second in point of collegiate attainment to no one in the class, and his subsequent eminence, and the nature of his daily occupations, render his testimony as to his classmate's character, and scholarship, and genius, not a whit less important than that even of Judge Napton. The modesty of Mr. McCall would throw a cloud over the fact that in the college studies he was himself considered, by the faculty. at least, and without hesitation the equal of Mr. Alexander.

CHAPTER III.

It was while in college that he seems to have formed the habit of keeping a commonplace-book, and employed for this purpose a huge folio volume of stiff paper bound in heavy, rough leather of the colour of gingerbread. This volume I have carefully inspected. It was afterwards used by one of his brothers as a scrap-book, and much that the original owner wrote in it is thus blotted out. What remains consists of catalogues of the various classes and honour-men for a number of successive years, fragments of speeches, curious autographs, snatches of poetry, and bursts of ineffable nonsense. Several of his brothers wrote in it at a later date, and one day in 1830 as he sat in the window his brother James inscribed in it some very pretty original verses. Among all the treasures of this old register none are more valuable than the first draught of Addison's now famous valedictory, and another very remarkable effusion of his entitled the Peruvians. This piece is one of the most florid and rhythmical of all his productions. The tune of the sentences is peculiar—something like that of Ossian. It is nothing but a fragment, or rather a succession of fragments, some of which are broken off in the middle of a sentence. It is highly and richly imaginative, and some few of its descriptions are very chaste, reminding one of those of Prescott. The whole is exceedingly impassioned, and admirably suited to the purposes of college declamation. I am informed on the best authority that the finished oration was actually pronounced by one of his comrades, on the college stage. The piece originated in this way. His brother William one day brought him a poem on "the Incas," which he seemed to admire and made the basis of a speech he had been asked to write for one of his distressed mates.*

---

* The admiration Dr. Addison Alexander had for the poet Cowper was constantly showing itself, and in ways that would little be suspected. The allusion

In September, 1826, Mr. Alexander, as we have just seen, was graduated at Princeton, with the valedictory honours of his class, having divided the *spolia opima* of scholarship at the rather early age of seventeen.

About the same time in the following year, viz., on the 27th of September, 1827, he was appointed a tutor in the College of New Jersey, but declined; probably because he was already making great strides in his Oriental studies, and wanted ample time for still greater. He was also enjoying the luxury of vast but discursive reading. Certain it is, that the interval between his graduation and his acceptance of the post of teacher in Mr. Patton's Seminary, in 1829, was spent in almost incredible linguistical toils, and especially in prosecuting his early researches in the Asiatic languages. He was also beginning to pay more attention than formerly to the languages of the West. He joyously seized this opportunity of comparative leisure, to perfect his knowledge of those tongues with which he was already acquainted, and to extend his inquiries along every shining radius of the great circle which embraced so

---

in his Isaiah to Cowper's free paraphrase of the 137th Psalm, ("By the rivers of Babylon there we sat down"), and to his application of some of its noblest imagery to the case of the Incas, is evidently to the superb passage in "Charity:"

> "Oh could their ancient Incas rise again,
> How would they take up Israel's taunting strain?
> Art thou too fallen, Iberia? Do we see
> The robber and the murderer weak as we?
> Thou that hast wasted earth, and dared despise
> Alike the wrath and mercy of the skies,
> Thy pomp is in the grave, thy glory laid
> Low in the pits thine avarice has made.
> We come with joy from our eternal rest,
> To see the oppressor in his turn oppressed.
> Art thou the god, the thunder of whose hand
> Rolled over all our desolated land,
> Shook principalities and kingdoms down,
> And made the nations tremble at his frown!
> The sword shall light upon thy boasted powers,
> And waste them, as thy sword has wasted ours.
> 'Tis thus Omnipotence his law fulfils,
> And Vengeance executes what Justice wills."
>
> *Grigg & Elliot, Philadelphia*, 1841, p. 35.

many subjects with regard to which, at present, he had but slight information, or none at all.

A gentleman of Virginia writes that he had often heard the praises of Addison Alexander sounded by a very lovely young female relative of his, who had "left no common picture" in the mind of her listener "of a young prodigy of intellect and scholarship." This gentleman, on going to Princeton as a student of the college, found that the picture of Mr. Alexander's fair kinswoman was not overdrawn. He says, "I was very naturally led to visit at his father's; and, besides the pleasant, gentle welcome which Dr. Archibald Alexander always gave one coming from his native place, I always felt when I saw that bright, genial, sincere-looking face of Mrs. Alexander, on which the roses of youth had not yet entirely faded, and heard her talk in her kind, earnest manner, that I was in some measure back again in Virginia. But Addison was very much of a recluse, and I was pressed with college studies, and I did not make up much acquaintance with him during that period; though my appointment along with him on a very important special committee, which, for some time, had frequent sessions, brought me at that time into a good deal of intercourse with him. One thing, however, impressed me then, as I believe it has universally impressed people in regard to him, I mean the unpretending simplicity of his character. Nobody could have seen in him the exhibition of any consciousness of his extraordinary superiority, and so it was always in my observation of him."

This must have been either during or just after Mr. Alexander's own connexion with the college as a student. I think it not unlikely it was in 1827 or '28, when he was a resident-graduate in the town and before he became connected with Mr. Patton and Edgehill.

There are but few incidents relating to this transition-period between his life as a college student and his life as an usher or schoolmaster. "Some years after graduating," writes Mr. Campbell, "I happened to pass a week or two at the Rev. Dr. Archibald Alexander's, in Princeton. I observed that

Addison did not eat with the family, but after them and by himself. He glided into the dining-room with noiseless adroitness, his singularity in this particular being apparently acquiesced in by the family without comment. The presence of visitors or company in the house, as a general rule, he appeared to ignore." This he attributed to an extreme constitutional diffidence and reserve. "In general he was, at this time, remarkably taciturn, without being at all morose. He was 'swift to hear and slow to speak.' Yet no one took more pleasure in conversation than he, only he confined it to a very few." During this sojourn of Mr. Campbell's at Dr. Alexander's house, he occupied the same room with Addison, and the two sometimes lay awake talking till a late hour. "His pent-up thoughts, when they found vent, flowed in a strong current. In the upstairs room, where we slept, he had his manuscripts arranged on the floor around the room, along the washboard, where he could readily lay his hand on any one that he wanted. He was at this time writing for a paper published in Princeton. I remember reading a humorous account of Commencement-day, at Princeton, in which Addison, who spoke to so few persons, seemed to know not only what the country people, who were present on that occasion, talked about, but also how they talked."*

It is with lively pleasure that I now have recourse to the memory and kindness of Professor John S. Hart, LL. D. of Trenton, formerly of the Edgehill school. "From the year 1826 down to the date of Addison's death," writes Dr. Hart, "no student I suppose ever came to Princeton, without having his imagination excited by stories bordering upon the marvellous, in regard to the prodigious learning and the mental endowments of the studious recluse who was seldom seen, but who was known to dwell somewhere in the neighbourhood of the Theological Seminary." He well remembers "the impression this intellectual giant made upon my own youthful imagination. The traditions of the town in regard to him, and

---

* This is an exact description of the letters of Job Raw, in the Patriot.

the occasional glimpses I had of him, gave me my first idea of *genius*, in the highest meaning of the word, and in my intercourse with him in later years, which at times was entirely free and familiar, that first impression was only confirmed and deepened. No man that I have ever met filled so entirely my conception of mental greatness of the very highest order."

The first actual evidence of Addison's abilities that came under Professor Hart's notice was in the formation of the Philological* Society in the college, in the year 1828. Professor Patton, who then occupied the chair of ancient languages in the college, and who was a great enthusiast in his department, it seems endeavoured to infuse some of his own enthusiasm into the young men under his instruction. "For this purpose he called Addison to his special assistance, and with the coöperation of the other members of the faculty and of the students, the Philological Society was formed, and Professor Patton generously placed upon its shelves for the free use of the members the entire contents of his private library, which was particularly rich in rare and costly works on philological science. One part of the plan was to have stated meetings, at which papers were to be read on various subjects." The first paper that was read, and the only one of which he had any distinct recollection, was by Addison. "From his reputed antecedents I expected to hear an essay, learned indeed and able, but dry and abstruse, on some nice point of philological inquiry. Instead of that, we were treated to a discourse on the duty of studying our own English classics, dwelling with particular emphasis, I recollect, upon the noble diction and the gorgeous imagery of Edmund Burke; and, as I listened to the rich racy English of his own glowing periods, and noticed the peculiar Addisonian grace and elegance which marked the youthful composition, it seemed as if it must have been not accidental, but by some mysterious prescience, that he had been named Joseph Addison." He remembers at all events,

---

* This is Professor Hart's name for it. If there were not two societies of like name, this was called the Philologian.

that it was a common remark among the students, after hearing that essay, that Addison Alexander was well named. "Such was the effect produced on my mind by the youthful performance. I dare say there are scores of others still living who would testify to the same effect having been produced on them."

This love of the best English classics for their own sake, and not at all because other people admired them, was always a marked trait in Mr. Alexander's intellectual character. Johnson, Swift, Steele, and Addison were in his youthful fancy almost worthy to be rivals of Sir William Jones himself in the estimation of scholars and men of taste. What struck him in Johnson was not idiomatic elegance, as in the charming essayist and critic of the Spectator, but Herculean sense, knowledge, and energy, and musical cadence. Burke, and the whole school of fresh original writers who overlapped or succeeded the age of Sir Joshua Reynolds and Garrick, filled him afterwards with a sense of new and increasing enjoyment, as well as that Cicero of the English pulpit, the incomparable Robert Hall. As to Burke, he was in his esteem more than a second Johnson, with a magnificence of his own, and without Johnson's faults. It was just like the writer of the essay here noticed to defeat the expectations of those who looked for an abstruse philological disquisition from the young linguist. He rejoiced at every chance of thus baffling curiosity.

It cannot now be known when Addison first became a contributor to the public press, but probably when he was at school with Mr. Baird. We know that he used to print newspapers with a pen at that time. A paper was published in Princeton called the New Jersey Patriot. In less than three months after leaving college, at the age of seventeen, he contributed to that paper an article of two columns and a half on Persian poetry, which attracted attention, and was especially commended to the notice of the public in an editorial article of the paper in which it appeared. He wrote during the ensuing winter some caustic political squibs over the signature of "The Jesuit," in reference to the election of a United States Senator for New Jersey, which had just taken place and caused great excitement in the state.

In the following summer the Patriot ceased to be a political paper, was enlarged and placed by its proprietor under the editorial charge of Mr. Alexander and one of his brothers. This position afforded full scope for his prolific pen. In addition to editorial matter and current news, he almost covered the broad sheet with essays, poems, tales, and communications, to which various signatures were attached.

It was at this time and at this early age that some of the articles at a later day published in the Philadelphia Monthly Magazine appeared, such as "The Fall of Ispahan," "Greece in 1827," and "The Tears of Esau." He wrote for this paper a tale called "The Quaker Settlement," of which I can discover no vestige. He wrote also a tale called "The Jewess of Damascus."

The Patriot soon ceased for want of patronage.*

About this time a literary weekly paper known as the Souvenir had a short existence in Philadelphia. The editor offered prizes for the best Essay, Poem, Tale, and Biography. Addison went in for all of them, and on the sealed envelope identifying the author, placed the name of "Horace Seaford, care of J. A. A.," &c. The publisher not finding it convenient to pay the prizes offered, announced that he would give a certain number of copies of his paper to the successful writer; and on the opening of the seals, Addison was inundated with

---

* During the days that the Patriot was at the height of its circulation, a protracted controversy, occupying column upon column, in weekly instalments, was carried on in successive numbers of that journal, on the vexed subject of Dancing. The contending writers were a leading clergyman and a distinguished layman. After the matter had gone to great lengths, and the readers of the paper were becoming excessively weary of the conflict and of the topic that had provoked it, Addison, who was then one of the editors of the Patriot, brought the matter to a sudden close with the characteristic remark in large type, that "he presumed the spirit of St. Vitus himself must be satisfied by this time with what had been said on both sides of the question."

copies of the paper addressed to "Horace Seaford, care of J. A. A."

I am so fortunate as to be able to give some extracts from the article on "The Persian Poets." It is signed "Ali." It will be remembered that it was written by a youth of little more than seventeen, and who was generally supposed to know nothing of oriental literature at first hand. How erroneous this conception was, we have already had occasion to remark.

After touching upon the wide difference in nature and degree between the influences that tend to promote works of science, and the circumstances which foster works of imagination and taste, he affirms that no country has abounded in the latter more remarkably than Persia. She has not indeed, he admits, afforded to her sons those artificial aids which constitute the apparatus of the western scholar, but on the other hand, he urges, she has richly furnished them with all that tends to develope the latent elements of poetic talent, and raise them to maturity. "It has been justly observed," he continues, "that the *Age of Poetry* lies midway between barbarism and complete refinement. It is neither to freedom from all mental discipline and application, nor to the immensity of public libraries, or to the ease and excellence of public instruction, that the poet owes his inspiration. It is neither among the restraints of elegant society, nor the wild excesses of savage life, that the muses work their wonders. It is rather among scenes where the revolting harshness of unsubdued ferocity has been removed, but the gloss of excessive refinement has not yet neutralized the energies of genius—where nature herself wears a poetic garb, and the manners of men are modelled after her. There the spirit of poetry is not a shy and haughty power, inhabiting the retirements of the learned, and looking on the multitude only to despise them, but a gentler influence, which though it bends in the exercise of its power to the lowest intellects, gives *them* elevation, while it loses none itself; like the Peris of Persian romance, which feed on the flowers and perfumes of earth, though they dwell in the regions of the air."

How far this description may be applied to Persia, he proposes to determine by an unerring test as he thinks, in literature as in morals, by the degree of privilege and opportunity enjoyed. This he does by considering the advantages which she has afforded to her poets. After speaking of the fertility of fancy to which must be ascribed the hyperbolic tendency so visible in the style and conceptions of their authors, he proceeds to restrict his review to their exclusive advantages, which have aided the natural powers of the poet; and these he proposes to consider without regard to intellectual endowments.

In the midst of the discussion of this point there occurs the following passage:

"The genius of the Persian was never compelled to struggle with disadvantages of geographical position—to borrow his ideas of verdure upon earth and cloudless serenity in the skies, from the writings of another age and nation—to outrage the sensibilities of his auditors or readers by singing the praises of perpetual spring amidst the horrors of Arctic winter, by planting roses beneath the avalanche, and rearing bowers on the shores of a frozen sea. His eyes were opened on scenes where the loftiest flights of his imagination were matched by the glories of the world around him—where his boldest pictures of the majesty of nature were but copies of the mountains which he climbed in infancy, and his most luxuriant descriptions of fairy scenery were drawn from the realities of his native valleys.

"In perfect accordance with the face of nature were the manners of the people. In the character and customs of most Mohammedan nations, but especially the Persians, there ever has been and still may be observed that rich peculiarity so exclusively appropriated by the people of the East, as to have acquired almost universally the name of *Oriental*. It is the same poetic cast of manners portrayed in the sacred scriptures, that picturesque simplicity of language, that figurative expressiveness of action, which is so interesting to every cultivated mind from the power of association; whether it occur in the record of eternal truth or in the trivial page of Asiatic fiction. The very dress, food, and colloquial phrases of the East are objects of lively interest, from their poetic character and their correspondence with the pictures in that book, whose sacred precepts and sublime descriptions fell so early and so often on the unconscious ear of infancy that we cannot trace their introduction to the mind, but retain them like the shadowy image of a half-forgotten dream. It is this early familiarity with the Bible, that causes the imagination (though schooled and chastened by the nicest art and subjected to the control of the soundest understanding) to yield without resistance to the spell thrown over it by the witchery of oriental romance. We may cling to the familiar state of things around us, or shrink from the thought of transition to another. But while we retain our early impressions of camels, caravans, and deserts —of dwelling in tents, and sleeping on housetops, we must feel that these are the modes of life most congenial to the poet, and the scenes most susceptible of poetic delineation."

It was in such a situation, he goes on to say, that the Persian poet undertook the task of perpetuating the history of his native land by the power of immortal verse; and there could not be a subject more fitted, as he conceives, for the wildest flights of the most exuberant fancy. " The historical legends of ancient Irán, which survived the Arab conquest and are still fondly cherished by the modern inhabitants, are full of appropriate themes for the loftiest efforts of the muse. Songs of chivalry and love, which are often thought peculiar to the European bard, have ever been favourites with the populace of Persia; and no troubadour or minstrel of the west ever tuned his harp for the recital of exploits more wild and daring than those of Firdúsi's heroes." Nor are their characters, in his opinion, entirely void of that species of refinement which was the glory of the European knight in the golden age of chivalry, and which so strongly distinguished him from the rude and bloody warriors of other lands and eras. " So much nearer indeed," he protests, " does the modern knight approach to the ancient heroes of the East than to the huge but childish characters in Homer, that we can scarcely help concluding, that between the former there exists a natural affinity, while the latter are of a different race." The attachment of the Persians to the memory of those primeval warriors he thinks is strongly evinced by the tenacity with which they have preserved the fragments of their early history. " Though the triumphant Khalif, with his Arab troops had introduced the

Koran, and converted every fire-temple to a mosque—though the religion and the laws of Mohammed were universally diffused, the vanquished, while they adopted both, retained their national affections. While they heard with indifference the triumph of Omar and Othman over Greece, Syria, and Egypt, they cherished the recollection of their native conquerors; and while the Arab bard found little in the character or actions of the prophet and his successors to be the subject of poetical embellishment, the exploits of *Zab* and *Rustam* furnished an exhaustless theme to the minstrelsy of Persia."

But the most remarkable advantage enjoyed by the bards of Persia, he believes, is unquestionably to be found in the rich and romantic mythology peculiar to that land of poets. "It may be regarded as a singular phenomenon, that the inflexible spirit and uncompromising bigotry of Islam should have allowed itself to be entwined with so wild a relic of ancient Paganism. Though the sacred cross was trodden, with the crown of Constantine, beneath the foot of the Moslem —though every remnant of Arab idolatry was exterminated by the unsparing zeal of the prophet and his Khalifs— though the sacred fire was extinguished upon every altar, from the Caspian to the Persian Gulf; the mythology of Irán was too elastic to be trodden down, too ethereal for annihilation. The mind of the Persian seems constructed for the reception of poetic images and the enjoyment of romantic fiction; so that although, when the alternative of 'Death, Tribute, or the Koran' was presented to the vanquished, with wonted flexibility they preferred the latter, yet the fanciful dreams of the Gebr poets and the beautiful superstitions of the Gebr populace were not forgotten — they were blended with their imaginative efforts. They were strangely intermixed with their devotions; a paradoxical alliance was formed between these dreams of fairy-land and the dogmas of the Koran. The holiest saint could subscribe to both, and the devoutest *Shiah*, who five times a day repeated the solemn profession, 'There is no God but God, and Mohammed is his Prophet,' in the midst of his genuflexions could tremble at the power of malignant genii and listen for the waving of the Peri's pinion in the breeze. Nor is the Persian's preference of his own mythology surprising or absurd. Apart from national and habitual feeling, it possesses a charm peculiar and delightful. The imagination of the Arab is teeming and almost uncontrollable. But its only flashes are flashes of lightning, and its flights are the flights of an eagle among storms and tempests. The fancy of the Persian is more delicately formed. Its creations are less bold and vigorous, but far more airy and enchanting; and we can scarcely wonder that the gross delights of the Prophet's Paradise should have been despised for the charms of Gebr's Elysium." What follows will shock some readers. His fancy had been perhaps too much wrought upon when a child by the stories of the Arabs, and more recently by the fervid descriptions of the Koran. There are some, however who may agree with the bold young critic. "But this is not all. The most fastidious taste, on a fair comparison of this mythology with the orations of classic genius or Grecian superstition, cannot hesitate in a preference of the former. There is, in the fantastic theology of the Greeks and Romans, a coldness and a coarseness, which even the fire of Homer could scarce animate, and the delicacy of Virgil could not wholly refine. The incongruous mixture of human and superhuman attributes, and the inconceivable vicissitudes in the fortunes of their immortals, united with the disgusting excesses of human vice, and the ridiculous extremes of human folly, by which they are so often distinguished, render the Olympus or the Pantheon a poor field for the wanderings of genius — how poor in comparison with the *Jinnistan* of Persia! with the shadowy possessors of that imaginary region, the Peris and the Dives, those good and evil beings who fill the intermediate space in the scale of animated nature between the inhabitants of earth and the inhabitants of heaven! These beings which may be regarded as the originals of the *fairy* and *giant* of European taste— possessed of bodies, but bodies formed of the element of fire, powerful but not almighty, intelligent but not omniscient;

the Peris, pure but not impeccable; the Dives, sinful but not without hope, engaged in mutual war, but not upon earth, neither dwelling among men, nor entirely removed from participating in his fortunes; sometimes courting his assistance, and often guiding his steps and directing his destiny; beings like these may well be made the subject of poetical romance. They are precisely the species of intermediate intelligences, which might be made the machinery of an epic poem, and possess this twofold advantage over the creations of classic mythology, that while they are far more pure, ethereal, and poetical, more like the phantasms of a "poet's phrensy," they are still subjected to a paramount authority, and not like the gods of Homer, clothed in the vileness of mortality, and then disgraced by the sceptre of the universe. Their existence and character were wholly poetical. They were unconnected with religious faith, so that the wildest fictions respecting them detracted nothing from the Gebr's reverence to the Deity.

"Surrounded, then, by the most impressive and enchanting scenes of nature; by boundless deserts and cultivated plains; by frowning cliffs and verdant valleys; beneath a sky which was never clouded, and among a people who 'lisped in numbers,' the Persian poet sang of the most chivalrous exploits of ancient heroism, the most romantic fictions of a beautiful mythology. In such a situation what might we not expect? If anything more can be conceived, as requisite to complete the picture of the *Poets' Paradise*, it is that which we have already seen abundantly supplied in the munificent patronage of the great and the enthusiastic admiration of the populace. The inferior bards of other lands may plead with justice the insalubrity of climate, the ruggedness of nature's works around them, the rudeness of their countrymen, the want of encouragement, and the absence of applause; but when the classics of the land of poets shall be subjected to the impartial scrutiny of Western taste, deficiency of genius alone can be the apology of those who may be said to have been born in the precincts of Parnassus, and to have drawn their first breath in an atmosphere of poetry."

It will probably be agreed that this was "a right masterful" effort for a lad of not over the age at which many go to college. Indeed, it is by no means unlikely that this production, like many others of the same hand had been composed at an earlier period and laid aside for future use. But of this there is no certainty. We know, however, that the writer who here subscribes himself "Ali" was as careless of the fate of such accidental effusions as the ostrich of her eggs which she deposits in the sands of the desert.

It would be incorrect to suppose that Dr. Addison Alexander in after life adhered in full to the opinions expressed in this remarkable juvenile critique, nor is it outside the limits of conjecture to surmise that the opinions are in some respects as imaginary as the signature. While it is true that no man was more volatile than he in many of his personal tastes and preferences, being full of unaccountable caprices, it is also true that he loved to wear a literary mask, and to mystify his readers in every ingenious manner possible. It was also well known that he was fond of espousing sentiments which were at once novel and hard to defend. Thus his depreciation of the characters of Homer in comparison with those of Firdusi, and his sallies at the expense of the Olympian divinities as contrasted with the fabulous creations of the *Jinnistan*, may or may not be genuine. He may have been carried along impetuously (as was his wont) by the heat of his youthful admiration (which was unquestionably intense) of the Persian poets, even to the disparagement of poets the most illustrious of other countries; or, which is almost equally agreeable to what is known of his whimsical humours, he may have been merely actuated by a wish to puzzle the *literati* of Princeton, and to excite a hubbub among the cultivated readers of "The Patriot." There is good evidence in the piece itself that the writer sought for some purpose or other to conceal his hand. It is not written in his usual style; at least not as a whole. There is in some of these balanced sentences an evident and exquisite imitation of the great literary dictator of the previous century. No one who is at all familiar with Rasselas and the Rambler can hesitate to come to this conclusion. What could be more like the old "Bear" of Bolt Court and the Mitre Tavern than the following: "The incongruous mixture of human and superhuman attributes, and the inconceivable vicissitudes in the fortunes of their immortals, united with the disgusting excesses of human vice, and the ridiculous extremes of human folly;" or this: "Surrounded, then, by the most majestic and enchanting scenes of nature; by boundless deserts and cultivated plains; by frowning cliffs and verdant valleys; beneath a sky which was never clouded, and among a people who lisped in numbers;" or this: "If any thing more can be conceived, as requisite to complete the picture of the Poets' Paradise, it is that which we have already seen abundantly supplied in the munificent patronage of the great, and the enthusiastic admiration of the populace."

We can almost see before us the unconscious lexicographer as he rounded off this sentence turning his candle upside down at Mrs. Boswell's, and blowing with delight at the happy finish he had given this ponderous period. Mr. Alexander's intuitive taste prevented him, however, from pushing this imitation to the verge of caricature, and thus spoiling his essay. The consequence is that the style of the production taken as a whole, though resembling that of the early Ramblers, is as vigorous and original as Johnson's own, and where his own native qualities break out, much superior to it on literary grounds. Whether this imitation of Johnson was wholly accidental, or not, is another question: but it will be remembered that Addison and Johnson were in every body's hands then, and one of his classmates tells us that the young collegian was much given to voluntary imitations of the most admired of the English classics. The young graduate's overweening partiality for Oriental studies and the masterpieces of Oriental genius, had, as we have seen, already begun to wane, and was destined to be almost entirely superseded, or at all events overborne, or held in abeyance, by his enthusiastic devotion to the languages and still more to the literatures of ancient and modern Europe. The literature of the Greeks, which is here spoken of with a dash of contempt, was afterwards and soon to become the theatre on which, after the sacred text of the Old and New Testaments, he employed his best powers through life. Yet he never ceased to go for an occasional solace and entertainment to the tales of the Arabs and the sweet numbers of Persia. One of my earliest recollections of him is that he taught me a Persian song (which I have not yet forgotten), and that he used to read me wonderful legends and fabulous and romantic stories from certain ancient rolls inscribed with characters which I subsequently learned were Arabic. I also well remember reading for hours at a time in his study and under his approving eye (and that day after day till I finished the volumes), from the pages of the "Green Book," as we both loved to call it; which was nothing less than Lane's larger edition of the Arabian Nights with English notes, with the golden shields and Moorish spears on the back, and the superb illustrations on the inside. The impression made upon my boyish imagination by the dark features and spreading wings of the Jinn drawn in the broad margin, will never be effaced. But when the ruddy scholar placed me in a corner of his cane settee, and regaled me with recitations, songs, tales, descriptions, and dialogues of his own, I recognized in him a being possessing powers not unlike those of "Sulliman the son of Daoud," who could command the genii and the Afrik at pleasure; for no captivation was ever more complete or genuine than that under which he held me whenever he chose to do so, a willing prisoner.

But the Patriot during the time he contributed for it, or rather, as I might almost say, wrote it, contained very different material from that of which a specimen or sample has just been given. The number before me (vol. ii. No. 59) is dated September 29, 1827, and bears this title: "New-Jersey Patriot, Princeton. Printed and published by D. A. Borrenstein." Underneath this superscription is the motto, "The Safety of the People is the Supreme Law." It is a quarto sheet of moderate size, but well-shaped and closely printed. The first piece is a communication in verse signed "Roland," and is an address "to Music." This I suspect to be from the pen of the invisible editor, and is an obvious imitation of the style of poetry which was so much in vogue before Scott and Byron, and which continued a sickly existence even after the appearance of Wordsworth. This is just such poetry as Burke was not ashamed to indulge in before he became an orator and a statesman.*

The next is some idle stanzas which surely must have sprung from a very different brain! They are in a totally different measure, are to "The Morrow," and are signed *Trochilus*. They are puerile and worthless, and are the type of thousands like them. Yet when we read the fine prose satire which immediately follows, and find it too signed Trochilus, a piece marked by all the energy, vehemence, and wit of Swift, we are led almost insensibly to the conclusion that the lines to "The Morrow" are also from the editor, and are either intended as a burlesque upon the general mass of fugitive newspaper poetry of the day, or else merely to throw the reader off his guard; and that the satirical effusion is perhaps a conscious and if so quite successful imitation of the Dean of St. Patrick's. This however is pure conjecture. It is possible some of these pieces are by other hands. Remarkable and innocent as this production is, it is not exactly quotable. It contains among other laughable things some sly and characteristic hits at the mathematicians and natural philosophers. This was doubtless to teaze the curiosity of the Princeton professors. Then comes an exposure of a coloured charlatan by the name of Rusworm, who had betrayed the confidence of the venerable Dr. Miller and others. Then we have a letter, "the original of which is in the possession of a gentleman of Princeton," from David Garrick, in relation to a tragedy by William Julius Mickle, the translator of the Lusiad.† It is

---

* And specimens of which are given in his biography by Pryor.

† The real name of the translator of Camolus was simply William Mickle. Julius was an afterthought of his own.

addressed to George Johnstone, Esq.—a friend and patron of the poet. "The Exile of Scio," which follows, and purports to be from the "New Monthly Magazine," exhibits strong signs of the same authorship. My conviction is that Mr. Alexander had previously written it and contributed it to the Magazine, with which he was certainly in communication; as another romantic and descriptive piece in this paper is undoubtedly by the editor.

The letter of Sir Walter Raleigh which figures on the same page is believed to be genuine. Two pieces, one on "Visitation of Schools," from "an American Journal," and one on Archimedes, fill up the side. The inside is taken up with Princeton matters and domestic news. In the middle of the page, however, are two editorials, one of which is in the usual serious style of Mr. Alexander, much affected in this instance, it must be confessed, by the Johnsonese swell. I give a part of it, as it affords us a transient glimpse of the Princeton Commencement. There is a full account of the exercises, in another column of the same issue. The annual oration before the American Whig and Cliosophic Societies in joint-meeting was delivered by the Hon. Theodore Frelinghuysen, Attorney General of the State of New Jersey, in the presence of an unusually large and respectable audience. The annual exhibition of undergraduates took place on the evening of the 25th. This was exactly a year from the time of Mr. Alexander's own graduation, so that he was not yet ready to take the master's degree. The Alumni Association of Nassau Hall held its first annual meeting in the college chapel on the morning of Commencement. A letter was read from his Excellency James Madison, President of the Association, expressing his interest in the prosperity of the college, and the objects of the Association. At this meeting it was resolved, that "it is expedient that a history of Nassau Hall be prepared for publication, and that the members of the association be requested to furnish during the ensuing year such biographical notices of the Alumni, as in their opinion will be useful to the college and interesting to the public." Also, "that all such biographical notices be forwarded to Mr. J. Addison Alexander, of Princeton."

This history, if ever entered upon by the young student, was, it is believed, never carried out.* These pleasant assemblages of the Alumni have been one of the most interesting features of the Princeton Commencement ever since the meeting of which record is here made.

The editorial article to which reference has been made, begins thus: "We are gratified to state that the number of persons attracted to Princeton by the ceremonies of the annual Commencement, during the present week, was unusually large.

---

* The following names comprised the officers of the association at the time referred to above:

PRESIDENT.
James Madison of Virginia.

VICE-PRESIDENTS.

Aaron Ogden of New Jersey, William Gaston of North Carolina,
Richard Stockton   "   John Henry Hobart of New York,
Andrew Kirkpatrick "   Henry W. Edwards of Connecticut.
Ashbel Green   "

TREASURER.
Samuel Bayard of New Jersey.

SECRETARY.
John Maclean of New Jersey.

COMMITTEE OF ARRANGEMENTS.
Professor Maclean, Samuel T. Bayard, Esq. and Mr. William C. Alexander.

It may be interesting to some also to know that the members of the Executive Committee of the New Jersey Bible Society at this time were: Dr. Archibald Alexander, Chief Justice Ewing, General Frelinghuysen, Dr. Miller, the Rev. George S. Woodhull, James S. Green, Esq. and Samuel Bayard, Esq.

There is still another item which may have an interest for practical men. The delegates to the Convention for the promotion of Internal Improvements, assembled on the 25th inst. at the hour appointed, in the upper room of the Academy. The honourable Richard Stockton, of Somerset, was appointed President, and the honourable William Coxe, of Burlington, Vice-President; John M. Sherrerd, Esq. of Warren, Secretary, and Daniel C. Croxall, Esq. of Hunterdon, Assistant Secretary. Delegates were present from eight counties. The business discussed was of considerable importance, but we have no room for further allusion to it.

A larger audience has seldom been witnessed here on a similar occasion, than that which occupied the church on Wednesday morning and the preceding night. It would give us pleasure to regard this as an indication of assuring interest in the prosperity of the college." And after some very strong writing comes this sentence of unmistakable Johnsonese: "In almost every State, public means of instruction are maintained by public patronage, and are esteemed and cherished as invaluable instruments of public prosperity. We may readily imagine then the judgment which an enlightened people in an age of great and progressive illumination, will be prepared to pass upon a community which blindly forgets the means of its existing greatness, and wilfully rejects the only means of future elevation."

The fourth page is mainly occupied by Foreign News. This department of the paper is in the stately Gazette style of the same columns in the London Times. It is no doubt a genuine extract from some English paper. The tidings from Greece, in particular, are given in a very sonorous and spirited manner. Redshid Pasha had turned towards the interior. The Constantinople fleet had returned a second time to Navarin, leaving four Greek brigs under Lord Cochrane to blockade the entrance of the Gulf of Corinth. Tidings also had arrived from Napoli that some Greeks occupying a convent had beaten and driven back 1500 Arabs whom Ibrahim Pacha had advanced against them. Four hundred of the Barbarians had been slain on the declivity of a hill, where the descendants of Leonidas had prepared an ambush.

The last piece in the paper, which is on "The Sea," is certainly by some writer after the discovery of steam, and if not already appropriated, may be safely attributed to the young scholar whose pen we have seen to have been so busy on the first page. The treatment of the subject is very brief and yet very exhaustive. The style is so altered, as not to be recognizable. That very summer he had made his first visit to the sea-shore, having gone to Long Branch with his parents. He always used to say that what most impressed him on the sea-beach was the thought that he was on the edge of a great continent.

THE SEA.

"There is something in being near the sea, like being on the confines of eternity. It is a new element, a pure abstraction. The mind loves to hover on that which is endless and forever the same. People wonder at a steamboat, the invention of man, managed by man, propelled by man, that makes its liquid path like a railway through the sea. I wonder at the sea itself, that vast Leviathan, rolled round the earth, smiling in its sleep, waked into fury, fathomless, boundless, a huge world of water-drops. Whence is it? Whither goes it? is it to eternity or nothing? Strange, ponderous riddle! that we can neither penetrate nor grasp in our comprehension, ebbing and flowing like human life, and swallowing it up in 'thy remorseless womb': what art thou?— what is there in common with thy life and ours who gaze on thee?— Blind, deaf, and old, thou seest not, hearest not, understandest not; neither do we understand, who behold and listen to thee! Great as thou art, unconscious of thy greatness, unwieldy, enormous, preposterous, twin sister of matter, rest in thy 'dark unfathomed cave' of mystery, mocking human pride and weakness. Still it is given to the mind of man to wonder at thee, to confess its ignorance, and to stand in awe of thy stupendous might and majesty, and of its own being that can question thee." *

---

* In singular contrast with this successful essay in the sublime style is a critique that appeared in another issue of the Patriot, of Shelley's Poems; which were then agitating the literary world of Europe. We do not scruple to make a few extracts.

* * * "The particular composition of Shelley's which forms the subject of this review, is *Prometheus Unbound,* which its author denominates a *Lyrical Drama,* although, as its author observes, it has neither action nor dramatic dialogue. It may be observed by the way, that writers of this school are exceedingly apt to miscall and misapply. The 'Prometheus Unbound' may be regarded as a text-book in this style of composition. The dramatis personæ are as follows: Prometheus a *male* nondescript, being neither god nor man. Asia, Panthea, and Ione, *female* non-descripts; Mercury and Apollo, gods; the Furies, and a Faun. To these add several voices—as the voices of the mountains, voices of the air, voices of the whirlwinds, and a large assortment of spirits, such as the spirit of the moon, of the earth, of the human mind, of the hours; who all, says the Reviewer, attest their superhuman nature, by singing

At the time Mr. Alexander assumed the editorial charge
and saying things which no human being can comprehend. As a specimen of
the Lyrics, take the following speech of a cloud:

> 'I silently laugh at my own cenotaph,
> And out of the caverns of rain,
> Like a child from the womb, like a ghost from the tomb,
> I arise and unbuild it again.'

And the following song by the spirits of the human mind:

> 'Earth, Air, and Light,
> And the spirit of Might,
> Which drives the stars in their fiery flight,
> And Love, thought and breath,
> The powers that quell death,
> Wherever we soar shall assemble beneath.'

"In imitation of this wonderful production, I once projected a Lyrical drama of my own, which I entitled 'Flibbertigibbet in Liquor.' After so long a preface, it may be unpardonable to insert a portion of the first scene. I shall do so however at all hazards, and appeal to any impartial judge whether the imitation even approaches to caricature.

SCENE I.

ENTER TWO SPIRITS.

[*Spirit of Turpentine sings.*]

> We come! we come!
> From the hidden recess of a puncheon of rum,
> Our fragrant breath,
> On the wings of death,
> Is building a house for the deaf and dumb.

[*Spirit of Wine sings.*]

> Hark! Hark!
> On the breast of the waves the seadogs bark,
> The frantic boy,
> In his senseless joy,
> Leaps into the jaws of the hungry shark.

[*Spirit of Turpentine sings.*]

> Sleep! sleep!
> Spirit of Wine, thy mighty watch keep,
> The billows sigh,
> While the phantoms fly,
> To their cold wet home in the gloomy deep.

ENTER THREE SPIRITS.

[*Voice of Grog sings.*]

> Down! down!
> Where the Spirit of Wine and his train have flown

of the Patriot, party politics were running high.* The fierce canvass between John Quincy Adams (then President of the United States) and Andrew Jackson was in agitation. The paper was to be neutral; but the people expected some politics; and so, to meet this demand, the masked editor would write an editorial arguing the questions on both sides and in a manner so adroit that it was not only impossible to discover on which side the new champion was preparing to do battle, but even to detect where his private sympathies lay.

>The soul of the world,
>In darkness furled,
>Has passed to its tomb with a speechless groan!
>
>[*Voice of Grary sings.*]
>
>The Spirit of Moisture comes flying abroad,
>And his train is borne by the Cyprian god,
>Behold, Behold,
>The voice of the ghost
>Of a murdered toast
>Sings an anthem of praise in the palace of gold.
>
>[*Voice of Garlic sings.*]
>
>Fire! fire!
>Rise on the wings of blue desire!
>The billows laugh,
>For the spirit of sleep,
>In the lowest deep
>Is building a snowy cenotaph.
>
>[*The Three Voices.*]
>
>The hour is come—from the puncheon of rum—
>I see the spirit come flaming around.
>'Tis done—'tis done—on a beam of the sun—
>We pass to our graves with an earthquake of sound.
>
>*Music*—The spirit of sleep playing upon the Solar system."

This extravaganza is signed W. The letters of Job Raw, on Commencement Day and other topics, are full of the adventures of an absurd greenhorn who makes as many mistakes as Yellowplush or Mrs. Partington.

* Numerous allusions to this contest will be found in the "Forty Years' Familiar Letters" of the Rev. J. W. Alexander D. D. The members of the family were amicably divided on this question. The subject of these memoirs was a political Gallio.

The truth was he was as strictly impartial as he professed to be, but not so warmly interested in the clash of weapons. All *that* was a ruse. A specimen of these puzzling political (or anti-political) leaders is subjoined. It is enough to show how keenly observant Mr. Alexander was of what was going on in the world.

The following editorial came out in the Patriot of the 18th of August, 1827, and excited much curiosity as to its authorship:

"As we have already intimated our intention to abstain from any participation in the political conflicts which divide and agitate the public mind; and as neutrality is, in these days of violence, regarded as more questionable and suspicious than the utmost extravagance of party zeal, we submit to our readers the following considerations, which we trust will serve both as an exposition and vindication of the course which we have adopted. It is to be lamented, that, while there is little or no essential difference of opinion among a large majority of the people as to the fundamental principles which ought to govern the councils of the United States, the political warfare of the present day is waged in a spirit which to every man of impartial and unbiased judgment must appear unnecessary and even prejudicial to the character of our country. The privacy of domestic life has been invaded;—alleged offences, which time had consigned to oblivion, have been raked from mouldering records;—conflicting and recrimitative accusations of the most startling magnitude and importance are urged by hostile partisans with a zeal and vehemence which makes it difficult to ascertain the truth. On one side it is averred, that General Jackson is a 'Military Chieftain,' regardless of the constitution and laws of his country;— that he is no friend to the policy by which the industry and resources of the several states can be most successfully employed;—that he is supported by men of desperate character and 'vaulting ambition;' that his private history is sullied with crimes;—that the principles on which he would administer public affairs are in a great measure unknown, and, so far as they can be penetrated, at variance with those which alone can conduct the nation safely in a career of prosperity and greatness. To Mr. Adams it is objected, on the other side, that he has been tried and 'found wanting;'—that his adherents have made a party question of that which ought to have been supported merely on national grounds and left to rest upon its own merits; that by this course they have not only put in jeopardy the due encouragement of national industry, but have thrown the apple of discord amongst the members of the Union;—that he has not redeemed the pledges which on various occasions he has given, with respect to the principles which should govern him in the execution of his responsible trust;—that he has employed the patronage of his office, merely to secure his re-election, and without due regard to the qualifications of the candidates, and has thereby sacrificed the public weal in seeking to promote his personal interests;—that from vanity, or want of correct judgment, he has excluded us from a most profitable branch of foreign commerce;—that the means by which he attained his present elevation were such as render his future exclusion from office necessary to vindicate the purity of the elective franchise, and essential to the honour and future safety of the country.

"Such are the charges proclaimed against both the candidates for the presidential chair through the medium of the press. Many of them have been recently promulgated, and are yet to be sustained by evidence, or demonstrated to be groundless. Independent of both parties, wishing to decide aright, and anxious only to serve the cause of truth and of our country, we cannot consistently with the dictates of conscience, at the present stage of the controversy, take a side with either of the contending ranks.

"Such evidence may hereafter be adduced that General Jackson is hostile to the plan which when properly modified will, we think, promote the welfare of every part of the Union, as will satisfy us that the public good cannot be advanced by a change of the administration. Nor is it beyond the bounds of possibility, that such testimony concerning the means by which Mr. Adams came into power may be made public, as to render it our duty to oppose his further continuance in office. Such being the state of the question, and having more than a year before us, we shall await with patience the developments of the future, without pledging ourselves to any man or set of men. We shall use the prerogative of a free press, and utter, with independence, but with becoming deference, our sentiments respecting public men and public measures. Measures which we think calculated to promote the public good we shall never condemn, whatever may be their origin. The honest acts of a wise, firm, liberal and independent government, shall receive whatever aid our feeble exertions can afford them. We shall conclude this article, already perhaps too much extended, by an enumeration of the qualifications which in our humble opinion should distinguish the chief magistrate of this republic. He should possess firmness enough to do what he knows to be right. He should regard more the interests of the country than the stability of his own power. He should have courage and wisdom to call to his assistance the wisest counsellors, and select for office the most able men of unsullied integrity within his reach. The rays of executive displeasure should never be concentrated on the humble citizen to consume and destroy him, because in the just exercise of a freeman's right he condemns measures of doubtful expediency. Wasteful expenditures he should discountenance and resist. The interests of every section of the country it should be his study to promote; nor should he, to extend his influence and perpetuate his power, patronize measures detrimental to one portion of the Union for the benefit of another. In short, THE COUNTRY, THE WHOLE COUNTRY should occupy every affection and actuate every measure of a President of the United States. We now submit the matter to the judgment of our readers. When the proper time arrives for us to choose a side, we hope to be able to give satisfactory reasons for the opinions we may then maintain, so as to merit the countenance and support of just and impartial men. In the mean time, we will gather for our own information, and lay before our readers all the important political information from both sides which may have a proper bearing upon this great controversy, in the full persuasion, that fearless neutrality where both parties are in fault, is the duty of every Patriot.

"The great Bacon, describing the qualifications and duties of a chief magistrate, declares it to be essential that ' he set not to sale the seats of justice, for that oppresseth the people,'—that *inutilis æquitas* sit not in the chancery, for that is *inepta misericordia ;* that *utilis inæquitas* keep not the exchequer, for that is *crudele latrocinium ;* that *infidelis prudentia* be not his secretary, for that is *anguis sub viridi herbâ.*"

The last extract I shall make from the Patriot, is the concluding chapter of the beautiful eastern tale entitled, The Jewess of Damascus. This is the best specimen now extant of Mr. Alexander's style in serious oriental fiction. It bears a certain resemblance in some of its characters, and in the general diction, to Ivanhoe. But it is still more like one or two chapters in the Talisman,* and may have been to some extent a deliberate imitation. There is little doubt that in comprehensive force and grandeur of imagination, and in fertility of invention, as well as in observation of nature and manners, in knowledge of human character, in genuine healthy passion, and multifarious though not exact and critical learning, and in quality of style, considered as admirably suited and proportioned to his subjects, Scott has had no equal since the days of Shakespeare. But of Mr. Alexander it may be said that he also had rare gifts of imagination, and a productive power of untold fecundity and versatility ; and a knowledge of human nature that for one who was regarded by many as a mere village recluse was truly wonderful ; and he possessed in addition this notable advantage over the wizard of the North, that he was intimately and even critically acquainted with the history, literature, and tongues of the lands of the Syrian, the Persian, and the Arab, of which he wrote. This is said merely in the

---

* The Tales of the Crusaders came out in 1825, while Mr. Alexander was a Junior in college.

way of introduction to the concluding passages of the story itself, and to indicate the opinion that certain extracts drawn from the two writers may be compared without serious injury to the reputation of the stripling scholar. Let it be borne in mind, however, that writing novels and poems was the main business of Scott's life; whereas it was Mr. Alexander's occasional pastime, and the pastime of his younger years and idlest hours. The attention of the reader is specially invited to the magnificent description of Damascus as it lay sparkling in an oriental sunset. It reminds one of the opening paragraphs of the Talisman:

THE JEWESS OF DAMASCUS.*

(*Concluded.*)

"The Aga of the Janissaries paused. The workings of a better spirit were visible in his countenance. 'I know not,' said he, at last, 'whether I ought to release you upon any terms. But you seem a stranger; and I will take it upon myself. You are free, if you will profess the faith in the presence of these witnesses. Speak quickly, rise, and begone.' A sentence of death could scarcely have been more dreadful to the Jew than this unwonted indulgence of the Turk. 'Ah,' thought he, 'the tender mercies of the ungodly are cruel. No, let me die, rather than again abjure the covenant of Abraham.' But as he formed this mental resolution, the recollection of the enchanting prospects it would blast, and the agony which his imprisonment might occasion to more than one affectionate bosom, rushed upon his soul. He reverted to the horrid stories of long captivity and dreadful death in the dungeons of the Turkish Empire, and thought of the many chances against his ultimate deliverance, and of the ruinous sacrifices by which, if obtained at all, it must be purchased,—his bosom was rent by an agonizing conflict.—Truth, honour, devotion to his God, and a solemn pledge to earthly friends, impelled him to refuse; while the dread of unknown sufferings and of certain disappointment, urged him to obey. The struggle was transient, however, though terrific. He buried his face in his hands, and seemed absorbed in prayer. He was, indeed, beseeching pardon for the falsehood he had resolved to utter, and

---

* The final chapter of the Jewess of Damascus stands next in the column to the critique on Shelley.

breathing at the same time to Heaven the profession of his true belief. Then without raising his eyes, after several fruitless attempts to articulate, he muttered in Arabic the solemn confession, 'There is no God but God, and Mohammed is his prophet.'

"'He has spoken it, Aga,' said a surly Janissary, who stood directly by him, 'but we know not what he has muttered to himself besides.' 'Hast thou confessed the Prophet, Ishaak,' said the Aga, who now sat upon his horse and overlooked the multitude, 'Dost thou acknowledge thyself a Moslem?'

"It was only by a mighty effort that the Jew could give utterance to the words 'I do.' 'Thou art free,' said the Aga; and applying to his mouth the silver trumpet which was suspended at his saddle-bow, he gave a single blast, and turned his horse's head in the direction of the castle. The Janissaries gathered around their leader, and in a few minutes the distant sound of their horses' feet had wholly died away.

"Never, perhaps, did a release from danger occasion so little satisfaction. Ishaak now reflected that he had violated his duty to heaven, broken his pledge to his dearest friends, and abjured the religion of his fathers. He was wholly unable to rise from his knees till the last of the spectators who had remained to pity and insult him, grew weary and departed. At last, when the crowd seemed finally dispersed, he arose slowly from the earth. But when he lifted his eyes he remained petrified and aghast. In the middle of the street stood a camel bearing on its back a litter of that description used in journeys by eastern females of superior rank. The curtains of this litter were withdrawn, and within, the astonished Jew beheld unveiled and fixed upon him the countenance of Miriam. Grief, anger and amazement beamed from her kindled eye, and contempt sat quivering on her lip. As her look met his, she dropped her veil, the curtains were hastily closed, and the camel proceeded on his journey.

"The emotions of the Jew at this unexpected sight would defy any attempt at description. An hour or two passed by, during which he remained in a state of torpid frenzy. He was wholly insensible of present objects, and without a distinct recollection of the past. At the end of this time he found himself again before the door of Asher Ziddim. Again he kissed the threshold, and again gave the signal for admission. The door was opened cautiously as before, and by the same grave domestic; but the visitor was not received with the same cordial and respectful welcome. The servant came out to receive his commands, and gave him no invitation to come in. Ishaak mechanically named his master. 'He seeth no one to day.' Ishaak muttered some

incoherent questions respecting Miriam, and her journey to Sidon.—
'The damsel goeth not forth to Sidon,' was the laconic answer, and the
frantic Ishaak departed in despair.

"It was sunset—a glorious hour in that land of unclouded skies—
when a traveller journeying towards the sea, paused to look back upon
Damascus. It was the same stranger who had surveyed the landscape
when glistening in the freshness of the morning. But the man seemed
not the same. The lofty bearing of his front and the proud glance of
his eye were exchanged for the contraction of inward pain and the fitful gleam of terror and conscious guilt. He gazed long in silence on
the city as it lay gilded by the parting rays of a rich autumnal sunset.
The splendour reflected from its domes and spires, though less dazzling
than that which appeared in a morning view, was more beautiful and
chastened. Instead of the unvaried golden tint which then overspread
the scene, the different objects now displayed an endless variety of
hues. Over one was spread a colouring of purple. Another was
arrayed in a robe of fiery red; while the highest points in the view,
the pinnacles and spires, were still gleaming in the simple brightness
of unmingled sunshine.

"'Thou art still beautiful,' said Ishaak, 'but the glory in my eyes
has departed. I look upon thy palaces, but I no longer covet them:
I survey thy groves and vineyards, but I desire them not. Thou hast
been to me a blasting and a curse, and now thou smilest in thy scorn
upon him whose peace thou hast destroyed.'

"He turned aside to a fresh and sparkling fountain which threw up its
liquid columns from a marble basin in a neighbouring enclosure; and
having bathed his throbbing head in its crystal waters, bade farewell
forever to Damascus, and journeyed on.

"There are few spirits so exempt from the debasing imperfections of
humanity as to endure the severing of ties which once seemed inter-
woven with the heart-strings, and still retain perfect equanimity of
feeling. If there is any principle in action among men which can
accomplish this in even a moderate degree, it is the principle of religion. It is such a sense of devotion to the service of heaven as makes
its subject forget and undervalue the affections and associations of
earth. Yet even this principle, all-powerful as it is, has seldom the
effect of producing entire oblivion or indifference. This was sensibly
felt by Father Isaac, the revered and holy monk of the Convent of
St. ——. He had long since renounced the obstinate unbelief of
Judaism. His heart had been subdued by the energy of grace, and his
understanding had bowed to the omnipotence of truth. He had

retired to the duties and enjoyments of monastic seclusion, and by the holiness of his life and the warmth of his benevolence had gained the reverence of his order and the grateful affection of the poor. Yet there were times when, in spite of all his efforts to suppress it, the memory of former days would rise upon his view. His sins and follies he voluntarily recalled as subjects of repentance and self-abasement before God. But with them there often came inseparably mingled images of joy and pleasure which he would gladly have forgotten. Among these, there was a dream-like form which though sedulously excluded from his waking thoughts would often flit across his mind amidst the airy pageant of some delightful vision. He tried to look upon it as an angel; but memory and conscience whispered that it was a woman.

"The summer of 18— brought an influx of Jewish refugees to the city of Genoa. Among the rest were a considerable number of exiles from Damascus. The oppressions of the Moslem had become intolerable, and even the venerable Asher Ziddim, though far beyond the appointed goal of threescore years and ten, chose rather to brave the danger of a boisterous voyage and become in his old age a stranger in a strange land, than to endure contempt and suffer persecution in the contaminated city of his fathers. His daughter clung to his side. They were all to each other. She renounced every other association to be the solace and companion of her aged parent; while he had made it the object of all his efforts and designs to create and preserve the happiness of his only child. The arrival of these emigrants was not long a secret, even in the cloisters of St. ——. The monks in succession visited the city to labour for the conversion of these unbelieving strangers. Yet there was one who steadily refused to aid in this pious enterprise—and, strange to tell, that one was the most revered and loved for piety, benevolence, and zeal, the self-denying, devoted Father Isaac.

"Weeks and months rolled by, and each as it passed brought tidings of the humanity and kindness of the devoted Damascenes. The aged Asher had fortunately rescued a large proportion of his riches, which by the hands of his daughter, at once his almoner and steward, were freely dispensed to feed the bowels of the poor. The name of Miriam, unbeliever as she was, soon furnished a theme of eulogy to every tongue; and it became at last a current saying among those who fed upon her bounty, that the balance of Justice would make no distinction between the good works of Isaac the Christian monk, and of Miriam the Jewess of Damascus."

This tale, like the panegyric of the Persian Poets, is printed under the signature of *Ali*. The indulgent reader will not forget that it was written hurriedly for the columns of a village newspaper. It appears to have been modelled in some degree, as regards its form, after the ingenious romances which were already beginning to fill the pages of the English periodicals. It would have been read with interest had it appeared in Maga. It is thought by some that this story would not have done discredit to John Wilson, or to Lockhart, on the score of imagination and diction, while it is doubted whether either of these could have more successfully preserved the oriental, and yet modern, *vraisemblance.*

But the New Jersey Patriot was not the only sheet to which Mr. Alexander was contributing these fugitive essays. He was also writing frequently, if not so constantly, for a journal known as the "Emporium." It is to be regretted that most of his communications in that quarter have been lost.

The Emporium was also a weekly paper, and was published in the city of Trenton, then as still the capital of the State. It was first of a literary and miscellaneous character, but afterwards became the leading Democratic organ in New Jersey. It was established, published, printed, and edited, by Joseph Justice and Stacy G. Potts, under the firm of Justice & Potts. Mr. Potts, then a young printer, afterwards became an eminent lawyer and a Judge of the Supreme Court of New-Jersey. He was in later years a gentleman of much dignity and suavity of manners, and of most agreeable social qualities, and withal a person of the highest probity and excellence of character. For this journal Mr. Alexander wrote copiously while in college, and after graduation published much which cannot now be recovered.*

It must not be forgotten that all this was the merest diversion. This tide of matter for the newspapers was wholly produced, one may say, while the other young men about Princeton were engaged in their walks and talks, were visiting

---

* A gentleman who has kindly examined the files of this paper for the period in question, assures me that there are pieces which "read like him," but he is unable to identify any of them.

their sweethearts, or were playing ball in the college campus. He too, it must be admitted, was at this time somewhat fond of walking, and would occasionally take a cheerful stroll, as we have seen, with his friends Mr. King or Mr. Napton. It was observed, however, that with the exception of Mr. Bolling's, he seldom entered a friend's room between recitations, or before the hour for college prayers, a degree of abstinence which was considered a sign of great self-denial in an undergraduate; nor did he usually encourage his fellow-students to visit him at his own home. This we may be persuaded was from no lack of hospitality on his part, and I have never heard that it gave any offence; but simply from a recluse habit already formed, and a passion for saving not only the precious ingots but even the golden dust and filings of time. He was remarkable for this peculiarity through life. He would rush from the breakfast table to his study as if an enemy were pursuing him, and slam the door as if he was angry: but the next moment he would be heard murmuring in an earnest rapid tone as he bent over the open books that covered his table. He also had a habit at times of snapping his eyes, as if involuntarily, perhaps unconsciously; first one and then after an interval the other; in a manner curious to behold, but which it would not be easy to describe. The movement did not distort, but gave a kind of pleasing sparkle to his face. The gentleman who sat next to him at Baird's Academy says he was even then the admiration and despair of the school; that his cheek was ruddy and his eye sparkling; that he was never known to make a mistake or a blunder in his recitations, or to fail to arrive at a perfect demonstration at the blackboard, and that no one ever saw him hesitate for a word. The impression of this gentleman was that "Addison could see through anything at a glance; that he could not help solving his problems, if he *tried*." At the time of which I am now speaking, the year after he took his Bachelor's degree, it does not appear that he was much changed in his appearance or characteristics and habits; except that he was visibly a little older, somewhat more sedate, more fully grown, and with a greater breadth of knowledge, cultivation, and experience of life. He was still, like the minstrel-warriour of Bethlehem Judah, "ruddy and withal of a beautiful countenance, and goodly to look to." Strange as it may seem, notwithstanding his reserve and bashfulness (for though the word bashfulness does not precisely express the shade of meaning intended, it is the only one except shyness that even verges towards a just description) and his solitary ways, he was among those who knew him well exceedingly popular. He was so modest and unassuming that no one envied him his growing honours. His compeers gloried in his successes as successes of the Academy, of the College, and of Whig Hall. He was not one of those who seem born to be admired and hated; but one of those who though named only to be praised are known only to be loved.

One of the very few records of Mr. Alexander's literary occupations at this time is furnished in the following statement with reference to the dates at which he finished the several books of Homer's Odyssey in Greek. He read it in the folio of Spondanus, Basle, 1533, the same copy which was afterwards perused by his brother James. He marked at the end of every book the time of his getting through it, and with the result exhibited in the annexed table:

No. of Book.				No. of Book.			
I.	January	22,	1827.	XIII.	February	10,	1827.
II.	"	23,	"	XIV.	"	19,	"
III.	"	24,	"	XV.	"	21,	"
IV.	"	26,	"	XVI.	"	27,	"
V.	"	29,	"	XVII.	March	6,	"
VI.	"	30,	"	XVIII.	"	7,	"
VII.	February	1,	"	XIX.	"	8,	"
VIII.	"	1,	"	XX.	"	9,	"
IX.	"	6,	"	XXI.	"	10,	"
X.	"	7,	"	XXII.	"	12,	"
XI.	"	8,	"	XXIII.	"	12,	"
XII.	"	8,	"	XXIV.	"	13,	"

I give here a letter which evidently, from its handwriting,

belongs to an early period of his life. It would not be recognized as his by those who were familiar only with his manuscript of a later day. The only date upon it is the month, September. The internal evidence corresponds perfectly with the external, in pointing to a period anterior to the time when his writing became round and elegant. There is a greater freedom and elasticity of style than he permitted himself afterwards. It was addressed to his brother James in Virginia and at Charlotte Court-House. Now his brother James went to Virginia in 1826 and returned in 1828, and did not revisit his old home in Charlotte till several years had elapsed. Moreover, the allusion in the letter to "a journey northward" is in such terms as necessarily imply a residence in the South, and not a mere visit to that region. This is further presupposed in the reference to a previous correspondence between the brothers. The mention of the elder brother's sickness, seems to fix the time as towards the close of his two years' sojourn in his native state. The repeated calling in of the name of Mr. Patton might seem to indicate the time the younger brother was that gentleman's assistant at Edgehill; but this was not till November of the year following the elder brother's return to the North. We are thus shut up to three years, 1826, 1827, and 1828. In the autumn of one of these years the letter was written. There are some things which might make one incline towards 1828. The letter shows him at work upon the Pentateuch. So does the journal for the winter of '28. The letter speaks of the recent completion of a poem entitled the " Tears of Esau," and the journal discloses the fact that he wrote off this poem for the columns of the monthly magazine on the 12th of January of that year. It is not necessarily implied, however, that he composed it then. It is more probable that he copied it. Besides, I find from his diary that on the 3d of January 1828, he was already deep in Exodus, whereas this letter though making copious references to the book of Genesis, makes no mention of any of the later books. Then again, in the letter he has a daily task of four languages; in the journal (unless his practice in the latter part of the year differed from that in the earlier), of five, six, and sometimes seven: in the letter he has just mastered the forms of Spanish grammar, and has merely sent for Don Quixotte; in the journal for Jan. 1828 he already has a daily task in Don Quixotte. This I think makes it certain that the letter was not written in 1828. It could hardly have been written in 1826, which was the year he was graduated. The little matters of Princeton news in the letter direct our view to the succeeding year. A minute comparison of the letter with the journal renders this conclusion almost sure. I shall therefore assume that in September 1827, the young scholar was pursuing the study of Hebrew, Arabic, and Italian, and had just possessed himself of the rudiments of Spanish. He at this time scorned chrestomathies, and collectanea such as Dalzell's. He thought the best way of mastering a new language was to open a great classic and go through it from cover to cover with the forms, the rules, and the lexicon. It was doubtless the best way for him. He had the knack of penetrating the secret of a mass of foreign idioms at a glance, and of moving on at once to the subjugation of the literature. The literature was his main quarry after all. In Hebrew, he was now poring over the sublime and inspired words of Moses. In Arabic he put himself under the guidance of Mohammed; in Persian, of Sadi and Hafiz; in Italian, which he was merely commencing, of Tasso. He soon after took up Cervantes, Ariosto and Dante.

The letter about to be given has a laughable mixture of the boy and the man in it. It is written with all the reckless ease of a youthful correspondence with a cherished brother. Yet the writer never in his life threw out more sagacious hints on the subject of philology, and never wrote better or more playfully on the defects of current English style; and he never expressed himself with more knowledge or a more pathetic tenderness in the way of criticism on the original Scriptures, regarded as a branch, and a most imposing one, of universal belles lettres. The critique on the Koran, that "bantling of Mohammed," is evidently the germ of the larger and later one in the Repertory. It is at once shrewd, subtle and humorous. As a whole the reader will find this learned, elegant, discriminating, free and easy, bantering effusion, as well worth reading as any of his similar productions in after years. It is very precious in a biographical point of view, as a fragment of records which have long since perished.

"DEAR JAMES,

"The manner in which you speak of a journey northward has encouraged us all to conceive a hope which you must take care not to disappoint. Meantime, let us have a little converse de omnibus rebus &c.

"I believe you have received no letter from me since the receipt of your philological mammoth. Cordially as I concurred in the sentiments which you there expressed, I thought it advisable to make allowances for the evanescent nature of violent emotions and not echo your rhapsodies till I was sure that they were likely to continue. The absence of philology in your subsequent epistles is, I suppose, to be ascribed to sickness. I trust you have not lost the noble enthusiasm. I am studying as a daily task four languages. In Hebrew, I read the Pentateuch; in Arabic, the Koran; in Persian, Hafiz and Sadi; in Italian. Tasso. You will not be surprised to learn, that my admiration of Hebrew grows continually. The exquisite and to me wonderful combination of primitive simplicity, and philosophical exactness in that mysterious tongue are without a parallel. The further I advance in the knowledge of it and its offspring Arabic, the more I am struck with the indications which present themselves, of their structure having been the result of elaborate research and subtle contrivance, and yet the simplicity which I have mentioned is so obvious and unequivocal as to preclude all hypotheses that might otherwise be formed. I am perfectly sincere when I assert that in *every* respect, the book of Genesis appears to me the finest specimen of historical composition that was ever produced. I never thought so when I read it in English, though I must add, that the fidelity of our version is far greater than I had ever conceived to be possible. The translation which comes nearest to it in this respect is Sale's Koran, but alas, longo intervallo. The reason of his inferiority is to be found in the character of the Koran itself; for I do declare, that of all the ridiculous exhibitions of ignorance, folly, and stupidity that ever saw the light, this bantling of Mohammed (even in its original swaddling clothes) is the most absurd. The only thing to recommend it, is the number of ethical truths which it contains well expressed; and occasional ebullitions of a fervid imagination in the way of description and apostrophe which no style nor subject can wholly suppress in the work of an Oriental writer. To return a minute to Genesis—how often have you ever read the 27th chapter in the original? It is beyond praise as a touching narrative; and nothing can be more pathetic than the point to which the story is brought in the 38th verse.

וַיֹּאמֶר עֵשָׂו אֶל־אָבִיו הַבְרָכָה אַחַת הִוא־לְךָ אָבִי בָּרֲכֵנִי גַם־אָנִי אָבִי וַיִּשָּׂא עֵשָׂו קֹלוֹ וַיֵּבְךְּ :

"I was so struck by the pathos of the story on a recent perusal that I threw it impromptu into very blank verse, which you will see in the Patriot. (By the bye send us some poetry.)

"I am reading Tasso with great delight. It is surprising with what graceful unconstrained ease his thoughts succeed each other notwithstanding the awkward restraint to which the ottara rima subjected him. The Italian, through its characteristic softness, seems admirably adapted to make the sound an echo to the sense. You know the verse which Blair quotes descriptive of the effects of a trumpet blown in the lower regions where tromba, rimbomba, piomba and similar words are admirably expressive. Mr. Patton says that no ancient or modern language is more rich in words descriptive of delicate and varying emotions, especially those of love. The following couplet by Tasso I have adopted as a valuable apothegm:

"'L'aspettar del male ò mal peggiore,
Forge, che non parebbe il mal presente.'

I have mastered the forms of Spanish grammar completely; and have just sent to Philadelphia for Don Quixote. M. Coulombe, a man educated under the auspices of Napoleon and possessed of considerable learning, has established himself in Princeton. He teaches French; and proposes to open a German school. Mr. Patton speaks well of him. As writing to you is the only vent which I find for my speculations on literature, I will set down two or three questions for your consideration. 1. Is not the imperative mood the root of the verb in all languages; i. e., Do you not suppose the first verb was used imperatively or oratively (*ut ita d.*), and that it will be found in a majority of the diverse tongues that this is the simplest form? Love—to love—I love. It is the only simple part of the English verb. 2. Ought not all collectanea on Dalzell's plan to be relentlessly proscribed? They have hurt *me* exceedingly. 3. Ought not the republic of letters to pass an act abolishing punctuation? Keep the period and the mark of interrogation; but let the rest go hang. I am glad to see you disapprove the dash. I loathe it as it is used by ———, e. g.: 'This work—and we wish we could say other works—came forth,' &c. No such form of a sentence should be tolerated. Dr. Johnson never used even a parenthesis. There is little news stirring. The family are well. * * * * William sends you the Report of the Colonization Society, and wishes you to read Vroom's address and give your opinion.

"Yours ever,

"A."

I have been so successful as to find the poem referred to in this letter, in an old brown fragment of the newspaper in which it originally appeared. The piece had been carefully hoarded by one of the author's playmates and oldest admirers. It possesses a high dramatic and exegetical interest, and is unlike anything else from Mr. Alexander's pen. It will be remarked that notwithstanding the protest in the letter to his brother he has not discarded the dash or the parenthesis. The piece sheds some light, too, on his own character. He too was one day to be seen in tears and helplessness—"*his* mighty frame" also "shuddering in anguish"; and was to excite a similar surprise. He too "loved not to be scanned so searchingly." It had been too long and injuriously thought of him that "from an eye so hard, so diamond-like, infusible, though bright, the kindly drops of pity, love, or grief, ne'er found a vent." "Yet have I seen him weep * * * and heard him cry aloud in sorrow, as a child."

The difference was this, Esau was really hard-hearted; but Addison Alexander, with all his force and brilliancy of character, had also the gentleness and softness of a girl.

THE TEARS OF ESAU.

[*From an unpublished Drama.*]

GENESIS, xxvii: 30—41.

Mark yon tall chief returning from the chase:
Canst thou not read in that deep wrinkled brow,
That quivering lip, that fiercely flashing eye,
The mingled characters of smothered grief

And rankling discontent? Thou readest well.
'Tis Esau, first-born of the ancient Isaac,
And monarch of the chase. There! did'st thou see
The sudden gleam his eye shot forth upon us?
Approach him not too nearly: drop thine eyes:
He loves not to be scanned so searchingly.
Yet men have guessed in vain what hidden crime
Preys on his soul, and makes his eye a coward.
The story which thou readest in his aspect
Is written in the process of his life,
And stamped on all his deeds. Proud, fearless, fierce,
Relentless—ever mindful of his wrongs,
Forgetful of the kindness which repays them.
Who would not say that from an eye so hard,
So diamond-like, infusible, though bright,
The kindly drops of pity, love, or grief,
Ne'er found a vent! Yet have I seen him weep,
Ay, seen him weep, and heard him cry aloud
In sorrow, as a child. 'Twas on that day,
When Jacob—but you know the tale of old.
Ah, Arioch! 'twas a sight to chill the blood,
I scarce believed it; though I stood in service
Upon the dying bed of Isaac. There
The rugged hunter knelt, and when he heard—
The savoury food still smoking in his hand,
And gently offered to his father's taste—
Yes, when he heard the old man's faltering tongue
In broken accents tell the treachery;
And saw those sightless eyes, with bursting tears
Of agony distended; and that hand,
That withered hand, whose hallowed imposition
Had laid on Jacob's head the promised blessing—
When its cold trembling touch, reminded him
Of all that he had lost—what did he then?
I stood in staring terror to behold
The wild and fearful bursting of his wrath
Come forth in frenzied action: but it came not;
I looked again: for how could I believe,
That Esau, the fierce hunter—that the Esau,
Whom I had known so terrible in anger,
Should bear his griefs thus meekly? When I looked,
His head was bowed upon his father's hand.
His own concealed his face; his mighty frame

Was shuddering in anguish: but anon,
Between his fingers, drop by drop I marked
The scalding tears were oozing, and I heard
Those strong convulsive sobs, which more than tears
Betray a *man's* proud grief. I could have wept
To see *him* humbled thus. The gentler Jacob
Might weep, and who would mark it? 'Tis his nature.
But to see tears upon the manlier cheek
Of rugged Esau—'twas a moving sight.
Long did he weep in silence, but at last
There came from him a wild and bitter cry,
And then in deep and hollow tones he said,
"Hast thou for me no blessing, O my father!"
What could the old man say? Before him knelt
The eldest born—his best beloved son,
Him whom he would have blessed, but for the arts
Of Jacob and his mother. Once again,
He murmured forth "thy brother—'twas thy brother."
Again wept Esau, and again he asked,
"Hast thou reserved no blessing for thy son?
Thine Esau, Oh my father!" Then once more
The biting, blasting thought, that he had lost
That mystic benediction, by whose virtue,
The favour of Jehovah seemed ensured,
Rose on his mind; and as it rose he cried
In bitterness of soul. But with that cry,
His weakness ended, and his agony
Passed from him as a dream. Across his brow,
He drew his hand impatiently, then sprang,
As if in anger, to his feet. His eyes,
No longer bathed in grief, were fired with rage;
And on his quivering lip there seemed to hang,
Unutterable things. The child was gone,
And vengeful Esau was himself again.

ALI.

During the year 1828 in the intervals of study he was also a frequent writer for the "Philadelphia Monthly Magazine," edited by Dr. Isaac C. Snowden.* Some of these contributions were in verse. The world of romantic literature, and especially poetry, and the world of severe scholarship, seemed now to press their conflicting claims upon him. He may be thought to have stood for a moment as if irresolute, like Garrick between tragedy and comedy, or like the hero in the Choice of Hercules.* Judge Napton assures us that his friend was certain of success, if he had chosen to enter the domain of fiction. He probably never dreamed of this, but he had a strong yearning towards the poetic muse. There is no evidence, however, that he ever gravely meditated the pursuits of mere literature. The real conflict in his mind was between Arabia and America, the Orient and the Occident; and, at a later day, between the law and theology. His efforts in verse were merely for the sake of mental diversion, or to please his friends. Alas, that we should have so little from his pen in the way of serious stanzas! What we have gives us the strongest evidence of what we might have had, if he had not bent his whole mind on other things. The huge labours of the philologist and commentator, left little room for those of the bard, or even of the polite littérateur. Thus law checked the literary aspirations of Lord Mansfield:

> "How sweet an Ovid, Murray, was our boast!
> How many Martials were in Pulteney lost!" †

And the speculations of moral philosophy proved too much for the genius of John Wilson, which hardly ever after blossomed into verse. The fairies, as an anonymous writer in "Black-

---

* The following is a list of his contributions to the "Philadelphia Monthly Magazine" in 1827 and 1828. I do not think he ever wrote for it afterward.

Volume I.

Page 125. "The Fastidious Man."
" 170. "Oriental Literature."
" 187. "The Complacent Man."
" 212. "Archy McMorrow."

Volume II.

" 74. "A Vision of Greece" (poetry).
" 76. "Aut Cæsar aut nullus."
" 89. "Anecdotes of the Barmecides. From the Arabic."
" 152. "Hurt Feelings."
" 351. "Father and Son; a Love Story."

† The Dunciad, Book IV., lines 169, 170.

wood" predicted at the time, were smothered in the Professor's gown.

He had a good deal of private correspondence, too, at this time with Dr. Snowden, under whose good management the "Monthly Magazine" had reached a creditable degree of excellence, though it was never widely circulated. In Philadelphia, however, it was read by many cultivated people, and was to be seen upon the tables of most of the public libraries and lyceums. I have not rescued a single one of Mr. Alexander's notes to the editor, but several of Dr. Snowden's letters to the Princeton essayist have fallen into my hands, and two of them are here given. They are all gracefully and happily expressed, and are good specimens of the old quill-pen hand then in vogue. They are all about the Magazine and Mr. Alexander's varied contributions, which were sometimes grave, sometimes gay. The distressed editor commonly beseeches his young friend to send him light and playful pieces, for which he knows he has a cunning gift, but is almost always willing to publish even his most learned essays. These kind and intelligent letters were sacredly kept by Mr. Alexander under the endorsement "Snowdeniana."

"PHILADELPHIA, *Jany.* 14, 1828.
"DEAR SIR,

" The fourth number of the Philadelphia Monthly Magazine is just completed, and will appear as usual on the 15th. The conduct of a work like this is certainly a task, but to me a very pleasant one; and would be still more so, if *all* my correspondents left me so little to correct as you. I have the same pleasure in receiving the communications of several gentlemen, which I have in yours; but some, the *matter* of which is excellent, I have to subject to modifications, which are sometimes very troublesome.

"'The Fastidious Man' is quite a popular paper here, as it deserves to be: the counterpart in No. 4 will I think please also. I am much pleased with the short article on Oriental Literature, and take this opportunity to remark, however strange it may appear, that subjects of an elevated character had better be deferred for the present, until the Magazine has acquired, by means of light and pleasing papers, that popularity which will enable a learned article to stand its ground in the crowd. It may afford an author some satisfaction to know, that four or five thousand readers have access to his writings every month, which is the case with the Magazine—not that it has so ample a patronage,—(the subscribers, though consisting of the first citizens, are comparatively few) but so many libraries, athenæums, &c., &c., have placed it on their tables, that the whole world seems to use it without contributing a cent to its support. This is a disadvantage to new publications—but it cannot be prevented. I think you might promote its interests by placing a copy of the third number (of which I send you two) on the tables of the Cliosophic and Whig Societies. The result would be totally different in this case from that of those which I have just mentioned, since the students will only see it long enough to know its character, by the time they leave college, when, it is probable, many may think of subscribing for it on their return to their homes. This however I leave to your discretion; if the societies should not think proper to subscribe for a copy each, I will *present* them with one. I thank you for the paper on Self-importance, it is excellent in its kind; but not, as you have intimated yourself, exactly the thing that I wished. It wants some of the raciness of your first paper, as well as variety and point. Self-importance, as it manifests itself in a thousand forms *in a city* would admit of many choice touches. You have, however, treated the subject well, and in a style of much perspicuity and elegance. It will appear in the fifth number.

"Let me request, if perfectly convenient to you, another short article in the course of two weeks, or earlier. Take any light topic that may occur to you, and *play* with it, in your ancient namesake's vein; and I will consent to your being learned, after a few more numbers of the Magazine have appeared: I have held my own tongue (pen I should say) on classical matters ever since the first number, when I was informed, to my great surprise, that it was too learned. This is a droll age, but we must humour it a little, if we wish to make it wiser.

"I am, dear Sir, with great respect,
"Your unknown friend,
"J. C. SNOWDEN."

"PHILADELPHIA, *May* 3, 1828.
"DEAR SIR,
"I received your pleasant letter of May 1st duly. You desire me to indicate what class of subjects I prefer for the magazine, 'grave, or lighter articles suggested by fancy.' As you say it rests with me to say

what species I prefer, I will remark, that however agreeable it would be to me to insert graver papers, yet the success of the Magazine requires gaiety: your grave papers would be very acceptable to me, but I and all my readers would prefer your gaiety. That faculty is rare. I have but two besides yourself who play in that vein. The mass of my correspondents are your grave gentlemen; they abound; I am at no loss for sober sense, in good taste: the inference then will be that efforts of fancy, playful essays or sketches, would be more desirable to me and my readers. People in this age do not read magazines to get wise; e. g. Blackwood, Campbell, &c., &c. Choose then, my good friend, whatever subject you please; and if at any time you have on hand something of the graver sort which *you* may think a 'confounded good thing' and which you would like to see inserted, be sure to send it to me; and if I entertain the same opinion I shall be happy to give it a place. This induces me to reply to a query in your letter and which you did not wish that I should answer: I have never inserted an article—I will say line—I had almost said word (such has been my care in these matters) which I did not approve of; or under the influence of any one. My control over the magazine is absolute; for, while I am Editor, I am also the sole Proprietor, and my correspondents are numerous—e. g., seventy and more rejected papers (among which, to my grief I say it, is one by the worthy friend to whom I am at this moment writing, and which he sent me three or four months ago (Conrad and Anselmo).

"With respect to the article on Self-Importance, which appears to have given you a little trouble, I may say that It did not meet my wishes: but then, the style, the diction, the flow of sentences, and other matters redeemed it, and I gave it place, *of right*, not as a perfect guest, but as one who deserved to be in good company. The piece, I assure you, was not without its friends—among them Dr. Franklin Bache. So much for 'Self-Importance.'

"You say, you could give me a trifle on 'Hurt Feelings' Good! the subject will take.

"You mention in a postscript 'Historical Romances in miniature,' founded on colonial and revolutionary legends. Such papers would be particularly interesting.

"I hereby request my worthy friend 'A. J. A.' alias 'A. L. I.' to accept (for kindnesses already rendered), 'a complete set of the Philadelphia Monthly Magazine' for five years, commencing from October, 1828.'

"I am, Sir, your unseen but sincere friend, J. C. SNOWDEN.

"J. A. ALEXANDER, *Princeton.*

"I am still unwell—a chill and fever yesterday and much debility to-day—Twenty to one I have written as bad English, ay and Latin, scraps as that Irish gentleman who swore that no one could write grammar with such a pen. Pass over such foibles as those of an invalid.

"God bless you, and mend your manuscript:

"Good-night, J. C. S."

It is interesting to read what he composed at this critical period of his life, whether in one mode or the other; but the poetry has this charm, that these were in a manner farewell efforts. I give below two of the pieces contributed by him to the "Monthly Magazine." Though published later, they were both written about this time.

The first implies a probable acquaintance with the literature of the East and especially of Persia. The second shows a growing enthusiasm for that of the West. We shall soon be convinced on still better grounds than any that have yet been given, that Mr. Alexander was neither a tyro nor a pretender in these matters. Moore has written Oriental verses *ad nauseam* without ever seeing the Orient or reading any one of its numerous languages. Kinglake and Beckford have written on the same subjects and with the same success in prose. But none of these has written such a Diary as the one on which we are about to enter.

THE FALL OF ISPAHAN.*

(*From the Persian.*)

THE whispers of the morning breeze
Through nodding groves of spicy trees
Have roused the bulbul from his rest;
And springing from his fragrant nest
He skims in search of luscious food,
Thy crystal waves, fair Zenderoud! †
But save the flight of that lone bird,
No sound nor sign of life is heard;

---

* The City of Ispahan was sacked by the Afghans in the early part of the last century.—J. A. A.

† A stream running through the city.—J. A. A.

FALL OF ISPAHAN.

Nor voice of mirth nor busy hum
Nor trumpet's blast, nor roll of drum,
Nor horseman's march, nor camel's tread:
But silence reigns, as deep and dead
As when the march of time began,
Through all thy dwellings, Ispahan!

Again 'tis morning; but no more
The silence reigns that reigned before;
The dying child's expiring cry,
The dying mother's farewell sigh,
The groans of famine and disease,
Are now the burden of the breeze;
The bulbul wheels his rapid flight
Away, with wonder and affright—
To see the dead by thousands strewed
O'er the polluted Zenderoud!
To feel the hot contagious breath
Of the stern messenger of death,
To hear the murmur of despair
Which agitates the troubled air,
As famished beast and starving man
Throng through the streets of Ispahan.

Once more 'tis morning, and again
The voice of nature and of men
Is hushed in silence, such as reigns
Through death's unvisited domains;
But not that calm and holy rest
Which soothes to peace the troubled breast,
And guardian vigils loves to keep
O'er the defenceless infant's sleep:
The pause that now enchains the air,
Is the dead stillness of despair:
No more to greet the sun's first rays,
The bulbul tunes his thousand lays; *
His song no more shall be renewed
Along thy waters, Zenderoud!
For see! o'er citadel and moat,
The Persian flag has ceased to float,
And struggling with the adverse air
A stranger's flag is floating there.

---

* One of the epithets applied to the bulbul by the Persian poets is that of *Hezer-avaz* or thousand voices, in allusion to the variety of its notes.—J. A. A.

> The strife is o'er; the deed is done:
> The Persian warrior's race is run;
> His sword is broken, and he lies
> In death, still gazing on the skies;
> While o'er the dying and the dead,
> In sullen mockery is spread,
> The banner of the fierce Afghan,—
> And thou art fallen, Ispahan!"

About the same time appeared the following:

A VISION OF GREECE.

Calm twilight o'er the Grecian isles
  Has thrown her veil of sombre gray;
The dying sunset's farewell smiles
  In golden pomp have passed away.

No sounds the solemn silence wake
  Save ocean's deep and distant roar,
As his chafed billows dash and break
  In sullen murmurs on the shore.

But as that dull and dream-like song
  Subsides in momentary rest,
A strain of music creeps along,
  As from the islands of the blest.

Whence flow the sounds? It is a lyre—
  And swept by none but Grecian hand;
In mingled tones of vengeful ire
  And sorrow for his native land.

As he pursues a theme so dear,
  Hark! how the ancient cliffs prolong,
With all their echoes far and near,
  The burden of the minstrel's song.

"Is this the land," he faintly sighs,
  "Where glory reared his crest of old,
And freedom to the cloudless skies
  Her crimsoned flag in wrath unrolled?"

"Is this the land," he fiercely asks,
  As memory goads him with her sting,
"This land where bondsmen ply their tasks
  And kneel before an alien king?

"Is this the land where Xerxes fled
   Alone, unarmed and in dismay?
Is this the noble Spartan's bed?
   Can this be proud Thermopylæ?"

As the last echo dies away,
   A hollow voice responds to his—
"Can this be proud Thermopylæ?"
   The answer comes—"It is, It is!"

And see! above the hallowed tomb,
   Where sleeps the Spartan and his men,
Their ghosts seem mustering in the gloom,
   And rallying for the fight again.

Behold! behold! the grisly band
   Have seized upon their ancient pass;
Before them stalks in stern command,
   The spirit of Leonidas.

One shout—one shout of ancient days,
   And all is silent as before;
While from the cliffs a sudden blaze
   Its blood-red light begins to pour.

Enough, enough, they work their will;
   No sooner is the signal given,
Than from the crest of every hill
   An answering beacon flames to Heaven.

But what portentous sound is this,
   Which rises with the rising dawn?
Half-stifled shouts from Salamis,
   And cries of war from Marathon.

The spell is broken! Arm for fight!
   Vengeance is sure, for God is just!
Greece has arisen in her might,
   And spurned her fetters to the dust.

Again, again, from every height,
   The war-cry sends its dread alarms;
Again the sun's returning light,
   Sees renovated Greece in arms.

She invokes no more the fabled powers,
   Whom erst her magic minstrels sung;

> But to the wind from all her towers,
>   The banner of the Cross is flung.
>
> No more the heathen anthem rings,
>   To Mars from her embattled posts;
> Her sovereign is the King of kings,
>   Her patron is the Lord of Hosts.
>
> See land and ocean, tower and mast,
>   Teeming with countless throngs of men!
> The dream of servitude is past,
>   And Greece is now herself again.

The constellation of poets that about this time continued to fix the attention of the world and dazzle the eyes of the critics, could hardly fail to be an object of considerable attraction to the author of these verses. As canto after canto, book after book came out, they were eagerly read by Mr. Alexander, as well as by his two older brothers. None of the gifted writers whose productions swarmed during this period and filled so much of the labours of Mr. Jeffrey and his coadjutors in the Edinburgh Review, seems to have exerted a more decided impression on the style of Mr. Alexander than those of Lord Byron. The American student was richly qualified to appreciate intellectual excellence of this sort, and his quick soul must have kindled under the inspiration. The correspondence, therefore, can hardly be altogether accidental between the stirring numbers of "the Childe" and the nervous diction and peculiarly sonorous rythm of every scrap of verse that fell from that young scholar. And yet the poetry of Addison Alexander is as original and *sui generis* as his prose. Some of the very themes* on which Byron loved to write were also favourites of Mr. Alexander's. Much of this was doubtless due to a partial similarity of tastes, and perhaps

---

* To say nothing of such familiar pieces as "The Isles of Greece," I need only point to the LXXIII. stanza of the second canto of Childe Harold, and the spirited translation of the Greek war song Δεῦτε παῖδες τῶν Ἑλλήνων of Riga, "Sons of the Greeks, arise." Both of the last named contain like allusions to Leonidas and Thermopylæ. The stanzas given in the text will not suffer in comparison with this animated lyric.

a resemblance of native talents. But he was now about to enter more and more heartily upon the business of a translator and interpreter of foreign tongues, and to turn his back upon the captivating East and the blandishments of poetry. Like the Shepherd in Lycidas after a wistful retrospective glance, he was soon to cease his song.

> He touched the tender stops of various quills,
> With eager thought warbling his Doric lay;
> And now the sun had stretched out all the hills,
> And now was dropped into the western bay;
> At last he rose, and twitched his mantle blue:
> *To-morrow to fresh woods and pastures new.*

CHAPTER IV.

THE first records which I have been able to find of Mr. Alexander's studies as preserved in his own journals are now to be laid before the reader. The earliest allusions to his literary employments are contained in the two letters to his brother James, which have already been given.

"Jan. 1.—Arabic, Al Koran, Sura 19. Hebrew, Exodus, chap. xix. Italian, Tasso, Ger. Lib. Canto 12. Latin, Cicero in Q. Cæcilium. German, Rules of pronunciation; Greek, Matthew, chaps. 1–4."

" Jan. 2.—Hebrew, Exodus, chap. 20. Persian, Hafiz (Nott's Ed.) ode 16. French, Auxiliary verbs. Spanish, Don Quix. chaps. 27–28. Greek, Matt. ch. 4–8."

"Jan. 3.—Hebrew, Exod. chs. 20–21. Arabic, Al Koran, Suras 19–20. Latin, Cicero in Cœlio, and pro Lege Manilia. German, Declensions of art., subs. and adj. Greek, Matthew, 9–12. Italian, Tasso, G. L., Canto 12 ; wrote paradigm of reg. verbs."

"Jan. 4.—Hebrew, Exod. chs. 21–22. Persian, sundries. Spanish, Don Quix. chs. 28–29. Syriac, Michaelis gram. alphabet, points, regular verbs. Greek, Matthew, chs. 13–16. French, wrote paradigm of eleven regular verbs (bis)."

" Jan. 5.—Hebrew, Exod. chs. 22–23. Arabic, Al Koran, Suras 20–21. Latin, Cicero Orat. pro Lege Manilia. Greek, Matt. chs. 17–20. French, Description de l'Arabe, par Neibuhr. English, Byron's poems. Italian, wrote translation of Historia Sacra. German, wrote paradigms of ten auxiliary verbs."

"Jan. 6.—Hebrew, Genesis chs. 1–10 ; Exodus, 19–23. Greek, Matt. 1–6 and 20–28. English, Butler's Analogy, Intro. and ch. 1. Italian, Tasso, Ger. Lib. canto 13."

" Jan. 7.—Hebrew, Exodus chs. 23–24. Persian, Persian controversies, xlix–liii and Gulistan of Sadi. Syriac, Matt. chap. i: 6–17. Spanish, Don Quix. chs. 29–30. Greek, Homer's Odyss. Lib. 1. Mark 1–4. French, par. eleven regular verbs."

"Jan. 8.—Hebrew, Exodus, chs. 24–25. Arabic, Al Koran, Suras 21–22. Latin, Cicero's orations. German, revised nouns, adjs. and verbs. Greek, Mark, ch. 5-8. Italian, wrote translation of Historia Sacra."

"Jan. 9.—Hebrew, Exod. chs. 25-26. Persian, Pers. contro. and Gulistan. Syriac, Matt. ch. i. v. 18-25. French, Levizac's grammar and irregular verbs. Spanish, Don Quix. chs. 30-31. Greek, Mark, chs. 9-12."

"Jan. 10—Hebrew, Exodus, chs. 26-27. Arabic, Al Koran, Suras 22-23. Latin, Cicero, pro Archia poetâ. German, the whole of Wenderbork's grammar. Greek, Mark, chs. 13-16. English, Otway's plays. Italian, paradigms of regular and irregular verbs; translation of Historia Sacra."

"Jan. 11.—Hebrew, Exod. chs. 27-28. Persian, Gulistan of Sadi. French, regular and irregular verbs. Spanish, Don Quix. chs. 31-32. Greek, Luke, ch. i."

"Jan. 12.—Hebrew, Exodus, chs. 28-29. Arabic, Al Koran, Suras 23-24. Latin, Cicero. Greek, Luke 1-3. English, wrote* communications for the Philadelphia Monthly Magazine, viz.: 1. A dramatic fragment. 2. The Fall of Ispahan. 3. A Vision of Greece. 4. The Tears of Esau."

The diary of the next few days presents more fully his method of studying the various languages which now occupied his attention. What is extracted from these entries is a specimen of all.

"Jan. 14.—Read: in Hebrew, Exodus, chs. 29-30.—May not our *canopy* be derived from the Hebrew כָּנָף, a wing? The *shadow of wings* is a frequent expression in the Bible. There is another derivation, more curious, and I think much more certain: I mean that of *each* from אִישׁ: The use of this word as a distributive pronoun in Hebrew is very remarkable. One to another would be properly translated אִישׁ אֶל רֵעֵהוּ *a man to his friend or brother*. Nor is this mode of expression confined in its application to human beings, nor even to animals in general; We find it used in Exodus with things which it would scarcely be possible to personify. For example ;—'The five curtains shall be coupled' אִשָּׁה אֶל אֲחוֹתָהּ '*woman*, (or generically *female*) to her sister,' i. e. one to another. 'And other five curtains shall be coupled *woman to her sister*.' Another peculiar idiom which occurs to me is that in which the word *son* is used in connection

---

* That is, I think he means, revised, copied and posted them.

with the number of years to express a man's age. To give one example out of many נֹחַ בֶּן־שֵׁשׁ מֵאוֹת שָׁנָה 'Noah was the *son of six hundred years*.' This may perhaps be explained by the fact that the terms expressive of natural relations among men, such as *father*, *mother*, *son* and *daughter*, are frequently used to express relations of a different kind and between different objects; a large proportion of the Arabic proper names being formed by this rule. For example—'Father of power,' i. e. the powerful. I have never, however, met with this idiom in the books of Moses in reference to any thing but the length of life."

"2. In Spanish. Don Quixote, chs. 32-33. The most elaborate passage in this work of Cervantes which I have yet met with, is, 'La Novela del curioso Impertinente.' Indeed, from the pains which he takes to introduce all his episodes, it is evident that he laboured them with a care which he did not give to the main story. To this fact he seems to allude himself when he speaks of the enjoyment which his hero had been the means of affording to the world, 'no solo de la dulzura de su verdadera historia, sino de *los cuentos y episodios* della, que la misma historia.' If the author had any partiality for this episode, 'La Novella,' it was certainly not a blind one. This story is finely conceived, ingeniously developed, and elegantly expressed. The speech of Lothario in opposition to the proposal of his friend is so fine a specimen of ethical argument and eloquence, that the reader is tempted to exclaim, as Sancho to his master—'Mas bueno era onestra merced para predicadore que para cabellero andante.' The following sentence contains a strong but most expressive description of the effect of suppressed sorrow,—'No exensaras con el secreto tu dolor; antes tendrás que lloras contino *si no lassimas de los ojos, lassimas sangre del corazena.*'

"3. Persian. The Gulistan. Persian and Hebrew are radically distinct, in their genius and structure, as well as vocables. They agree however in this remarkable circumstance, that the government of one substantive by another is denoted by a change in the latter and not the former as in almost all other languages. The cardinal number for *six* is the same also in both the Hebrew and Persian languages. The Persian agrees with the Syriac (a derivative of Hebrew) with respect to the definite article, which is formed in both by adding a vowel at the end of the noun. The coincidences between the Persian and English are very numerous and striking, and are rendered more remarkable, by the fact that many of the words common to both are simple, original, primitive terms used in ordinary intercourse, and not mere technicalities."

"4. In English. (1.) Sir William Jones's anniversary discourse on the Philosophy of the Asiatics. I read this with a view to the composition of an article on the same subject. Sir William, however, speaks principally in reference to the Hindus. I should confine myself to the Mohammedan nations. (2). The Edinburgh Review. Review of the Hamiltonian System. I find I have adopted this system unconsciously in teaching J. A. and P. S. C. the Italian language. The principal difference is this that I introduce grammatical inflexions at an earlier period. My rule is to give a short lesson translated word for word. When the meaning and combination of words is learned, to give the paradigms of the verbs contained in it to be committed to memory, and explain the other grammatical difficulties before proceeding further. (3). The Red Rover, vol. 2, chs. 1-7. I am fond of beginning with the second volume of a novel. It makes the first doubly interesting. I think the comparison, or rather the equalizing, of Cooper with Scott is highly unjust for these causes following :—1. Scott, it is evident from every page of his works, is a man of taste, Cooper not. (2). Scott is always at his ease; Cooper, constrained, and apparently striving after something unattainable. (3). Scott is always perspicuous. His pictures are not only striking in distant view, but perfectly intelligible in all their parts. Cooper, on the contrary, is often obscure, and that when he has no intention to be mysterious—and his descriptions frequently leave the mind confused and clouded without any definite image to occupy it. Cooper may be a man of more depth and strength of feeling; but Scott is vastly his superior in liveliness and fertility of fancy. Cooper relies on the interest of his scene, and, at most, on variety of incident, to arrest the attention of his reader. Scott enchains it by the delineation of character. All Cooper's passages may be resolved into one or two varieties; and of these few, some are unnatural and even monstrous; while Scott has an endless diversity, and all of them true to nature. The only passage in Cooper's writings I have met with approaching to sublimity, is the description of the storm in the first volume of the Pilot; but although the advantages as to scene and circumstances would appear to be on his side, that description is nothing when compared with the escape of Sir Arthur Wardour, his daughter and Edie Ochiltree from the sea, in the Antiquary."

"5. French. Telemaque, pp. 1-5. Wrote paradigms of all the verbs occurring in the above passage of Telemaque, being, in number, thirty-five regular and sixteen irregular verbs; total, fifty-one."

"Jan. 15.—The finest passage which I have seen in the Koran is the comparison of the excellence of the wicked to the *lake of the desert* (an optical illusion in sandy and hot countries), which occurs in the chapter of light. I differ in toto from all writers who assert that Mohammed, in devising a religion for his followers, proceeded upon any regular plan whatever. We are too apt to ascribe motives to those who never felt them, and regard as deep-laid contrivance what probably arose from accident. He was first an enthusiast; a half-mad visionary. In this character he began his revelations, and afterwards finding their effect, became an ambitious aspirant after power. The idea that he endeavoured to adapt his doctrines to the belief and propensities of particular sects, I think unwarranted: not only from his ridiculous anachronisms, but from the character of the stories which he gave as sacred history. All that he has borrowed from the Scriptures has the appearance of being caught from oral narration. When we consider the fondness of the Arabs for story-telling, we may readily believe that the Jews and Christians who were among them found abundant employment in rehearsing impressive narratives of the Pentateuch and Gospel. That these should take strong hold of Mohammed's mind, then in a low condition is not surprising. By nature imaginative, he may have brooded in secret over these historical facts, till he felt their influence in a rising desire to emulate the ancient prophets. This I believe to be the source of his Scriptural information. That he was actually assisted in the composition of the Koran by either Jew or Christian, I think improbable; because either would have given more connected narratives. In his own, not only is the truth diluted, but the facts confused and out of order, like the attempts of a man to repeat a half-forgotten story."

The following criticism gives us an insight into his early tastes, confirming also the impressions and justifying the inferences which we have already drawn from other sources, as to his amazing intellectual energy:

"Jan. 17.—Read the 'Red Rover.' After reading this novel through, I am inclined to think it the best, as a whole, of Cooper's writings. The interest is far more intense and better supported than in any of the rest. There is a sameness, however, in his descriptions which nothing but the comparative novelty of *naval romance* enables us to tolerate. The ships are forever 'bending their tall spars as if to salute' this or that object, and then 'gracefully recovering their erect position.' He is too fond, moreover, of 'lurking smiles,' and 'struggling smiles,' and other cant phrases of his own, which would appear to indicate, that he had no very vivid impression of the object in his own mind; but described rather by rote; so that his descriptions, especially of men, are like set speeches, differing only in minor particulars, but capable of being adapted, by a little alteration to any character. In denouement he is never successful. The winding up of his novel is wretched in itself and rendered more so by its resemblance to the closing chapters of the 'Spy.'"

This plan of writing down his thoughts on the studies and readings of the day he kept up for several weeks. I continue to quote from the journal:

"Jan. 26.—I have been reading the past week nine chapters in Hebrew; seven chapters in the Koran, and one in the Arabic New Testament; twelve chapters in the Italian Bible; two in the Persian New Testament; two in the Spanish do.; one in the German do.; three chapters in Don Quixote, and several passages in Telemaque."

"Jan. 31.—During the month which is now closing, I have read thirty-two chapters in the Hebrew Bible, all of them twice and most of them three times; seventeen Suras in the Koran—all of them twice except the first and last. I have also, within this month, begun the study of the German language, and made such progress as shall be mentioned hereafter. I commenced reading the Greek Testament on the first of the month, but discontinued it after finishing two gospels. On the 11th inst. I commenced the practice of repeating what I read in Hebrew in Martini's Italian version, which I have regularly continued. On the 25th inst. I procured the 5th volume of Walton's Polyglot, and since that date, have read the Scriptures in six languages on the following plan. 1. Leviticus in the morning; in Hebrew critically, (i. e. with grammar and lexicon). 2. The Gospel of John in the morning in German—critically; at night in Spanish cursorily. 3. The Gospel of Matthew in the morning in Persian—critically; at night, in Arabic cursorily; repeating every day the readings of the preceding. These readings have, since the 25th, been my standing orders of the day, which I was not at liberty to set aside. My moveable orders of the day, which might be dispensed with, if necessary or shifted from one day to another, were—1. The critical reading of Don Quixote in Spanish. 2. The reading of Telemaque in French. 3. All English reading; and lastly, composition. On Sundays I have been in the practice of repeating the portions of Scripture read during the week."

"Feb. 2.—During the past week I have read, *critically*, 1. In

Hebrew nine chapters in Leviticus. 2. In Persian, five chapters in Matthew. 3. In Arabic, eight chapters in Matthew and four Suras in the Koran. 4. In German, five chapters in John. 5. In Spanish, eight chapters in Don Quixote. 6. In Italian, nine chapters in Leviticus. 7. In French, all the first book of Telemaque."

"Feb. 9.—During the week which began on Monday the 4th and closes to-night (for I exclude Sundays), I have read critically—that is to say, with strict philological attention, and with the usual aids of grammar, lexicon, &c., as follows:—In Hebrew—Lev. 14–23; In Persian, Matt. 9–14; in German, John, 8–13; in Arabic, Koran, 39–42; in Spanish, Don Quixotte, 39–41. In French, Telemaque, one Book. During the same period I have read *cursorily*—that is to say, with a view to philological improvement, but with less strict attention to verbal accuracy and grammatical niceties, (besides repeating in this way every day the portion read critically the day before) as follows:—In Arabic, Matt. 9–14; in Italian, Lev. 14–23; in Spanish, John 8–13. In addition to the above I have read attentively, 'Goode's Book of Nature,' ii.-vii., and skimmed over Dunham & Clapperton's Discoveries in Africa. To conclude, I have recovered my knowledge of the Syriac Alphabet, and acquired the Ethiopic."

"Saturday night, 12 M., Feb. 16.—I have, during the past week finished in Hebrew, Leviticus, the third book of Moses, having been employed upon it since the 25th of January. It was not so pleasing a task as the perusal of Genesis, and Exodus (I speak more critico)—so many words occur of which the meaning is at best uncertain and the whole is so generally confined to a single subject, that there is comparatively little room for philological [investigation]. The 26th chapter, however, is very eloquent, and it is very interesting to observe the difference in the design and character of the different books of Moses thus far. The first is a picture of the ancient world and patriarchal times; a history of the chosen people while favoured by the Deity but still living in the midst of other nations and complying with their customs. But the second begins the story of their sufferings and their wrongs, their deliverance and their government, and their journeyings toward that land where they were about to be established as a peculiar people. The third contains the detail of those singular ceremonial observances which were to be the badge of their distinction from the rest of the human race.—I have also finished, during this week, the same book in Martini's translation, having read every day since the 16th of January (Sundays excepted) the same portion critically in Hebrew and cursorily in Italian."

These records, spreading before us as they do an exact chart of his course at this time, give one a good idea of his thoroughness and system in laying the foundations of his subsequent attainments. He continued to work under this schedule through the summer months. His labours are summed up in the quarterly retrospect following, viz.:

"March 31.—The first quarter of the year 1828 is this day completed. A detailed review of all my studies during that period would be but a repetition of the foregoing pages. Laying aside therefore the consideration of subjects attended to accidentally, or on particular occasions, and of those which I have begun, and for various reasons abandoned, I shall confine myself to a consideration of my advances in the six languages which have been the regular and special object of my attention.

"I. Hebrew. In Hebrew I have read since the 1st of January, the last twenty-one chapters of Exodus; the whole of Leviticus, Numbers, Deuteronomy, and the first fifteen chapters of Joshua; in all a hundred and thirty-three chapters.

"II. Arabic. In Arabic I have read the last ninety-five chapters of the Koran, and thirty-three pages in De Sacy's Arabic Chrestomathy, besides the Gospel of Matthew in Walton's Polyglot; making (exclusive of De Sacy) one hundred and twenty-three chapters.

"III. Spanish. In Spanish I have read the last twenty-six chapters of the first part of Don Quixote, and the first eighteen chapters of the second part—in all forty-four chapters.

"IV. French. In French I have read the whole of Telemaque; the 'Avare' of Moliere, and two acts of Racine's Andromaque, besides a number of minor tracts.

"V. German. The study of German I have begun within the quarter, and besides Wenderbork's and Noehden's grammars, have read the gospels of Matthew and John, in Luther's translation, and five chapters in the gospel of Mark—in all fifty-four chapters.

"VI. Persian. In Persian I have read since the 1st of January the Gospels of Matthew and John in Walton's Polyglot—and various parts of the Gulistan of Sadi and the Tooti Nameh.* The last two works I use in MS. To these facts it may be added that I have regularly instructed P. S. C. and J. A. in Italian; and have written sundries."

* Or Tales of a Parrot.

"April 24.—I was born on the 24th of April 1809, and am consequently nineteen years old this day. Since my last birthday, besides parts and parcels of other works, I have read the following classical works entire:

"1. In Hebrew. The Pentateuch of Moses; the books of Joshua, Judges and 1st Samuel.—2. In Arabic. The Koran of Mohammed, the Gospel of Matthew, and parts of Abulfaraj and Facklibeddin. 3. In French. The Telemaque of Fenelon, the 'Avare' of Moliere and the Andromaque of Racine. 4. In Spanish. The Don Quixote of Cervantes. 5. In Italian. The Gerusalemme Liberata of Tasso and the Novelle of Soave in two volumes. I am an enemy to all chrestomathies, collectanea, and other scrap-books for the students of any language. Where no other books can be had, the use of such substitutes is compulsory; but when entire classical works can be obtained, no student ought to hesitate. The Quarterly Review very justly says, that a young man of sense and diligence will learn vastly more Greek by one perusal of the Iliad than by any attention to such compilations as those of Andrew Dalzel. This has been my principle. When about to learn a language, I have endeavoured to obtain a standard work of acknowledged merit, and read it from end to end; and if no other such could be immediately obtained, my rule has been to read the first again. To the above list I may add a sixth: 6. In German. The four Gospels, in Luther's version. I have determined that in the ensuing summer, in addition to my philological pursuits, I will read law, beginning with Blackstone's Commentaries."

The following entries give a minute history of his studies for some time longer:

"June 30.—1. Since the 31st of March I have read in Hebrew, the last nine chapters in the book of Joshua, the two books of Samuel, the two books of Kings, the prophecy of Isaiah, and twenty-two chapters in that of Jeremiah;—in all, one hundred and forty-four chapters.

"2. In Spanish, I have read during the same period the last fifty-six chapters of Don Quixote, and some numbers of 'El Mercurio de Nueva York,' a weekly newspaper published every Saturday.

"3. I have read in French the last two acts of Racine's Andromaque, the first two acts of Corneille's Menteur &c., and one satire of Boileau's; also, the second volume of De Sacy's Arabic grammar.

"4. I have read in Persian twelve tales (or chapters) of the Tooti Nameh.

"5. In German I have read the last eleven chapters in Mark; all of Luke, Acts, Romans, and two chapters in Corinthians—in all eighty-six chapters.

"6. In Italian I have read the last seven cantos of Tasso's G. L., and the first eighteen cantos of the Orlando Furioso—in all twenty-five chapters.

"7. In Latin, The Institutes of Justinian.

"8. In Greek, The tenth book of the Odyssey.

"In English, Coke upon Littleton and the second book of Blackstone's Commentaries—the latter a second time."

"Aug. 23. The Philological Society was formed this day composed of graduates and students."

The studies of the quarter are thus summed up:

"Sept. 30. 1. In Hebrew. Since the 30th day of June I have read the last thirty chapters of Jeremiah—the prophecies of Ezekiel, Hosea, Joel, Amos, Obed, Jonah, Micah, Nahum, Habakkuk, Zephaniah, Haggai, Zechariah, Malachi, and thirty-six Psalms;—in all, a hundred and sixty-nine chapters.

"2. Italian. The last twenty-eight cantos of Orlando Furioso.

"3. Spanish. Twelve numbers of 'El Mercurio, &c.'

"4. French. The funeral orations on the death of Maréchal Turenne by Fléchiea and Mascara; the last two acts of the 'Menteur' of Corneille; other plays by same author and four comedies of Moliere.

"5. Arabic. Sundries in the Koran and Lokmân's Fables.

"6. Persian. Sundries in the Gulistan and the Tooti Nameh.

"7. Greek. Homer; Ilias, I., II., XVIII.: Odyssey, I., II. Sophocles, the Antigone, several hundred lines. No more.

"8. Latin. The first Book of Cicero, de Inventione Rhetorica.

"9. English. Vattel's Law of Nations; the Federalist; the first two volumes of Stewart's Philosophy of the Human Mind; the first two volumes of Kent's Commentaries on American Law; the third volume of Blackstone's Commentaries (for the third time); and sundries."

There are several allusions to Mr. Alexander's astonishing progress in his studies, in his brother's letters to Dr. Hall. On the 4th of April he writes, "Addison has just completed the Koran in Arabic, a work which few have attempted in America. He has added Spanish and Italian to his list of languages;"* and on the 28th, "Addison has finished

---

* See Familiar Letters, Vol. I., p. 66.

Ariosto, and is now at Boccacio. He has read about half of Corneille, which I have also read. In Spanish Addison began with Don Quixote and read it over and over."* He was, like every other person of taste, a great admirer of the serious and gay creations of Cervantes, and laughed uncontrollably at the absurdities of Sancho Panza. He was almost equally amused with Gil Blas, and despised the practice of reading such books in translations.

It would be delightful to be able to look in upon the young student as he bent his eyes over these tasks, murmuring the while like a swarm of bees in the warm sunshine. Princeton, the Princeton of that day especially, had attractions alike for old and young people. The society of the place was refined, intellectual, various, and agreeable, and would have been pleased to receive the noted graduate, editor, and magazinist to its bosom. Princeton is and was famous for its fine level prospects, and beautiful sylvan walks along the banks of streams that were still lovely, if not so fair and beguiling as Cam or Isis; rustic shades which would have well befitted the speculations of Plato, and verdant undulations displaying the fantastically wreathen roots of the beech-tree, or the summer shadows of the oak or dogwood or sassafras,—with many a shining surface of reflected sky and softly delineated cloud—where Isaac Walton might have pursued his sweet meditations, or Virgil or Theocritus piped to their imaginary shepherds. Every observing alumnus of the college or resident in the town, has noticed the rare glory of the sunsets. Morning and evening, in good weather, nearly all the young persons of the place seized the occasion to take pedestrian rambles over the village roads and into the surrounding country. A wide lane shaded for a considerable distance by noble elms led immediately from the college, through green fields, to Stony Brook with its grassy meadow margins, and its isolated groups of trees, or denser forest stretched along the stream for miles. This lane commanded the rear view of the old grey building yclept, at the suggestion of good Gov-

---

* See Familiar Letters, Vol. I., p. 109.

ernor Belcher, Nassau-Hall. This was from the college, south as the crow flies. The main thoroughfare ran east, through the open country to Kingston. The prospect to the west was at that time full of umbrageous charm and shelter. To the north was Rocky-Hill, with its immense boulders and precipitous acclivities. Nor were these various localities without their actual or traditionary associations.

But the cloistered enthusiast was not vulnerable to any of these influences. "None of these things moved him." His passion for literature, the rapid progress he was making in different departments of science, his love of cheerful, indoor solitude, his wonderful health and unflagging spirits, and his native shyness, and repugnance to the awkward contacts of the world, overmastered every thing else. The Spring might be never so balmy, the early Summer never so florid and inviting, the autumnal coolness never so crisp and bracing, and the autumnal forests never so dreamily brown and crimson. What were these things to "Addison"—as he was still known among his old companions of the college and academy? He was a citizen of the world of mind. He wandered in the fields of thought. He took wing, and hovered over the continents of literature. He was deaf to the voices of ordinary ambition. He coveted none of the intoxications of mere pleasure. "What"! he might exclaim, as he swept the pages of the Gulistan or the Cyropædia, "what! crave ye wine, and have NILUS to drink of"?

Time was too short, it seemed to him, for any dalliance. Some might have to exercise their bodies to preserve their health; but it was different in his case; he was, as Wilson used to say, "as strong as an eagle." He was as great a prodigy of flesh and colour as of intellect. Why should *he* exercise his body? Of recreation, other than in the pursuits of philology and belles-lettres, and in making fun for the bevy of children that was always at his beck and call, he needed none, he cared for none. His duty evidently was to inform and discipline his mind. No! let others do as they liked; he would keep his room; he would read the Bible, and the Koran, and Firdusi, and Dante, and Tasso, and Xenophon, and Sir Walter Scott. This was to him, not hardship but joy; not slavery but freedom; it was his element. "Stone walls do not a prison make." No swallow was ever happier in the sky, than he was among his morocco-covered tomes. "Fishes that tipple in the deep, know no such liberty"!

Of course his library was as yet but the nucleus of the large collection he afterwards amassed. He was pretty rich in English history, biography, criticism, poetry, and essays of the Rambler and Spectator kind; in the Latin and Greek classics; and in the learned helps in classical and philological study, and in the principal modern languages; he had enough in Arabic, but was poor in his darling tongue, the Persian. What he lacked he could mostly find in his father's library, or at the seminary, or at the college, or with his brother James (who was devoted to books), or in the hands of Mr. Hodge, Mr. Hall or some other friend. He was not much addicted to the habit of borrowing, and what he borrowed he invariably returned. A new poem from Lord Byron, or a new story by "the great unknown," would excite his interest as it would that of every cultivated reader of English; but he became still more enthusiastically interested if he found (as he once did) an Arabic manuscript or got wind of a new Arabic and Persian dictionary.* The soft light of his candles fell upon characters of the most uncouth description, and upon walls already burdened with folios and odd-looking grammars and lexicons. Yet the bow was not always bent. He had his own peculiar pastimes. He would revel in the romantic poems of Spenser and Tasso and Ariosto and in the wonderful chapters of the wonderful book of Cervantes; and the boys and girls were nearly always welcome, whether for a romp or story.

During the month of October, he read in Hebrew a hundred and seventeen Psalms, and thirteen chapters in the book of Proverbs; in French, all the comedies of Moliere; in Italian, the whole of the Decameron of Boccacio; in

---

* He obtained access to Richardson.

English, the Paradise Lost and the first volume of Chitty on Special Pleading; in German, Ruth, Esther and Jonah; and in Arabic, all the historical passages of the Koran.

The months of November and December were occupied in the study of the same subjects, with this addition—the commencement of the study of Chinese; as appears from his note under Dec. 12.—"Learned the first six of the two hundred and fourteen keys; to wit, those formed by a single stroke." Whether he continued this study is not here recorded. He took it up again at a much later period, and prosecuted it far enough to understand the structure and genius of the written language. One of the volumes in which he kept his first diary in Europe is marked with very many of the Chinese* word signs.

I now give his review of the past year:

"In reviewing the memoranda of my studies during the year 1828 contained in this book, the first circumstance which strikes my attention is that they are almost exclusively philological. They have, perhaps, been too much so; but I do not regret it for two reasons:—1. My taste is, at present, strongly inclined toward philological pursuits; if I were to postpone the indulgence of it, it would perhaps change its direction, and leave me unwilling, and therefore unable to pursue philology even so far as would be necessary. 2. Languages are the keys to science, philosophy, literature, history, &c. &c., and should be mastered early. The languages to which I have attended during the past year are—Hebrew, Arabic, Persian, French, Italian, Spanish and German." †

"1. Hebrew. I have, since the 1st of January, 1828, read the whole of the Old Testament in the original, with the exception of the book of Genesis and eighteen chapters in Exodus, which I had read in 1827.‡ In the perusal of the Hebrew Bible, I have not been very strict or systematic. I have freely used the English translation as an auxiliary, and have seldom resorted to the grammar. I find, however, that I

---

* The reader will remember that it was this language which threw Mezzofanti into the brain fever, that caused him for a time to forget all his tongues.

† He for some reason omits to catalogue Syriac and Latin.

‡ This seems to confirm my judgment as to the true date of the letter to his brother respecting the "Tears of Esau," etc. See above.

have insensibly acquired that sort (not degree) of familiarity with the language which we get of our own tongue by colloquial practice. I cannot run through the paradigm of any one verb perhaps, correctly; but I recognize the individual inflexions when I meet with them, and find little difficulty in translating simple sentences from the English into Hebrew. But although this mode of acquiring the knowledge of a language is the most agreeable, and perhaps the best foundation for subsequent improvement, I feel that it is not, in itself, sufficient. I therefore intend to accompany my second reading of the Bible (which I expect to commence to-morrow) with an attentive study of Hebrew grammar; always excepting the accentual system, which I design to leave untouched. I also design to adopt the practice of writing Hebrew exercises; which practice I have found exceedingly improving in French and other languages. I am surprised that this is neglected by Hebrew students, since the exactness of our English version furnishes the greatest facility for doing it with pleasure and success. [In a note to this, dated Dec. 31, 1832, he says:—"I afterwards changed my opinion on this subject, and my mode of study too."]*

"2. Arabic. In Arabic I have read during the past year, the last ninety-six Suras of the Koran; one or two articles in De Sacy's Arabic Chrestomathy, and the Gospel of Matthew as contained in Walton's Polyglot. The early age at which I commenced the study of this language (nine or ten), and the almost constant attention which I have given to it since, have made me perhaps as familiar with its genius and construction as those of any other I ever studied. It is, however, very difficult as to its grammatical forms and rules, while its vocabulary is like an ocean. I wish to pursue it further. I have lately copied out of the Koran all the historical passages upon which I intend to write explanatory notes, and add a glossary and compendious grammar. The exercise will be useful to myself and may enable me to afford assistance to others.

"3. Persian. In Persian I have read, during the past year, the Gospels of John and Matthew contained in Walton's Polyglot; about fifteen tales in the Tooti Nameh, or Tales of a Parrot, and sundry parts of the Gulistan of Sadi. Of this charming language I am passionately fond; and nothing but the want of proper and necessary books prevents my pursuing it extensively. I have written for one or two, but have heard nothing yet respecting them.

---

* This probably refers to the scheme as a whole. He never undervalued the importance of writing every language that is to be really learned.

"4. French. I have been accustomed from my infancy to read French books without a dictionary, and, like most persons who have any previous acquaintance with the Latin, found little difficulty in catching the general idea, in ordinary cases. As I felt, however, that I was acquiring a pernicious habit of superficial study, and had various reasons for desiring an accurate knowledge of the language, I began in January the study of the grammatical forms and rules, which I mastered without difficulty; and have since read—Le Telemaque de Fenelon; six tragedies and une comedie de Corneille; Toutes les comedies de Moliere; Le Siécle de Louis XIV.; Le Petit Carême de Massillon; and various detached articles in different books. Since Dec. 1st, I have also taken lessons from M. Louis Hargous of Trenton, a Frenchman, educated for a priest, but now a teacher of French and Spanish. I am already sensible of the advantages arising from the instructions of a living teacher, and intend to continue my attendance upon him, in conjunction with my private reading of the best authors."*

It is unnecessary to make further selection, as the rest of this retrospect consists merely of the names of the books he read in Italian, Spanish, German, English, Greek and Latin, which have already been inscribed on these pages.

An admirable view of what Mr. Alexander was at this period of his private and social relations, may be obtained from the following extract from a letter of the Rev. John H. Rice, D. D., of Mobile:

"I saw Addison Alexander for the first time in July 1828. I was then just ten years old. I had come on from Petersburg, Virginia, in order to go to school at Amherst, Massachusetts. My father, mother and elder sister accompanied me. We came to Princeton by stage-coach from Trenton, and stopped at Dr. Alexander's, where we spent several weeks. I think it was the evening of the day of our arrival, that I met Addison on the back porch of his father's house. I can recall his appearance as vividly as though it were yesterday. He was unusually fleshy, as he continued to be until a short time before his lamented death, and wore at that time the glasses which continued to be a necessity for him during his whole life. I was told that he had lately graduated at Princeton College, though at the time I did not

---

* Mr. Alexander thought a great deal of Mr. Hargous, and they were much together; as his diaries attest.

know what that meant. He was then the same shy, diffident, retiring person that he was in after life. He seemed averse to going into the house, where his strange uncle and aunt were; but I, being a boy, was running about the house everywhere with the boys who were a little younger than myself. Upon going out upon the back porch I found Addison there. He greeted me cordially, and very soon began to tease me about Virginia, my provincial dialect, and the enormous use of calomel which he affected to believe was the chief article of the diet of the eastern Virginians. I had heard that he was a great student and very learned, and at first was a little afraid of one who was then regarded as a prodigy. You know how fond he was of children, and with what wonderful skill he would entertain them for hours when he had the requisite leisure. I had been but a day or two at Dr. Alexander's, when I felt as familiar with Addison as though he had been a boy of my own age." [He was a few months past nineteen.] "He very soon, I believe it was the second or third evening after my arrival, began to tell me his celebrated story of 'Old Black,' which every child who ever enjoyed his intimacy will remember. It kept us all in a continuous roar of laughter, so that I often rolled over the floor of the room beyond all power of self-restraint; which seemed to afford him a great deal of quiet amusement. This story of 'Old Black,' which consisted of a series of ludicrous mistakes and blunders of an old serving woman, he evidently improvised, inventing the incidents as he related them. These alternated with a similar story of a serving man, whom he called 'Peter Arun.' He also took occasion of our intercourse to impart in the pleasantest way a great amount of valuable information, some of which I retain to this day. Before I left Princeton he presented me with my Life, printed with the pen in a number of small volumes neatly stitched and bound in blue covers. It was written with all the formality and seriousness of an actual biography. These I kept with great care until they were literally worn out. You know how children always loved him. So I became devotedly attached to him during the few delightful weeks that I spent at Princeton in the summer of 1828, weeks made delightful chiefly by his wonderful skill in entertaining children. I left Princeton for Amherst, Mass., in September. Soon after I received a letter from Addison written on folio post paper, giving me a playful account of everything that had taken place in Princeton since my departure. He continued to write these large letters to me, at intervals, during the four years that I remained at Amherst. Among them were several which seemed to me then to be the most wonderful productions of human genius. And I confess that they still appear very extraordinary. They were written in the form of poetry or verse; and being read entirely across the page, were in verse of one measure and one sense, but being read half-way across, made poetry of another measure and the opposite sense. With him such a performance required no labour, it was dashed off with greater ease than I can scribble these recollections. I kept all these letters with affectionate care, but in the lapse of time and my many interruptions, they have disappeared. They would be worth to me now more than their weight in gold. They were all written on the largest sized folio post paper."

The above sketch presents a true picture of Mr. Alexander as he appeared to me when I was a boy; though as has already been said, he never appeared to any two persons in precisely the same way. There was doubtless, too, a greater effervescence of youthful spirits at the time referred to by Dr. Rice than at any time within my own recollection. The story of "Old Black" has been graven upon my memory with a pen of iron. I have heard it in one or other of its innumerable variations a hundred times. It is given in full, in one of its forms, in "Wistar's Magazine;" which was the most elaborate and curious of all the works he prepared for children. The story of "Peter Arun" was of a somewhat higher grade, and passed through full as many transformations. Old Black bore a shadowy resemblance to Mrs. Malaprop, and the whole thing was in a style of broad farce. As printed with the pen, it is given in the form of a dialogue between Old Black and Mrs. Bald. The two characters are as distinctly drawn as those of Dickens or Fielding, and are natural and unexaggerated like those of Goldsmith. The characteristic of Peter Arun was shrewd mother wit combined with a sort of hilarious *insouciance*, which ventured to the most reckless lengths, yet without a particle of fear, without real malice, with imperturbable *sang-froid*, and with no serious ill consequences. Seldom was a character better sustained or managed with more adroitness or humour. Peter's repartee is as poignant as it is endless. The "Wistar's Magazine" contains the correspondence between Mr. Arun and a gentleman whom he had wilfully but in perfect good humour offended, and whom he had provoked to a challenge. It is a ridiculous burlesque on the duello and the code of honour, and in point of rich, intellectual, mirthfulness deserves a comparison with some of the best parts of "Le Bourgeois Gentilhomme." Another of his famous stories was "Linn Lane," and still another, "Wickliffe, Johnson, Crow, and Lane." These were delivered orally and were indefinitely varied to suit the character of the circumstances and of the auditors. They were chief favourites with the younger children, and have seldom if ever been surpassed by the most renowned caterers for the little boys and girls. They were as original and showed genius as plainly and decidedly as his lectures in the seminary. Linn Lane was sometimes introduced alone: sometimes in company with W. J. and C. He had a voice that still rings in my ears, and that was as inimitably peculiar and laughable as some of the cries of the parrot. Sometimes it was Linn Lane among the Indians: sometimes it was Linn Lane at school: sometimes it was the incorrigible little wag and mischief-maker following and with his comrades mocking the unfortunate Wickliffe, who had a squeaking voice. When the bass tones of Johnson were mingled with the bland tenor of Crow, the shrill pipe of poor Wickliffe, and the forever indescribable quavering outcry of Lane, all uttering the same words, and all but one of the performers uttering them in the way of gibe and mockery; the effect was sometimes perfectly irresistible. It was often a wild burst of laughter, a chorus of shouts, and a series of delighted childish questions. The result was in part a triumph of ventriloquism, or at least of histrionic mimicry, in which the face and throat were changed to meet every emergency. Sometimes the *raconteur* would laugh himself in a quick uncontrollable way, as if the fun of the thing had just struck him for the first time. More commonly, however, he was perfectly grave, and only showed his interest in what was going on by the animation with which he told his tale.

The year 1829 was entered upon with the same studies which occupied his mind during the preceding. Particular attention was paid to the Greek. We shall still find him going to foundation principles; mastering all the grammars he can lay his hands upon, and reading critically all the best Greek authors. He also acquired the modern Greek.

Specimens of the diary, showing the way in which he spent his time at this period, may not be considered out of place here, and will be read without weariness by a large class of book-lovers, and students of strange biography.

"Jan. 14. After breakfast went to consult Prof. Hodge about a proofsheet of the Repertory, and remained there in conversation till 11: then returned and read the twenty-first chapter of Genesis in Hebrew; then read a review of Gieseler's Kirchengeschichte in the Studien und Kritiken of Hamburg, written by himself; then removed my book-case and a number of my books from my chamber above stairs to the dining-room below; then read the general catalogue of the Seminary just published, and looked at the National Gazette of yesterday; then glanced at the British Critic for July 1828—particularly at the account of the proceedings of the two Universities; then glanced at Ewald's book on Arabic Prosody; then read the preface to Rosenmüller's Arabic grammar; then wrote an abstract of Gieseler's article aforesaid, to be inserted in the Repertory; then read the 27th chapter of Isaiah in Hebrew; then read a part of chapter five in De Sacy's Arabic grammar; comparing it with Rosenmüller's, which appears to be a translation of De Sacy; then read the 28th chapter of Isaiah; then wrote a foolscap-sheet of French exercises; and then— to bed."

Another specimen is from the journal of the next day:

"Jan. 15. Read a part of the 29th chapter of Isaiah in Hebrew; the 4th chapter of Louis XV.; the 4th chapter of the 2d section of Condillac's Essai sur les Connaissances humaines, in French, and the 12th chapter of Don Quixote in Spanish; then wrote the 6th and 7th exercises in Josse's Spanish grammar; then read about a hundred lines in the Clouds of Aristophanes; then read about the same number in Chaucer's Canterbury Tales; then went to the Philological Hall, to attend a meeting of the Board of Criticism of the Philological Society, and received from the President an anonymous translation of Horace's Book 1., ode 22, to criticise. Read in the Hall the 14th canto of Dante's 'Inferno,' and finished the article on Arabian Literature in the Foreign Quarterly Review; returned home and examined the anonymous translation aforesaid, noting down some observations on the same; then read a review of Hase's Dogmatik and Gnosis in the Theologische Studien; then read the remainder of Isaiah 29 in Hebrew; then read De Sacy's Arabic grammar; then read Shakspeare; then read Genesis 22, 23, in Hebrew; then wrote a sheet of French exercises—and to bed."

I find, under date of Feb. 10, 1829, in a detached fragment, in the shape of a little manuscript book, in Mr. Alexander's early hand, the following critique upon the two dramatists mentioned above:

"I have finished the famous Clouds of Aristophanes, but can scarcely say what my feelings and opinions are as I close the book. Such a combination of extremes, intellectual and moral, I have never before known. Such transitions from earth to heaven, from Parnassus to the dunghill, are to me new and startling. Shakespeare is unequal, but his inequalities are nothing to the fits and starts of Aristophanes. The English poet never dives so deep into pollution, nor rises, in point of artificial elegance, so high as the Athenian. Shakespeare's genius is obviously untutored. His excellences and his faults are perhaps equally attributable to his want of education. It is altogether probable that many of these original and most significant and poetic modes of expression which he has introduced into our language, arose entirely from his ignorance of grammar and of foreign tongues. Had he been familiar with technical distinctions and etymological analogies, his thoughts would have been distracted between *words* and *things*. The dread of committing solecisms, and the ambition to exhibit that sort of elegance which results from the formal rules of an artificial rhetoric, would have cooled his ardour. His 'muse of fire' would never have reached 'the heaven of invention,' but would have stayed its flight amidst the clouds and mists of puerile conceit. I never read any of Shakespeare's real poetry (for much of his verse is most bald prosing) without feeling, in my very soul, that no man could write thus, whose heart was fixed on propriety of diction, as a principal or even a secondary object. He seems to have let his imagination boil, and actually to have taken the first words which bubbled up from its ebullition. Hence his strange revolt from authority in the use of ordinary words [in senses] as far removed from common practice as from etymology. And that reminds me of another circumstance. In the common blank verse of his dialogue, not only is he habitually careless, but seems not to know (in many cases) the method of constructing a harmonious verse; and perhaps his broken measure is more dramatic than one smoother would be; certainly more so than the intolerable tintinnabulum of the Théâtre Français. But let him rise into one of his grand flights, and his numbers are as musical as the 'harp of Orpheus.' I defy any man to bring forward any specimen of heroic blank verse, where the rhythm is as melodious as in some passages of Shakespeare, and the sense at the same time within sight—I mean comparably good in any degree. Milton, you say, &c. But who can read the Paradise Lost without thinking of the square and compass? Even when we admire, we admire scientifically—we applaud the arrangement of the cæsuras and pauses, and are forever thinking of iambuses and trochees and hypercatalectics, and all the hard words that Milton himself would have dealt forth in lecturing upon his own versification. Whereas, I do verily believe, that Shakespeare knew no more of Prosody, than of Animal Magnetism or Phrenology. Thompson, again, is among our finest specimens of rich and musical blank verse, but Thompson is laboured too; not in Milton's way, by weight and measure, but in a way no less artificial and discernible. He is always labouring to make his lines flow with a luscious sweetness: Every body knows that he succeeds, but every body, alas, knows how. He does it by presenting words in profusion, which are at once dulcet to the ear and exciting to the imagination. The method is the only true one, but he carries it too far. One strong proof that Shakespeare was a genius and a unique one, is that his excellence is not sustained and equal. Moonlight and candlelight shed a uniform lustre, but who ever saw or heard of a continuous flash of lightning? Our bard trifles and proses and quibbles, and whines (but always without affectation) till something (whether accident or not I cannot tell) strikes a spark into his combustible imagination, and straightway, he is in a blaze. I think a good rocket is a capital illustration of his muse of fire. First we have a premonitory whiz—then a delicate but gorgeous column of brilliant scintillations, stretching away into the bosom of heaven and at last dying away in a shower of mimic stars and comets of tenfold—of transcendent brightness. What then? Why then comes darkness visible, or at best a beggarly gray twilight. But in talking thus to myself, I forget what I am about. I began with Aristophanes, and have been raving about Shakespeare. All I have to say, however, about the former, is, that he is a perfect contrast to the Englishman. He is evidently a master of the art of versifying, but he knows how to temper the formality of systematic elegance with the charm of native poetry. Compared with the Greek tragedians, his flights of choral and lyrical inspiration appear to great advantage. More coherent and intelligible than Æschylus, more vigorous and nervous and significant than Sophocles, more natural and spirited than Euripides; he notwithstanding excels them all in the music of his numbers, and the Attic purity and terseness of his diction."

No one can pursue these records far without acknowledging the astonishing industry and versatility of the stripling scholar. And then the effrontery with which he marches up to a new language with which perhaps few of his seniors are at all acquainted, is fairly startling. His taste in letters, too, is peculiar certainly, but also at once robust and refined.

"Feb. 17.—The historical style of the Arabs is very curious. It varies indeed, in different cases. Some of their histories are florid, inflated, and verbose. Others, and, I suspect, the great majority, are hasty, confused and crude enumerations of heterogeneous facts. I was amused in looking over some of the historical facts in De Sacy, to observe the exquisite taste exhibited in the arrangement and enumeration of events; e. g. Makrizi says, speaking of Hakem, the Imaum of the Fatemists, 'He commanded that all dogs should be killed, in consequence of which a multitude were put to death. He founded a college called the "House of Wisdom," to which he transferred the royal library. He was very cruel to his running footmen; and a number of them he put to death.' What a circumflective climax, pour ainsi dire? Dead dogs—colleges—libraries—running footmen!"

His notions about the literature of English metaphysics are fresh and unusual, but not ignorant.

"Read the 5th and 6th chapters of Brown's Lectures on the philosophy of the human mind. The first four I read last summer, and was then disgusted with the book. I know the reason; for reading Stewart's Philosophy just before, I had been drawn off from that elegant writer's statements to his style, which, in my opinion, merits well to be regarded as a model of purity, elegance, and perspicuity. When I took up Brown, I judged him rather rhetorically than philosophically; and finding his sentences (though full of meaning) to be long, involved, sometimes obscure, and often awkward, I grew tired of him. On this second trial I view him with other eyes. I can recognize at once, the fire of genius and strength of intellect. I should imagine that the lectures were posthumous, and published as he pronounced them. A good delivery might have made them captivating, and perhaps they were so.* On paper they are not so well, in point of style. There are too many parenthetical expressions, and some excessively *intelligible* explanations of his meaning, which, however useful and necessary in the lecture-room, or when orally delivered, the author's task would have curtailed in revising for the press. As to *matter*, though metaphysics is a terra incognita to me, I can readily perceive he shows power and skill in drawing nice but strong distinctions and detecting latent fallacies."

The next day he writes thus of Brown:

"He is a wonderful man, it must be owned. For length of sentences and fulness of illustration—rather, of explanation—he is remarkable. He holds up an idea in all imaginable points of view, and never seems satisfied till he has exhausted all explanatory ideas and expressions. But he never loses nor forgets himself; and, what above all pleases me, he never *cants*, i. e. he never uses phrases just because other philosophers have used them, though they may mean any thing or nothing quoad hoc. As to his doctrine of Cause and Effect, it sounds well and *seems* true; but I am not satisfied. He seems to deny, though not directly, that we can *conceive* of any *power* or *causation*, except immediate invariable antecedence. Now I certainly can *conceive* of a power which has never yet been exercised, and which, perhaps, never will be.

"I admire Brown's ease and vivacity, especially as it exists in combination with so much depth and penetration. There is no scholastic stiffness, nor repulsive technicality about the annunciation of his most important doctrines. And what other metaphysician since the world began would have quoted Gulliver and Martinus Scriblerus? This marks the man of taste, judgment, and independent spirit. An inferior writer would have been afraid of lowering his subject by citing such authorities. The true philospher takes a just idea of a striking illustration, even from the mouth of a buffoon."

I find him next engaged with Dante. About the middle

---

* Everybody is of course familiar now with the enthusiasm they awakened at the time, and with the fact that they were commonly dashed off in a heat, the night before.

of February he was occupied reading the Purgatorio. Here are some of his remarks in the way of comment:

"Feb. 19.—This part of the Divina Commedia begins with a metaphor in which the poem is represented as a ship and the subject as the sea upon which it sails. I felt a good deal relieved on finding that he calls the argument of this second part *miglior acqua* in comparison with the preceding one. I feel now more than I did when actually reading the Inferno, that the poetry of Dante, like all truly original composition, produces an *original*—I mean, peculiar and unique impression on the mind. His conceptions of Hell, revolting as some of them appeared (I mean poetically revolting to the taste and judgment) have left their traces on my memory and fancy more strongly than the refined but less substantial and tangible creations of Milton's genius. The Purgatorio opens where the Inferno ended, at the exit of the poet from the infernal regions. I must confess that I have no precise idea respecting the locality of the aperture; though Dante described it, or intended to describe it, with becoming accuracy. For, of all poets, past and present, he is the most trigonometrical that I have ever met with."

To show still further his versatility, I give another record made on the same day:

"Read the 4th Canto of the Faery Queen. I cannot but admire, more and more, Spenser's wonderful descriptive talent. His pictures of the six passions, in this canto, exceed in vividness and truth any description that I have ever read, without exception. I begin now to suspect that Spenser's forte was in describing loathsome objects, and he certainly does it with a master hand. I feel his excellence the more on comparison with Dante. I may, through ignorance, do the Italian bard injustice, but it does appear to me that he was deficient in a talent which Spenser possesses in a singular degree—the talent for discriminating and appropriate description. How striking is the adaptation of the six beasts to the character of their respective riders themselves. A few characteristic traits and circumstances are selected as the prominent features of each portrait, and are exhibited in strong relief, without the aid of vague generalities and cant terms. I can actually see Sloth 'still drowned in sleep and most of his days dead,' nodding along upon his ass;—Gluttony, sweating and vomiting upon his swine;—Lechery, suffering the reproachful pain of that foul evil, 'that rots the marrow and consumes the brain;'—Avarice, counting o'er his pelf; and, above all, Envy, with a snake in his bosom and a toad between his teeth, 'the poison running all about his jaw,' weeping that cause of weeping one he had; but when he hears of harm, waxing wondrous glad. I forgot Anger. That picture too is very fine, especially the redeeming and afflictive circumstance thrown into the description. The poet goes as far as nature goes and no further. He does not unite a fierce and irritable, with a cold-blooded and deliberate malignity (traits seldom, if ever, actually found in combination), but with exquisite truth and knowledge of the heart, after telling us that 'of his hands he had no government, ne cared for blood in his avengement,' adds, that 'when the furious fit was overpast, his cruel facts he often would repent.'"

"Feb. 20. Read Isaiah 54, and Genesis 43 in Hebrew. At the Philological Hall, read the 3d and 4th cantos of Purgatorio; also examined Kennicott's Hebrew Bible and Wetstein's Greek Testament. I wish they were both upon my table. [The books from this library could not be taken away.] The former is a noble work. After reading the Hebrew Bible with the points, I find it much more agreeable to read without them. In the historical parts I can supply most of the points which affect the etymology, and the whole seems much more neat and simple without such a multiplicity of marks.

"At home again; wrote the 25th exercise in Josse's Spanish grammar. Finished the 3d chapter of Levizac's Grammaire Francaise. Read the first chapter of Voltaire's Histoire de l'Empire de Russie sous Pierre le Grand. Finished the 2d chapter of Horne. Finished the extracts from the books of the Druses. Read the 33d chapter of Scott's Napoleon. Notwithstanding the literary faultiness of this book, there is much that is valuable in it. The nature of the subject makes it interesting, malgré lui, and the good sense and acute observation of the author, make it frequently instructive. His reflections, particularly those derived incidentally from individual facts, are often worthy of preservation. No attributes can contribute more to the popularity of a new government than an appearance of conscious strength combined with clemency; since the spirit of opposition, despairing of success but not of personal safety, gradually sinks into acquiescence. As a specimen of style, it does Walter Scott no honour. His phraseology is often rendered vulgar by excessive straining after classical simplicity and colloquial ease. He is sometimes ungrammatical and frequently inelegant. But nothing disgusts me more, than the frequency and stiffness of his similes and illustrations, which, however well they might appear in an epic poem, or even in a higher species of romance, are too recherché and affected for a work like this. In a word, they are too *good*. I observe, too, a disposition similar to that of Brown, to borrow illustration from works of burlesque humour. But oh, how far different the modus operandi! There is no work of a historical description, which exhibits such a multitude of striking, ingenious, but unreasonable illustrations, as this of Scott's—always excepting Tom Moore's Life of Sheridan, which may be regarded as a perfect model of the far-fetched, pretty style, and John Q. Adams's Ebony and Topaz toast, which, sonorous as it was, is a sealed book, I believe, even unto this day. My impression, on the whole, is that Scott wrote mainly in the hope of reward; which accounts for the crudeness and rudeness of the composition; unwisely availing himself, however, of the opportunity to surfeit the public with a profusion of good sayings, which if retained in his commonplace book might have eked out a thousand dialogues in a hundred new Waverleys to come."

"Feb. 23. Read ten sections in the first book of 'Cicero's Academical Questions.'—My dabblings in the modern and oriental languages must have vitiated my taste most lamentably; for I protest that this Ciceronian Latin is to my eyes, ears and understanding the most lumbering, clumsy, formal style imaginable. Every thing seems elaborate and artificial; the terms and expressions that are meant to be most colloquial and familiar, are so studied and distorted, and the inversions are so wilful, wanton, and grotesque, that I have no patience with the thing at all. How is it, and why is it that the Latin verse of Virgil, and especially of Horace, is much more natural and easy, and consequently so much nearer the language of common life, than the Latin prose of Cicero? Why, because neither Horace nor Virgil was a conceited, affected, pedantic, pompous, egotistical, verbose, jack-of-all-trades."

He had now become sufficiently familiar with the Hebrew to be able to distinguish and appreciate the styles of the different Bible writers. His observations on this head will be found to possess a fascinating and even popular interest:

"March 4. Read in Hebrew the 3d chapters of Exodus and Jeremiah. I can now perceive distinctly the diversity of style in the Hebrew Scriptures. Isaiah and Jeremiah are as unlike as any two classical or modern poets. The genius of the former is characterized by vigour, elevation and impetuosity. He deals much in animated exhortation and severe invective. Jeremiah on the other hand is calmer and more equable. There seems to be a vein of melancholy running through his composition. One thing is common to them both, as it is indeed to all oriental writers; a figurative mode of expression. Even in this, however, they are different. Isaiah's metaphors are lively and animated; those of Jeremiah more subdued: both are graphic and impressive. I prefer the Pentateuch to any other book, as a genuine specimen of primitive, unsophisticated simplicity of style. There is nothing puerile on the one hand, nor inflated on the other. The exodus of the Israelites from Egypt is one of the finest subjects in the world for an epic poem."

"April 18. Read in Hebrew, Exodus and Jeremiah xxxv. Looked through Jorton's Life of Erasmus.—Rezeau Brown* returned to-day from New Haven, after an absence of ten days. He brings as curiosities two Arabic letters written in Syria, and brought over by Mr. Brewer as waste paper. They are apparently addressed to a Mr. Bird. I am surprised to find the hand so much like my own. With a little practice, and a good pen, I could equal it—I think. He has also brought Henry Martyn's Persian Testament, borrowed from Professor Gibbs of Yale. I have long wished to see this book, and am delighted to obtain it. I have no printed Persian books, and should prefer a version of the Bible; because with my familiarity with its contents, and, in some measure, with the original, I can gather more instruction from it than from any other book. The Polyglots, it is true, contain Persian versions; but their purity and correctness, are, to say the least, equivocal. Now Martyn's version has been made within the last twenty years, and in circumstances which afford good ground for the presumption that it is a good one. 1st. Martyn was a man of genius and a scholar; an upright man and devoted to his work. 2d. He had previously finished a version with great labour which was thought too *Arabic* (his assistant having been an Arab) whereupon he instantly resolved to recommence the task. From this circumstance I infer, 1st, that his whole soul was in the thing, which ensures fidelity and accuracy; 2d, that although his first translation was imperfect, it must have qualified him for the second, in a very great degree; 3d, this version was prepared at Shiraz which has been called 'the Athens of Persia,' where the purest Persian is spoken,—and with the assistance of an intelligent, refined and educated native; 4th, it was read before the Shah, who signified his approbation of its execution. It has also been approved

---

* His bosom friend, of whom we shall know more presently.

by many of the Persian literati. The first edition of this translation was printed at St. Petersburg, soon after Martyn's death. This impression, I have seen it somewhere mentioned, abounded in errors of the press which rendered it not only partly unintelligible, but in some cases even blasphemous. Even this edition I should have been pleased to see, though it would not have answered all my ends. I am pleased to find, however, that the one before me is a Calcutta edition of later date. Persian literature is so zealously and thoroughly pursued at the metropolis of British India, and the latter has given to the world so many valuable impressions of oriental works, that I feel little doubt that this book, though by no means elegant, is perfectly correct. It is an octavo of 741 pages, with the following title-page in English: 'The New Testament of our Lord and Saviour Jesus Christ; Translated from the original Greek into Persian, at Shiraz, by the Rev. Henry Martyn, A. B. Late Fellow of St. John's College, and chaplain on the Bengal Establishment; with the assistance of Meerza Sueyed Ulee (Mirza Seid Ali) of Sheeraz, Calcutta: Printed by P. Pereira, at the Hindoostanee Press for the British and Foreign Bible Society in the year 1816.' The leaves are uncut, and Prof. Gibbs did not recollect that the book was in his library. It is probably the only copy in America."

The continuation of the journal will afford the reader an agreeable change of topics. The extraordinary character of these youthful records must acquit them of the charge of monotony.

"April 27. This is my Greek week; and I have begun to-day at the foundation, reviewing Moore's grammar through and through, and reading Valpy's Delectus Sententiarum Græcarum, an excellent book for beginners. It is not only perfectly intelligible, but contains a chosen selection of golden sentences. Some of the sayings of the old philosophers are wonderfully striking. As I extend my acquaintance with the classic writers I am surprised to find so much acuteness and wit, as well as wisdom, in their sayings. We are apt (I mean the ignorant and partially informed) to think them admirable only by comparison—a sort of silly naiveté as their chief characteristic; at least this has been my own case. When I think of the Greek writers whom I have not read, I think of them—but no matter, I am every day more and more disabused. The little book above mentioned I have read through to-day."

"April 29. I have finished to-day the fifty chapters of Neilson's

Greek Exercises, and am sensible of having derived great benefit from the perusal. The Latin sentences I have passed over, as also the supplemental exercises on the dialects and poetry, because I intend, at present, to confine myself to *prose* and to *Attic* prose. I shall take up the book again hereafter and go through with it. I have also revised again to-day, Moore's rules for the formation of the tenses. I am more and more convinced, every day, that this grammar is the best for elementary instruction that was ever written. It does not twaddle like the German books, about the original forms and progressive changes of the etymology, but gives rules for deducing the parts of the language as they are."

"May 4. Read in Greek about five hundred lines in the first book of the Cyropædia. My object is to recover and extend my acquaintance with the forms of the Greek Grammar. For this purpose I run over the tenses of every verb on its first appearance, and often afterwards. This requires a frequent recurrence to the lexicon."

About this time he received the following letter from his brother James. The date on the outside is May 5. His brother sends him Botta,* and had previously sent the Greek Prayer-Book concerning which we shall presently find him writing to Mr. Hall. The letter contains so many allusions that it would be hard to sum them up in a sentence.

"Hoping that William will call again I venture upon a few lines. I send you Botta, which will be exactly in place after Scott. [Scott's Napoleon which he was reading]. I think you will admire it, especially as it is not marred by the absurdity of fabricated speeches. The Greek prayer-book I also sent. I imagine it is made for the Greek Catholics of the islands near Venice. See Carter's travels. Also, a letter of John Hall's which contains some notices which may interest you. John is an excellent correspondent in all such matters. He spares no pains in answering every question I send him, even when he has to turn over whole volumes in the library. As to the Review, all I know is this: Walsh called at Littell's and said that he thought the whole edition would sell, and that a very favourable review of it would be in the next American Quarterly Review. I very highly approve of your devotion to the Greek, and of your ardour in the pursuit, as well as the mode of critical study which you have adopted. You would probably find all

---

* I presume, his "Floria d'Italia," etc.

Xenophon's works interesting, and then might be prepared to undertake Plato. 'Das pou sto' is attributed to Archimedes, as 'Richard is himself,'—'So much for Buckingham,' are to Shakspeare, and 'a sweet morsel under the tongue,' is to the Bible. Who invented the sayings I know not. I have found the origin of Byron's 'hell of waters,' the expression which he applies to the cascade of Vellino (Childe Harold, iv., 69). When the German poet Lenz visited the cataract of the Rhine at Schaffhausen, he smote his thigh, (a classical gesture as per Homer,) and cried 'Hier ist wasser-hölle.' Stolberg's Travels, I., 85. Next to Mitford's Greece will stand Halsey on antediluvianism, for chasteness and harmony of language. I have sent for an Italian Les-Buch on the Hamiltonian plan, this being the nearest approach I can make to a living teacher; thus I hope to learn the vexatious niceties which puzzle one so much in a new language."

I again resume my extracts from the journal:

"May 6. Read in Hebrew, Numbers 1, and Ezekiel 13.—Read in Greek and Persian, Matt. 16. Finished the first book of the Κύρου-παιδείς, and read the whole over. Finished the second volume of Scott's Life of Bonaparte. On page 18 there are two attempts at illustrative allusion, so to speak, which is his favourite method in this work. One of these is pretty good; it is about vengeance and dragon's teeth. The other is horrible; it is in these words: 'Every obligation according to the making of the civil law, is made void in the same manner in which it is made binding; as *Arthegal, the emblematic champion of justice in Spenser's allegory*, decrees as law, that what the sea has brought the sea may resume.' I can scarcely believe that a man of taste and genius could be guilty of such absurdity. Appealing to a character in an allegorical poem for proof of a maxim in law, and that, not in the way of a direct quotation, but with all the formality of a pleader citing an adjudged case. Here is a match for it: 'Every thing projected from the earth will, by the law of gravitation return to it again'; as the little ragged boy who cleans my boots says, when he plays *sky-high*, 'What goes up must come down; let every man take care of his crown!'"

"May 14. Read the 8th and last book of the Cyropædia. I have read this book with great satisfaction. My principal object has been to recover and extend my knowledge of the Greek etymology, but my interest in the subject and admiration of the style diverted my attention in a great degree from mere grammatical forms. Xenophon is one of those writers whose personal character seems to be exhibited in all their compositions. Throughout this book I have conceived an idea of the author as a man particularly amiable. There is a suavity of temper which pervades and characterizes the whole work that is very charming. No harsh or intemperate terms are used, even in his censures of vice; nor is there any thing biting or sarcastic in his humour. He is indeed more like Addison than any modern writer whom I know. As to his style, I am struck with its transparent perspicuity and dignified simplicity. By-the-bye, the words *simple** and *simplicity* are very equivocal in English. They have become, by usage, almost contemptuous, a character which does not belong to the primitives in Latin. We are apt, therefore, to attach to the expression *simple style* an idea of something stale, flat and unprofitable. But the genuine simplicity of classic writers is not the simplicity of *simpletons*. It is not the childish naiveté of unsophisticated ignorance. It is the simplicity of men who had ornament at command, and exhaustless sources of rhetorical embellishment, whose taste forbade an undue use of them. In every page Xenophon shows himself to be familiar with the highest learning that was known in the times in which he lived; as well as endowed with elevated intellectual powers. His simplicity is therefore the result of an exquisite refinement which entitles him to the epithet which has been given him, Αττικωτατος.† This book, which I have read as a romance, without making any research pro. or con. in relation to its character, deserves the highest admiration. The purity of moral principles, which it formally inculcates, and what is still more important, the perfectly unexceptionable character of the work itself, astonish me. I cannot help feeling some amazement at the wonderful superiority of the best heathen writers over the infidel authors of modern times. That the former, in an age of gross superstition and idolatry, and in the midst of the blackest abominations, should have breathed a spirit so much purer than that of men born in an enlightened age, reared in a state of society, hostile, at least, to external vice, and with all the advantages of Christianity, is truly wonderful. What a figure does Voltaire make by the side of Xenophon! This charming writer delights me also by his delicate wit, and his nice discernment of character."

In May the Directors of the Seminary held their semi-

---

* There are some fine remarks to the same purport in the Greyson Letters.

† This is directly in the teeth of the strange assertions of Macaulay in his Essay on History.

annual meeting. At this time he heard several distinguished preachers. A strong impression was made upon him by Dr. William Nevins, of Baltimore. The record of fact and feeling is interesting:

"May 17. Morning sermon by William Nevins of the First Church, Baltimore. 'What is a man advantaged if he gain the whole world and lose himself?' A fine specimen of studied oratory. The mode of uttering every word seemed to be preconcerted; yet the preacher had so much tact, taste, judgment, and, above all, unaffected earnestness and tenderness of feeling that he was truly eloquent. As to the matter, the plan of the sermon was ingenious and to me noble. Instead of explaining the question in the text as denoting an absolute negation, he undertook to answer it by setting forth the advantages of sin in all their strength and breadth. This was, of course, a very hard thing to do well. The general strain of the discourse was necessarily half ironical, and it was necessary, here and there, to throw in a solitary caution in order to prevent the fascinations of iniquity from having more effect than the countervailing benefits of holiness, which were only exhibited by implication. And this the preacher managed wonderfully well."

On the evening of the same day, in contrast with the former, he heard a sermon from another preacher of some distinction whom he thus describes:

"He seems to be a sincere honest man, but is one of the new school of preachers, who place more dependence on the way in which they say a thing, than on the intrinsic weight of the thing itself. He seemed to be always making use of stage tricks for the production of effect, an artifice rendered more apparent and ridiculous by the homely simplicity of his *improvisations* in point of style. Thus he tried to startle the assembly by interspersing divers observations between the verses of the introductory hymn. He even talked about the philosophy of the mind, in this appropriate and decorous connexion. Then in his sermon he placed great dependence on the mystical repetition of the same thing thrice, thus: 'Will you tell a lie? Will you tell a lie? Will you tell a lie?' accompanied with an equal number of hard slaps upon the Bible. He also thought proper to display some specimens of weeping on a grand scale, so obviously forced, if not feigned, that they did more harm than good. How unfortunate that a man apparently sincere and unquestionably zealous should resort to such poor trickery to bolster up the weakness of the gospel! His text was, 'Is there no balm in Gilead?' The introduction consisted of a question in the rule of three, the answer required being the relative number of souls lost and saved since the beginning of the world. It was as regularly stated and worked out as it could have been by Pike."

On the 18th he heard a sermon preached before the Directors, and thus notices it:

"May 18th. In the evening, semi-annual sermon before the Directors of the Seminary by Joseph Sandford, of the Arch Street Presbyterian Church, Philadelphia. Nothing original in the conceptions or new in the mode of expression; but the most finished taste and sound judgment in the selection and arrangement of the materials. The delivery was fine. I had heard of Sandford's pulpit eloquence, but supposed him to be an oily, measured, studied speaker. On the contrary, there is no appearance of artifice in his manner. He has a noble voice and commanding figure. The unimpassioned parts of his discourse were pronounced in a subdued tone, with great dignity and distinctness; the animated passages, with great richness of intonation and admirable spirit. He cited and applied to America the Scriptural allegory of the cedars of Lebanon. This part of his sermon, could not, I think, have been delivered better. Text: 'And while Paul tarried at Athens his spirit was stirred within him.'"

"May 30. Read in Hebrew, Numbers 25-26 and Ezekiel 36-37. Read in Greek the first book of Xenophon's *Anabasis*. I can easily perceive that this is not such a book as the Cyropædia. It is evidently written with less care and less attention to rhetorical elegance. From the abruptness of some of the transitions, and the baldness of some of the narratives, I should think it was a transcript of the author's memorandum book. Still it has all the excellences of the Xenophontic style. And the very circumstances which I have here mentioned render it the best Greek book for beginners, as Professor Porson used to say it was. Read in French the second and third books of Voltaire's Charles XII. Read in Persian and Greek Matt. XXVII.

In the absence of other data relative to this period, except those which are furnished by the diary, and a hint here and there in letters, it will doubtless be agreeable to the reader to be put in possession of the full particulars which have been kindly communicated by Dr. John H. Rice. The description which this gentleman gives of Mr. Alexander's habits at this time, will answer in some degree as a flowing outline sketch of his habits when making visits to the city at a later day. The minutiæ of the pictures are not the same. Indeed his plans and occupations during these visits were as different at different times as one can well conceive. Sometimes he had taken his carpet-bag in his hand and gone on to preach a sermon for one of the city ministers, by special request. Sometimes he had arrived in town with the absorbing purpose of making a commentary before he left it. On such occasions he kept himself very close. Sometimes again, he went merely to disport himself amidst the fantastic excitements of the crowded streets; to make trial of the various hotels; to step into restaurants and cafés; to move noiselessly and unobserved in the throngs of men; to see the signs and listen to the street-cries; to refresh his eyes with the spectacle of the flashing shop-windows; to gaze upon bannered pageants and military processions; to lose himself in strange places and strange scenes; to avoid the officious notice to which he was sometimes subjected at Princeton; and to read in the many-leaved volume of human nature, which in the city always lay open for his inspection.

But I will not detain the reader from the reminiscences of Dr. Rice.

"In 1829," he says, "my father moved from Petersburg, Virginia, to New York city. During our residence there Addison made us frequent visits, which were usually extended from two days to a week. He was at that time diligently engaged in the study of the French language, in which he afterward became a proficient. I had enjoyed unusually favourable opportunities for learning to speak French, and Addison seemed to think that he could gain something by conversing with me. As I had nothing to do at the time, and was not going to school, we spent almost every day in wandering over the city together, going to the least attractive and most obscure portions of it, and observing the manners and habits of the poor and vicious classes. We frequently walked through the Five Points and the adjacent purlieus, and saw a great deal of the street-life of the destitute and abandoned. You perhaps have remarked that his local acquaintance with the city of New York was such as hardly any one ever attains who has not been born and brought up there. Much of his knowledge of the various phases of human nature, which seemed so wonderful in one who was generally regarded as a man of the study and of books, was probably picked up in these and similar rambles through New York, and other great cities in both hemispheres. Though very short-sighted, yet by the aid of glasses he could see more than most persons whose vision is perfect. Our intercourse was carried on entirely in French, neither of us ever speaking English, except to discuss some question of French idiom or pronunciation. His observation was exceedingly quick, and his memory the most extraordinary I ever knew, unless it be that of his brother the Hon. Wm. C. Alexander, now of New York. I recollect that once, as we were walking near the Five Points, he called my attention to a sign over the door of one of the most dilapidated houses, the floor of which was below the level of the sidewalk. The sign read, 'P. Brady's school.' Upon looking in we could see no sign of school of any kind: the front room was one of the lowest of low grog-shops. That school seemed to make a great impression on his mind, and he referred to it in my presence years afterwards.

"You know how much he delighted in the solitude of a great city; where he could see, yet not be seen. While my father's family resided in New York, he felt free to come and stay with us. He stayed in my room, and we spent a good portion of every night, after we had retired, in talking over the adventures and rambles of the day. His conversation at that time was characterized by the same sprightliness, unaffectedness, and exuberant flow of humour. I never could perceive that he intentionally undertook to teach me anything, but you know he was the most skilful of instructors, and I doubt not that he made ineffaceable impressions on my mind at that time, and in a good measure gave direction to my thinking; so that I am to this day reaping the benefit of our familiar intercourse. I continued to see him thus occasionally at New York and during visits which I made to his father's house in Princeton, until he sailed for Europe."

CHAPTER V.

MR. ALEXANDER's only intimate friend at this period, and the only bosom friend he ever had, was Rezeau Brown,* a son of the Rev. Isaac V. Brown, of Lawrenceville, a village in the neighbourhood of Princeton. During the course of the year 1829 the two young men studied Hebrew together. It is nowhere asserted, but is not intrinsically improbable, that Mr. Brown received the rudiments, or perhaps the first suggestion, from Mr. Alexander, and that afterwards they proceeded together in delightful and congenial co-operation.

The character of this lovely youth was in some respects so remarkable, and his relation to the subject of this biography so close and tender, that no apology is needed for the insertion of what follows.

Rezeau Brown was born September 30, 1808, at Lawrenceville, Hunterdon (now Mercer) county, New Jersey, and was consequently about seventeen months older than his Princeton friend. Not long before Rezeau's birth, his father had assumed the pastoral charge of the Presbyterian congregation in the little hamlet, which is only five miles from Princeton. A few years after, though without relinquishing his duties as pastor, he became the head of a flourishing classical school at the same place.

Rezeau entered a common English school in his native village at the age of four years. His precocity was remarkable, and he made rapid advances; being especially distinguished for his aptness in ac-

---

* A pretty extended memoir of Rezeau Brown (of which I have made free use in preparing the above account) will be found in the Bib. Rep. for October, 1834, from the pen of the Rev. J. W. Alexander. The accuracy of this account is confirmed by short but eulogistic letters from the Rev. I. V. Brown, Dr. Miller, and Dr. Archibald Alexander.

quiring the knowledge of arithmetic. He was fond of study, but even at this early period had a feeble constitution. It was noticed that (like Alexander) he was not much addicted to the usual boyish amusements, but derived his "chief entertainment from intellectual pursuits." When it became proper he was admitted to his father's classical seminary, where for a number of years he enjoyed the direction and judicious care of this affectionate parent. The facilities here afforded were not wasted upon him. He was very soon distinguished in every branch of study. Especially in the various lines of mathematical pursuit, he displayed a quickness and a maturity of understanding which were rare; passing through the details of arithmetic, algebra, geometry, not only with ease, but with delight, in no case requiring to be urged, and in scarcely any to be assisted.

At this time the greater part of those who were connected with Mr. Brown's academy were young men approaching to manhood, and some of them of adult age. Yet even these, we are assured, were accustomed to look up to Rezeau for assistance, while he was yet a child.* There are those still who remember "the pleasing appearance of this promising boy, his symmetrical form, his manly grace of motion, and that beauty which arises from the light of intelligence playing upon features of perfect regularity."

In the autumn of 1823, being then fifteen, he was admitted to the Junior class in the college of New Jersey; thus being at the same age and entering the same collegiate class with his friend Addison, who at the expiration of a year strictly followed his bright example. Addison was at this time at the Academy. During the period of his connexion with the college, Rezeau was much absorbed in the appropriate studies of the course, and like his young compeer, was uniformly in the first rank of distinguished scholars, and received the highest literary honour at the close, though a number of his competitors were young men more advanced in years. There are but few particulars of his college life that have been preserved, but it is known that his favourite studies were the mathematical and physical sciences, and that "his deportment was such as to win the regard of his friends and teachers." In his strong partiality towards the exact sciences he differed strikingly from his friend. About this time he was so fortunate as to be domiciliated in the family of his uncle, the late Dr. John Van Cleve, "who will long be remembered in New Jersey as a skilful practitioner of medicine, a proficient in science, a citizen of probity and talent, and a

---

* Memoir in the Repertory.

church officer of wisdom and piety." Rezeau was employed by Dr. Van Cleve, who was at the time delivering a course of lectures on chemistry, as an assistant in his laboratory. This engagement covered the period of two successive winters, and the manipulations to which it gave rise not only tended to develop his taste for the science, but also helped to give perfection to "that manual tact for which he was always distinguished," and to "awaken in him a desire to enter the medical profession."

The severity and long continuance of his studies proved greatly prejudicial, and subsequently fatal, to his health, which was always extremely precarious. His physicians accordingly put an interdict upon his scientific schemes, and encouraged him in a purpose to seek mental and bodily improvement in a tour to Ohio and Kentucky, where he passed the autumn of 1825, and the following winter, in active travel in company with a college friend. On his return, in the spring of 1826, "he was seized with a violent affection of the lungs, which reduced him to the brink of the grave."

In March, 1826, having in a measure recovered his health, he proceeded to carry out his cherished purpose of becoming a physician, and entered the office of his uncle. In March, 1827, he met with a "change in his spirit," which gave a new direction and a new colour to the remainder of his life. It was to this time that he and others were accustomed to date his conversion.

At the time referred to there was a much-awakened feeling about the soul's interests, both at Lawrenceville and Princeton. Rezeau had stood out with positive and sturdy defiance. He was opposed to the good work itself, its instrumentalities, and its conductors. At length suddenly overwhelmed with a sense of God's mercy, he sank to the earth. He was admitted soon after to the communion of the church in the little rural village where he was born; to wit, in June, 1827.

The following winter he passed in New Haven, his main inducement being a wish to attend the lectures of Prof. Silliman, a gentleman from whom he received much kind attention, and for whom he ever afterwards entertained an affectionate respect. He frequented the lectures of the medical department, and particularly the course in chemistry and mineralogy. "At the same time, the example and aid of Professor Gibbs strongly incited him towards the pursuit of the Oriental languages." It may be that his Princeton friend had already somewhat stimulated his taste for these unaccustomed studies, though on this point there is no certainty. He also went through a course of gymnastics, which in his case, if in any, was absolutely essential.

But above all, during his residence at New Haven, he "grew in grace and in the knowledge of our Lord and Saviour Jesus Christ." Great revivals were at this time agitating New England.

The summer of 1828 was spent in studies preparatory to a regular course in theology, especially of the original Scriptures. In the spring of 1828 he received and accepted the appointment of tutor in the college of New Jersey; which situation he held two years and a half. His progress in religious things was now becoming more and more marked.

In the spring of 1831 Mr. Brown renounced his literary employments in Nassau Hall, "under an ever-deepening conviction that he ought to enter without delay upon the work of the ministry." He had been for a year or two engaged in theological studies, and his name was now enrolled among the young men of the Theological Seminary at Princeton. He revolved in his mind the plan of going as a missionary to the heathen; but the state of his health was an insurmountable impediment. 'His health was even then radically impaired, and his spare frame, and mild but bloodless countenance, were signals of distress by which nature seemed to warn him from any further seclusion.'

As a college officer he was "conscientious, faithful, and acceptable." He was often known to "assist in various social meetings in the vicinity of Princeton: in one of these his prayers and exhortations, and private admonitions, were made instrumental to the awakening of souls."

The cause of Sunday schools was very dear to him, and "among other important services, he prepared for the American Sunday School Union the *Memoirs of Augustus Hermann Francke*, which has proved to be one of the most popular of useful works."*

In the month of April, 1831, Mr. Brown was licensed to preach by the Presbytery of New Brunswick as a probationer for the gospel ministry. Soon after this event a great awakening of religion began to manifest itself in the county of Somerset, and not less than one hundred and twenty-five persons were thought to be converted. The zealous and unflagging labours of Mr. Brown were largely instrumental in the hands of Providence in the production of that gracious result. In the month of October of the same year, he received an appointment from the General Assembly's Board of Missions, to preach

---

* The German work of which this was little more than an English abridgment, was reviewed by Mr. Alexander in one of the early numbers of the Repertory.—See Bib. Rep., 1830, p. 408.

the gospel in Virginia. The scene of his labours was the village of Morgantown, in Monongalia county. He greatly endeared himself to that whole community, and shed the fragrance of his piety into the most secluded parts of the territory covered by his ministrations.

In June, 1832, he returned from the theatre of his painful toils in Virginia, to his father's house. The bleak winters of the mountain country had been too much for him. He was in as delicate a condition of body as at almost any former period. "Shortly after his return, he again connected himself with the Theological Seminary in Princeton, and sat down to study with an intensity of application" which gave well-founded alarm to all his friends. He busied himself in all kinds of researches. His health again gave way. He refused a number of flattering invitations, and among the rest a professorship of chemistry in a southern college.

Mr. Brown pursued the regular course of study until the summer of 1832, and after preaching a few weeks with much acceptance in the city of Trenton, he was then prevailed upon by the solicitations of the Rev. James W. Alexander (who was at the time the editor of the "Presbyterian," a religious journal published in Philadelphia), to assist him in that work. That winter was a season of deep sorrow for the young editor, who was himself in dreadful health, and whose distant home was in Trenton. Those were the days of the old coaches, when the public vehicles in use were very slow and uncertain; making travelling no easy matter in cold weather, and rendering it almost impossible for one to reside at a distance and transact business in the city. It was under these circumstances that he had recourse to his affectionate and tried friend, Rezeau Brown, whose willingness proved equal to the emergency. "He repaired to Philadelphia, and for a number of months persevered in the faithful and assiduous performance of the duties which he had assumed. The friend whom he came to aid could never forget the generous ardour with which he wore himself down in this employment; nor the pious principle by which he seemed to be actuated. Even those minute drudgeries of the editorial life which are almost mechanical, seemed to be conducted by Mr. Brown with a direct view to the glory of Christ."

No Lord's day passed in which Mr. Brown did not preach at least once. He was universally respected and beloved, and visibly improved as a public speaker. "In spite of bodily infirmity Mr. Brown continued to study, to write, and even to preach. Towards the end of March, 1833, he was seized with catarrh, and while under its pressure conducted two public services on the Lord's day. In the interval of services, he was observed to lie upon a sofa, pallid and exhausted. The next day a hectic flush mantled his cheek, and his pulse was alarmingly accelerated. There was no time to be lost, and he hastened to his father's house. The pulmonary disorder was evidently seated and confirmed. It was no small aggravation of his solicitude that he had matured a plan for a voyage to Europe, in company with an early and most intimate friend." There can be little doubt that this friend was no other than the subject of the present memoir. "For such a visit he was eminently prepared by his course of study, his avidity in pursuit of knowledge, and his acquaintance with the French and German languages. His object was to travel through the most interesting literary fields of Europe, and to repair to the chief universities of Germany, to acquire the languages, and to complete his familiarity with biblical and classical antiquities, Oriental letters, and the natural sciences. There was every reason to believe that on his return he would have received a professorship in one of our most distinguished colleges. His passport was already obtained, his companion was awaiting his recovery, and letters of recommendation were furnished. "In some of these letters, kindly furnished by Professors in Yale College, he is characterized as "a young man of extensive scientific and literary attainments, well skilled in the Hebrew language, and otherwise learned." But Providence was opening his way to "a better country, even a heavenly."

His symptoms from this time forward grew gradually worse. He became weak and emaciated; "his visage assumed the hue of death," and no one could fail to recognize in him the victim of pulmonary consumption. All remedies failed; and he was evidently drawing near his end. "He was generally exempt from acute pain, and complained chiefly of a lassitude which was almost insupportable." He was fully prepared to lay aside the frail earthly tabernacle. All his hopes were fixed on Christ and heaven.

In the month of July, he set out in company with a younger brother, for the Red Sulphur Springs of Virginia, which have been supposed to possess a specific virtue in such cases. Just before his departure an intimate acquaintance, with whom he cherished a confidential intercourse from childhood, embraced a last effort of drawing from him a statement of his religious views. Rezeau Brown was much interested, and though he lay panting for breath upon the sofa, entered into a free conversation. His friend addressed him thus: "Tell me frankly, Rezeau, what is the prospect which you entertain of recovery?" He answered much as follows:

"'I have no expectation of recovery. I am fully acquainted with the nature of my disease, and aware that I am a dying man. Sometimes an illusive hope plays about me; but my prevalent judgment is, that I am not long for this world.'

"'And now, my dear R., what effect has this expectation on your feelings? Do you regard death with terror?'

"'Not at all,' he replied; 'I am relieved from all fear, and entertain a calm hope of heaven.' He then proceeded, in words not now remembered, to give a clear and satisfactory account of his trust in Christ, and his resignation to the will of God. There was no rapture, nor any strong excitement of feeling; indeed this seemed, in his case, to be precluded by the sedative and benumbing influence of the disease; but every word indicated a serene waiting till his change should come.'

"He came back from the Springs without benefit. This was on the 4th of September; and though he had talked delightfully and peacefully during the homeward journey, he was now too ill to speak. He declined the visits of any friends, except two, with each of whom he conversed a few moments."

Who can doubt that these were the brothers James and Addison Alexander; who were the two friends of his bosom, and who clung to him in mournful apprehension that they should be soon called upon to receive his last adieux?

"To a brother who inquired after his spiritual frame, two days before his departure, he replied: 'I have experienced some seasons of fluctuation and depression, but my prevailing state is one of established confidence and hope.' There was no visible indication of the change until a short time before he fell asleep in Jesus. His departure was then without a struggle or a groan."

The funeral was largely attended by the people of the neighbourhood and a collection of persons from the literary institutions of Princeton. The discourse was delivered by the Rev. J. W. Alexander, from Rev. xxii. 3–5. Much and tender feeling is said to have been exhibited on this occasion. There was no one who knew him that did not love and admire, and at the same time honour, Rezeau Brown.

In concluding the sketch of his life, his friend and biographer adds, among others, the following interesting particulars:

"It may not be out of place to say that with regard to personal appearance, Mr. Brown possessed every advantage. Though slender, he was above the common height, and had the appearance of greater strength than he really possessed. His whole exterior was marked by graceful dignity; and his calm and somewhat pensive countenance, in which regularity of feature was joined with an expression of intelligence and gentleness, was highly prepossessing of his manners; it is enough to say that he was in every sense of the term a Christian gentleman."

A survivor, confirming every part of this statement, informs me that Rezeau Brown had black hair and very dark eyes, and before his health became hopelessly bad, a clear, delicate, rosy complexion, of the kind which often suggests genius, and in his case painfully betokened an early death. The same person says that he had a sweet face, and was one of the most generous and one of the best-hearted of men.

"His intellectual traits have already been exhibited to some extent. Quick and discursive rather than profound or commanding, his mind attempted almost every department of literature and science. Indeed, such was his inquisitiveness with regard to all useful knowledge, that we may doubt whether his reigning fault was not the diffusion of his powers over too wide a field. Languages both ancient and modern, belles-lettres, criticism, chemistry, physics, anatomy and physiology were his favourite pursuits. In the acquisition of these he manifested a readiness which was astonishing. The versatility of his genius made every subject soon familiar; and the tenacity of his memory rendered these stores available. This was strikingly exemplified in his examination for licensure before the Presbytery of New-Brunswick; on which occasion those who were present were astonished at the compass and precision of his knowledge, and the promptness and pertinency of his replies on every subject.

"As a preacher he was hindered in some degree by constitutional frailty from becoming eloquent. Yet it is not here meant that he was not both acceptable and impressive. Indeed, his improvement in pulpit exercises was rapid and constant, even until his latest public performances. And there was in all his addresses a solemn sincerity, and sometimes a natural pathos, which endeared his ministrations to all who enjoyed them.

"His adversaria and common-place books attest the care with

which he made collections for future labours. Epitomes, criticisms, abstracts and reflections form the greater part of these manuscripts.

"But it is to his character as a Christian, dedicating all his talents and acquirements to the service of Christ, that we turn with most satisfaction. * * Of the spirit and character of his preaching, as truly as of any man's that I have ever heard, I think the description of the Apostle Paul's preaching to the Corinthians may be sued: 'For I determined to know nothing among you, save Jesus Christ and him crucified!' His labours were incessant—too great for his debilitated state of health. It is well known that a desire to do good, and a love for his Master's work, would not allow him to enjoy the relaxation which was necessary. A respectable number were added to the Church during his six months' labour, and many—even the most lawless and thoughtless—were occasionally made to feel and reflect under his discourses."

It was impossible that Addison Alexander should not be most painfully affected by the death of his nearest and best friend. He was in Italy when the sad event occurred; but five months after, at Berlin, in a moment of restless and characteristic longing for change, and a strong desire for home, "or ever he was aware," he seems to have been overwhelmed by a sudden rush of recollections, and at once poured out his whole soul in the following pathetic poem, which it may be well to say, was immediately suggested by a conversation in which he had just been engaged with some friend on the closing scene of Schleiermacher. It was written with great rapidity, in his ordinary journal. The handwriting, by its irregularity and fiery speed, shows the presence of some vivid emotion.

"The plan was laid. The hour was nigh.
  Both were resolved to brave
The tempest's terrors and to try
  The swiftness of the wave.
To-day where art thou? where am I?
Alone, beneath a foreign sky,
  And thou art in thy grave!
While I careered before the gale,
  And the auspicious blast

> Filled the deep bosom of the sail,
>   And bowed the sturdy mast;
> Thy pallid cheek became more pale,
> Thy secret springs began to fail,
>   Thy life was ebbing fast.
> While I, through Latium's blasted plain
>   Approached the walls of Rome,
> Where o'er a thousand spires and vanes
>   The antichrist's proud dome
> Like an imperial giant reigns;
> Disease had well-nigh loosed the chains,
>   Which kept thee from thy home.
> And while I hastened to explore
>   That world so new to me,
> That grave of empires now no more,
>   How fared it then with thee?
> Ah! thy captivity was o'er.
> Death had unbarred thy dungeon door
>   And set thy spirit free!

There is as much sonorous passion in this verse as in anything he has written. The gates of his soul were not often thus lifted; but when they were, the torrent that came forth was at flood-tide, and bore him impetuously onward, till the gush of feeling had spent itself. He was not known to revert very often to the decease of this amiable and attractive being, but there is every reasonable certainty that he continued to hold his image in his heart, and that for a time it exerted a quickening influence upon his life.

Such was "the manner of man" that the young scholar grappled to his soul with hooks of steel, in the scholastic retirement of Edgehill. Brown, or "Rezeau" (as he called him), was not only the sharer in his literary raptures, but also in joys and sorrows which he imparted to no other outside of his own family.*

---

* As Mr. Alexander commonly burnt his letters, I have succeeded in discovering one only of Rezeau Brown's. It possesses a melancholy interest, now that he is gone, and has been for years forgotten.

"My Dear Friend,

"I am sorry that I am unable to be punctual to our appointed time for

A few words in the journal for June, 1829, show the stout scholar busy upon a book of sacred geography, which he and his brother James afterwards published through the American Sunday School Union.

"June 25. I have undertaken to prepare a book of sacred geography for the American S. S. Union, and am now abridging Rosenmüller's Alterthemskunde.

He had prepared about half when he became "disgusted" with the work and placed his MS. in the hands of his brother James to finish. The following letter from his coadjutor bears upon the subject:

"*September* 2, 1829.

" CARISSIME,

"I wrote to Porter according to promise and informed him that I was about completing your geography. On looking over the ground I find that I have a hard path to travel—for instance, the ethno-genealogico-geographico-mythico representations about the early settlers. Is it possible to concrete or abstract Rosenmüller's discourse into any thing tolerable? I beg you, notwithstanding the disgust you have acquired for the labour, to achieve *l'impossible*, and, without delay, make out an abstract of *Phœnicia*, and such other parts as you have in the second volume. N. B. I have put the references into parentheses, for your brackets will disfigure the book exceedingly, and I find that small letters look the best: e. g. (Josh. xliii; 10, 11. Hab. lxxxviii. 7, 9). Set about this, and we may hope to have the whole thing accomplished this month. Make yourself a paper book and leave an inch blank at the fold of the sheet. Your MS. is almost intangible (ut ita dicam), one must handle it as tenderly as a scroll of Herculaneum.

I have got all done (errors excepted) except Band I. Theil I. and *Die biblische west*, in the end of the green one. I have carefully verified all the references, many of which, either from typographical errors or different division of chapter or verse, are irrelevant. I have taken a reading together. The sickness of my mother called me to Lawrence on Saturday evening, and I think of going again to-night.

"Nothing but a duty of such a kind—or one equally important—would induce me to be absent from these exercises. Yours,

"Monday evening. R. B."

good deal from Mansford, who, by-the-way, is wrong wherever he is original. Rosenmüller strangely says (upon Tarsus) that Gamaliel had a school *there*. Paul's words are: "brought up at the feet of Gamaliel in *this* city." * By the first opportunity I will send my MS. as far as done. I have numbered the folios consecutively after yours. Leave what you may write unpaged.

"J. W. A."

The advice here given was taken, and the book appeared as the joint work of the two brothers.†

So far as I am aware this little book was the pioneer of its class in the country. Other and fuller works have since appeared; but probably none so compendious, and few more carefully built up upon ascertained facts.

"Sept. 2. Read in Job, 34–36 chapters. Read in German the fifth (and last) act of Schiller's Wallenstein. This play, though a very fine one, is too long. Schiller had not in perfection the faculty mentioned by Pope 'of rejecting his own thoughts.'‡ His plots, too, are somewhat obscure. The characters in this play are not so strongly marked as in Don Carlos, nor the tragic interest so deep and overwhelming. I rank it therefore below that notable tragedy in the scale of merit, but, at the same time, infinitely above the common run of modern dramas. Read in Spanish 'La Conquista de Mejico IV: 17–20.' Read in English the remainder of the 'Essay on Criticism,' 'The Rape of the Lock,' and the 'Elegy to the Memory of an Unfortunate Lady;' also a few chapters in Denham and Clapperton's 'Travels in Africa.' Read in Latin half of Schultens's translation of Extracts from the *Hamasa*. Read in Hebrew with R. Brown, 2 Samuel, 7–9. Received a note from J. W. A. with his MS. of the Sacred Geography.

* See a full account of this matter in Conybeare and Howson.

† In a letter dated September 14, 1829, his brother James thus refers to the joint literary task in which they had been engaged:

"Addison has consigned to me his papers and notes upon Sacred Geography, and I have been engaged in finishing the book [for the A. S. S. U.], so that we shall have it between us. The labour has been very irksome. I spent twelve hours last week verifying the texts of Scripture referred to, by looking for all of them. The mere geographical part is very interesting. Altogether it is discouraging to find how little is really known of the site of many ancient places."—Familiar Letters, vol I., p. 134.

‡ Oddly enough, Goethe somewhere attributes to Schiller this very power.

"Sept. 3. Read in Hebrew Job, 27-28: in German, 'The Sorrows of Werther': about forty pages. Goethe has in eminent degree the quality which I thought was wanting in his compeer Schiller. Though minute in his descriptions and details, all seems compact and condensed; there are no loose ends—no *purpurii panni*. He has also the enviable power of describing simple familiar things without the least tincture of mawkish affectation. Read in Pope's works: 'Sappho to Phaon,' 'Eloisa to Abelard,' and 'The Temple of Fame.' In Eloisa to Abelard there are abundant specimens of rich and polished diction; but what particularly charms me is this exquisite paragraph, especially the last couplet, which I think inimitably beautiful:

> "For thee, the Fates, severely kind, ordain,
> A cool suspense from pleasure and from pain;
> Thy life a long, dead calm of fixed repose,
> No pulse that riots, and no blood that glows;
> Still as the sea, e'er winds were taught to blow,
> Or moving spirits bade the waters flow;
> Soft as the slumbers of a saint forgiven,
> And mild as opening gleams of promised heaven."*

"Read also Denham and Clapperton.—In Hebrew, 2 Sam. chaps. 10-12, with R. Brown.—Finished Schultens's Extracts from the *Hamasa*."

"Sept. 4. Read in Hebrew, Job, 39-40. In German, the beginning of the chapter on Phœnicia in Rosenmüller's Alterthumskunde. Read in Pope's works: 'January and May,' and 'The Wife of Bath.' I cannot help feeling contempt for a great genius who would select such passages for imitation as these obscene absurdities of Chaucer. The grossness is considerably refined, but enough remains to make them disgusting. J. W. A. came with the remainder of the Geography. Read and abridged Rosenmüller's chapter on Phœnicia.

"Sept. 15. Read in Hebrew 1 Kings, 5-6. Revised and corrected Sacred Geography (in part). Read in Spanish El Fray Gerundio. Read in Hebrew with R. Brown, 1 Chron. 16-19. Read the Dunciad. I have lately read over all Pope's poems, except his Homer. He has far more wit than I supposed, but very little splendour or elevation of genius, it appears to me. He seems perfectly cold and heartless too. Johnson's remark is just that Pope does not seem to have composed with ease. His rhymes are often imperfect and his epithets ill-

---

* Lines 250-255.

chosen. All his writings are elaborated with much pain and difficulty. He uses upon elevated subjects more colloquial language than a poet of these times would. Finally, like Swift, he is evidently fond of obscene images."

Mr. Alexander had about this time more serious employment for his pen than scribbling random paragraphs for the Patriot and the Emporium, or writing verses and essays for Dr. Snowden's magazine. He now appears for the first time as a contributor to the pages of the Biblical Repertory, which has since, and largely through his influence, become well-known, and which was afterwards to be adorned by some of the maturest results of his scholarship and genius.

His brother, writing to Dr. Hall from his room in the college, where he was then tutor of mathematics, thus refers to the projected publication. The letter is dated September 20, 1828, just about the time that Mr. Alexander was admitted to the Junior class.

"You have here another prospectus of another Princeton work, which I trust will prove honourable to us, and useful to the cause."*

This plan was fully and successfully carried out, and resulted in the appearance of the *Biblical Repertory*, which, begun in 1825, is still continued under the charge of its original editor.

If my memory serves me, the first volume was entirely filled by the Rev. Charles Hodge and the Rev. J. W. Alexander. This I was told once by the latter. The second volume, besides a number of reprints from foreign sources, contained translations from the pen of the editor Mr. Hodge, Prof. Patton, President James Marsh (then Professor at Hampden Sidney), and others. The first appearance of Mr. Alexander in the pages of the Repertory was in 1827, in an article translated from John Alphonso Turretin, entitled, "Refutation of the Hypothesis of the Papists in Relation to the Interpretation of the Scriptures." † This article at once

---

* Familiar Letters, Vol. I., p. 65. † See Bib. Rep., 1827, p. 275.

excited notice, and was attributed in Boston to Dr. Archibald Alexander. This was immediately followed by a translation from Justin the Martyr, entitled "Exhortation to the Greeks." The style of this article is exceedingly mature, and the rendering of the Greek idiom not only of the Christian Father but of the classical authors to whom he copiously refers, exceedingly happy. The diction is pure and terse, and the language for the most part Saxon, or remarkably strong and idiomatic English. While he availed himself freely of the helps at hand in interpreting Homer, the translations from less familiar writers seem to be his own. I may cite by way of example the words of Orpheus to Musaeus and his other children (p. 341), commencing,

$$\Phi\theta\epsilon\gamma\xi o\mu a\iota\ o\hat{i}s\ \theta\epsilon\mu\iota s\ \epsilon\sigma\tau\grave{\iota},\ \theta\upsilon\rho as\ \delta'\ \epsilon\pi\iota\theta\epsilon\sigma\theta\epsilon\ \beta\epsilon\beta\eta\lambda o\iota$$
$$\Pi\acute{a}\nu\tau\epsilon s\ \acute{o}\mu\hat{\omega}s\cdot\ \sigma\upsilon\ \delta'\ \ddot{a}\kappa o\upsilon\epsilon\ \phi a\epsilon\sigma\phi\acute{o}\rho o\upsilon\ \ddot{\epsilon}\kappa\gamma o\nu\epsilon\ \mu\acute{\eta}\nu\eta s,$$

of which he gives a literal and yet spirited and nervous version : *

The Repertory was at this time temporarily in the hands of Professor Patton, who performed the duties of editor in the absence of Mr. Hodge in Europe. Mr. Alexander does not appear to have contributed any thing in 1828. In 1829 the Biblical Repertory, which had been up to that time little more than a series of reprints and translations, was given up

---

* I will speak to those to whom it is allowed. Let the uninitiated be excluded: Listen thou, Musaeus, child of the shining moon, while I utter the truth, nor let that which has before been infused into thy breast, deprive thee of thy precious life. Behold the Divine Word, and give thyself wholly to it, ordering aright the intelligent receptacle of thy heart. Come up hither, and contemplate the sole King of the universe. He is one. He is self-existent. He alone created all things. Though good himself, he gives evils to his creatures, bloody wars, and lamentable sorrows, and besides him there is no supreme king. I cannot behold him; for clouds are round about him, and the mortal pupils of mortal eyes are unable to look upon the ruler of the universe. He is established upon the brazen heavens. He sits upon a golden throne and treads with his feet upon the earth, and stretches out his right hand to all the ends of the ocean. Then the lofty mountains tremble, the rivers, and the depths of the hoary sea.

by Mr. Hodge its founder into the hands of "an association of gentlemen," to be published as a quarterly Review.*

The change in the form and aims of the Journal took place, as was contemplated in the new prospectus, at the beginning of the year 1830. With 1830 also commences the present numbering of the volumes. The periodical from this time until 1837 bears the title of "Biblical Repertory and Theological Review," and may be considered as embracing in its plan the whole range of theological and religious subjects. The ninth volume, which was issued in 1837, is the first of the whole collection which bears the title Biblical Repertory and Princeton Review. It had already fallen under "the direction" of the coterie of Presbyterian clergymen and literary gentlemen of Princeton and its environs, as early as the beginning of 1829. Mr. Patton seems to have been the most active spirit of the new management, though the Professors of the Seminary and College, and such men as the Rev. Mr. Yeomans, Professor Marsh, Professor Bush, the Rev. (now Doctor) R. J. Breckinridge, to say nothing of a host of others, lent valuable assistance. Mr. Hodge returned from Europe, where he had been pursuing a course of study at the German universities, in 1828, and delivered his introductory lecture to his class in the Seminary on the seventh of November of that year. He began by saying:

"In entering anew upon my duties in this institution, I feel constrained to acknowledge the goodness of God, by which I have been so kindly preserved, and restored to the field of labour to which he has called me. As it was a desire to become more useful to you, that led me to leave for so protracted a period, my friends and country, my heart has been continually turned towards this institution; and it frequently occurred to me, that should I live to return to my native land, I would endeavour to impress upon your minds the practical truths which the circumstances of foreign states and countries had deeply impressed upon my own. It is true the vividness of these impressions has faded away, but the convictions in which they resulted remain." . . . .

* See advertisement to the fourth volume.

It is no doubt to the personal influence of Mr. Hodge that the Repertory is indebted for the original labours of Professor Tholuck, by which its columns were about this time occasionally enriched.

From the date of his return from Europe Mr. Hodge again gave much time to the Review, and after the removal of Mr. Patton from Princeton became once more its sole editor, and has continued to this day to be one of its chief writers and its sustaining and animating spirit.

Some of the very best things ever written by Dr. Archibald Alexander and Dr. Miller, were written in the first instance for this publication. The same may be said of that brilliant genius and lamented clergyman, Prof. Albert B. Dod, of the College of New Jersey. The brothers James and Addison Alexander also continued their connection with the periodical, and now began to write original articles. In after years, as long as they lived, they were still accustomed from time to time to make use of "the Repertory" as the chosen vehicle of their learned and graceful disquisitions upon all subjects which were suited to the pages of such a Journal. In 1838, we learn from his own diary, Mr. Alexander became for a short time one of the editors, and wrote more copiously than ever. A number of these articles were afterwards republished, with strong eulogy, in the pages of an eclectic quarterly which made its appearance periodically in Scotland. The volume for 1829 contained, besides Professor Hodge's Introductory Lecture, and a number of valuable criticisms and dissertations, a biographical sketch of Erasmus, drawn mainly from sources furnished by Adolph Müller in his "Leben des Erasmus von Rotterdam," &c. This life-like portrait of the great scholar of the Reformation has been attributed to the subject of this memoir, and is claimed by him in a catalogue of his own articles which he made years after. * The only articles

---

* This is possibly a mistake, as Mr. Alexander said he was uncertain about some of the articles on his own list of his own contributions, and as in his brother's copy this article on Erasmus bears the characteristic signature, in pencil, "By J. W. Alexander." It is possible that both had a hand in it.

certainly contributed to this volume by Addison (as he was and still is, fondly called by the various members of his father's family) were the translations from the Latin of Flatt on the Deity of Christ, and an elaborate effort entitled "The History and Religious Opinions of the Druses." Of these articles the former was in reality one, but was divided into two parts which appeared at different times, the first part constituting the leading treatise of the volume. This performance does not fail to show the same acquaintance with the technical terms of the seventeenth century which had led the literati of Boston to attribute the translation of Alphonso Turretin, which came out the year before, to the father; never once suspecting that the article in question was by his precocious son. These able reproductions of the theological Latin writers of the post-Reformation period may, however, be safely set down to the guiding influence of Dr. Alexander, who had more to do than any one else in giving shape and direction to his son's studies, and who, as is well known, was himself a devoted admirer of the old vellum quartos and folios of the age immediately succeeding the times of Erasmus and Luther.

But in his second article for the year 1829, Mr. Alexander must have broken away from all restraints, however wise and gentle, and followed the bent of his own strong inclinations and enthusiastic genius. The essay on "the Druses" is one of the most singular and startling demonstrations, among the many that he has left us, of his learning and capacity. The theme was one which exactly suited him. It was strange, mysterious, difficult, romantic; calling for all the hidden resources of his historical and linguistic attainments; as well as for all the acumen of his intellect, and delicacy of his critical judgment; and bringing into play not only his powers of reason and analysis, but his impassioned energy, his talent for rapid and graphic description, and his talent, no less surprising in one who was still scarcely out of his teens, for the mere construction of a sentence. The aim of the article is to arrive, if possible, at an approximate solution of the vexed questions touching the origin and early history of this mysterious fraternity or sect of the *Mowahhidûn* of Mount Libanus. The treatise is mainly historical and critical, but it is marked by broad outline views, and vigorous generalizations, together with a marvellous acquaintance with the repositories of oriental learning, and with every thing relating to the oriental people, and particularly the Arabs; as well as by masterly sketches of character, and lively and engaging but condensed narrative. As a specimen of his narrative style, there are perhaps some who will be pleased to have their attention directed to the following extract:

"The notorious prince just mentioned (Hakem Biamrillah) was the fifth Fatimite sovereign after Obeidallah, and the third who reigned in Egypt. He ascended the throne, A. H. 386, at a very early age; and after some years of fickle and inactive government, began to exhibit symptoms of the wildest madness, combined with the most extravagant impiety. His official acts at this period of his reign, as recorded by Makrizi, are pitiable specimens of mingled folly, insanity, and wickedness. In one of his edicts he commanded all the dogs of Cairo to be massacred; in another he forbids the women of the city to leave their homes on any pretext or at any time. On one day he required that the names of the first three khalifs should be cursed at public worship, and on the next revoked the order. In one decree he would regulate with minuteness and precision the distinctive dress to be worn by Jews and Christians, and before the change could well be made, would issue another altering the fashion and requiring strict obedience upon pain of death. As his malady increased, he grew restless, and passed whole nights in pompous marches through the streets of Cairo, requiring the bazars to be kept open and the shops to be illuminated. With an intellect thus crazed, and under the influence of the wild speculations of the wildest shiahs, it is not surprising that the unhappy monarch became a tool in the hands of ambitious and fanatical impostors, who availed themselves of his insanity, to forward their own schemes of proselytism or aggrandizement." *

So far as I am able to ascertain, he wrote no more for the Repertory that year.

It would be interesting to know precisely when Mr. Alex-

* Bib. Rep. 1829, p. 218.

ander commenced the study of Arabic. It was probably even before he had mastered the Hebrew grammar prepared for him by his father, that is when he was a very little boy. He says himself it was when he was nine or ten years old.*
I have a strong impression that he found an old Arabic grammar on a shelf in " the study," or else in the litter of the attic room already spoken of, and that he had familiarized himself to some extent with its outlandish characters, and, I, think gone through it from cover to cover, before any member of the family knew that he was acquainted with a single orthograpic sign. My impression is that I was told so by a near relative, many years ago. He speaks himself of his "early and almost unnatural proclivity to oriental studies" as belonging to the period of his "boyish dreams," and says that he continued his labours in this strange field, after his college course, at which time he "read the whole of the Koran in Arabic, and the Old Testament in Hebrew." His brother James, in a letter to Dr. Hall dated April 4, 1828, announces that Addison had then just completed the Koran in Arabic, and speaks of it as a work which few had as yet attempted in America. Soon after learning Arabic, he took up Persian, Syriac and Chaldee, but exactly at what time or in what order I cannot tell.

The journal sheds abundant light on these later studies. His first entry so far as is known was on the first of January of that year, on which day, as we have seen, his portion of Arabic was the 19th sura al Koran. The same day he read also the 19th chapter of Exodus in Hebrew, and the day following, the 20th chapter of Exodus in Hebrew and the 16th

* Dr. John S. Hart has substantially confirmed this statement, in a letter to the writer of these pages. He says, " The department of knowledge which he early selected was that of language, and it was as a linguist that he was chiefly known. While reading Arabic with him, I questioned him once as to the origin of his familiarity with that copious tongue. He told me he began the study privately, of his own accord, when he was but ten years old, having found accidentally an old copy of the Arabic grammar on one of the top shelves of his father's library. He seemed as familiar with the Asiatic tongues as with Latin or Greek."

Ode of Hafiz in Persian; and this in addition to allotted work in Italian, Latin, German, Greek, French and Spanish. These records would seem to imply some previous acquaintance with the Arabic and Persian. There can be no doubt that he was somewhat versed in both of these languages from a very early period of his boyhood.

There is a tradition still current among the old students of Princeton Seminary that somewhere about the year 1821 a prize was awarded to Dr. Archibald Alexander for the best essay on Arabic literature, and that the fact was published in the newspapers. The story runs, that alluding to the matter, as was his wont when any thing interested him, at the dinner-table, Dr. Alexander expressed unbounded astonishment that such an error should have been committed, as it was well known that he possessed no special acquaintance with the language; whereupon to the surprise of all present Addison, then a boy of twelve, and who was not supposed to have studied Arabic, admitted with some confusion that *he* had written the article in question, and had signed it A. Alexander, never dreaming that he should get the prize. I only mention this story to contradict it. There is certainly not a word of truth in it: it bears its own refutation on its face; though in different forms it has obtained much currency, and has been repeated in my hearing by a number of highly respectable clergymen. The young scholar would hardly have assumed his father's name in print, or even his favourite initial. Besides this, the facts if true would have been treasured in the family.* The whole thing probably grew out of a mistake of

---

* Since writing the above I have received the following account of the matter from his oldest surviving brother. A comparison of these statements with those of Dr. Beach Jones will probably bring out the full truth relative to the report in question:

"The ground of the rumour about the prize essay was doubtless this. A translation from the Latin made by him was published in the Repertory, then conducted by Prof. Patton during the absence of Prof. Hodge in Europe. A Boston Magazine in speaking of this translation attributed it to Dr. Archibald Alexander, not supposing it likely to be the production of a youth still in his

Mr. Robert Walsh with regard to the authorship of an article in the American Quarterly Review on the subject of *Persian* literature, which will be explained presently. *This* article was written by the son, though at a somewhat later period, and was attributed by Mr. Walsh to the father. It is quite certain, however, that Addison was somewhat acquainted with Arabic literature at twelve years of age; perhaps better acquainted with it than many who were at that time regarded as learned men. It is absolutely certain that he had studied both Arabic and Persian to some degree, and probably also Chaldee and Syriac, before he entered college.

An intimate friend says, in an editorial notice of his death in the Central-Presbyterian, "From his childhood he exhibited the rarest talent. His father removed to Princeton in 1812, and evincing even at that early age great fondness for study, he was allowed to take his own course. From *ten to twelve* he commenced the study of the Arabic, and before fourteen years of age had read the Koran." Dr. Moore has good authority for these statements,* though, as we have seen, Addison did not *complete* the Koran until he was nineteen. The alleged date of his commencement of the study is doubtless sufficiently exact. Mr. Alexander's own expression is "nine or ten." Dr. Moore is of the impression that he commenced the study of Persian very soon afterwards, and in this opinion I agree with him. Indeed he must have done so, if we are to account upon any intelligible hypothesis for the commonest entries in his diary.

It is a sad commentary upon the evanescence of fame that

---

minority. The article may be found in one of the numbers of the Repertory for 1827."

It is a translation from the younger Turretin, and will be found in the volume of the Biblical Repertory for that year, p. 175. The writer was at that time eighteen years old.

* Dr. Hall in the Funeral Sermon. Dr. Hall writes that he cannot vouch for the minute accuracy of these statements, having merely spoken to the best of his recollection on these and similar points.

the name of such a man as the editor of the Philadelphia Gazette and American Quarterly should now be strange to many who think themselves versed in the literature of the day. Mr. Robert Walsh may be said to have been at one time the prince of elegant letters in this country. He was the pioneer of that robust American scholarship which has since made itself felt to the extremities of Europe. His great work in defence of America against England * is one of the most vigorous and cogent arguments that has ever been penned. He was a close student and happy imitator of the Latin classics. His knowledge of current literature in the various languages of the Continent was amazing. His English style seems to have been influenced by that of Canning, for whose talents as a writer he entertained an extravagant admiration. It has been said of Macaulay that he is almost the only master of modern English who has left no sentence that cannot be strictly parsed. The same high praise is perhaps due to Mr. Walsh.† He was in his generation honoured by the crowned sovereigns of France, and performed his part in the cultivated society of the French capitol with grace and dignity, and with a singular measure of affable tact and *savoir faire*. He was the Mæcenas ‡ of tasteful art in every form, in an age that did not lack its Maros. He encouraged every

---

* The title-page now before me runs as follows:

"An Appeal from the Judgments of Great Britain respecting the United States of America. Part First. Containing an Historical Outline of their Merits and Wrongs as Colonies; and Strictures upon the Calumnies of the British Writers. By Robert Walsh, Jr.

'Quod quisque fecit, patitur: autorem scelus
Repetit, suoque premitur exemplo nocens.—*Senec.*

"Second Edition: Philadelphia, published by Mitchell, Ames & White. William Brown, Printer, 1819,"

† Mr. Walsh is described by Dr. Hall as being a man below the medium height, with sandy hair and a dignified, intellectual face. He wore spectacles.

‡ "Sunt Mæcenates, non deerunt, Flacci Marones."—*Martial*, 8. 56.

honourable aspirant, and many a modest young man owed his success in life to this generous protection. Mr. Walsh was not slow to perceive merit; and was one of the first to give a helping hand to the two sons of Dr. Archibald Alexander, who were then just struggling into print. His letters to the elder of these youths are full of kindness and wise counsel. There is an admirable and affectionate account of him in the pages of the Princeton Magazine,* which is the work of his friend Dr. Hall of Trenton.

There are numerous allusions to the great *littérateur*, in the Familiar Letters to Dr. Hall. Writing from Trenton, May 4, 1829, his correspondent says:

"I entertain lively anticipations with regard to the results of your introduction to the modern Johnson. There are few men in the country whose acquaintance would be a greater prize. May you have many profitable and pleasant hours in his conversazioni. I hope that you will come forth from the den of lions, unscathed as Daniel."

Again, April 17, 1835, he says:

"I shall miss Walsh very much if he goes abroad, for his pithy paragraphs have become a necessary condiment."

On another occasion he points out a single error in Walsh's English, viz., the saying "I doubt *that*," for "I doubt *whether*." (Vol. I. p. 246.) On still another occasion, writing from Princeton, he says:

"I would subscribe two prices for a bona fide old-time Walshian gazette. I owe something to that man.

"'But why then publish? Granville the polite
And *knowing Walsh* would tell me I could write.'"—POPE.

Writing from Charlotte Court-House, Oct. 27, 1840, soon after a visit to the University of Virginia, he says:

---

* Princeton Magazine, p. 361. The single volume of this periodical has been long out of print.

"Their professors do more, especially in the way of lecture, than any I know. Bonnycastle is a wonderful man for genius and learning. Tucker is a man of elegant *English* gentlemanhood; just like Walsh in the cast of his mind, and his talk."

Still again he writes to Dr. Hall:

" One of the few things I can read is Walsh's Letters to the National Intelligencer."

And on Jan. 6, 1843:

"Walsh writes with as much vigour and pith as ever for the National Intelligencer. He gave Baird a grand *feu de joie* in his last. His health is quite good."

And in 1844 he writes, still in the same strain:

"I rejoice that Walsh has the Consulship. * * I never tire of his *ana*, which are copious during the vacation of Congress."

And in 1846:

"Walsh's letters in the National Intelligencer are equal to his best days."

On the 30th of June, 1851, we have the following interesting entry in the epistolary journal kept by the older brother when he was in Paris:

"Mr. Walsh has gone out to St. Germain-en-Laze. He sent me a most warm and characteristic letter, *mistaking me for Addison*, and went to the Director of the National (once Royal) Library, *and requested that I might be introduced to the principal Orientalists of Paris.*" *

It was with unalloyed pleasure that the vigorous and kind-hearted old man looked back years after upon the start of these young writers, whom he had helped on to fame.

It was doubtless with a certain sense of satisfaction that Mr. Alexander found that his venturous efforts in unaccus-

* The Italics are mine

tomed fields of literature were not slighted by the famous Philadelphia critic, but were inserted among the essays of well-known scholars, and suffered to make their way in the world, under the most favourable auspices. Little did he know, however, what a sensation he had created in the higher circles of American criticism. A thrill of surprise would no doubt have shot through his heart, if he had been informed of the terms in which the terrible and fastidious Mr. Walsh was speaking of his contributions, and especially those on Oriental studies and literature. No further evidence is needed of Mr. Alexander's great proficiency at this time in Arabic and Persian, and indeed the Oriental languages in general, than will result from a simple perusal of his very earliest printed articles on these subjects. These efforts were universally admired for the "reach of scholarship" they displayed and their comprehensive yet easy mastery of the topics handled. Astonishment was expressed that so much genius and learning had lain so long *perdu* and almost unsuspected. The reminiscences which immediately follow are from the pen of Dr. S. B. Jones of Bridgeton, N. J. Referring to the subject of this biographic outline, he says:

"My earliest acquaintance with the fame of this illustrious man dates back as far as the year 1831. In the fall of that year I removed to Princeton; where I resided for four years. Young as Mr. Alexander was when I went to Princeton" [twenty-two years old], "he had even then acquired the reputation of a prodigy in scholarship, and especially in his acquaintance with Oriental languages and literature."

Among the articles furnished by him for the American Quarterly Review, edited by Mr. Walsh of Philadelphia, was one on the Persian Language or Literature.* The number of the Review containing this article the writer of the recollec-

---

* "Mr. Alexander reviewed Mohammedan History in the American Quarterly Review, March 1830, and the Gulistan of Sadi, and Anthon's Horace, in *September* 1830."—Forty Years' Familiar Letters of J. W. Alexander, D. D. Vol. I., p. 135.

The article on the Gulistan may be the one referred to by Dr. Jones. If

tions I am now using has unfortunately lost: but he well remembers reading it with wonder and admiration; and was induced to peruse it by the following incident, which goes to show the maturity of Mr. Alexander's views, as well as the extent of his erudition, at a very early age.

Mr. Walsh was professedly a Romanist, but of a Rationalistic type. It is Dr. Jones's judgment that as such he could have little affinity for so decided a Protestant and so prominent a Calvinistic divine as Dr. Archibald Alexander; while for various reasons he was inclined to depreciate and stand aloof from Presbyterians. I give the rest in his own words: "Upon one occasion, after expressing to a friend disparaging opinions of the Presbyterian clergy, he remarked that there was one Presbyterian minister with whom he would like to be personally acquainted; and this was Dr. Alexander of Princeton. Somewhat surprised that Dr. Alexander should possess attractions for one of such opposite views and tastes as Robert Walsh, the friend enquired his reasons; when Mr. Walsh replied, that 'he was so rare and eminent an Orientalist.' Knowing that Dr. Alexander was not preeminent in this department, the friend informed him that he must have confounded Dr. Alexander's son with his father; that the younger Alexander was familiar with several Oriental languages with which the father had no acquaintance. Mr. Walsh, however, questioned the correctness of his friend's opinion, on the ground that the article, or articles, sent to his Review evinced a maturity of mind and a thoroughness and reach of scholarship which clearly indicated that they had been written by an old rather than by a young scholar."*

The letter I am now to give, from Mr. Alexander to Mr.

not, all trace of it is now lost. The Doctor has since informed me that my conjecture as to the missing number is correct, and that the only gap in the series is for September 1830; which seems to put the question at rest. If there were another link necessary to the chain of demonstration it is furnished by Dr. Hart of Trenton, who has seen the article on "Gulistan and Sadi" in the Philadelphia Library, and says it is in the number in question.

* One of Mr. Alexander's brothers writes: "I know nothing of the article

Hall, refers to another contribution from the pen of the former, and which I take to be the same which is mentioned in the Familiar Letters under title of "Mohammedan History." †
Mr. Walsh was evidently much pleased with it.

"DEAR SIR,
"I have just received your obliging letter dated yesterday, for which accept my thanks. I am heartily chagrined and sorry, that my evil fortune should have led me to write upon a subject any how allied to that selected by an abler writer, and then to aggravate the evil by adopting the same text. It will certainly look very strange to have

to which you refer. * * * From the first establishment of the American Quarterly Review, my brothers James and Addison were regular contributors, and the articles forwarded by them were varied and numerous. They had at an earlier day contributed articles to the columns of the National Gazette, a paper established and edited by Mr. Walsh. I imagine that the desire of Mr. Walsh to meet Dr. Alexander, was not caused particularly by the article to which you allude. Mr. Walsh spent his life in a state of bewilderment on this subject, always confounding the father with the sons. He would write to my father on the subject of articles furnished by my brothers, and sometimes sent him a cheque in payment for articles written by them. There is no person living who is fully informed on the subject of these early contributions except the Rev. Dr. Hall of Trenton. Dr. Hall then resided in Philadelphia, and I am under the impression that all articles passed through his hands on their way to Mr. Walsh. The subject of Persian Literature was a favourite one with Addison. I think that long before the establishment of the American Quarterly he furnished an article on the subject to the Philadelphia Monthly Magazine, a periodical published and edited by Dr. J. C. Snowden in 1827 or '28. This was immediately after his graduation. A series of Persian Proverbs and an article on the Persian Language were also written by him and published in the Princeton Magazine."

The article in the Princeton Magazine on the Persian Language not only gives a sketch of its grammatical peculiarities but also of its relations to the Semitic and the Indo-European Group. The article is short, and so far as the nature of the subject would admit, eminently popular. The other contribution to the Princeton Magazine is nothing but a string of translated proverbs.

Dr. Hall thus alludes to the point, in a letter dated March 27, 1867: "You refer to his connexion with Mr. Walsh and the American Quarterly (not North American) Review. I do not think this went beyond his furnishing a few articles. I know that Walsh was always confounding the three Alexanders."

† Vid. sup.

two nominal reviews of the same work in a single number. I have even felt some disposition to withdraw my article; but if the editor is content to have such a duplicate, I suppose I might as well agree to it. The English of the titles is as follows:

1. Thousand and One Nights, in Arabic, &c. Edited by Dr. M. Habicht.

2. Thousand and One Nights, translated in full by M. Habicht, von der Hagen, and K. Schall.

The running title might be 'Rise and Progress of the Khalifat.'

With respect to the sheets, I entrust them cheerfully to your inspection if you will undertake the task.

I must beg to have two notes inserted, which are wanting in the MS. I cannot designate the proper place of either, but leave that to your judgment. The first relates to the opinion expressed of the character of the Koran, and is in these words. 'It may be asked how this view of the case is to be reconciled with the enthusiastic admiration of the Koran as a literary composition, which prevails among Mohammedans. The answer is, that its merit, in their eyes, or rather in their ears, is altogether metrical and musical. To use the words of a distinguished orientalist: 'Sa superiorité consiste moins dans l'invention et dans les images, que dans le charme inexprimable de la diction, dans l'admirable harmonie du rythme, et dans le retour des rimes redoublées, qui produisent un si grand effet sur une oreille arabe.' (Von Hammer.) The writer, whom we quote, cites this, indeed, as a proof of genius. To us it is just the contrary; but we cannot enlarge.

The other has reference to the remarks upon the Arabic historians. There are no doubt some exceptions to this sweeping censure of these, Abulfeda and Abulfaraj are among the most respectable.

I cannot conclude without again lamenting my ill luck in seizing upon the Arabian Nights as a victim, at the same time with another critic. It has frightened me effectually out of all the oriental articles which I had projected. The ground is pre-occupied and I relinquish it. Excuse my detaining you so long upon so slight a subject.

Yours, respectfully,
J. Addison Alexander.

Princeton, N. J., Oct. 14, 1829."

The two brothers wrote a few articles for the National Gazette under the same signature, that of "Didymus."* It is

---

* Dr. Hall referring to the articles of "Didymus" in the Gazette, of which

likely enough these articles were remembered by the editor as those of their father. One of these essays is before me now, and is entitled "Coffee."* It appeared in the number of the paper which was issued on the 31st of October 1829, and is complimented, together with another of the series styled 'Plautus,' in one of Mr. Walsh's pithy editorial paragraphs, in the words following, to wit:

"We thank the author of the curious communication on *Coffee*, which we ourselves honour the most among the berries. It is the 'slow poison' that vivified Voltaire's wit until the age of ninety, and would have inspired Lord Byron longer and better than his favourite spirit of the juniper. We can never pardon those who degrade the sovereign grain by giving its name to a powder of rye. The excellent essay on *Plautus*, with the same signature as that of the article on Coffee, shall appear next week."

this one on Coffee was one, testifies that the two brothers wrote under the same signature. The article on Coffee, however, I am assured by another gentleman was by the elder brother. The former says:

"Your father and uncle undertook to write for the National Gazette of Philadelphia (Mr. Walsh's) both under that signature. I do not remember whether it went further than this on 'Coffee,' and two by your father; one on 'Plautus'—which, with some other of his (James's) articles in the Gazette, &c., I find copies of."

* The Coffee article is a lively recital of the causes leading to the condemnation of this beverage in the Koran, and winds up with an old Sheikh's expression of wonder that it should be possible ' to extract from a husk such an exquisite drink with the odour of musk and the colour of ink."

CHAPTER VI.

In the month of November 1829, Prof. Robert Patton opened a high-school in Princeton, and Addison Alexander, then a youth of nineteen, became the teacher of Latin, Modern and Ancient History, Ancient Geography and Composition. As no man, with one exception, had more influence than Mr. Patton in moulding his intellectual character, a notice of that gentleman will not be out of place here.

Robert Bridges Patton, the man to whom Mr. Alexander was so deeply indebted in his philological studies, was the son of a gentleman who had been at one time the post-master of Philadelphia. He studied law with Alexander James Dallas, and afterwards (in 1814) entered Middlebury College. He was graduated at Yale in 1817. Soon after his graduation he was appointed tutor at Middlebury. In 1818 he sailed for Europe, and spent some time at the German Universities, and on his return was appointed Professor at Middlebury. In 1825 he received the appointment of Professor of Languages in the College of New Jersey, a position he held till 1829, when he resigned and set up the Edgehill School. This school was most successful, and he abandoned it when in its most successful state. After leaving Edgehill he became an enthusiast in Natural History and especially Ornithology, and soon after an equally great enthusiast in Anatomy. While at Edgehill he put forth an edition of Donnegan's Greek Lexicon, in the preparation of which the principal burden of the work fell to the share of his gifted associate, Addison Alexander. In 1833 Mr. Patton sailed for Europe, and returned in 1834 in the ship with Mr. Alexander. On his return he was appointed Greek professor in the University of New York. He was undoubtedly a learned man, though his learning was confined mainly to the ancient and modern languages and natural history.

In regard to Mr. Alexander's connection with the preparation of a new edition of Donnegan's Greek Lexicon,* the Rev. S. B. Jones, D. D. of Bridgeton, N. J., writes:

"How well he had established his reputation as a Grecist is proved by the fact that so distinguished a scholar as Professor R. B. Patton, in preparing his first American edition of Donnegan's Greek Lexicon, sought the assistance of this precocious young man; of whom in his Preface, dated June 13th, 1832, he thus speaks: 'I have received also much valuable assistance from my esteemed friend, Prof. J. A. Alexander of Nassau Hall; and while I make my most grateful acknowledgments of his services, cannot but regret that much of his assiduous and faithful labour was in a measure lost; inasmuch as the second English edition had anticipated to such an extent the additional articles prepared for the American edition.'"

An account of the sort of work it was which is here briefly alluded to will be found in the young professor's diary for that period. German scholarship was ransacked by the as yet unknown critic and made to yield many valuable additions to the improvements suggested by the American labourer.

In the early part of the year 1829, the Rev. Isaac V. Brown, the principal of a classical school at Lawrenceville, N. J., had invited Mr. Alexander to become the teacher of Greek in his academy. This invitation he accepted conditionally, but never entered upon the work. It nevertheless stimulated him to lay the foundation of that wonderful knowledge of Greek, which in connection with his Biblical studies, and especially the study of the New Testament, was the glory of his life.

A gentleman who often walked the streets of Princeton in those days,† thus writes, in a letter from which a few extracts are taken:

---

* See Donnegan's Greek and English Lexicon: Boston, Hilliard, Gray & Co.; New York, G. & C. Carvill & Co.

† The Rev. J. B. Adger, D.D., now a professor in Columbia Seminary, S. C., but then a student at Princeton.

"I had no personal acquaintance with Mr. Alexander except of the slightest kind. But I well remember the reverence I had for him as a *great scholar* even when he was a young man, and I was a boyish student at Princeton Seminary in 1829-33. He was at that time I believe not even a professor of religion, but we all knew that he was skilled in the Oriental tongues, and a thorough Biblical critic. How often have I gazed in admiration at the mysterious recluse who once in a couple of months perhaps crossed my track as at long intervals he took his unaccustomed walk. They said of him that he was full of fun among children, but neither men nor boys, so far as I know, could approach him. And I believe he had hardly any lady acquaintances. He was deep in love with books, and his communion was with the mighty dead and in outlandish tongues. The church in these days has had few such lights as Addison Alexander."

But fortunately on some of these points we have a better witness than has yet been brought to the stand, and the only one who could speak with absolute decision—I mean Mr. Alexander himself. I here insert out of chronological order a letter to his brother James, which covers in a general way all this ground, and darts a strong and steady light into the past and into the future. It certainly makes the period of which I am now treating, brightly luminous. This letter, to change the figure, is indeed the master key to the writer's intellectual history. It derives a peculiar interest from the fact that it was written on the completion of his half-century, and only a few months before his brother's death. From it we gather, what we should not otherwise have known, that he really thought at one time of emulating Lane and Burckhardt, and becoming a denizen of the East ("not New-England but הַקֶּדֶם," perhaps) in the garb of a turbaned sheikh, and that he was originally impelled to form this purpose not from any fervour of piety, but simply and solely to study the languages and become acquainted with the scenery and manners. The joke about his fear lest the Moslems should be Christianized before he got there, will be enjoyed with a relish impossible in other cases, by those who were thoroughly acquainted with the writer, and can remember his quick, half-bashful utterance at such times, and the quizzical gleam of his eye. He informed one of his connections subsequently that he had at one time intended going to one of these countries as a missionary, and was only deterred from doing so by the strenuous exertions of one of his most valued friends. This must have been at a somewhat later period, for he says that he was not actuated at this time by any zeal for souls. Whether his usefulness in the Church would or would not have been impaired by such a step, it is impossible for man to determine; he himself did not undertake to decide. If he had gone to Constantinople, or India, or Persia, it is hardly a frivolous thought that the fame of such Orientalists as Sir William Jones and Eli Smith might have been equalled—possibly eclipsed; or if he had ventured to penetrate, like Burckhardt, in disguise into the strong fastnesses of Idumea, or like Carsten Niebuhr and Palgrave to plunge into the depths of the Arabian Desert, it would not be difficult to believe that with his store of proverbs, his rich acquaintance with the Koran, his knowledge of Eastern history and geography, his early sympathy with the Mussulman's tastes and feelings, his strong imagination, and his glowing eloquence, he might have shaken the souls of the sons of Esau or thrilled the wild heart of the Bedouin, with emotions to which they had before been strangers. Who knows how many poor Mohammedans he might not have succeeded in turning from the crescent to the cross, and in bringing them to a better and more perfect knowledge of him whom they already honour under the title of "Issa Ben Mariam"? But it is idle to speculate about such things. The past is irrevocable, and few would in this instance wish it recalled. The sorrow of the romantic youth when he turned away from this dream (for whether to be lamented or not, it was nothing but a dream), was as short-lived as that of his namesake when his advisers restrained him from crossing the Ganges, and pushing his victories into the heart of India. There were more smiling fields to be entered and other memorable trophies to be won. The joy of new and successful achievements in a very different quarter of the hemisphere soon obliterated every trace of despondency from his mind, if any such remained, with regard to the bursting of this bubble.

It should seem, however, from this letter that notwithstanding his lingering admiration for the literatures of the East, our student at the time to which it mainly refers had already given himself, heart and soul, to the study of that noble language which has embalmed forever the thoughts of Homer, and Herodotus, and Xenophon. This was owing in part to the influence of Professor Patton and of the Edgehill school, with which Mr. Alexander was now connected, and perhaps still more to the more thorough acquaintance with Greek which he obtained in preparing himself to be a teacher of that language in Mr. I. V. Brown's school, a position however which he never filled; as well as to other causes which are detailed in the letter.

The Greek grammar and lexicon now became his constant companions; and a translation of parts of Passow for the new edition of Donnegan, greatly improved his previous acquaintance with the vocabulary and idiom. This change of tastes was not suspected by his friends generally, and yet, when he was appointed tutor in the Seminary (as he tells us himself) he "had already left his first love for a second," and reproached himself for not making this fact known to the Board. Hence, as he thinks, he "began his course with a divided heart," and though he liked the Hebrew, he greatly preferred the Greek, and in private devoted to it a large part of his time and strength. Few will agree with him in supposing that he did wrong thus to follow the strong bent of his genius and feelings, or that the hours taken from the Oriental languages which he had already mastered, were misapplied. If *this* be idleness, or "unfaithfulness to official obligations," would that we had more of it! There is singular modesty and an inimitable *naiveté* in these surprising confessions. In the remarkable autobiographical document which is now to be spread before the reader, the writer lays his whole heart bare to the inquisitive and impartial eye of his sick brother. The opening words speak volumes as to the close and affectionate intimacy that subsisted then, as always, between the two, and the very peculiar and beautiful relation in which they stood the one towards the other—as elder and younger—as adviser and advised. Here is a man at whose word, when that word was stern, the classes trembled, and for whose emphatic voice his colleagues eagerly waited, bending with gentleness and dignity to the judgment of a meek and sorrowful spirit who yet did not hesitate to give candid opinions and express peremptory convictions. They were pleasant in their lives, and in their death they were not far divided. There is much more in the letter, all of which I leave to speak for itself.

May 5, 1859.

My dear Brother:

"Though I never should have made the recent move without your strong concurrence and advice, and though I have consulted you at every step, I feel that I have not yet put you in complete possession of my views and feelings, and, more particularly, of my reasons for adhering to a form and title not entirely in accordance with your better taste and judgment. This I cannot do without being a little autobiographical; to which I am the less averse because this is a critical juncture in my history, not only on account of the proposed change in my position, but because I have just finished my half century. I need not remind you of my early and almost unnatural proclivity to Oriental studies; but it may be news, even to you, that, under the potent spell of Scheherazade and Sir William Jones, it was my cherished wish for several years to settle in the East,—not New England but הַקֶּדֶם—and so far from having any missionary zeal, that I was really afraid the Moslems would be Christianized before I could get at them. This boyish dream was early broken and succeeded by a no less passionate desire to be a lawyer; but my Oriental studies were continued after my college course, at which time I read the whole of the Koran in Arabic and the Old Testament in Hebrew. It is nevertheless true that I had begun already to be weaned from Anatolic to Hellenic studies. The exciting cause of this change was the influence of Patton—first as a teacher, chiefly by his making me acquainted with the German form of classical philology; then by means of his Society [the Philological Society] and library; and lastly, by association with him at Edgehill. This influence, however, would have had no permanent effect, if I had not been led to lay the foundation of my Greek more firmly than it had been laid by Salmon Strong, Horace Pratt, or Robert Baird. Whatever accurate Greek scholarship I have is three years subsequent in date to my graduation, and owes its origin to my having undertaken to teach the language in Brown's school, for which I endeavoured to prepare myself by thoroughly mastering Moore's admirable grammar, which contains the germ of all the late improvements. This I almost learned by heart in Latin, going over it a thousand times as I walked up and down in the old garden, where I am often now reminded of that toilsome but delightful process. Having got the grammar fairly in possession, I read every word of the Anabasis and Cyropædia for the purpose of grammatical analysis, and, having done this, for the first time felt that I was a Greek scholar, even of the humblest rank. All this labour seemed then to be thrown away; as I did not go to Brown's but to Patton's, and not as Greek but Latin teacher! This was more than made good, however, by my lexicographical labours, in translating parts of Passow, for the new edition of Donnegan; and although in this case too, my hard work answered no immediate purpose, its value was inestimable to my own improvement, as I found when I began the next year to teach Greek at College. One effect of all this, never known to others, was, that when I was appointed tutor in the Seminary, I had already left my first love for a second; so that when I heard of John Breckinridge's saying, in the Board, as an apology for moving me, that I was not a classical, but an Oriental scholar, my conscience smote me as a literary hypocrite, for letting the mistake continue. Thus I began my course with a divided heart, and though I never disliked teaching Hebrew, but preferred it much to all my other Seminary duties, I still spent much time upon Greek in private; not without a secret feeling of unfaithfulness to my official obligations. It was this, together with my strong distaste for prophetical studies, and the crushing load of authorship which Dr. Hodge had laid upon me from the first, that made me catch with a sort of eager desperation at the first suggestion of a change in my professorship (in 1845) as promising to free me from a very heavy burden, not so much of labour, as of responsibility, and to bring me somewhat nearer to the studies which I really preferred. A great stride was taken in the same direction when I was unexpectedly, and as I now see providentially, compelled to study and expound the historical books of the New Testament; the most delightful labour of my life, and the direct source of my latest and best publications. I still felt, however, that my studies were not classical; and cherished my old, childish prejudice against the Biblical Greek, as something illiterate and ungrammatical, a mere corruption and abuse of the first language in the world. My earliest glimpse of the modern German doctrine on this subject was afforded by Schaff's admirable chapter in his history, containing little of his own except the clear and captivating mode of presentation, but collecting the best thoughts of the best writers, in relation to the claims of the Hellenistic dialect, as a co-ordinate branch of the Hellenic tree, with a distinctive independent character, and no small merits of its own. From that time (about ten years since) these have been my favourite studies; none the less because connected upon one side with the vast domain of classical philology, and on the other, with the sacred field of Biblical learning. My interest in the language soon extended to the literature of the Hellenistic Jews, inspired and uninspired, as a distinct and well-defined department of ancient learning. It is this that I have always had before my mind, as my proposed field of study and instruction in my many schemes and efforts to attain my true position. It is not merely the New Testament literature, strictly so called, that I wish to cultivate—though that does lie at the foundation, and gives character to all the rest; but I covet the privilege of making excursions, without any violation of official duty, into the adjacent fields of Hellenistic learning, having still in view as my supreme end, the defence and illustration of the Bible, but at the same time opening a new field for literary culture in this country, and thus gaining for myself a more original position than that of simply sharing Green's professorship. I wish it to be fully understood, if the proposed change should be carried out, that while the New Testament department will have greater justice done it than was possible at any former period, it will have something new connected with it; which can only be suggested by a new name, the novelty of which is therefore an advantage, if it be not otherwise objectionable, which I cannot see to be the case. The more I reflect upon it, therefore, the more clearly I perceive that no description could more perfectly express what I have carried out for myself, than that of 'Hellenistic and New Testament Literature."

Affectionately yours,
J. A. A.

It was while at Mr. Patton's school that Mr. Alexander's mind first became deeply impressed with religious things, and that he was led, as he and others believed, to put his trust in a crucified Saviour. Indeed the change in his feelings and purposes was, in his own judgment and in the judgment of his father, directly owing to his first removal from his father's house, to which he was attached with a passionate devotion.

Of his exercises previous to conversion there are no trustworthy memorials. It was hardly to be expected that one whose advantages had been so extraordinary, should not have embraced the truth intellectually at a very early period, and this presumption is rendered almost a certainty by his own subsequent allusions, as well as by a multitude of collateral proofs, of slender weight if estimated separately, but of convincing force when put together and examined in combination. He was remarkable when young for his punctilious morality and outward respect for the great subjects of the gospel. It will be remembered that all the friends of his boyhood testify to his singularly exemplary character, and pronounce him one of the purest and most reputable youths with whom they were ever acquainted. But it will be seen from the diary to which the reader is now to be introduced, that Mr. Alexander himself confessed and bewailed his utter sinfulness, and saw no hope of salvation but in the merits and shed blood of Jesus Christ. The work of restoration was gradual, and unaccompanied by strong terrors or remorse. These solemn records possess a strange and mournful interest from the fact already mentioned that with one or two exceptions they are the only extant registers of his religious feelings.

The only glimpse, aside from matters of reasonable conjecture, which I have been able to obtain of the precise state of Mr. Alexander's feelings on this subject before he became an avowed believer in Jesus, is afforded in the obituary sketch by Dr. Baird. The picture of Addison's reticent and cautious father melted to tears over the evidences of his son's conversion is affecting, and the fact recorded of him is remarkable and stands alone in Dr. Archibald Alexander's history.

"While he was a student of the Academy, Addison was a punctual and serious attendant upon the religious services of the Institution.

Seldom, if ever, was he absent from the daily opening and closing prayer, and the reading of the Scriptures. He was always present at the Bible class on Sabbath afternoon, and the season of special prayer on Thursday afternoon, at the close of the usual exercises of that day. But whilst there was much attention, respect, and even seriousness, there was no special manifestation of deep interest in religion as a personal matter. It was not until he had finished his studies in the College, and had become an assistant teacher in Professor Patton's Edgehill School in Princeton, that his heart became savingly engaged in the subject of religion. I shall never forget an interview which I had with his father about that time. Dr. Alexander was a man of strong feelings; but he also had great control over his emotions, and I never knew him to give way to them excepting on that occasion. After speaking of the business respecting which I had called to see him, he remarked that as I had taken a great interest in his sons, he had a piece of intelligence to communicate which he was sure would give me much delight. He then stated that he was well satisfied, from a conversation which he had had with Addison the evening previous, that he was a converted man! This he said in a tone of voice which manifested the deepest feeling. Indeed, for some moments afterwards he could not speak, but covered his face with his handkerchief, and gave way to his deep emotions of joy and hope. He had a high opinion of the talents of Addison and James, but he did not think that either of them was naturally the most gifted of his sons. On this point I think he was right, distinguished as both unquestionably were for their great mental endowments."*

But let us recur to his journal. These revelations of fierce and remarkable spiritual conflicts will not greatly surprise the admirers of his experimental sermons. They are however of a nature so unusual that I shall give them to the reader with but little abridgment.

"Jan. 1830. During the month of January, besides attending to my duties in the school, I have been employed in assisting Mr. Patton

---

* This statement needs great qualification. The father considered Addison as on the whole inferior in point of ability and character to no member of his family, and in many respects in advance of every one within the range of his acquaintance. Witness his own words in the letter to Mrs. Graham which will be found on page.

to collect materials for his Greek lexicon. My part of the work consists in translating from Passow's Greek and German dictionary the definitions of words omitted by Donnegan. I have also completed the rough draught of a review of Sadi's Gulistan for the American Quarterly Review, which I began in December. I have contributed some trifles to the Philadelphia Morning Journal. But in addition to these literary pursuits, I have been deeply engaged in a study new to me, and far more important than all others—the study of the Bible and my own heart. I humbly trust that I am not what I was. I have still my old propensities to evil, but I have also a new will co-existing with the old, and counteracting and controlling it.* My views respecting study are now changed. Intellectual enjoyment has been my idol heretofore; now my heart's desire is that I may live no longer to myself, but in Him in whom I have everlasting life. God grant that the acquisitions that I have been allowed to make under the influence of selfish motives may be turned to good account as instruments for the promotion of His glory. May it not be that my strong and unaccountable attachment from a very early age to unusual studies, &c., was intended as a preparation for God's service in some foreign land? Oh! if I were thought worthy of bearing such a message—but I desire to abstain from all attempts to order my own steps. I have indulged my imagination formerly too much. It must be mortified. My God, for such I, even I, may call thee in the name of Christ—my God, into thy hands I commit myself! In life or death, at home or abroad, in peace and joy or in the dark valley, I design to be thine—thine with a devotedness proportioned to my meanness, misery, ingratitude, infirmity and utter unworthiness of favour. Oh! deliver me from my worst enemy—myself."

"Feb. 4. For some days I have been suffering the pains of melancholy—an evil from which I have been heretofore exempt. It has no reference to my religious views, which continue substantially unchanged; but seems rather hypochondriacal in its character, engendering dark apprehensions of disease and death. Its worst effect is that it begins to establish an association in my mind (I cannot conceive how), between religious duties and these gloomy fears. I am sometimes tempted to believe that it is a device of the adversary intended to throw a shade over the subject of religion, and alienate my thoughts from it.

---

* This may indicate his opinion as to the true meaning of Gal. vi: 17.

I was somewhat relieved by conversing with my father last night,* but find myself still under the dominion of evil spirits, especially as night comes on. After all, the best explanation of it is that it arises from my languor and neglect in the discharge of duty and the cultivation of a spiritual temper. It is probably no more than a black vapour from the stagnant pool of my own corruptions, eclipsing the little light which had begun to shine upon my soul. O, Sun of Righteousness, arise with healing under thy wings. When I look back upon the doings of a day and count over my remembered transgressions and deficiencies (to say nothing of the numberless offences which my blunted conscience takes no notice of) I feel that I have no right to wonder or complain when I find myself at night wrapped in spiritual darkness.

"I am reading the epistles of Peter, slowly but with great satisfaction. The nature of my occupations obliges me to read the Bible at intervals and in very small portions at a time. This, which at first troubled me, I find to be an eminent advantage. Instead of running over a whole chapter with divided attention, and without being able to retain any portion of it accurately in the memory, I can dwell upon one text for half an hour or more, and in this way see not only more meaning and derive more instruction from it, but give a wholesome seasoning to my secular pursuits. Happily my business is not of such a nature as to exclude all thoughts of other things. While hearing a boy parse a sentence in Latin, or copying the definition of a Greek word, I have abundant opportunity to turn the word of life in my mind and apply it to my conscience. What shall I render to the Lord for placing me in circumstances so propitious to my spiritual welfare! I look back with shame to my discontented feelings on first coming to this place, and bless God that my wish to be released from my engagement was not gratified. I am satisfied that my removal from my father's house, by breaking the associations which had been growing stronger and stronger for twenty years, and turning the current of my thoughts into new channels, was highly instrumental in directing my attention to the subject of religion. I expressed this idea to my father, who concurred in it, and observed that the removal of a young man, from his father's house, is always a critical event, producing powerful effects, good or bad, according to the situation into which he passes."

"Now, thanks be to God, a better situation, quoad hoc, could not

---

* May not this have been the very interview referred to by Dr. Baird? and may not the father have counselled the son on the subject of Satanic temptations?

have been selected than the one in which I find myself. The heads of the family are both exemplary Christians; religion is treated by all the household with respect, and I am wholly delivered from the company of any whose contempt or opposition might retard my progress. Bless the Lord, O my soul, and forget not all his benefits.

"I have been reading Augustin's Confessions as abridged in Milner's Church History. What a wonderful conversion! Like most other practical works which I have read, it contains something parallel to my case. The difficulty which the historian appears to look upon as something very singular (viz., of forming a conception of the Deity as a spiritual substance) gave me no small trouble sometime since, and is not yet conquered. Most of his conflicts too I have felt, though not in the same circumstances. The statement which he makes in the last book, of his temptations through the different senses, I might almost transcribe and make my own. Does not this coincidence in the experience and language of men separated by such intervals of space and time, prove the truth of their religious sentiments?

"I finished yesterday Ellerby's abridgment of Edwards on the Affections. I am happy that I read it. It put me on my guard against some delusions into which I should have been very apt to fall. I am reading slowly Owen on Spiritual Mindedness. Large portions of it cannot be digested well at once; but it is evidently well worth the perusal.

"10 o'clock, P. M. Thank God! I feel myself much relieved from the irrational and sinful melancholy which has been oppressing me. I have been enabled, in some measure, to obey the precept in 1 Peter 5.7 (Ps. 55.22). O my God, $\kappa\alpha\tau\alpha\rho\tau\iota\sigma\alpha\iota$ $\sigma\tau\eta\rho\iota\xi\alpha\iota$ $\sigma\theta\epsilon\nu\omega\sigma\alpha\varsigma$, $\theta\epsilon\mu\epsilon\lambda\iota\omega\sigma\alpha\iota$! I am weak but thou art strength itself. I do, Lord! humbly cast my burden upon thee, knowing that thou WILT sustain me, for I dare not disbelieve thee.

"I have no longer any right to wonder at the darkness and discomfort which have lately troubled me, when I find myself so prone to yield to every temptation, however feeble.—O my Father who art in Heaven, when shall I feel humbly grateful for the privilege of calling thee my father? Oh, how canst thou who art holiness itself endure the approaches of an impure worm? Save me from the presumptuous folly of ascribing it to my own merits, and give me a deeper and deeper conviction of the truth that it is only through the intercession of a great High Priest that I am not spurned from thy footstool;—Hallowed be thy name;—strike me, in mercy strike me to the earth under a deep sense of thy holiness and majesty; Oh! save me from the blasphemous impiety of trifling with thy name.—How often, O Lord, I have taken it in vain! How needless do I utter it even at this moment! Keep me, O Lord, for I have not even holiness enough to look upon thee with reverence! Oh! blast this pride and insensibility, not with the lightnings of thy wrath, but with the breathings of thy Holy Spirit. Let me no longer come into thy presence reeking with the vanities of life, or wallowing in my own native filthiness, and in such a state presume to take thy name, even thine O God, upon *my* polluted lips! But enable me to say with my heart as well as with my lips, hallowed be thy name!—Thy kingdom come! Oh enable me to rejoice with joy unspeakable at the very thought that thy throne is forever and ever: knowing and believing that the sceptre of thy kingdom is a right sceptre, and that from everlasting to everlasting thou art God! Oh, when shall thy kingdom come among the nations? When shall our God and Saviour have the heathen for his inheritance? Come, Lord Jesus, come quickly! Oh, that my eyes might see the salvation of the world! And, O Lord, when thou comest in thy kingdom, remember me—remember me!

"Feb. 5. I have read to-day with great pleasure and benefit the fourth chapter and part of the fifth in Owen on Spiritual Mindedness. The perusal of it was permitted to be instrumental in dispelling somewhat the black cloud of selfish melancholy which has hung upon me for some days. Alas, alas, I yielded this evening to a temptation which I vainly imagined I had gained power to resist. Who shall deliver me from the body of this death! A short time since such surprises, by making me despair of my own strength checked my progress toward a life of obedience. But now I thank God I have learned two lessons that before were foolishness to me; one is, that my own strength is perfect weakness; the other that I can do all things through Christ that strengtheneth me. I arise from this fall with new convictions of my own inability to think a right thought, and, I trust, with renewed dependence upon God.

"Feb. 7. Read an abridgment of the life of Henry Martyn. I have so often read this biography for its almost romantic interest, that I expected to derive no entertainment from it. But in this perusal my attention was abstracted to the account of his conversion; and I was surprised at its remarkable resemblance to my own. It was equally gradual, without strong terrors or remorse, and seems to have resulted as immediately from study of the Scriptures. The fragments also of his subsequent experience, contained in extracts from his journal might be transcribed here as narratives of mine; I mean his unfavourable pictures. Would to God I had his—and far more than his—love, faith, devotion, patience, deadness to the world, meekness and charity toward all men! But as Martyn himself says, 'The gospel was contrived to meet the case of sinners, and no sins can get beyond its redeeming and purifying power.' Oh for light; God is light; Oh for more love—God is love; and he that dwelleth in love dwelleth in God and God in him. Oh let me dwell in thee eternally!"

"Feb. 8. Though I awoke at an early hour sloth and the severe cold made me break my resolution as to early rising and devotion. Would to God my senses had less influence upon my spirit! Notwithstanding this delinquency, my mind was graciously brought into a more comfortable and, I hope, more spiritual state than it has been for some time, if at all. The evils which I have most reason to complain of are distrust in God's goodness* and a proneness to unbelief. A delightful letter from the dearest friend (as to community of feelings, sentiments, &c.) that I have on earth, stirred up my feelings not a little. Six weeks ago I should have been annoyed by such a letter; as it is, I desire to bless God that I have such a brother. I have lately been oppressed with a feeling of solitariness arising from my situation; for I have intimate communion with no one in the same house, and my occupations are exceedingly confining. In my anxiety about my own state, too, I have forgotten others. I have unconsciously regarded myself as the only one on earth who stood in just such a relation to God. In some respects this has been beneficial. It has enabled me to make up my mind, and lay my plans, independently of mere human considerations, and to regard personal religion as an affair between God and my own heart. The views which I have entertained and the resolutions I have taken, have rested on the supposition that I stood alone; I hope, therefore, that they will be less likely to be moved by any change in external circumstances. But now that I begin to feel some confidence that I am in the right way, I find it to be a privilege as well as duty, to look at others. Archbishop Leighton's observations on the first sentence of the Lord's prayer, brought the duty to my mind with new liveliness and force; and this letter makes me feel the value of the privilege of Christian communion more forcibly.

"2 P. M. I have constantly new warnings against putting confidence in the stability of my own resolutions, and the permanence of my feelings. This morning I felt confident, resigned and spiritual. At

---

* The letter of his eldest brother, which is here referred to, is not now in existence.

this moment, I am not only cold in my affections, and indistinct in my views of truth, but plagued by a return of my old feelings of false shame, attachment to mere worldly objects, &c. I thank God, however, I am still enabled to feel that it all arises from the want of faith and watchfulness, and to believe that it is possible to obtain other states of mind, by unwearied diligence combined with humble reliance upon Divine assistance. This remedy I am determined to apply; fighting my way through all difficulties, and waging war especially against myself, as my most treacherous enemy. Oh my God! though thou canst not but abhor the unbelief and corruption which produces these vicissitudes, yet thou knowest that my heart's desire before thee is to love thee with a fervour, and serve thee with a zeal, above and beyond all that I have yet imagined or designed. Oh, aid me in the struggle with my own heart and with sin!

"11 P. M. I am hourly made to feel my weakness. I vainly imagined that my religious feelings were not likely to be influenced by outward circumstances; but on going home to-night and finding my father low-spirited and my mother unwell, though both spiritually well and rejoicing in my change, I felt my spirits sink within me as if my prospects of eternal life depended upon them. When shall I be delivered from this bondage to mere natural affections, and mere worldly objects? Lord, this struggle is too hard for my unassisted strength. Oh, fan my dying faith into a flame with the breathings of thy Spirit! Oh, sustain me with the arms of thy everlasting love; I feel my own shortcomings. In this single day how little have my thoughts been with God; how little have I thought of His omnipresence; how little have I tried to wean my affections from the world and fix them upon Christ; how little have I been actuated in my conduct by a regard to duty and a sincere desire to do the will of God. Lord, thou hast searched me and known me; thou knowest my downsittings and my uprising; strengthen my weakness; animate, excite, invigorate me! In humble confidence that thou wilt not reject this prayer, I desire to resolve in thy presence that I will endeavour, if permitted to behold another day, to spend it in a way more agreeable to thee and beneficial to myself. What a mercy is it that our duty and our interests are so united. God might justly have required us to submit to torments in his service, but no—the very duties which we render, if performed aright, are sources of delight."

"Feb. 9. Cold, languid, earthly—O Lord, how long? But is it not one of my habitual sins to expect God's aid without the use of means;

and then to complain of my deficiencies, as if they did not spring from my own sinfulness?

"10.—11. A little comforted, strengthened and enlightened by the latter part of Romans xiv; but still tormented by a dread of ridicule, disgrace, &c. My imagination works too much; one of Owen's rules struck me forcibly; to take from our most valuable time for God's service, not palm the scraps and refuse on Him.

"The fifth of Romans is a glorious chapter—even my blindness could perceive its brightness! O my God apply thy Word to me the chief of sinners. I have obtained the first volume of John Newton's works and hope to derive much advantage from it. He always speaks from his heart and from his own experience.

"Who hath bewitched me? Though rationally satisfied that this world contains nothing commensurate with my capacity and desires, and that if I will, I may obtain a crown of everlasting life, I am harassed by constant disposition to fall back into my old pursuit of worldly happiness; and even when I feel no relish for the 'beggarly elements around me, I am equally devoid of taste for spiritual good; so that I am left in a miserable state of fluctuation and dissatisfaction.

"11 P. M. From some cause I feel much relieved from melancholy, &c. I am thankful for the comfort, but distrust its source. I find by recent experience that when I emerge from gloom, it is commonly to run into the opposite extreme of negligence and levity. God grant that I may soon be brought into the golden mean of cheerful obedience and unhesitating confidence in His fidelity and goodness!"

"Feb. 10. To my surprise I awoke this morning with an agreeable impression on my mind of the words, 'Though I walk through the valley of the shadow of death, &c.' I am struck with this because I begin to see that my melancholy feelings may be all resolved into an undignified fear of death. I take comfort, however, in the reflection that my dread is not simply that the terrors of death are great, but that they may be so great as to overpower faith and love. From these forebodings I derive at least temporary relief from such passages as the latter part of Romans viii (a glorious revelation). I am also comforted, strengthened, and encouraged by the experience of John Newton which teaches me that my want of deep sensibility, strong convictions, &c., though a melancholy defect, is no proof that I am not in Christ. May God preserve me from unbelieving despondency, on one hand, and presumptuous confidence on the other.* I feel that I need trials and

---

* This was an almost daily petition with him, long afterwards.

troubles to make me feel, as well as know, my dependence upon God. Every little circumstance distracts my thoughts, and throws me back into my old associations; and yet when I read of temptations, &c., I am ready to say, my mountain stands firm.

"11 P. M. By engaging in long and somewhat frivolous discourse, I find that I have lost much even of the spiritual taste and feeling which I had this morning—little as that was. I do, indeed, want something to wean my affections altogether from the trifles of this life. I am apt to think sometimes, that if placed in such or such a place, I should be more spiritual. The truth, no doubt, is, that without new supplies of grace, I would carry the same worldliness into any situation. My own strength is perfect weakness—when shall I learn to lean upon my all-sufficient helper? O God, humble my proud heart, crucify my lusts, subdue my obstinacy, melt my insensibility, and bring all my powers into captivity to thee only! I shall be satisfied when I awake with thy likeness."

"Feb. 11. I derive much pleasure, and I hope advantage, from the writings of John Newton. He evidently grounds his opinions on the Word of God, confirmed by personal experience. I find it necessary, however, to beware of placing my dependence on human aids. Men are fallible; and their fallibility is everywhere apparent. I value religious books because they bring into a single point of view, truths which are detached in the Scriptures; and because they show the effects the religion of the Bible has, actually, upon the minds of men. In almost every book, however, there is a tincture of some personal infirmity or error—an overstraining of some one point in preference to others. Thus Owen, who wrote his book on Spiritual Mindedness in his old age, when waiting for his last change, was too apt to underrate the social relations and man's duties as a member of society; while Newton, who was wonderfully changed from a wicked slave-dealer to a Christian minister, naturally set too little value on learning, education, &c. It is only in the Book—the Book of Books, that all is symmetrical and consistent; Oh may I love it more and more! I have felt some grateful emotions this evening in reflecting on the mercies of God in arresting my sinful projects and opening my eyes. A year ago how many resolutions had I broken as to my conduct during the ensuing year! But alas, such feelings with me are but transitory. Light conversation and mere literary employments distract and dissipate my thoughts till I feel as if there was no spiritual life within me. Lord, quicken me!"

"Feb. 12. The book of Ecclesiastes is an exact expression of the feelings which I have lately experienced as to the vanity of earthly things. How true is it, that though the experience of men is infinitely various, the Bible contains a description of every possible and imaginable case.

"I have reason to be continually upon my guard against internal enemies as well as those without. On reading the report of the Oriental Translation Fund of London, I found myself at night carried back by a current of strong associations into my old train of thought, my literary projects, &c. This I must watch and pray to be delivered from; for I am fully persuaded that I am more in danger from literary pursuits than from any other quarter. Sensual gratification I always despised, even when I was a slave to it; but intellectual pleasure has been the idol to which I have deliberately sacrificed my interests and my duty. I cannot recollect a moment in which the prospect of any sensual enjoyment could have induced me to have abandoned my acquisitions and the hope of more; whereas I would at any time have given up forever the pursuit of all bodily enjoyment to procure some favourite objects of the other kind. But amidst the turmoil of my passions I can still take refuge in the consciousness that my supreme desire is to make God's glory my first object, and to use all things else as instruments. God preserve me in this disposition for Christ's sake."

"Feb. 13. O Lord, what a blank is the past week! What progress have I made toward heaven and toward thee? I am not even so peaceful nor so single-eyed as I was a week ago. Though I have overcome the temptations of old lusts which gave me trouble, the *lust* of the understanding—the most plausible and insinuating of all unsanctified affections, seems to be creeping back upon me. The thirst for mere literary pleasure, which was one of my besetting sins, seems to threaten a return. I can only guard myself by making sacred literature an object of attention, for which reason I design to study Hebrew de novo. Greek I study with exclusive reference to the Scriptures. After all, my surest dependence is on Him who is, and was, and is to come; to Him be glory forever and ever, Amen."

"Feb. 14. I have not enjoyed much light or peace to-day, because I have not sought it with sufficient zeal and diligence. Unbelieving fears or wild imagination, and the natural aversion of the heart to God have kept me from the throne of Grace. The greatest difficulty which I have to encounter is a perfect resignation of myself—life, health, reputation, talents, acquisitions, time, and all, into the hands of God. I feel willing to do great things, and make costly sacrifices in His service; but it seems as if my proud heart would not be contented without having some share in ordering my steps. Hide me, O Lord, under the shadow of thy wings!"

"Feb. 15. The evil I have most to complain of to-day is dissipation and distraction of mind. Every thing seems vague and undefined. Though I have no spiritual distress, I have no clear views of truth, nor elevated affections. I have not yet learned to be sufficiently jealous of myself. I am too apt to fall back into my old trains of thought and association. When I do so, and in consequence forget God and spiritual things for many minutes, I invariably feel a painful void which can only be filled by turning my attention to religious matters again. And, I thank God, I feel something like a relish for His service, and though hypochondriacal still, feel little attachment to my own life, or the world in comparison with that which lies beyond."

"Feb. 16. At times to-day I have enjoyed considerable peace of mind; but for the most part, I have been distracted between intellectual exercise on one hand, and hypochondriacal apprehensions, on the other. From the latter plague I never feel so free as when I am engaged in prayer. Yet, strange to tell, it is with difficulty that I can constrain myself to go upon my knees. What an enigma of wickedness and folly do I daily find myself to be! I am astonished that I could live so long without any discovery of my own character—its selfishness and meanness, its weakness and inconsistency. But I console myself with 1 Corinthians, xx. 51."

"Feb. 17. At different hours on this as on every other day, my feelings vary. Occasionally I am quite resigned and contented to repose upon God's wisdom and goodness. These are my happiest moments, but they are few and transitory. Would to God I were rid of this selfish solicitude, which not only mars my comfort by diffusing gloom through all my feelings, but engrosses so large a share of my attention that there is none left for God."

"Feb. 18. I have hardly patience to continue this monotonous and meagre record. My experience on one day is the same as on another. Still I desire to take all the shame and grief of my darkness and discomfort to myself, while I give all the glory to God. The occasional intervals of satisfaction which I enjoy are evidently produced by communion with Him, while the disquietude and apathy of other moments as evidently spring from a neglect of religious duties—$\kappa\bar{\upsilon}\rho\iota\epsilon\ \dot{\epsilon}\lambda\acute{\epsilon}\eta\sigma o\nu$."

"Feb. 19. I began this day in considerable peace and comfort, and though I have had returns of my dejection, I have reason to be thankful for my general tranquillity. At noon, when alone, I felt some emotions of sorrow in reading the account of our Saviour's agony."

"Feb. 20. During the past week I have finished Canticles, and read forty-four chapters in English. I have also finished Matthew, read all of Mark and eight chapters of Luke in Greek. In the Septuagint I have read eighteen chapters of Genesis; in Martyn's Persian New Testsment the remainder of the Apocalypse and five chapters of Mark. I have also studied Stuart's Hebrew grammar and Rosenmüller's Arabic grammar, and have finished the revision of thirty-three pages of the Greek lexicon; lastly, I have read much of the first volume of John Newton's works, and several other books, such as 'Advice to a young Christian,' 'Jowett's Christian Remembrancer,' &c.

"This is little enough, but when I turn to spiritual things, and ask what progress I have made during the past week I am dumb with confusion. One sin stands forth with especial prominence—my ungrateful and presumptuous neglect of intercourse with God. I have scarcely prayed regularly during the whole week. Sloth in the morning combined with other delinquencies would drive me from the mercy-seat, were it not for such grand revelations as Isaiah lxiii. 25. If it was for my sake the Lord showed me favour, I might well despair of ever gaining it, but since, as he expressly declares, it is for His *own* sake, I submit—my defections make me cling closer to the throne of God and to the cross of Christ. Still I must do something, and therefore with reliance on Divine help I resolve that in the coming week I will arise as soon as I awake, and devote the time so gained to secret prayer. If the immaculate Saviour rose 'a great while before day,' and spent whole nights in prayer, surely I ought to pray without ceasing."

"Feb. 21. I was enabled to-day, after a slight struggle, to gain the victory over sloth, and rise a little earlier than usual. Read the Scriptures with great pleasure and I hope Divine illumination. I am astonished to meet with such multiplied and convincing evidences of the deity of Christ. I never saw them before because I looked for direct, positive declarations, whereas the most satisfactory proofs are, apparently, minute and accidental. In fact, the strongest argument, it seems to me, is that the supposition of Christ's divinity gives a harmony, consistency and beauty to the Scriptures which they cannot have without it. The point to which my attention has been chiefly called to-day, in relation to this matter, is the fact that God is repeatedly declared to be the only *Saviour*, and that this name is as strongly claimed by Him, as one of His inalienable titles, as any other; while, on the other hand, it is so expressly given to Jesus Christ in the New Testament, that it has become his most familiar and appropriate epithet throughout the Christian world. Under the influence of these considerations, I cannot help regarding Christ in God, when I examine in connection the following texts, which I have been able to turn to without a concordance (multitudes of others tend to the same point) Isaiah xliii. 11; xlv. 42; Jude, 25; 1 Tim. i. 1; 2 Peter i. 1, 3, 18. Two of these (1 Tim i. 1, and 2 Peter i. 1) admit of an interpretation which amounts to positive assertion of Christ's deity, but even waiving this, they satisfy me.

"Read the 9th chapter of Luke with feelings altogether new. What a glory is thrown upon the gospel history by keeping constantly in view its connection with the former dispensation! I have been too apt, in spite of the Saviour's own admonition, to suppose that he came to destroy the law. I have commonly looked upon his advent &c. as a plan formed subsequently to the revelations of the Old Testament. But now, when I read the predictions of a Messiah in the prophets, the types of him in the ceremonial law, the promise of him in paradise, and then turn and read the gospel as nothing more nor less than a continuation of the history; recognizing in Christ the Messiah foretold of old, and all that he did as steps taken to accomplish the grand scheme—it is unutterably glorious. In reading our Lord's instructions to his apostles, Luke ix. 1-6, I was more than ever, or rather for the first time, struck with the fact that he did not heal the sick and raise the dead for mere sympathetic feeling for the sorrows of the sufferers, but as means for the accomplishment of the great end of his incarnation. I read the account of the transfiguration with new emotions, heightened by a recollection of the intercourse between God and Moses and Elias in former times. Two circumstances struck me: Moses talked to Jesus of the ἐξοδος which he should accomplish at Jerusalem;—what a contrast must there have been between the feelings of Elijah, when he stood with his face wrapped in his mantle at the entering in of the cave, trembling at the still small voice of his unseen God, and those which he experienced on the summit of Mount Tabor hearing the same voice proceed from the excellent glory, and conversing with the same God, incarnate, face to face! Moses was a great man—Elijah was a great man, and the simple inscription given in the gospel of their intercourse with the Saviour, at this time, gave me some impressions and strong feelings of the Saviour's glory which I never had before, but which I never wish to lose. Is it not strange that my conceptions of the Saviour should be still so gross—that even Moses and Elias could reflect light upon Him?

"11 o'clock, A. M. Heard Mr. Woodhull on Jesus Christ and Him crucified. At 4. P. M., Mr. Bush lectured at the school on the Ten Virgins and the Talents. Went home and attended the religious conference in the Seminary—subject, *zeal.* I have enjoyed, to-day, unusual peace and satisfaction. These feelings were less strong toward evening; probably because I trusted too much in my own ability to keep up such emotions at my pleasure. The Lord preserve me from self-confidence! I have read, to-day, in Greek, Luke 9–12; in English, Isaiah xliv–xlviii; Newton's letters, Force of Truth, Jowett's Researches."

"Feb. 22. I feel a sensible declension from the elevation of feeling which I enjoyed yesterday. It arises partly, no doubt, from my necessary return to secular business, but also, in a great measure, from my proneness to self-confidence and to forget that of myself I can do nothing. Oh, that I had attained that stage in the progress of the soul in which the only motive is the love of God; the only end, the glory of God, and the only dependence on the grace of God! I also need to be constantly reminded of the emptiness of this world, and its tumult of affairs! Oh, that it were written indelibly in my heart —ενος, ενος, εστι χρεια."

"Feb. 24. I am backsliding very fast; the change is very sensible. I find the impression which I had of the vanity of earthly things fast wearing off; the little sense which I had gained of the excellence of holiness becoming less and less lively, and all my feelings setting back towards their ancient current. The worst symptom of all this is, that I feel no grief on account of this declension. And yet amidst it all I feel that I could cheerfully sacrifice all the pleasures, gains and honours of the world for an increase in holiness. Lord, save me—I perish.

"Feb. 25. It pleased God to rouse me from the lethargy into which I was sinking, by a deep wound in my pride; occasioned by the contemptuous treatment of one of my large pupils who has always behaved to me with great respect. I bless God I was enabled to defer my anger, to repress all resentful feelings and to pay the boy's impertinence with kindness and forbearance. It was, indeed, of great use to me, by giving me a clearer view of the precarious tenure by which men possess the respect and esteem of others, and so leading me to renounce the world as a source of happiness. While under the influence of this incident, I read Jeremiah ii., and was astonished at its appropriateness to my own case. A personal address on the subject of my backsliding could not come more home. Verses 13, 17, 23, 34, 37, struck me particularly as precisely applicable. Oh, that the Lord would sanctify this portion of His work as a means of awakening, convincing, and humbling me!"

"Feb. 27. For some days past I have been vexed by a return of some old feelings which I thought had quit me long ago. Their first effect has been to agitate and disturb me; their second to drive me back to God as the only source of true felicity. I conversed this afternoon with Mr. Patton on the subject of religion. He gave me some account of his experience, which, in some respects, resembles mine. One observation of his struck me, viz.—that when the soul is harassed with doubts and difficulties as to the evidences of its state, peace may often be obtained by asking itself a simple question: 'Would any thing induce me to give up my hope, such as it is?'

To-morrow is the blessed Sabbath. How little did I think, six months ago, that I should ever hail its return with joy; not as a season of mere relaxation, but a precious opportunity of waiting upon God. I thank the Lord that he has enabled me to look upon His Sabbath as a delight and as honourable. Oh, may He give me grace to sanctify the coming day aright!"

"Feb. 28. I went to sleep last night with a delightful impression on my mind of the relation between Christ and His followers, as represented by the figure of a shepherd and his sheep. There seemed to be a force and beauty in the allegory which I had never before observed. This morning I awoke earlier than common. It is somewhat singular that for some time past, though I have generally slept till late, I have been awakened early Sabbath morning by the crowing of the cock. Through the day I have been generally comfortable and have had much more enjoyment in secret prayer."

"March 1. After reviewing my recorded experience during the month just past and endeavouring to feel some of that humiliation which my coldness, sloth and inconsistency afford so much reason for, I venture, in reliance upon God's assistance to resolve: 1. That during the present month I will endeavour to watch with redoubled vigilance against the beginnings of evil; especially against those temptations which I know by experience to be most dangerous. 2. That I will endeavour to act more upon principle, with more regard to the will of God. 3. That I will endeavour to avoid with equal diligence, an irreligious levity, and an unprofitable despondency and gloom. 4. That I will watch with more care against sloth; endeavouring to improve the time more than I have done. 5. That I will endeavour to cultivate a principle of Christian benevolence and love. 6. That I will endeavour to mortify my pride; especially those latent forms under which that evil principle conceals itself. 7. That I will guard against my old enemy— the love of intellectual pleasure; by studying with regularity, and with constant reference to the grand object of all study. 8. That I will endeavour to study God's Word with more reverence, attention, patience, faith, and love. 9. That I will pay such attention to my own health as duty seems to demand, by moderation in diet and regularity in exercise. 10. That having done all I will throw myself, always and forever, on the gracious aid of the Almighty, without which I cannot stir a step in my progress toward perfection.

"And now, O Omniscient Searcher of hearts! if thou seest any insincerity in these resolves, purge it, I beseech thee, from my heart; and if I am indeed sincere, Oh, enable me to keep the vow which I now make in thy name and presence: for the sake of Christ. Amen."

"March 2. I have had something of a struggle to-day between my literary lusts, so to speak, and a sense of duty. I fully believe, from experience as well as testimony, that an exclusive devotion to intellectual pursuits is one of the worst enemies with which the renewed soul has to grapple. I am not certain that I ought not to relinquish my Arabic; at least for the present; as I have relinquished French, Spanish, German and Italian reading."

"March 7. How seldom do we know what we are praying for, when we ask God, upon our knees, to humble us, show us our vileness, wean us from dependence on ourselves, &c! For my own part I know that when I offer such petitions, I commonly expect them to be answered by an immediate operation on my heart, without the intervention of external means. No wonder, then, that I am often taken by surprise by the answer to my own earnest supplications. On Tuesday (Mar. 1,) I vowed, among other things, to endeavour to mortify my pride; especially those latent forms under which that evil principle conceals itself. At the same time I besought the Lord to assist me in adhering to this resolution, and to detect any insincerity by which it might be vitiated. On Tuesday all went well, but on Wednesday a trifling occurrence was permitted so to stir up the corrupt mass of my bad passions, especially my pride, that I stood amazed at the mingled folly, wickedness and helplessness of my own heart. Yet, strange to tell, it never occurred to me until this evening, that this occurrence was in answer to my own request and was graciously designed to show me what a risk I run whenever I presume to make a vow or resolution in dependence on myself. If this be indeed so, I bless God for the timely warning, and hope to profit by it. The two great evils I have to complain of are, my proneness to act upon mere impulse, without regard to principle, and my inability to view things temporal and eternal in their great proportions."

"March 15. O Lord! Thou knowest me altogether; when I look

back through the past week and consider my neglect of thee, my discontent, my ungrateful and rebellious murmurings against thy providence, how can I appear before thee? And yet, when I look further back and remember my presumptuous self-confidence, my fancied preparation for all trials, I cannot but acknowledge in the dust before thee, that I did indeed need a lesson such as thou only canst give. With shame, too, I confess, O thou long-suffering and gracious Lord! my selfish reservations in giving myself up to thee. Thou hast opened my eyes to see that in all my acts of self-devotion, I have constantly prescribed conditions unto thee; consenting to serve thee if thou wouldst let me choose the circumstances; submitting to thy will, provided it coincided with my own; and professing myself willing to undergo all sufferings, provided I should never be required in *practice* to submit to them. Even now, O Lord! with my eyes in a measure open to the wickedness and folly of such dealings with a holy, merciful and jealous God—even now my corrupt, my rotten heart suggests that these confessions will bribe thee to deliver me from the natural evil, with the fear of which I have been long tormented. Against this diabolical and mad corruption, I would strive; but where is my strength? When I should have clung to the throne—to the cross—to the promises, with most tenacity, I have foolishly forsaken them; what wonder then that I am weak, blind, unwilling and unable to confide in thee—all-faithful as thou art? O God, thou art just! I deserve it all: but in the name of one whose intercession thou canst not despise, I pray—with agony pray, that I may be made willing to do or to suffer any thing! Amen."

"March 16. O Lord, God of infinite compassion! words fail me when I undertake to express my gratitude—or rather obligations to thy goodness. I can hardly believe that I am spared, preserved, exempted from excruciating torments. What am I, O Lord! that thou shouldest regard me, even for a moment, with forbearance. O Lord! extirpate this hypocrisy that taints every exercise of my soul. Save me, I implore thee, from the damning sin of uttering words before thee which belie my thoughts. When I say that I am vile. Oh drench my spirit in an overwhelming flood of shame and unfeigned humiliation at the thought of my pollution! When I confess my enormities, O suffer me not to confess them with my lips alone!—make me feel that I am viler than any language can describe me."

"March 17. This morning little Harriet Patton died of the scarlet fever. On Sunday she was at church, and appeared as well as usual. How shall I derive any personal advantage from this melancholy event?

The Lord seems to be teaching me, by repeated lessons, the shortness and uncertainty of life; the folly and meanness of mere hypochondriacal depressions; when the occasions of real sorrow are so numerous around me; the necessity, the absolute necessity, of providing sources of relief and consolation altogether independent of mere human circumstances. From the gloom which at present clouds this house of mourning, I feel constantly disposed to take refuge by visiting or thinking of my father's family; where all are well, and where I might no doubt, obtain a temporary and unprofitable interval of freedom from unpleasant thoughts. But when I begin to make the supposition that death might enter even that asylum; that one and another even of that circle, to which all my affections have so long been selfishly confined, might be removed as suddenly as this poor child; when I merely imagine these events as possible; my very soul grows sick and revolts from the painful thought. But why? It must be so at some time! Nothing can be more certain than that sooner or later I must either die and leave my friends, or must survive the last wreck of my family. Where, then, is the wisdom of shutting my eyes to the consideration of such truths? The fact is, at least in my case, that strong remedies are necessary to overcome this sickly tenderness. Men must die: they are dying every moment; and the very unavoidableness of the event seems to tempt us all to labour to forget it. In no circumstances do men hew out broken cisterns with such perverse diligence as when shrouded in the gloom produced by the death of friends. And, indeed, this would be the height of wisdom, if death were the closing scene. If we ceased to exist at death, and death were inevitable, it would be gross folly to torment ourselves with apprehensions which could only multiply our pangs. But is it so? Or if salvation was a hopeless thing; if death must necessarily plunge us into misery; I cannot see what better course we could pursue than to exclude it altogether from our thoughts. But if it be true (and multitudes who act thus will at least profess to believe it), if it be true that one ray of light from heaven beaming into the soul, one single ray of spiritual light, could dispel this darkness perfectly; if it be true that thousands have enjoyed this beatific sunshine in the midst of sorrows—nay, amidst the pangs of death; if it be true that the Holy Spirit is as willing now as ever to impart this delightful gift; and indeed only shuts up the apertures through which the dim light of this world shines in order to lead us to another source of illumination; if it be true that we have only to resign ourselves to God, disputing nothing—leaving ALL to Him in absolute defiance of appearances and of ourselves; why should we be depressed at all?

"Noon. I have been to-day inexpressibly gloomy. The concurrence of so many melancholy circumstances tinges my imagination with a dye of tenfold blackness. The death of this child; my hypochondria; my slight indisposition; the gloomy weather; but above all, the unsettled state of my mind as to religion. I find there are two kinds of assurance necessary to religious comfort: 1. An assurance of the truth of Christianity. 2. An assurance of personal interest in its advantages. On both these points I feel a corroding anxiety entirely incompatible with joy or peace or even resignation. My doubts as to Christianity itself are not so much settled and habitual misgivings, as occasional suggestions of distrust and scepticism. I have good evidence that this state of mind arises from corruption and is radically sinful; because I feel myself continually prone to lay a thousand times more stress on difficulties and objections, than on arguments that lean the other way. My perplexities on the other matter are more constant and abiding. I have so little evidence *within* me (and where that is wanting what external indications can avail) I feel so little evidence *within* me of a renewed heart, and a principle of grace, that I am continually tossed about in miserable uncertainty. I think internal evidence of one's acceptance far more valuable by itself than the most ample satisfaction of the understanding as to the verity of Christianity. For it seems to me that the former, where it exists at all, must be founded on a consciousness of changes wrought in the character and feelings which no lower cause than a divine operation can produce; and consequently must include, in some degree, a lively conviction of the truth of the gospel. The other, on the contrary, may be wholly unattended even by a belief in one's conversion—nay, a man may preach and convince others and be a cast-away. What then are the necessities which press most heavily upon me in my present circumstances?

"To-night it pleased the Lord to give me some stability of confidence in the Scriptures; through the reading of Scott's preface to the Bible.

"April 24. I am this day twenty-one years old, and after looking back upon my past life, and forward to eternity, having also sought instruction in God's Word and at the throne of grace, I desire with few words, but with a fixed heart, to consecrate myself, soul and body, now and forever, to the God who made me. With this intent I now most solemnly renounce the service of the devil, my late master; abandoning not only certain sins, but *sin* itself; with all its pleasures, honours and emoluments; desiring and beseeching God never more to suffer me to taste the least enjoyment of a sinful nature. I also bind my conscience in the presence of the jealous God who searches the heart and cannot look upon iniquity without abhorrence, to watch against all temptation; and, if necessary, to resist unto blood striving against sin. At the same time I renounce all dependence upon any thing I may be, do or suffer, here or hereafter, as a ground of deliverance from hell—trusting for mercy in the cross of Christ. And having thus discharged myself from all allegiance to the Prince of Darkness, I submit myself to God in Christ; desiring and consenting to be His forever, to do and suffer all His will, in the joyful hope of an eternal recompense. And now, having learned by sad experience, the deceitfulness of my own heart, the weakness of my resolution and the craft of Satan, I throw myself at thy feet, O Lord! and claim the promise of thy strengthening and illuminating grace to aid me in the performance of these vows. Oh, let me not, I pray thee, be forsworn! Let me not insult thy majesty by perjury so gross—so impious—so damnable! Keep me, O God, in the hollow of thy hand! For the sake of thy dear Son impart to me the gift of thy free Spirit to purify, enlighten and transform my heart! Through life may I be thine, and in death, O Lord, in death be thou my God! Again, and again, and again I solemnly devote myself to God the Father, God the Son, and God the Holy Ghost; desiring nothing, hoping nothing, fearing nothing if I may but be accepted in the name of Christ! Amen."

"April 25. Read the epistle to Titus in Greek and English. What a comfort it must be to ministers that the apostle Paul has left such particular directions in relation to their office, the character of the incumbents and the subjects of their preaching! I was much struck with the explicit charge he gives to Titus, to insist upon the great doctrines of redemption by the blood of Christ, and regeneration through the influences of the Spirit, and to avoid vain controversy. What a rebuke to the zealots of the present age! who, as Robert Hall says, forget the things about which they agree, in disputing about those in which they differ. I am also struck with the fidelity in adhering to his own directions by frequently and repeatedly summing up the essentials of Christianity in a few words. This is done with wonderful brevity and force in verses 3, 4, 5, 6, and 7 of the third chapter of this epistle. In this short passage we have: 1. A clear exhibition of universal depravity. 2. Of God's free grace. 3. Of the offices of the Son and Spirit in the work of redemption and sanctification.

" Read the Section *Daleth* in the cxixth Psalm. I have derived great satisfaction, within a few days, from perusing this masterpiece of devotion. It is not to be read like the epistles; which I find are most intelligible and impressive when perused upon Locke's plan, continuously and as a whole. The Psalms must be taken piece-meal; and drank in drop by drop. Every verse seems to be full of meaning, and to become more so the longer it is pondered. I find it advantageous to read each verse in the original, and, also, in such versions as I have at hand. This I have read in Hebrew, Latin, French and English.

This is the end of his experimental journal so far as it has been continuously preserved. Detached entries reappear, but from this time nearly all his diaries of this nature were kept in separate books which were afterwards destroyed. The inner history of his soul can be truly read only in the light of these fragments which have escaped the flames. He seldom spoke about his own spiritual state. The silence of his journals as to this important subject for so long a course of years cannot be compensated. It is "hiatus maxime deflendus."

CHAPTER VII.

In the month of July of this year, Mr. Alexander was dangerously sick with scarlet fever. It was seldom indeed that he suffered from any thing that could be called illness, and he was hardly ever known to be confined to his bed. On this occasion he was very patient, and a survivor distinctly recalls his placid face and quiet grateful ways. This attack though sharp was soon over; and upon his recovery he was, on the 29th day of the same month, appointed by the trustees Adjunct Professor of Ancient Languages And Literature in the College of New Jersey, with the understanding that he was to reside in the College and act as tutor. This position was one which afforded many advantages in the way of self-improvement. The College tasks were not burdensome to him, and left much leisure for the prosecution of other and still more congenial studies. The rigid sameness of the academic routine no doubt fatigued and possibly fretted him; but its methodical regularity was exactly what he liked. The scholastic repose of certain hours, the lively noise of others; the unbroken seclusion of his own apartments; the verdant or frozen lawn, that was spread like a carpet of velvet, or snow* under his window; the grateful early summer shades; the occasional intercourse of men of learning and talents, or at any rate of extensive information and experience; must for a while at least, have been agreeable to his tastes and disposition. But the truth was, when not fully employed, he became wretched in any situation of unvaried repose. He loved to be surrounded by excitement, and was never so happy as

---

* He lived in the college; No. 59 of the old college, now burnt; next to the bell-rope.

when the sport of painless vicissitude. It may be inferred that he soon wearied of his work at the College.

If by this is meant, that he was often restless in his new employment, and at times thirsted for a change, the inference is probably correct. But if it be meant, that he was on the whole dissatisfied with his new situation, or that he was soon induced to give up the post, the impression is a mistaken one. His diaries lend no countenance to any such notion; and he remained at the College till he set sail for Europe, that is for a period of two years and five months, and then (to use a political phrase) he gave up his portfolio in obedience to the dictate of obvious and imperative duty.

His journal contains a transcript of his feelings at this time, and presents a somewhat detailed account of his mental operations, as well as the series of his regular tasks in the College.

"Dec. 16. On the 11th day of November I entered on my duties as actual* tutor and nominal Professor in the College of New Jersey. My official labours are not so burdensome but that they leave me considerable time for study. Indeed, I should not have accepted the appointment, except upon the supposition that I should be able to continue my professional pursuits. Having finally resolved upon preparation for the ministry, I feel the satisfaction and advantage of having some one definite object in my studies, instead of wandering amidst a thousand, under the mere guidance of capricious inclination. I have set before me as the specific end of my toils, to become thoroughly acquainted with the *Scriptures;* philologically, theologically, practically; and so to qualify myself for interpreting them properly to others. My studies having this for their chief end, will, at present, fall under three distinct heads: 1. Biblical criticism. 2. Systematic theology. 3. History. To the first I shall for some time devote one whole day in each week; to the second, four; and to the third, one. The first and third will however receive some attention every day. My course of study in the first branch will consist in studying the original Scriptures, and in reading approved works on criticism, under the direction of Mr. Hodge. Before taking up theology proper, my father advises a course

---

* He acted as tutor so far as discipline in the building was concerned, but was never tutor by appointment.

of Metaphysics; upon which I have already entered. My historical reading will, of course, be chiefly in the Ecclesiastical department; but I have determined to embrace this opportunity of laying a firm general foundation. This I shall do by reading the best *original* historical authorities in the languages with which I am acquainted. I shall avoid compilers and second-hand retailers. Content adire integros fontes. My object is to survey for myself the raw stuff—the material from which historiographers have wrought their patch-work. I shall begin with the historical books of the Bible, and then probably proceed to Herodotus. Further I have not yet looked ahead."

The following statement will show what progress he had already made in these departments, and what his scheme was for the future. In Biblical criticism he had begun the gospel of Matthew in Greek; pursuing the method of thorough-going analysis—sifting every syllable and letter, and not even forgetting the accents. He had also begun the Epistle to the Galatians, of which he declares his intention to read it over and over again; first repeatedly in Greek, with critical care, but not with such minute regard to grammatical niceties as in the other exercise; then in all the versions that he finds accessible, comparing the best commentators. When he should think himself well grounded in Galatians, he proposed to go on to Ephesians. He had thus finished the first chapter, making use of "Robert Stephens's magnificent edition," and comparing the text with that of Griesbach. His lexicons at this time were Bretschneider's (Leip. 1829), and Robinson's translation of Wahl. He had also been revising Gesenius's grammar, preparatory to a course of critical reading in Hebrew. The plan he had thought of, was to take some short book and proceed inch by inch as he had done in Matthew. He should also be reading the historical books *pari passu;* but with more freedom. He was to use Kennicott's and Vanderhooght's editions and Gesenius's Hebrew-German Lexicon.

In metaphysics, he had read within a month, Beattie on Truth; Buffier's First Truths; the fourth book of Locke's Essays; the first book of the Novum Organum; Des Cartes's Meditations and the first book of his Principia; Hobbes's treatise on Human Nature; and Reid's Enquiry into the Human Mind. The last he had finished two days before, and was to attack Reid's Essays next.

In history, he had begun Genesis in Hebrew, merely as an exercise in historical literature. I find that he was reading it in Kennicott without the points, which he discovered was a very pleasant method in his unfettered excursions. For purposes of critical analysis he of course used the pointed text. He had this day finished the twenty-sixth chapter.

To metaphysics and theology, he was now devoting four days, viz.: Monday, Wednesday, Thursday and Saturday, or to speak more strictly, the best part of four days, from four to six hours each. To history he devoted Tuesday, and a little additional time on every other day—" say enough to read one chapter." Friday he gave up to the study of books on Biblical criticism. His critical reading in Hebrew and Greek was continued daily and revised on Friday. His chart also included a plan for amusement; nor did he suffer his literary tasks to crowd out his religious meditations.

"Besides these subjects of systematic study, I shall indulge myself moderately in lighter reading as a relaxation. For the present this shall consist in a partial survey of European periodical literature, beginning with the Monthly Review for 1758. I shall read no newspapers (regularly) except the Boston Recorder (a weekly religious paper), which I expect to take. As I know by experience the importance of distributing my time exactly, I have adopted the following scheme to serve till I form a better.

"1. My leisure time in the study hours of College, both before and after dinner; i. e. between nine and twelve in the forenoon, and two and five in the afternoon; I shall devote to the *leading subjects* of the day.

"2. The part of an hour after breakfast and dinner before study hours begin, I shall occupy with my critical reading of Greek and Hebrew.

"3. From eight to nine P. M. shall be sacred to devotion.

"4. The time before breakfast, between twelve M. and dinner, and between evening prayers and eight o'clock, are not appropriated above. The mode of spending this time will depend on circumstances. Sometimes I shall be in at these hours; sometimes not. During one of these intervals I must attend daily to my more cursory reading in Greek and Hebrew.

"The Sabbath is not included in the foregoing arrangements. My reading on that day must be confined to the Scriptures and practical divinity."

Here is a picture of the young scholar among his textbooks. We can almost hear him muttering over the odd-looking pages of his great open volumes.

"Dec. 23. This is my Hebrew day. My object, at present, is to obtain as accurate a knowledge as I can, of the lexiography and grammar of both languages. I choose a passage therefore, merely to serve as a text, and go over it twice. In Hebrew I do this first in Kennicott, without the points, looking for every word in Gesenius's lexicon, and reading the whole article upon it carefully. This is my way of studying the passage lexicographically. I then take the pointed text, and analyze it most minutely, reading at large every article in Gesenius's Elementarbuch which has a bearing upon the subject. By pursuing this plan I shall soon have read a large proportion of the lexicon, and grounded myself pretty completely in the grammar. In this sort of study, the grammar and lexicon are the real objects of attention; the Hebrew passage only serving as an index to the parts to be consulted. In another branch I shall make the exegesis of the passage my chief aim. Even in the former mode, however, I shall be slowly, but surely gaining a thorough knowledge of some parts of the Bible."

The boldness of the attempt to master the entire Hebrew dictionary in one course of study, does not seem to have once occurred to him. With him to resolve was to do; unless his mind was suddenly diverted to something else, or he lost interest in his labours. In the present case neither of these events happened. He was at this time not near so stout as at a later period, and was remarkably good-looking, with short, dark brown hair, and a clear, fresh, florid complexion. His fine blue eyes twinkled through a pair of strong near-sighted glasses. His face was clean-shaven, and he was exquisitely neat in his person, dress, and habits. A lady who saw him for the first time in June of this year tells me that he was very retiring, but very kind and pleasant. To her he was all that was cordial and agreeable, and she should never have dreamed that he was in any important respect different from other people. No one saw much of him, for he was buried among his books at Mr. Patton's school. His devotion to his mother was unbounded. During his illness he was observed again and again to turn his head and look up in her face with glances of wistful love and pleasure. His admiration for her understanding, and the winning charm of her society, was almost as great as his affection for her person.

The uniformity of testimony as to his leading characteristics at this period, leaves no doubt as to what they were.

"From my boyhood," writes one who has travelled far and met with a variety of men,* "I had been accustomed to hear of Addison Alexander through a relation of his who was married to one of my brothers, and who having spent some years in Dr. Alexander's family had, of course, enjoyed the most favourable opportunities for an intimate acquaintance with his son Addison. The minute details thus given me of his manner of life and his various sayings and doings greatly impressed me, and excited a strong desire to see him."

This was before he became known to the public, but even then this writer had learned to look upon him as an intellectual prodigy.

"My personal acquaintance with him was made on my going to Princeton as a student of the college, in which he then held the place of adjunct Professor of Languages. He had previously been carrying on a correspondence with my brother George to induce him to accept a tutorship in the college during his course in the Theological Seminary which he was about to enter; and as I accompanied my brother to Princeton, this circumstance immediately brought me into contact with Mr. Alexander."

He found him affable and kind, unassuming and apparently much like any other educated and pleasant gentleman.

* The Rev. John Leyburn, D. D., of Baltimore, but for many years of Philadelphia, and at one time one of the editors of the *Presbyterian.*

Subsequently he was himself a member of one of his classes in college, and was smitten with the general admiration for his teacher..

"The students among themselves always called him 'Addy,' but they never ventured on familiarity with him. His extraordinary mental gifts and wonderful scholarship were perfectly understood and commanded their respect, while his prompt and decided manner in the recitation-room showed that he was not to be trifled with. He had but little patience at this time with the indolent and negligent, and sometimes cut them up with sharp words."

Occasionally too, it struck him that Mr. Alexander's own gifted and luminous mind had elevated him so far above the common range of intellect as to some extent to incapacitate him from appreciating the difficulties of a naturally dull student.

"One in our class of this description he used to be quite hard upon. He would allow him to flounder along through the lengthy and complicated sentences of Cicero, making the most hideous blunders; the Professor never correcting them, but once in a while casting a glance of mingled astonishment and displeasure at the poor fellow; until having completed his tissue of incomprehensible nonsense, the latter came to a pause. 'Now Mr. ———,' the Professor would say, 'what do you understand by *that!*' The tone in which the question was put, in connexion with the exhibition just made, rendered the thing so ludicrous as to call forth a general titter."

A year or two after the graduation of the Rev. George W, Leyburn of Virginia, it was proposed to him to take a tutorship in the college, and Professor Addison Alexander, as a member of the faculty, conducted the correspondence with him. While, for the next year or two, as tutor and as a student of the seminary, Mr. Leyburn was again at Princeton, he and Mr. Alexander exchanged occasional visits, and the former has never ceased to regret that he did not more fully improve the opportunity he then enjoyed of cultivating acquaintance and intercourse with a man whom he " so much admired, as one of the greatest geniuses of our own or any age. But, though I believe his condescension would have encouraged it, my own diffidence as to seeking such a privilege, and my absorption in the studies of the seminary course, too much restrained me."

That was really the period at which the writer of these reminiscences saw most of him. But that part of his life was spent in the quiet, unconspicuous walks of his college subprofessorship. Nothing of a striking character in regard to it, presents itself to the memory of the survivor.

"He was then pious, though not a minister," and was sometimes at faculty meetings called upon to make an opening or closing prayer; and scarcely any thing in regard to him, during that period, impressed the young tutor more than the rich and easy flow of thought and diction, which marked those prayers.

It will be noticed that Dr. Burrowes bears the same testimony.

Mr. Leyburn then goes on to say that to the eye—*his* eye, at least—the two brothers were men of quite different appearance:

"The one being a man of pale, pensive face of oval shape, the other having a fair complexion and a rotundity of face and person which made me think of the phlegmatic German students, according at least to my idea of them, who fatten upon study. I once thought of Professor Addison Alexander as one who could almost do the same, a real salamander as to the capability of endurance in this respect."

But on his renewing his acquaintance with him on his second sojourn in Princeton, Mr. Alexander expressed to him the opinion that no man of sedentary habits could do without seasons of relaxation, and told him that he had himself suffered in health from too great confinement and labour in study, during the time he was at Mr. Patton's. He appeared to allude especially to the severe work he had had in getting ready the edition of Donnegan.

"But," continues Mr. Leyburn, "though dissimilar in some things of the outer man, the two brothers were much alike in others: in that musical tone of their voices, their eminently high and varied culture, and the remarkable fecundity of thought and flow of correct and elegant language which made them such attractive and even fascinating men to those who listened to them publicly or privately or read the rich productions of their pens.

"They were to me, I believe, the two men who of all that I have ever actually known, threw over me the spell of an admiration amounting to a kind of charm; and I think of them with a peculiar sadness, oft-times, as taken away just in the glowing ripeness of those high powers and graceful accomplishments which clustered so richly about both of them. 'Was it,' I sometimes ask myself, 'in their cases the realization of the idea of an early, rapid, and astonishingly beautiful efflorescence, to be followed by a correspondingly early and what would seem to us premature decay and dropping of the leaf?' But I felt as if the whole church of God, this western continent that gave them birth, and this generation at large, had to mourn the death of the two Alexanders."

Mr. Alexander wrote but two articles for the Repertory this year; for the July number, a Review of Guerike's Life* of "August Hermann Francke;" and for the October number, a most lively, racy, entertaining, and skilful showing up of Madden's "Travels in Turkey, Egypt, Nubia, and Palestine in 1824, 1825, 1826, and 1827." The article on Francke is mainly biographical, and is bright and vivid in its character.

Among the students of this time was Parke Godwin, Esq., of New York, the well known editor and historian. He has politely furnished me with the following recollections of his old teacher, who at the period referred to was in years barely a man. Mr. Godwin writes that the impression which the

---

*The following is a list of his contributions to the Philadelphia "Morning Journal" in 1830:

"I cannot positively in every case distinguish them from J. W. A.'s, but am pretty confident of the following.—J. H."

Jan. 15. "Carsten Niebuhr."
" 16. Several literary paragraphs.
Feb. 24. "The Child of Mystery, translated from a Persian MS."
" 27. Literary paragraphs.
March 31. A humorous letter for an ambitious author.
April 14. "Arabic Anecdotes, translated from the original."

young professor made upon him is still very distinct. It will be found that Mr. Godwin's ideas as to the attainments of his youthful instructor do not differ materially from those of others who were better acquainted with him.

"I shall never forget the abruptness as well as the sagacity of the first remark he made to our class, during the Sophomore year.' 'Young gentlemen,' he said, in a quick but positive way, 'all knowledge is pleasant.' He then stopped for a moment that we might digest the truth. 'All knowledge is pleasant,' he resumed: 'and I shall therefore take it for granted, when I hear that any one does not like any particular study, that he does not know any thing about it.' That was about the whole of his address, and you may infer from it that he received few complaints from us, during his incumbency at least. "Addy" as we called him familiarly, was held in the profoundest respect by all the students; and for two reasons: the first was, that nobody ever saw him, except in the class; and the second, that we imputed to him a marvellous amount of human knowledge of all sorts. He was supposed to study about eighteen hours a day, adding to his already prodigious acquirements; and these acquirements were computed at no less than thirteen different languages, and all the then known Natural Sciences.* You may imagine that we always approached him with a feeling of awe and veneration.

"I found afterwards that these popular estimates of the students' halls were scarcely exaggerated; he was a marvel of erudition; his learning was no less accurate than comprehensive; he seemed to find no difficulty in mastering any tongue or any science; and what was better than this mere facility of accumulation was the thoroughness with which he assimilated his omnivorous gatherings. It could not be said of him, what Robert Hall said of Dr. Kippis, that 'he had so many books on his head that his brains couldn't move.' His brains did move, and moved to great effect. When he either wrote or spoke, his matter was original, well-considered, apt, and vivacious. You wondered alike at its fulness, its fluency, and its fervour. His lectures and sermons were models of chaste and elegant composition, as well as of a complete mastery of the subject. He was not eloquent in the sense that his brother James Waddel Alexander was, but he was always instructive, elevating and moving; and no student willingly

* It is due to truth to say that Mr. Alexander's knowledge of the natural sciences was but slight.

staid away from chapel when it was given out that he was about to occupy the pulpit."

Of his personal traits Mr. G. can give no account. The professor was always hard at work, and was as shy as a fawn.

"He was then so close a student that none but the members of his family saw much of him, and when a chance encounter brought you into his presence he was generally very shy and reserved. It was the ambition of all of us to become intimate with him: but we were not permitted the opportunity. I regret that I cannot furnish you other particulars, as I have never ceased to love and admire the man, as one of the noblest and most gifted of our fellow countrymen."

The plan of study indicated in the foregoing journal of 1830, Mr. Alexander carried out faithfully during the year 1831; and his diary consists of nothing but a view of his daily employment under this rigid scheme. The following list embraces most of the works upon which he was engaged: in psychology and kindred sciences, Reid's Essays, Brown's Lectures, Stewart's Elements, Payne's Elements, and Edwards on the Will; in Persian, Bakhtyarnameh;* in German, Gesenius's Handbuch, Gesenius's History of the Hebrew Language, and a large part of Conversations Lexicon; in the ancient languages, Thucydides, Herodotus, parts of Plato, parts of Demosthenes, and parts of Aristophanes, besides many pages of the Latin classics; in Biblical criticism and theology, Wetstein's Prolegomena, and New Testament in Greek; parts of Schramm's Analysis Patrum, Stillingfleet's Origines Sacræ, Kennicott's Disertatio Generalis, Pictet, Herbert Marsh's Lectures, Watson's Institutes, and Turretin; in history and upon miscellaneous topics, Dunlop's History of Roman Literature, various works on the History of India, the New Monthly Magazine, and the Boston Recorder; besides whatever fell into his hands during his idle moments, if any of his moments could be so called. He was moreover a faithful at-

---

* Or the story of Prince Bakhtyarnameh and the ten viziers.

tendant upon his father's lectures on metaphysics, which were delivered to one of the classes in the Seminary.

In addition to all this, he continued his study of Portuguese and Danish, and commenced the study of Turkish. This last item is gathered from the following record :

"October 22. — Began to study Turkish in an old *Grammaire Turque*, which may be regarded as a typographical curiosity; as it was printed a hundred years ago in Constantinople. I have examined it before, but never studied it with care. I went to-day through the chapter on adjectives; the language appears to be remarkably free from grammatical anomalies."

And on the 25th :

"Learned the personal, possessive, and relative pronouns, the cardinal, ordinal, and distributive numerals in Turkish. I think this language more remarkable, so far as I am yet acquainted with it, for regularity than any other which I have attempted.* It takes precedence of the Persian, quoad hoc, because the latter is remarkable for paucity of changes and inflections, whereas Turkish has a multitude, e. g. five cases of nouns distinctly marked. I shall wait, however, till I enter on the verb, before I pass judgment."

The common opinion was then and still is, that he not only had a dislike for metaphysical reasoning, but was wholly unacquainted with what had been done in this department. It will be seen from the extract which follows, as is evident from the many like it, that this opinion was erroneous. He was well read in the writings of the English and Scotch schools, and though he never lost an opportunity of satirizing the German idealists, few persons were better informed as to their names and the nature of their speculations; and no one, unless Henry Rogers, has given us a better parody of their† manner than he has done in the "Diagnosis of the I and the Not-I," in the Princeton Magazine,‡ or has made them the

* See Max Müller Sc. Lang. First Series, pp. 108, 109. Ch. Scribner, N. Y., 1862.

† See the Grayson Letters.

‡ "'DIAGNOSIS OF THE I AND THE NOT—I.'—Assuming as we safely may that all the reflex actings of the rational idea towards the pole of semi-entity are

butt of a more intelligent and refined ridicule, than he has done casually in his Seminary lectures, and his review articles, as well as in various squibs in his children's books. There is a trace of this raillery in the subjoined burlesque on the disproportionate zeal with which writers often advocate their hobbies.

"PRIZE ESSAY UPON NOTHING.*

"The apparent incongruity of coming forward, at the present crisis, when the minds of men are agitated by the fear of fiscal and political convulsion, with a systematic treatise upon nothing, will, it is fondly hoped, be found excusable, on a deliberate examination of the principles maintained and the practical inferences thence deduced.

CHAPTER I.

"1. Nothing may be defined not any thing.

"2. It naturally divides itself into two species, positive nothing, and negative nothing.

"3. Positive nothing includes every thing of which the non-entity is demonstrable.

"4. Negative nothing includes every thing, of which the non-entity may be presumed, but cannot be demonstrated.

"5. The principal use of Nothing, is to nullify every thing.

"6. Nothing may be converted into something, by abstracting its non-entity.

naturally complicated with a tissue of non-negative impressions, which can only be disintegrated by a process of spontaneous and intuitive abstraction, it inevitably follows, as a self-sustaining corollary, that the isolated and connatural conceptions, formed in this antespeculative stage of intellectual activity, must be reflected on the faculty itself, or, to speak with philosophical precision, on the I, when viewed concretely as the Not–I ; and in this reciprocal self-reproduction, carried on by the direct and transverse action of the Reason and the Understanding, modified of course by those extraneous and illusory perceptions, which can never be entirely excluded from the mutual relations of the pure intelligence on the one hand and the mixed operations of the will and the imagination on the other, may be detected, even by an infant eye, the true solution of this great philosophical enigma, the one sole self-developing criterion of the elementary difference between the Not–I and the I."—Princeton Magazine, p. 35.

*From Wistar's Magazine.

"7. Nobody may become nothing by being deprived of its negative personality.

"8. Any thing may become nothing, by annihilation. The only other remark which I propose to offer on this interesting and important point is—nothing."

His wonderful powers of analysis are as evident in some of these little whimsical effusions which he poured out almost spontaneously, as in his serious works. His mind moved as regularly as a planet.

His opinion as to the relative merits of two of the most eminent writers in this department may be gathered from the following record:

"Jan. 8. Read cursorily the first volume of Dugald Stewart's Philosophy of the Human Mind. I read this book once before. I liked it better then than now. He seems to me to have made himself master of all Dr. Reid's discoveries, and then to have busied himself in clothing them in elegant but diffuse expressions—just differing enough from his exemplar to escape the charge of servile plagiarism. From his studied attention to style and his frequent introduction of historical illustrations, I infer that he was more of a rhetorician than a philosopher. He appears to care more for the way in which he says a thing than for what he says."

His adversaria of this period evince the same shrewd, critical acquaintance with Reid and Brown, and the same discriminative appreciation of their philosophical labours. The literary merits of Stewart and Brown could not escape an eye that loved to wander over every pleasing territory in the domain of the belles-lettres, and it required but a single glance of so penetrating an intellect to discover the defect in Brown's Theory of Cause, which had already been conclusively pointed out by Dr. Archibald Alexander, and was afterwards more fully exposed by Sir William Hamilton. The son had probably read the father's article, but gives his own independent impressions.

Whatever else he did, or failed to do, he at no time neglected the study of the Scriptures in the original tongues.

Hebrew, whether with or without points, he could now read and write with somewhat of the ease of his vernacular. On the same day with the reference to Stewart, there is the following reminiscence of Mr. Alexander's early Oriental tastes, which were never entirely brought into subjection to his later views with regard to the Indo-European tongues in general and the importance of the Biblical or Hellenistic Greek.

"Read in Hebrew the historical parts of Exodus xv, and the whole of chapters xvi, xvii. Read a number of articles in Gesenius's lexicon. Read ten pages in Bakhtyar-Nameh (Persian). Read the first volume of the Mussulman, a novel by the traveller, Madden. Interesting from its illustrations of Oriental character and manners, but full of affectation and false taste. There seems to be a covert aim at satire upon European manners running through the work."

The subjoined entries explain themselves, and show very fully what he was doing in the way of generous excursion into various fields of knowledge.

"Feb. 3. Continued Payne's Elements of Mental Science. Read a portion of Thucydides. The second part of Matthiae's Greek Grammar (comprising the syntax) contains the most copious collection of authorities, I suspect, that is anywhere extant. The index of the passages cited occupies, of itself, above 200 pages. I think of reading the volume and analyzing the citations as I go along. Read the first section in this way to-day."

The discreet estimate here given of the great work of Matthiae, reveals only partially the thorough way in which Mr. Alexander prosecuted his researches in this and every other direction. He was versed also in such authors as Winer, Kühner, Wahl, Thiersch and Buttmann, and of nearly all of the English and American compilations which he thought worth his attention. But in Greek as in every other language he had his own, original, unwritten grammar and lexicon, derived from his own surprising recollection of the various meanings and relations of the words, phrases, and idioms he had met with in reading. There is no one but has been struck with this in perusing his "Matthew" or "Mark," or his work on "the Acts." A compendious but characteristic lexicon, as well as grammar, of the Greek language, especially in its Hellenistic form, might almost be constructed out of the hints that are thrown out in these three books. The plan of mastering the citations as well as the text of Matthiae, he fully accomplished. Sometimes the entries in his diary are in Greek, sometimes Italian, sometimes French, sometimes in Arabic or even Persian.

The items which followed enable us to trace him through the summer.

"Aug. 8. Read in Greek Ps. xxxviii–xliii. Read in Greek and English, Ephesians i. Read in Greek three sections in the Melpomene of Herodotus. Read in German the articles "Englische Poesie," "Engl. Theatre" and part of the article "Deutsche Literatur" in Conversations-Lexicon. Read in English Woodbridge's account of the maritime divisions of the earth. Read the 23d chapter of Matthew in ancient and modern Greek. Read the first chapter of John in Danish. Wrote three pages of Valpy's Greek Exercises.

"Aug. 18. Read Psalms xc–xciv in the Septuagint. Read Philippians ii. in Greek and English. Read Matthew xxvi in ancient and modern Greek. Read forty-nine sections in the Melpomene of Herodotus. Read the latter half of the Batrachoi of Aristophanes in Kuster's edition, referring to his Latin version and Greek scholia. This play is truly witty, and has this advantage that there is nothing immoral or indecent in the plot, and very little in the language. The satire on Euripides is very amusing, but that on Bacchus and the heathen mythology still better. I think, with a little expurgation and exposition, this comedy might be made an excellent text-book."

I find the following isolated experimental record.

"June 5. Read a considerable part of Halyburton's life with avidity and astonishment. I seemed to be reading a history of my own life. I speak within bounds when I say that up to the age of twenty his spiritual history is mine in almost every point. Both minister's sons, and both ministers of the same communion—both guarded, in an unusual degree, by circumstances from exterior temptation—both outwardly exemplary, inwardly corrupt—both led to seek religion by distress—both tormented with the fear of death! The coincidence is truly wonderful. The account of his vows and resolutions; his frequent breaches of them; his distress in consequence; his subsequent resorts and shifts—I might transcribe and make my own. I was obliged to pause sometimes and wonder at these strange coincidences; and I bless God that the book fell into my hands. From the experience of one whose early history was so much like my own, I have learned some precious lessons. Some enigmas have been solved; some mysteries of iniquity developed; some obstacles removed; some useful hints suggested. On one head particularly, I have been much edified. When my conscience has been wounded by relapses into sin, I have always been tempted to sink down into a sullen apathy, or else to wait a day or two before approaching God again. It has seemed to me, on such occasions, that it would be awfully presumptuous and insolent to ask God to forgive me *on the spot.* I never knew why I thought so until Halyburton told me. I had been trusting in my abstinence from sin, instead of Christ's atonement, so that when surprised and vanquished, by temptation, I felt that my foundation was removed, my righteousness gone, and I had no righteousness wherewith to purchase favour. It pleased God this afternoon to use the memoir as an instrument in fixing on my mind a strong conviction that the only reasonable course is to come at once, and ask forgiveness in the name of Christ. The remarks which particularly struck me as conclusive were these three :

1. After an act of known transgression, every moment that I spend without applying to the blood of Christ I spend in sin; and consequently aggravate my guilt.

2. It was my folly to suppose that I should never sin again. He that trusteth to his own heart is a fool.

3. Above all I seemed to have received new light upon a point which I never before thought of as I ought, viz. that God's chief end in dealing with men's souls is not to discipline them nor save them; but to promote his own glory. Now He chooses to glorify all his attributes together—His mercy as well as His justice. To distrust the extent of His forgiving mercy through Christ Jesus, therefore, is an insult. It is in vain that the sinner talks about his unworthiness and the greatness of his sins. Poor wretch;—if God thought of your unworthiness you might well despair; but it is to glorify Himself that He invites you! You may be sure, therefore, that He will receive you. This is an humbling but delightful doctrine. I feel, however, the necessity of guarding against an antinomian spirit. Self-righteousness and antinomianism are my Scylla and Charybdis."

At the close of a letter to one of his old pastor's sons, a friend* thus expresses his sense of obligation to the Reverend James W. Alexander, who was still labouring at the State capital:

"While writing this there have been constantly running in my mind remembrances of my youthful days, blended with your sainted father, when in that old church in Trenton with its lofty galleries and pulpit perched aloft between the doors, I took, in the depths of my soul, impressions from his then peerless preaching, which have done so much towards forming my literary taste and moulding my religious life; times when in my father's gig I drove him to some neighbouring church on Saturday, to preach on the Sabbath and return on Monday; and with what hearty pleasure, he would have me stop the horse that he might go along the banks of a brook to gather wild flowers and magnolias; and with what happiness he entered into the beauties of the green fields, and of the summer works of that God whom he adored and Saviour whom he loved so well. But my hand is weary and I must pause."

How pleasing it would be to be able to give a record of the words that fell from the lips of the brothers James and Addison in conversation! This is of course impossible. A few sentences of it has been preserved in letters and commonplace books. One day speaking of Watson the Methodist, whom he had just compared to Turretin, the younger brother exclaimed with vivacity, and I have no doubt with a beaming countenance, "He reasons like Paley and descants like Hall!" To this opinion his auditor heartily subscribes.† On another occasion, in a later year of this general period, the talk fell upon childrens' books and the younger scholar said to his delighted companion, "Don't try to vary the Bible language too much; say what you will it is the most intelligible to children. Don't try too much to improve upon the Bible; let what you add be exegetical and brief." He went on then to say that "a thousand books may yet be made out of the raw

---

* Dr. Burrowes, of Easton.
† Fam. Lett. Vol. I., p. 181.

Bible material, with very little alteration of the text. Thus one may take all that relates to the archæology of the Hebrew houses, and make a book of it; and that not by casting the scriptural parts into the pigeon-holes of formal artistical arrangement, but following the exact order of the scripture story. Take one subject and chase it through the canon."*

His thirst for knowledge was no less insatiable than when as a boy he devoured strange volumes in his father's garret. On the sixth of July he writes, "I was seized to-day with a strong desire to study geography, created probably by the perusal of Kotzebue and Stewart's voyages." He continued this investigation with some mental entertainment until he had finished one of Woodbridge's school text-books. He was always passionately fond of books of travels. "England's Forgotten Worthies," Drake, Raleigh, and the other early navigators, were as fascinating personages to him in his rural solitude, as they were ever to Froude. He lived largely, as in his boyhood, in an ideal or imaginary world. He could summon round him at will, the famous personages of ancient or modern history; the men and women of the Bible; the scenery and manners of the East or of the West; the fictitious actors in the story of Cervantes, in the dramas of Shakespeare, in the chivalrous ballads of Firdusi, in the glorious poems of Homer. His studies all ministered to the purest æsthetic as well as to higher forms of intellectual enjoyment.

During this time he was a contributor at intervals to Walsh's National Gazette of Philadelphia, and to the Princeton Courier, a weekly newspaper.† But in the midst of all his laborious and diversified pursuits he saved time for the most heart-searching exercises in his closet. He gave himself up to daily communion with his God. He might neglect every thing else, but he could not neglect his private devotions. In point of fact he neglected nothing. He moved as by clockwork. The cultivation of personal piety, in the light of the

---

* Fam. Lett. Vol. I., p. 219.
† None of these articles is in the *Courier* known to be extant.

inspired word, was now with him the main object that he had in life. The next most prominent goal that he set before himself was the interpretation of the original scriptures; for their own sake, and for the benefit of a rising ministry, as well as for the gratification he took in the work. The Bible was to him the most profoundly interesting book in the world. It was in his eyes not merely the only source of true and undefiled religion, but also the very paragon among all remains of human genius. He knew great portions of it by heart. He was now, or afterwards became, a consummate master of every one of its idioms, of the wide embrace of its contents, of the whole sweep of its doctrine, evidence, history, and literature, of much of the broad domain of exterior but kindred science and belles-lettres, of the innumerable manuscripts and versions, of the immense field of patristic comment and modern hermeneutics and criticism; and long before the close of his life, he had analyzed every book, every chapter, every paragraph, every sentence, every word, every syllable, every letter, of which an analysis was possible, with a degree of minuteness, precision, clearness, originality, force, and comprehensive fulness, and with an humble childlike reverence for truth as it is in Jesus, which, as exhibited in his printed volumes, have awakened the respect of pious scholars on both sides of the Atlantic, without distinction of creed or rubric. But more than this: the Bible was the chief object of his personal enthusiasm; he was fond of it; he loved it; he was proud of it; he exulted in it. It occupied his best thoughts by day and by night. It was his meat and drink. It was his delectable reward. There were times when he might say with the Psalmist, "Mine eyes prevent the night watches that I might meditate in thy word, I have rejoiced in the way of thy precepts more than in great riches." He succeeded perfectly in communicating this delightful zeal to others. His pupils all concur in saying that "he made the Bible glorious" to them.

On the twenty-first of May we have another isolated record of his religious experience:

"I have been grievously tempted to-day, and the temptation has not left me. It is on me at this moment; I take refuge in the act of writing, from its assaults. Oh, that I were delivered from this body of death!

How strange a conflict! between a man and himself! How strange the coëxistence of two wills in one person!—a will to do evil and a will to avoid it.

"When I look forward to temptations I am always confident of victory, and that an easy one. I have a vague idea that the foe to be contended with is something extrinsic to myself, and feel myself interested, therefore, in resisting unto blood. But when the trial comes and I find arrayed against me my own strongest propensities and tenderest affections, when every blow aimed at the tempter rends a fibre of my heart—then is my strength indeed found perfect weakness.

"It grieves me, too, and galls me to discover by experience, that the strongest deductions of my reason are of little use by themselves in the moment of temptation. During an interval of calm, dispassionate reflection, I revolve a moral question in my mind. I weigh all the arguments on both sides. I am satisfied—entirely satisfied that reason, conscience, gratitude, require me, una voce, to do this, or abstain from that. I foolishly imagine that with such convictions I can never be seduced into transgression. A strong temptation fastens on me—all my fortified conclusions seem to vanish into air! I no longer seem to be a rational creature. Instinct, passion, appetite, appear to be omnipotent. I may remember all my arguments, but I no longer feel their force. What then is to sustain me? The grace of God imparted at the moment and proportioned to the exigency. How is it to be had? By prayer and holy living through the Saviour's intercession. How shall I be assured of having it in season? Trust—trust—trust in God. Remember that you do not deserve to be sustained at all; that if you are, it is a mere favour. What assurance, then, is wanting but a knowledge of God's goodness and a firm faith in his promises?"

He does not seem to have written any this year for the Biblical Repertory.

The year 1832 was occupied very much as the last. Besides finishing, or continuing the perusal of the works already named, but not fully read, he addicted himself to Horne's Introduction, Paley's Natural Theology; Paley's Evidences; Murdock's Mosheim; Gesenius's Einleitung on Isa.; Stuart on Hebrews; Wolf's Bibliotheca Hebraica; Alexander on the Canon; Acts of the Synod of Dort; Clarendon's History of the Rebellion; and Milner's Letters on the Christian Ministry. He also studied Isaiah, in Hebrew, Chaldee, Syriac, Greek, Latin, English, Arabic, and German, with Rosenmüller's and Gesenius's and Lowth's notes; the Peshito, and the Targum of Jonathan; also Campbell's gospels; Hugo Einleitung; Bush on Millennium, etc.

I find the following record:

"March 11. At the conference last Lord's Day, my father urged upon the students the duty of storing their memory with Scripture. I resolved, by way of experiment, to get by heart a portion of Scripture every day, both in English and the original."

In pursuance of this purpose, during this year, he committed the whole of the Psalms in Hebrew and English, and the first few verses of each chapter in Isaiah; and the epistles of Romans and Hebrews in Greek and English. He also fastened in his memory the succession of events in the gospels of Matthew, Mark and Luke, so as to be able to give an analysis of each chapter from memory.

He had, during the previous year, studied critically, almost the whole of the Bible in that thorough and exhaustive way proposed in his plan of study. This work he now completed. He also thoroughly mastered several grammars of the German, Syriac and Chaldee languages. During most of this time he was giving instruction to two classes in the college in Greek; writing for Walsh's Review, the Biblical Repertory, and the Presbyterian; teaching one of his brothers and a young lady German and French, and reading the English poets with them; besides reading English reviews, many treatises on various subjects, and portions of many books, great and small, not enumerated above.

"PRINCETON, *July* 31, 1832.

"DEAR SIR,

"I happened to hear, not long ago, that you were editing the S. S. J. *pro tempore*. The thought occurred at once, that this arrangement might be rendered permanent with great advantage to the institution. I was not aware, at that time, of the purpose to employ another editor, which you have since informed me of. Your letter of last week affords me an opportunity of meddling in the matter, which I do at once by saying, that I think you called by Providence to undertake this business. I speak, of course, in deference to public interests. Those private relations and considerations which may bear upon the case, I know nothing about. Looking at the thing from the Sunday School side only, I should certainly have given you my vote, if qualified, even though I had never been called upon to do it by way of repartee.

"I do not deny, that arguments suggest themselves in favour of my doing what you ask. But I can truly say that there is not one of them (I mean of such of them as rest upon the ground of public utility) which does not reach you just as fully as myself. And then besides these, there are others which apply to you alone, and strongly too. Let me mention three as samples. (1.) You have experience and resources as an editor, which I have not. (2.) You are already familiar with the entire system, or, to use the new word, 'cause'—of Sunday Schools. (3.) You would not be forsaking one field of usefulness to rush, perhaps at no small hazard, into another. That many things in the life of an editor would please me, I admit. But you see how stoically I have set aside the dulce for the utile.

"I am afraid that you will find this a very informal and unscientific answer to your protocol. Please to lay the blame of its defects, in part upon a class of interesting youth who are awaiting me, and in part upon my own procrastination, which has left your favour unacknowledged for a week. With true, though tardy thanks for it, I now stop short.

"Yours, truly,
"ADDISON ALEXANDER.

"*J. Hall, Esq.*

"On stating the substance of the above to James, he graciously assented to it. He desires me to say that he has received your letter and may answer it (or *will*—I have forgotten which.)"

CHAPTER VIII.

DURING the year 1832, Mr. Alexander contributed no less than six articles to the Princeton Quarterly, viz. one on Hengstenberg's Daniel, one on Arabian and Persian Lexicography, one on the Historical Statements of the Koran, one on Gibbs's Manual, one on De Sacy's Arabic Grammar, and one on Hebrew Grammar. There is something in the profusion of his mind at this time that strikes one with fresh astonishment and admiration. His efforts of this period are equal in most respects to any of his life. His continued preference of Oriental themes to classical, would seem to show that whatever might be the ripening conclusions of his judgment, the governing bent of his inclinations was still towards the tongues that are spoken in the tents of Shem; though he tells us that he was now becoming daily more and more enamoured of Greek, and soon came to rate it as his first choice among all his studies. This was so at the time of his appointment as teacher in the Seminary; but as he says himself, he was already somewhat weaned from anatolic studies as early as 1829, when under the guiding influence of Patton he began to explore the wonders of modern German philology, and under the stimulus of new and better grammars to ground himself in the principles of profound classical scholarship. The years intervening between his residence at Edgehill and his first European voyage, was the transition period.

At the time these articles were published he was on the point of casting the slough of his Semitic tastes and proclivities, and to wear it no more as his favourite and almost exclusive vesture. He was in a short time to emerge from his youthful chrysalis apparelled in intellectual garments of scarcely less resplendent richness. He was (to modify the figure) about to clothe himself in raiment wrought out of the Indo-

European looms. But the language he was learning more and more to love was Greek. It was to become almost as easy to him as his native tongue. It was for it he was to give up his coat of many colours by which he had been distinguished from his brethren. If the languages of the East (and the remark is chiefly applicable to the Persian)* in their variegated splendour were his *toga prætexta*, the Greek in its snow-white purity may be said to have been his *toga virilis*, which still however bore its fringe of anatolic purple. He clung to the Hebrew and the cognate dialects, and to the Hellenistic Greek, with ever growing enthusiasm and unconquerable affection.

Perhaps the most remarkable of these contributions is the one on the "Historical Statements of the Koran," † though the one on " De Sacy's Arabic Grammar " ‡ is of the same general character, and exhibits the same sort of philological and critical ability; and, besides the remarks more strictly germane to the subject of De Sacy's volume, is distinguished by a luminous exposition of the relation between the Arabic and the Hebrew. The article on "Hebrew Grammar" is also very learned and able, discovering a thorough acquaintance with the writings of Jahn, Storr, Buxtorf, Gesenius, Lee, Michaelis, Hoffman, and Ewald. The article on "Gibbs's Manual Lexicon," is a short but appreciative notice of the admirable vade-mecum put forth by the Yale Professor, for the benefit of Hebrew and Chaldee students, in the year 1832.

It is interesting in this connection to note the fact that Mr. Alexander was afterwards a pupil of Gesenius and Nordheimer, and a bearer of despatches between De Sacy and Freytag.

The article on "Hengstenberg's Vindication of the Book

---

* I am aware that the Persian, though written in Arabic characters, is not one of the Semitic languages.

† Bib. Rep., 1832, p. 195.

‡ Bib. Rep., 1832, p. 543. "Grammaire Arabe, à l'usage des élèves de l'école spéciale des langues orientales vivantes; avec figures. Par M. le Baron Silvestre de Sacy," &c., &c. "Paris; imprimé par autorisation du Roi," &c.

of Daniel," * is equally attractive on similar as well as on very different grounds. Mr. Alexander, as we shall presently see, was afterwards somewhat intimately associated with this Coryphæus of Evangelical criticism in Germany, both as his pupil and friend. He probably owed more as a commentator to Hengstenberg than to any other man, unless it was Calvin. He was an early convert to the outlines of Hengstenberg's Messianic theory, as well as to his general views as to the structure of prophecy; and though he discarded many of his particular opinions and interpretations, believing them to be in some instances palpably incorrect and in others mere visionary crotchets; and while he never yielded himself up to the slavish guidance of any teacher; he yet held this great scholar in the most exalted estimation, for his learning, his bold sagacity, his strength of will and breadth of mind, his independence of judgment, vigour of logic, soundness of view, and eminent piety. His own work on the Psalms was in large part a reproduction in another form, of Hengstenberg's; and while in his "Isaiah" he often mentions the great German only to differ from him, he never mentions him in terms that are inconsistent with the highest respect and admiration.

But the article on the Koran is the one in which Mr. Alexander seems to have exerted the whole force of his mind, and gives what is possibly the best *coup d'œil* that can now be had of the grasp and reach of his acquisitions in Arabic literature. In this article he not only corrects many of the numerous blunders, loose translations, and wrong translations, into which Sale has wittingly or unwittingly fallen, but takes "the Perspicuous Book" to pieces precisely as a watchmaker takes to pieces a watch, rearranging and systematizing the historical portions of the volume on a plan of his own. It must have been a gigantic toil, but it was a labour of love. The same faculty of minute analysis which he afterwards

---

* Bib. Rep., 1832, p. 48. "Die Authentie des Daniel und die Integritaet des Sacharjah, Erwiesen von Ernst Wilhelm Hengstenberg, Dr. der Phil. und der Theol. der letzt. ord. Prof. Berlin, 1831, 8vo."

brought to bear upon the gospels of Mark and Matthew, is here brought to bear upon certain obscure or controverted passages of the Mussulman's Bible.

But what lends a popular interest to the article, and impresses upon it a strongly distinctive character, is the fact that it also exhibits a complete view of Mohammedanism and its relation to Christianity, and makes known the author's own conceptions of the great deceiver of Islam.* The reader will be richly rewarded by a perusal of the following extracts:

"The Mohammedan religion is, in some respects, the most remarkable of all false religions. The specious simplicity of its essential doctrines, and its perfect freedom from idolatry, distinguish it forever from the gross mythology of classical and oriental paganism. But besides these characteristics, it displays a third, more interesting still. We mean the peculiar relation which it bears to Christianity. Whether it happened from a happy accident or a sagacious policy, we think it clear that Islam owes a vast proportion of its success, to the fact that Mohammed built upon another man's foundation. Assuming the correctness of the common doctrine that the impostor was a brilliant genius, though a worthless libertine, and that his book is the offspring not of insane stupidity but of consummate contrivance, there certainly is ground for admiration in the apparent union of simplicity and efficacy in the whole design. The single idea of admitting freely the divine legation of the Hebrew seers, and exhibiting himself as the top-stone of the Edifice, the Last Great Prophet, and the Paraclete of Christ, has certainly the aspect of a master-stroke of policy. Besides conciliating multitudes of Jews and soi-disant Christians at the very first, this circumstance has aided the imposture not a little ever since. It relieves the Moslem doctors of the necessity of waging war against both law and gospel." * * *

Every discrepancy is at once conveniently resolved into corruption in the text.

* It is interesting to compare the impressions of this young scholar, impressions mainly derived either from admitted facts in the history or else from the naked text of the Koran, with the results of modern criticism and the investigations of such thorough-going workmen as Mommsen. A very striking view of these results is embodied in an article entitled "Mahomet" in the Ed. Rev. for 1866.

"It is not the policy of Islam to array itself against the Jewish and the Christian dispensations, as an original and independent system; but to assume the same position in relation to the Gospel, which the Gospel seems to hold in relation to the Law—or in other words, to make itself the grand dénouement of that grand scheme of which the old and new Testaments were only the preparatory stages. Indeed, if we were fully satisfied that the *Rasool Allah* * had any plan at all, we should be disposed to account for it in this way. He was acquainted with three forms of religion, Judaism, Christianity, and Paganism. Disgusted with the latter, he was led, we may suppose, to make some inquiries into the points of difference between the Jews and Christians. This he could not do without discovering their singular relations to each other." * * * "This fact might very readily suggest the project of a new dispensation—a third one to the Christian, and a second to the Jew. The impostor would thus be furnished with an argument *ad hominem* to stop the mouths of both. To the Jews he could say, Did not Moses tell your fathers that a prophet should rise up in the latter days, greater than all before him? I am he. Do you doubt it? Here is a revelation just received from Gabriel. Do not all your sacred books predict the coming of a great deliverer, a conqueror, a king? I am he. In a few months you shall see me at the head of a thousand tribes going forth to the conquest of the world.

"If this was the ground really taken at first, how striking must have been the seeming confirmation of these bold pretensions, when Mohammed and his successors had in fact subjected, not Arabia only, but Greece, Persia, Syria, and Egypt.

"To the objection of the Christians, that the line of prophets was long since completed, he could answer, Did not Jesus come to abrogate or modify the law, when its provisions were no longer suited to the state of things? Even so come I, to supersede the Gospel—not to discredit it but to render it unnecessary, by a more extensive and authoritative doctrine. So far from being Antichrist (as some no doubt objected) I am the very comforter whom Jesus promised.

"That such sophistry might easily have undermined the faith of renegadoes and half-pagan Christians, is certainly conceivable. Whether this was in fact the course adopted in the infancy of Islam will admit of a doubt. Be that as it may, it is certain that the Impostor considered it expedient to incorporate the leading facts of Sacred his-

---

* The Apostle of God. We are not aware that Mohammed ever called himself a prophet.—J. A. A.

tory into his revelation, so far as they were known to him. That his knowledge of the subject was imperfect, need not excite our wonder. The sources which probably supplied his information, could scarcely be expected to remit a purer stream than that which irrigates the pages of the Perspicuous Book."

In illustration of the way in which he could combine learning, exegesis, irony, keen criticism, wit, humour, sarcasm, caution, moderation, strong writing, and knock-down argument, in the same paragraph, I adduce the following:

"One thing more in this account of the creation may deserve our notice, 'He said to the heaven and earth, Come, either obediently or against your will.' This was obviously intended as a match for that inimitable sentence 'God said, Let there be light and light was.' One can hardly help smiling at the Irish sublimity of poor Mohammed's masterpiece, the alternative proposed to two nonentities, and their sagacious choice. It is but just, however, to admit, that the language may be considered as addressed to the heavens and the earth after they were created; but before they were arranged and beautified."

What follows sheds a new light on the Arabian tales with which we have all been familiar from our childhood:

"The Genii, we are told in the chapter of Al Hejr [c. xv.] were made of *subtle fire*, as Sale translates it. The original words are *nar semum*, the latter term properly denoting the hot wind of the desert called *simoom* by travellers. There is something poetical in this idea, which would no doubt strike the fervid fancy of a Bedouin with mighty force."

It is not proposed to follow out the writer along the various ramifying lines of this intricate but often alluring investigation. The concluding words of this article, however, convey such ocular proof of his capacity as a critic and philologist, and as a writer of flexible and muscular English, and show him in so many various attitudes and lights, that it seems proper to reanimate them from the dust which always envelopes the bound volumes of anonymous periodical literature. His inventive turn, or shall I say his planning faculty, which was always so prolific of new schemes and suggestions, finds full play in this learned essay. His views respecting translated grammars will strike many persons as novel and worthy of attention. His witty allusion to the Chinese tailor is characteristic. There is indeed an air of light-hearted gaiety about the whole performance. This was always his mood when he was in full health, and was interested in his work. He took the same joyous satisfaction in his folio Targums and Oriental dictionaries, that a sportsman does in his horses and dogs. His favourite studies were always an enthusiasm with him; he was either in love with a pursuit or had taken a disgust for it; and was never more ready to break out into fun than when he was most busy, and his mind was excited by his toils.

"We shall add a few words with respect to the study of Arabic. It is highly desirable, on various accounts that a knowledge of this noble and important language should become more common. Biblical learning and the missionary enterprise alike demand it. What we most need, is a taste for the pursuit, and a conscientious willingness to undertake the task. The great deficiency is not so much in grammars, as in men to study them. We observe that Mr. Smith, the American missionary at Malta, has declined to undertake an English version of Ibn Ferhat's grammar. His views are such as might have been expected from a man of sense and learning. It may, indeed, be stated as a general truth, that translated grammars are as likely to be hinderances as helps. A grammarian cannot possibly explain the phenomena of a foreign language, except by appealing to the structure of his own or of that in which he writes. Now as every language has its peculiarities, both great and small, no two can stand in the same relation to a third. Latin and French agree where French and English differ. The same form of speech in Latin, therefore, which must be explained to English learners, may be as clear, without elucidation, to the Frenchman, as if founded upon some fixed law of nature. Give the latter the same comments that you give the former, and you not only do not aid him, but you really confound him. For we need not say that the attempt to explain what is perfectly intelligible must have that effect. The same remark may be applied to another case. For a familiar instance, we refer to Josse's Spanish Grammar, as translated into English by Mr. Sales, of Cambridge. The original work was designed for

Frenchmen, and as the translator, we believe, is himself a Frenchman, many rules and statements in themselves just, and in their proper places useful, are wholly unintelligible to the English reader. Analogous cases will occur to every scholar, abundantly proving that the servile transfer not of language merely, but of rules, arrangements, proofs, and illustrations, is unfriendly to the only end which grammars should promote. While we believe, with Dr. Johnson, that the practice of translating (in the proper sense, and on an extensive scale) is injurious to the purity of language, we likewise consider it injurious to the interests of sound and thorough scholarship. To avoid the former evil, we would substitute the transfusion of thoughts for the translation of words. To remedy the latter, we would have bilingual scholars to study, sift, digest, remodel, reproduce. By this we should avoid the needless introduction of an uncouth terminology and the practical paralogism of attempting to explain ignotum per ignotius. By this means too, a freshness would be given to our learned works, very unlike the tang contracted by a passage over sea. This too, would serve to check the strong propensity of young philologists towards a stagnant acquiescence in the dicta of their text-books, which is always attended with the danger of mistaking form for substance, and forgetting the great ends of language in the infinitesimal minutiæ of a barren etymology. In Germany, that great philological brewery, the extreme of stagnation has been long exchanged for that of fermentation, and although we do not wish to see the eccentricities of foreign scholarship imported here, we do believe that much of their advancement may be fairly traced to their contempt of mere authority, their leech-like thirst for indefinite improvement, and their practice of working up the materials of their learning into new and varied forms without much regard to preëxistent models. Let us imitate their merits and avoid their faults. Let us mount upon their shoulders, not grovel at their feet. Let us take the *stuff* which they provide for us, and mould it for ourselves, to suit our own peculiarities of language, habit, genius, wants, and prospects. Let our books be English, not Anglo-French or Anglo-German. Let us not make them as the Chinese tailor made the tar's new jacket, with a patch to suit the old one.

"To return to grammars—though what we said above may seem directly applicable only to those written in one language to explain another, it applies *à fortiori*, to what are called *native* grammars, which are merely designed to reduce into systematic form the knowledge previously gathered by empirical induction. To those who have become familiar with a language in the concrete by extensive reading, such works are highly useful and need no translation. To beginners they are useless; for they presuppose the knowledge which beginners want. Besides, they are *untranslatable*, as Mr. Smith justly affirms—with special reference, indeed, to *Bahth El Mutalib*, of which we know nothing but through him. We may add, however, that even if that work admitted of translation, it would scarcely throw more light upon the subject than De Sacy's lucid digest (pre-eminently lucid after all deductions, drawbacks, and exceptions) the fruit of most laborious and long continued study of numerous authorities—a work, too, which has had more indirect influence on biblical philology than many are aware of. *

"When De Sacy has been mastered and exhausted, he may very fairly be condemned and thrown aside. To those who would prefer a shorter grammar and the Latin tongue, Rosenmüller's book may be safely recommended. It is Erpenius rewritten, with improvements from De Sacy. Meanwhile we look with some impatience for the forthcoming work of Ewald, whose acuteness, ingenuity, and habits of research afford the promise of a masterly performance.† It must be owned, however, that we do not need reading-books, or Readers, for beginners. Most of the chrestomathies prepared in Europe appear to presuppose some acquaintance with the Koran. For us this will not answer. Here, where the study is, at most, but nascent, we need an introduction to the Koran itself. We have often thought that a selection of historical passages from that book, reduced to order, with grammatical notes and a vocabulary, would answer the ends of a chrestomathy for mere beginners most completely. It is highly important that the learner's first acquaintance with the written language, should be formed upon the Koran. Amidst all the dialectic variations of a tongue which is spoken from the great Sahara to the Steppes of Tartary, there is a large proportion both of words and phrases, everywhere the same. These are the words and phrases of the Koran, which religious scruples have preserved from change, and religious use

---

* No one we think who is familiar with De Sacy's noble work can fail to recognise its agency in giving form, perspicuity, and richness to the famous Lehrgebååde of Gesenius.   J. A. A.

† There is in addition to the works referred to by Mr. Alexander, a valuable and very compendious handbook by Tregelles. There is also a grammar of note by Caspari. It has been translated into English by William Wright, Assistant in the MS. Department, British Museum, and published by Williams & Norgate, Covent Garden, London, 1862. It must be imported, and is a beautifully printed and yet really cheap octavo.

made universally familiar. He who is acquainted with the language of the Koran, has the means of oral access to any Arab, and to almost any Mussulman. He may not understand as yet the many variations of the vulgar from the sacred tongue, much less the local diversities of speech; but he has the foundation upon which these rest, the stated formula from which they are mere departures. He will also have acquired a measure of that knowledge, with respect to facts and doctrines, which no man can dispense with, who would either vanquish or convert the Moslem."

The writer of the above could be no smatterer; he certainly must have felt the firm ground of true and thorough knowledge, of a learning as solid as it was extensive, beneath his feet. We need not wonder then, if Mr. Walsh should confound this nameless young man who wrote the Persian article in the Quarterly with the well-known theological professor at Princeton, and suppose him to be one of the maturest orientalists in the country. He *was* one of the maturest orientalists in the country! "The study," as he says, "was then, at most, but nascent." Mr. Alexander had few companions at that day in those tropical voyages among the spice-islands, or in these violent inroads upon the domain of the false prophet. Persian was a greater luxury to him than Lalla Rookh. He had been reading Arabic from the time he was nine or ten years old, and had been familiar with the Koran ever since he knew anything about the language. He had read it through at least four years previously, and had committed parts of it to memory. He could write Arabic letters (Arabic epistles, I mean) with the same rapidity and apparent ease that he could English. He had a great talent for forming the characters of a foreign language. He wrote the Hebrew with singular elegance. The letters were made small and uniform, and looked nearly as well as print. Some of his Arabic is in the beautiful current hand in which accomplished dragomans write l'Arabe vulgaire:* sometimes it is carefully copied from the style which is seen in printed books; more commonly it is in the same

* See fac-simile in Byron's poetical works. Murray. 1815, vol. i. r. 303.

general style but dashed off with the masterly negligence with which a man, who feels at home in it, dashes off a familiar letter in his native tongue.

The young adjunct professor lived at this time in the house of Mr. Henry Vethake, the professor of natural philosophy. The building was situated at a point precisely in a line with the college and towards the dwelling of the President. On the other side of the college stood the steward's hall. It was now and there that Mr. Alexander gave his heart to God according to the terms of the everlasting covenant. Mr. Alexander had a decided admiration for his associate, as was the case with all others who knew him. Henry Vethake was an accomplished man, and in a great variety of ways. His forte was probably political economy, though in his time he honoured and graced many different chairs. He was a scholar of the type that is best known on the continent of Europe. He was a native of Prussia, having come with his parents to the United States when he was yet a child. His boyhood was passed in New York, where he afterwards received his academic degree from Columbia College. His first post as a teacher was in this institution. Subsequently he accepted the professorship of mathematics and natural philosophy in Queen's (now Rutgers) College, New Brunswick, N. J. In the year 1817 he was chosen to be the occupant of the chair of mathematics, natural philosophy and chemistry, in the College of New Jersey. He seemed for some time to be the sport of changes. The next year his department was divided and he became the professor of mathematics and mechanical philosophy. Two or three years later he resigned his chair at Princeton and went to Carlisle, Penn., as professor of the same branches in Dickinson College. There he remained till the autumn of 1829. The following year he returned to Princeton and was for two years professor of natural philosophy in the college. After the lapse of two more years he again resigned his chair at Princeton and accepted one in the University of New York, then just established. Two or three years after he was elected to the presidency of Washington College in Lexington, Rockbridge county, Virginia. He remained there about twelve months.

The last thirty years, or more, of his life was spent in Philadelphia, amidst the congenial society of men of letters, and chiefly in connection with the University of Pennsylvania, in which institution he was at first the professor of mathematics, and afterwards the Provost of the University. At the time of his death he held the same chair in the Polytechnic School, or College, of Philadelphia.

Dr. Vethake was a man of varied attainments both in science and literature, and an excellent teacher. He was withal an amiable man and a good companion. As a writer he is chiefly known as the author of certain contributions to the science of political economy. He prepared a supplementary volume for an edition of the American Encyclopædia, published some years ago in Philadelphia. The daily society of such a man must have been a great treat to the bashful linguist.

Professor Burrowes* of Easton writes, that when he entered Princeton College in the autumn of 1830, Mr. Alexander was adjunct professor of languages, living in the college and acting as tutor. His room was on the fourth floor of the old college building, next to the bell, and over what was then the chapel. He occupied afterwards the front room on the left of the entry of a house then standing on the now open space between the college and the old Library. "As my room," he says, "was on the same entry with his in college, he looked in on us daily in the visits made by the tutors to the rooms of the students. There was a marked difference between the air with which the other tutor threw wide open the door in his visits, and, pausing, looked around to see if any of the inmates had escaped since his last trip; and the quick movement with which the door was opened barely enough to let us catch a glimpse of the fresh, ruddy, handsome face of Professor Addison, and then closed again and he was gone. On one occasion a member of our class, pleasant and companionable, but not in danger of hurting himself with study, came into our room just

---

* The Rev. Geo. Burrowes, D.D. Professor of Biblical Instruction in Lafayette College.

after the professor had passed, mortified and saying—"I will try hereafter to avoid Professor Addison in his rounds. As I passed him in the entry he said to me, 'Mr. ——, you seem a bird of passage; I find you always on the wing.'" Even then, though a young man hardly one and twenty, this writer remembers that he carried with him great influence, and commanded unbounded respect. "No student ever dreamed of playing on him any of the pranks of which the other tutor had so bountiful a share. His great reputation for one of his years had thrown a something around him that caused him to be looked up to with a kind of awe by the poor hard-working herd, plodding our way along through jagged passes of the hill of science, over which we felt he had swept with an eagle's wing."

He mentions an amusing instance of this feeling. There were two rooms in the refectory, in one of which was a cheaper table where were gathered most of the pious students. The young professor took the head of the table in this room. "I noticed that his end of the table was for some reason deserted; and found that these good men, most of whom were candidates for the ministry, had crowded away from him to a most respectful distance, because they were absolutely afraid of him. They appeared to have the impression that he could not stoop from his lofty perch to anything short of Persian and Arabic roots. They seemed to look upon him as they might look on a Leyden jar heavily charged, as likely to give a dangerous shock to any one coming too near." No shadow of dislike, he is satisfied, had anything to do with this strange avoidance. "The thing was amusingly ridiculous, when the reason was known. He doubtless never knew anything of it." Seeing the way in which the table had been cleared at the professor's end—"really an instinctive tribute to his great reputation"—the writer says he took a vacant seat next to him, and, "to the surprise of the others, found this young man of whom they were so shy, to be gentle and pleasant, possessing great powers of conversation, and in his conversation most suggestive and instructive. I regret that I did not make a record of some conversations then had with him.

"Indeed," he continues, "both he and his brother, Dr. James W. Alexander, were such men that it was hard to come in contact with them without receiving some influence making itself felt in an enlivening power on the mind and heart. A single remark by Dr. James in a morning walk before I went to college, made an impression on me through life. He suggested the importance of resolving to read at least one verse of the Greek Testament every day; to read the Psalms through once a month according to the division in the Book of Common

Prayer; and to read a chapter daily in the book of Proverbs, which will take us through them once a month. The suggestion was a simple one; but the enduring effects have been among the most valuable on my religious life."

While sitting at the college table with Professor Addison Alexander he could not avoid noticing "how little indulgence he gave his appetite. He carried in his countenance every appearance of the best health, and was of full habit of body; but he ate less than any person I have ever known. One slender meal a day was all his healthy appetite seemed to crave. At the other meals in the refectory he would preside, but take nothing. The powers of his body were made tributary to the wants and higher ministry of the mind; and they received no indulgence on his part any further than was necessary for keeping the material enginery in fit condition for the demands of the service needed by the activity of the soul." *

He cannot forget the impression made on him as a student, by the prayers of Professor Alexander while officiating at morning prayers in the college chapel. "It was not that there was any attempt at display, or fine language. Like his father before him, everything of this kind he despised. The simplicity, fitness, and comprehensiveness of the language constituted its beauty and its power. It was the utterance o the feelings of humble piety in abasement at the feet of Jesus, by a mind which grasped those subtle feelings with the precision of a giant's strength, and expressed them in words of a transparency and fitness that genius only can command." And when he attended the meetings of the Philadelphian Society, a gathering of pious students only, he was struck with the same characteristics of his language. "Had it been possible to evaporate the ideas from the words, it seemed as though there would linger a nameless beauty and music still among the words. His language flowed easy and gentle; though strong, a stream

'Strong without rage, without o'erflowing full'—

full of the clearest, richest good sense and piety."

The writer, like most others, thinks it was a wonder that a man who had mingled with the world so little, could know so much about it; and that one who had so lately become pious, could pour out such a flow of sober, clear, rich good sense to professing Christians. "Good writing," he says, "and good discourse is the embodying of good sense in good language. In all this, he was even from that early age pre-emi-

* I am under the impression that he took some of his meals at home.

nent. To him, this was natural. He could not help it. He could not, if he would, have used any other than this clear, appropriate, precise expressive, unapproachable language. Of him I felt it was not true—

> Ut sibi quivis
> Speret idem; sudet multum, frustraque laboret
> Ausus idem:

For you had no disposition to try. You felt in listening, that try as you might, you could never hope to attain such a mastery of language."

The vigour and clearness of his mind were apparent in the class-room. He was a great teacher. The secret of successful instruction is to interest and rouse the mind of the student to work for himself. This he did. "He benefited his class not by loading them down with useless lumber, like an ass sinking under his panniers; but by stimulating and quickening their dormant energies. He was quick; sometimes perhaps too quick for the grade of scholarship in college-classes as they then were; and like all men of energy such as his, seemed to slower and more plodding minds, at times a little sharp: forgetting under the impulse of his own fulness and enthusiasm, the great interval there was between his own talents and attainments, and the talents and attainments of those before him. In any accidental case of this kind, a moment's reflection was sufficient to bring into exercise his lofty magnanimity, which soothed any wounded feeling."

The writer adverts to the fact that some men are fond of making an ostentatious display of their learning. To this the professor never stooped. "With a memory of marvellous power and all the varied riches of his great acquisitions at instant command with ease, he brought forth from his treasures only what was needed for putting in a proper light before the class the point requiring explanation, and what the grade of scholarship in his students needed and could appropriate with advantage." In his instructions in college, he says, the same characteristics appeared that are visible in his commentaries—"the results of the richest and most varied learning sifted from everything extraneous, and concentrated on the direct point at issue, always with reference to the wants and degree of advancement of those under instruction. He was the last man to suspect of Hezekiah's weakness in showing 'the house of his precious things, the silver, and the gold, and all that was found in his treasures.' All his intellectual treasure of whatever kind that might be needed, was, however, forthcoming at the right moment; and that too, refined, recoined, and bearing his own imperial impress and superscription."

If the testimony of Dr. Burrowes is worthy of credence, no man could command more respect. "He was respected for his abilities and attainments; and then his quick wit made those disposed to trespass feel there was a power behind the throne with which it was perilous to meddle. Self-conceit and presumption found instinctively their level, and were satisfied to keep it." In keen delicate wit and sarcasm he was, in the writer's estimation, unsurpassed. "This was never used unnecessarily; it was kept as a power in reserve. Like the colossal spectre touched by the wand of the magician in the Arabian tale, the unlucky wight of large dimensions in his own conceit, shrivelled up into pitiable littleness under the touch of this polished shaft. In his writings a passing flash of his sarcasm often carries more power than a labored argument. It may come like lightning from a cloudless sky; an unexpected flash, and the airy towers and battlements of pretension and sophistry have disappeared."

Mr. Alexander's eldest brother returned from Virginia about the time that the young philologist accepted the position at Patton's school. He was elected pastor of the congregation at Trenton in the autumn of 1828, and preached his first sermon to the Trenton people on the 10th of January 1829.

The letters of the Trenton pastor to Dr. Hall and others, and his copious private diaries, and ephemerides, of this period, are not only profoundly interesting for their own sakes and because of their connection with the contemporary history, but give many a passing glimpse of the life and manners of that day, as well as of the new teacher Mr. Patton had induced to join him at Edgehill, and who soon after became a sort of tutorial professor in the college, and a few years later buried himself from the observation of the idle villagers of Princeton, among strange people and strange scenes across the seas.

Besides finishing the books commenced the last year, Mr. Alexander read, during the winter of this year, Kleinert on Isaiah, Æschines, Hariri, (with Arabic scholia,) Luther's Letters, Rosenmüller on Isaiah, and Neander on the Primitive Church.

On Feb. 20 he began to read the Psalms again with some degree of critical attention; supplying the vowels in the unpointed text, and using the pointed text as a commentary. "This," he says, "is my general plan for Hebrew study now."

During the months of Dec. 1832 and Jan. 1833, he wrote forty articles for the Presbyterian, of which his brother was then the editor.*

---

* I am able to give the titles of these little articles, from a paper in the author's handwriting, labelled:

"PARAGRAPHS CONTRIBUTED TO THE PRESBYTERIAN," (by J. A. A.). "IN 1832–33.

DATE OF WRITING.

1. Nov. 27, 1832. On Verbal Orthodoxy.
2.   The Biblical Repository.
3. Nov. 29. The Art of Reading.
4.   Soliloquies in Church.
5. Nov. 30. Learning and Religion.
6. " Moderation.
7. " Princeton.
8. " Oxford and Cambridge.
9. Dec. 1. Excerpts.
10. " Anecdote of Gellert.
11. " German Criticism.
12. " Guardian Angels.
13. " Mode of Printing Poetry.
14. Dec. 3. Loyalty.
15. " Hastings.
16. " Public Worship.
17. " Introductions.
18. " Formality in Preaching.
19. Dec. 5. African Colonization.
20. " Charles I. and Scotland.
21. " College Discipline.
22. Dec. 10. Excerpts.
22. " Pascal.
23. " Dante.
24. " Imitation.
25. Dec. 17. Theological Libraries.
26. " The Sonna.

DATE OF WRITING.
27. Dec. 18.   The Sanhedrim of Paris.
28. Dec. 24.   An Article, Prejudice.
29. Jan. 5., 1833. A Sheet.
30. Jan. 13.   An article siged *Simon*.
31. Jan. 15.   An article signed *Peter*.
32. Jan. 16.   An article signed *McD*
33. Jan. 17.   A paper signed Holofernes.
34. Jan. 18.   A Churchyard Dialogue signed S. D. A.
35. Jan. 21.   An article signed *Idiotes*.
36. Jan. 22.   An article on Plain Preaching.
37. Jan. 23.   An Editorial on Imitation.
38. Jan. 24.   An Editorial on Missionary Facts.
39. Jan. 25.   An Editorial on the Advantages of Presbyterianism.
40 March 1.   Translation of an article on Cyril Lucaris.

W. S. MARTIEN to J. A. ALEXANDER,   Dr.
    To 40 articles at $1.   .   .   .   . $40.00
                           Received payment."

CHAPTER IX.

NEVER was there a greater mistake, than that Professor Addison Alexander did not care to know about the busy world beyond the limits of his study and class room; and he was now resolved, with Parnell's hermit,* "to find if books or swains report it right." Mr. Alexander's acquaintance with the learned and critical labours of Germany, and his knowledge of the valuable mental discipline afforded by her universities, had greatly stimulated in him the curiosity which every enlightened American feels with respect to Europe, and had awakened in his breast a strong desire to cross the seas, and spend some time in foreign travel, and in the search for intellectual improvement in the foreign schools. His friends all thought well of the scheme, and his father and those who were on his return to be his coadjutors in the seminary, heartily approved of it.

The Rev. Rezeau Brown, who was animated by similar views, and still more by a wish to corroborate his shattered health, made every preparation to accompany him; but was destined, as we have seen, for a shorter voyage to a better country. He was too unwell to start, and soon after breathed his last. This was a heavy blow to Mr. Alexander; though the voyage to Europe was, in his case, an accomplished fact before he heard of his friend's death.

Several distinguished gentlemen communicated with Dr.

* " To clear this doubt, to know the world by sight,
   To find if books or swains report it right,
   For yet by swains alone the world he knew,
   Whose feet came wandering o'er the nightly dew."
—Parnell, The Hermit. London, Strand, John Bell, 1774. p. 161.

Alexander on the subject of his son's projected voyage. Here is an extract from a letter of the Hon. William C. Rives, of Virginia, relating wholly to this topic. Mr. Rives had been the United States Minister to France.

CASTLE HILL, April 12th, 1833.

MY DEAR SIR,

* * * You will perceive that instead of a letter to Baron de Sacy, with whom I have not the pleasure of a persona acquaintance, I have written one to the Baron de Ferrusac, who, having been a long time at the head of the *Bulletin Universel*, &c., has familiar relations with the whole corps of literati at Paris, and whom I have particularly requested to make your son acquainted with Monsieur de Sacy. The deaths of the Count Chaptal, Baron Cuvier, &c. during the last summer, have narrowed considerably the circle of my acquaintance with the savans of France, or I should have added other letters to members of that fraternity. Those which I have written to General Lafayette and Mr. Niles, our late Chargé d'affaires, will, however, amply and more efficiently supply the deficiency.

I am, my dear sir, most truly, Faithfully yours,
W. C. RIVES.

On the 10th of April, 1833, having resigned for that purpose his chair in the college, Mr. Alexander sailed from New York, in the ship Samson, Captain Chadwick, for London. While making his final preparations for the voyage, he remained a day or two with Dr. Benjamin H. Rice, who had married his father's sister; and was attended by one or two of his kindred to the quay. During Mr. Alexander's absence, Dr. Rice removed from New York to Princeton, and became the pastor of the Presbyterian church, at that time the only church in the place, though the building of an Episcopal church, which was subsequently put up, was then in contemplation.

The following letter to his mother was intended to cheer her on his departure. It had been looked for with impatience.

SHIP SAMSON,
5 o'clock, Wednesday, April 10, 1833.

MY DEAR MOTHER:

Here comes your pilot-letter. I have as yet had no means of ascertaining whether I am proof against sea-sickness, the weather being so extremely mild and the water so smooth. Capt. Chadwick is one of the pleasantest men that I have ever seen. Dr. Cox pleases me well thus far. He is frank and cordial, but not obtrusive. He has read me whole passages from his book already and told me things without number. Our party includes Mr. Clay, Secretary to the Russian Embassy, on his way to St. Petersburg, two officers of the English army, two other Englishmen, two Canadians, and a Frenchman. We have thirty steerage passengers, mostly English people going home. There are chickens, ducks, and a cow on board. Dr. Cox, the English officers, and I, have the ladies' cabin to ourselves. The Captain is positive that we shall reach London before the "first proximo," and seems to anticipate fair weather throughout. Clay asked me if I had relatives at Princeton—said he knew a Mr. Alexander in Virginia.

I must go above now and see what is passing there. Farewell, be of good cheer, as I am and shall try to be.

Love to all and every one.   J. A. A.

During his year's absence, Mr. Alexander kept a minute journal of all that befell him. We shall select here and there from his diary interesting facts, without attempting to give a continued history of his daily life. He was much interested in the movements of the captain, the mate and the pilot, when they reached the Needles. I give his own words:

"In the midst of our exulting expectations of a speedy landing, we were becalmed just outside of the Needles. By the bye, the chief mate is a sturdy Yankee, and stands up for America with laudable intrepidity. As he was eating his supper to-night with the other mate and the pilot at the foot of the cabin table, I heard him speaking with great scorn of the English game laws, and the absurdity of a man's not being suffered to shoot on his own grounds, without a certain amount of property. He also mystified the old pilot about panthers and other beasts in America, in a very amusing style. He was at dinner to-day when the weather changed, and the pilot gave the orders for manœuvring, &c. The captain hearing the noise, ran up, looked about him, countermanded the pilot's orders, asked him what he was about, &c., and assumed the command himself; yet all this was done with perfect equanimity of temper. I never knew indeed, till I came to sea, how far peremptory decision and even rigour could be blended with uniform good humour. It is a fact, however, that both Chadwicks scold the sailors without a change of countenance. The second mate scolds the seamen, the first mate the second and the captain, all together, without any manifestation of surprise or discontent. But to return to the pilot; he was once a slaver on the coast of Guinea, and still speaks with satisfaction of his former enormities. His son was lately detected in smuggling, and was condemned to five years service in a man-of-war. The old man's dialect and manner are to me entirely new and strange."

Here is a lively description of an English stage coach, as these vehicles were thirty-five years ago; which may be read before, or after, those of Irving, Dickens, and De Quincey.

"Just imagine that you see us at the door of the hotel, surrounded by some six or seven men each asserting the immense superiority of his or his master's coach and directly contradicting what the others said. The 'Rockett is much the fastest coach, sir—we shall be in by half-past five.' 'The Rockett charges extra for baggage, sir—the Regulator never does.' 'We go at nine, sir—we shall be in first.' 'We go at ten, sir—but we arrive before the others.' 'How can you lie so? you are unable of speaking the truth.' During our negotiations, we changed our scene of action. One was taking us off to see his coach, when lo! another turned us back by his representative, and thus the thing proceeded until I began to think our situation rather ludicrous, and told Dr. Cox that if he pleased, I would assume the responsibility of deciding at once, which I forthwith did, in favor of the Regulator, the 9 o'clock coach, which, in the course of ten minutes was at the door.

"The coach, when it took us up, had only a pair of horses; but while we stopped at another inn to receive our complement of passengers, two horses were added; forming the noblest quaternion of steeds that I ever saw attached to a public conveyance. The harness, too, has the appearance of being perfectly new; and to complete the picture, a 'gentleman,' dressed in a black frock-coat, with drab trousers and gaiters, took his seat as coachman."

He continues to describe the ride through English country.

"We now paid our fare (15s.), and were dunned by a lad who pretended that he had 'loaded our luggage' at the Quebec hotel; though we all agreed in saying that we had never seen his face. A handsome young man, about my age, took his seat beside the coachman, and we set off at a smart pace through the streets of Portsmouth. This being the first time that I had travelled in the old world, I kept both my eyes wide open in search of novelties. The first thing that struck me was the antique look of the houses, built of dirty brick, as little like the brick of Philadelphia or New York as you can well imagine. The next thing that struck me was the variety of costume. Here was a man in pantaloons, there one in breeches, yonder one in gaiters; further on was one in a shirt or frock, &c., &c. Soldiers we saw at every corner; young and old; and I was much surprised at the smartness of their appearance; their red coats and white trousers seemed to have just proceeded from the tailor's hands. A ride of any sort, after our voyage, would have been a luxury; but such a ride as we were now to enjoy was more than luxurious; it was luscious. In the outskirts of Portsmouth we began to catch a glimpse of English cultivation; little gardens, exquisitely neat, grass-plots of the most delicious green, hedges and trees and shrubbery—all combined to make it overpowering. The milestones glided by us with surprising speed, and yet the motion of the coach was all but imperceptible. It was only when I looked at the horses that I felt convinced of our impetuous progress. The coachman made much entertainment by his dignified and gentlemanly air. There was not the least degree of that vulgar swagger which our 'drivers' commonly display; he did not crack his whip once, and very seldom lashed the horses, though when he did, he did it with a boldness quite alarming. He was loaded with commissions in the shape of bundles, letters, &c., both from Portsmouth and from places on the road. These he frequently took up without stopping at all; just as he paid his toll, while at full speed. We changed horses six or seven times, with great rapidity and elegance. Besides the variety of scenery, the frequent interchange of grain fields, pasture grounds and commons, we were pleased with the sight of flocks and herds, and the appearance of the country people. What struck me particularly in the latter was their fresh, healthy appearance; I do not mean mere ruddiness. Indeed, I was mistaken in my preconceptions. My ideas of English health and heartiness were associated with images of grossness. I find, however, that in the country the people at large, and especially the women and children, are remarkable for a clear, transparent complexion, smooth full skin, and smiling countenance. I am forcibly struck with the contrast between the boys whom we met in wagons and on foot, and the young rustics of New Jersey. I think I may say with truth that every one whom we met was fresh and handsome."

His first visit to the House of Commons was not altogether satisfactory.

"As the Doctor and I walked along the street at night, we felt a curiosity to know where the House of Commons was. The Doctor therefore asked a gentleman who passed us. He replied 'This is it. I will show you the way; but you can't get in without an order from a member.' 'I was not aware of that, sir; we are strangers.' 'If you wish to go in, I will give you an order with pleasure.' 'Are you a member, sir?' 'Yes—for Ireland." He then took us in through a number of halls and passages lined with two rows of persons waiting for admission, or something else, to a little office on one side, where he wrote an order. 'Admit the bearer. P. Lalor.' He gave this to Dr. Cox and said that he would go and get one for me; as no member can can give more than one. While he was gone, we were knocked about by the door-keepers, &c., telling us to stand, now on this side and then on that. At last he returned and took us up through a labyrinth of passages to a small, dark lobby in which a number of persons were crowded round two doors. Into one of these we at length contrived to peep, and had the happiness of seeing Mr. Manners Sutton, in his robe and wig. Mr. Lalor gave Dr. Cox his card and said that he took a particular interest in Americans, and would be glad to do us any service in his power."

He was a little more fortunate at Exeter Hall.

"As I was going in, a policeman at his door asked me the colour of my ticket. I told him I had none. 'You can't go in without one,' said he. 'Do they sell them?' said I. 'O no,' says he, 'if you wish to go in, I think I can get you a place.' He then took me round the corner into a postern door, got a ticket from the porter, and conducted me up-stairs, saying—'This is not customary, but I don't like to see a respectable person turned away.' In a moment I found myself in a sort of gallery opposite the platform where the speakers and other leading personages sat. I soon recognized Dr. Cox, who had gone out while I was dressing. Lord Bexley presided. A note was read from Teignmouth, and then an abstract of the report by the Rev. Mr. Brandram, one of the Secretaries. The Bishop of Winchester then rose, dressed in a frock coat and black apron. He was followed by J. J. Gurney, the Quaker. Then came Dr. Cox, then a member of Parliament, then Baptist Noel, then Dr. Morrison, then Lord Mountsanford, then the

Bishop of Chester. All the speakers were applauded more or less by stamping, clapping of hands, and occasionally, cries of 'hear.'"

Mr. Alexander's passion for courts and juries, judges, witnesses and barristers, was much indulged in England. Here is a description of the High Court of Chancery, and what he saw there.

"A guide introduced us to the High Court of Chancery—a room not near so large as the court-room at Trenton, but handsomely fitted up. Here we saw Lord Brougham, and had the satisfaction of hearing him utter a few words. I think I could have recognized him by the pictures I have seen, though they are all caricatures. He has a very intellectual physiognomy, and much sarcastic expression in the twitching of his face. Here, for the first time, I saw the counsellors' robes and wigs. In the latter I was agreeably disappointed; they are by no means so grotesque as I supposed. After hearing Sir Edward Sugden plead awhile, we left the court, and in the hall met counsel without number in their gowns and wigs. As the courts all sit at once, the lawyers are obliged to pass incessantly from one to another, with their green bags and enormous briefs."

The name of Edward Irving, who was now one of the lions of London, had recently become familiar to the two Americans, and they were both eager to see and hear him. The following account by the younger of the two, tallies precisely with that given by Lockhart in the life of John Wilson * by Mrs. Gordon, and with that subsequently printed by Dr. Cox. It possesses a curious interest now.

"After breakfast, having learned that Edward Irving was to hold a meeting at half-past eleven, we resolved to go; but without expecting to hear the tongues; as they have not been audible of late. Mr. Nott, who had called before breakfast, conducted us to Newman street, where Irving is established since he left the house in Regent square. As we walked along we saw a lady before us arm in arm with a tall man in black breeches, a broad-brimmed hat, and black hair hanging down his shoulders. This, Mr. Nott informed us, was Irving himself with his *cara sposa*. We followed them to the door of the chapel in Newman

---

* See "Christopher North." W. J. Widdleton, 1863. p. 271.

street; where Dr. Nott left us, and we went in. The chapel is a room of moderate size, seated with plain modern benches, like our recitation-rooms. The end opposite the entrance is semicircular, and filled with amphitheatrical seats. In front of these there is a large arch, and immediately beneath it a reading-desk in the shape of an altar, with a large arm-chair beside it. From this point there are several steps descending toward the body of the house, on which are chairs for the elders of the church. I mention these particulars because I think the pulpit and its appendages extremely well contrived for scenic effects. The following diagram may give some faint idea of the appearance."

Here follows a carefully drawn picture of the dais and chairs.

"Soon after we were seated, the chairs below the pulpit were occupied by several respectable men, one of them quite handsome and well dressed. Another man and a woman took their seats upon the benches behind. While we were gazing at these, we heard a heavy tramp along the aisle, and the next moment Irving walked up to the altar, opened the Bible, and began at once to read. He has a noble figure, and his features are not ugly; with the exception of an awful squint. His hair is parted right and left, and hangs down on his shoulders in affected disorder. His dress is laboriously old fashioned—a black quaker coat and small clothes. His voice is harsh, but like a trumpet; it takes hold of one and cannot be forgotten. His great aim appeared to be to vary his attitudes and appear at ease. He began to read in a standing posture, but had scarcely finished half a dozen verses when he dropped into the chair and sat while he read the remainder. He then stepped forward to the point of his stage, dropped on his knees and began to pray in a voice of thunder; most of the people kneeling fairly down. At the end of the prayer he read the 66th Psalm, and I now perceived that his selections were designed to have a bearing on the persecutions of his people and himself. The chapter from Samuel was that relating to Shimei. He then gave out the 66th Psalm in verse; which was sung standing, very well, Irving himself joining in with a mighty bass. He then began to read the 39th of Exodus, with an allegorical exposition, after a short prayer for Divine assistance. The ouches of the breast-plate he explained to mean the rulers of the church. While he was dealing this out, he was interrupted in a manner rather startling. I had observed that the elders who sat near him, kept their eyes raised to the sky-light overhead, as if wooing inspiration. One in particular looked very wild. His face was flushed, and he occasionally turned up the white of his eyes in an ominous style. For the most part, however, his eyes were shut. Just as Irving reached the point I have mentioned and was explaining the ouches; this elder of ye church who sat in the chair marked P on page 48, burst out in a sort of wild ejaculation, thus: 'Taranti-hoiti-faragmi-santi'*; 'O ye people—ye people of ye Lord, ye have not the ouches—ye have not the ouches-ha-a-a; ye must have them—ye must have them-ha-a-a; ye cannot hear—ye cannot hear!" This last was spoken in a pretty loud whisper; as the inspiration died away within him. When he began, Irving suspended his exposition and covered his face with his hands. As soon as the voice ceased, he resumed the thread of his discourse, till the 'tongue' broke out again 'in unknown strains.' After these had again come to an end, Irving knelt and prayed, thanking God for looking upon the poverty and desolation of his church amidst her persecutions. After he had finished and arisen from his knees, he dropped down again saying—'one supplication more'—or 'one thanksgiving more.' He now proceeded to implore the Divine blessing on the servant who had been ordained as a prophet in the sight of the people. After this supplementary prayer, he stood up, asked a blessing in a few words, and began to read in the 6th John about feeding on Christ's flesh. In the course of his remarks, he said—" The priests and churches in our day have denied the Saviour's flesh, and therefore cannot feed upon him. 'He then prayed again (with genuflexion) after which he dropped into his chair, covered his face with his hands and said — 'Hear, now, what the elders have to say to you.' No sooner was this signal given than the 'tongue' began anew, and for several minutes uttered a flat and silly rhapsody, charging the church with unfaithfulness and rebuking it therefor. The 'tongue' having finished, an elder who sat above him rose, with Bible in hand, and made a dry but sober speech about faith, in which there was nothing, I believe, *outré*. The handsome, well-dressed man, whom I have mentioned, at Irving's left hand, now rose and came forward with his Bible. His first words were—'Your sins which are many are forgiven you.' His discourse was incoherent, though not wild, and had reference to the persecutions of the church. The last preacher on the occasion was a decent, ministerial looking man in black, who discoursed on oneness with Christ. A paper was now handed to Irving which he looked at, and then fell upon his knees. In the midst of his prayer he took the paper and read it to the Lord, as he would have read a notice. It was a

* I do not pretend to recollect the words. —J. A. A.

thanksgiving by Harriet Palmer for the privilige of attending on these services to day. After the prayer, they sang a Psalm, and then the meeting was dismissed by benediction. The impression made on my mind was one of unmingled contempt. Everything which fell from Irving's lips was purely flat and stupid, without a single flash of genius, or the slightest indication of strength or even vivacity of mind. I was confirmed in my former low opinion of him founded on his writings. Mr. Nott, who knew him when he was in Glasgow, says that his first éclat in London was owing to the notes which he had taken of Dr. Chalmers' conversation; and that when he was cast upon his own resources, he appeared in his real character as a dunce. Dr. Cox and I flattered ourselves that he observed us, and preached at us. I saw him peeping through his fingers several times, and I suppose he was not gratified to see us gazing steadfastly at him all the time, for he took occasion to tell the people that it would profit them nothing without the circumcision of the ear. This he defined to be the putting away of all impertinent curiosity and profane inquisitiveness—all gazing and prying into the mysteries of God, and all malicious reporting of his doings in the church. We were, afterwards, given to understand that one of the elders was, probably, the Hon. Spencer Percival."

The ride in the stage coach from Oxford was a very picturesque and agreeable incident to look back to. He says:

"You never see here, as in America, a long string of stages; but there is a perpetual succession of coaches; so that you can choose your hour in almost every case. I do not know how many passed the Mitre, bound either to or from London, while I was waiting; and you must recollect, my dear readers, that an English stage coach under sail is a majestic sight. The number of passengers above, below and around; the pile of luggage on the roof, and the tremendous speed at which they are driven, make these vehicles a really sight-worthy spectacle. At length the Union arrived, but to my dismay the inside was full. This, however, is not so shocking in England as in America, where much disappointment would be seriously felt. The bookkeeper of the coach office assured me that the next coach would be along in fifteen minutes; and so it was. There were only a gentleman and lady inside, so that I got in very comfortably. Off we went at a tremendous rate, over the Oxford pavement; our guard shaking the houses with his trumpet. The silent but well lighted streets through which we rattled, and the moonlit fields through which we afterwards glided, made me quite romantic till sleep overcame me, and I dreamed of home."

Here is a pen-and-ink drawing of the dashing coachman who gave him the best notion he has ever had of the character of Jehu.

"Our coachman was of a different class from those I had seen—younger, more dashing, and extremely reckless in his air and manner. In driving he was a perfect Jehu; indeed, I never entered into Jehu's character before. The coach horses are invariably spirited, and there is always (at least so far as I have seen) one that is ungovernable: this is obvious from the cautious manner in which the vicious horse is brought out and put into the harness, and the mysterious hints which are given to the coachman by the hostlers and 'horsers.' Again, if there is any delay between the gearing of the horses and the starting coach, two men at their heads can scarcely hold them at all. When they do start, it is all at once and *fortissimo*. When any of the steeds begins to play the fool, the coachman increases their speed, and brings them to reason by galloping up hill."

"On the way we took up an old, old man, and when he alighted a woman had to take him in her arms. A toll-gate tacksman put his wife into the coach. 'Who's that, Jeremy?' said the coachman. 'A friend of mine,' quoth he. 'She's na rinnin awa yet?' 'Na.' Between two and three we hove in sight of Edinboro'. Villas and country seats began to make their appearance, and through the haze which hung upon the atmosphere we began to discern the steeples of 'Auld Reekie.' I shall make no attempt to describe my first impressions. I felt as if I were in another world. Hills, valleys, gardens, palaces—all brought together! The castle frowning from its cliff, the unfinished Parthenon on Calton Hill, the splendid churches, and the long, lofty ranges of stone building—well, what of them? Nothing."

He saw an odd thing in Edinburgh to which he thus refers:

"The first projecting house, a little, old, low and narrow one, was once the residence of JOHN KNOX, whose image and superscription are still upon the wall, with the date of his birth and death, and the name of God in Greek, Latin and English. It is now occupied by a fashionable hairdresser and wigmaker!!! named Dryden!!!

It would be tedious to follow him through mazes which

have been exhausted by the guidebooks. I prefer to retain the following vivid description of the celebrated view from Calton Hill:

"I now left Holyrood, and ascended Calton Hill by an elegant carriage road, winding spirally around it. Every turn presented a new scene, or a modification of it, but from the top I beheld one of unspeakable magnificence. On one side lay the New Town like a map, regular, spacious, splendid, interspersed with trees and gardens; on another stretched the hills of Fife, the Frith of Forth, and the German Ocean; on another lay a beautiful slope of rich and cultivated lands, bounded by lofty mountains. Last but not least, I had before me the Old Town, magnificent 'Auld Reekie.' The New Town is very noble in its way, and equal to any other place I ever saw; but if it were demolished, the old town would be a wonder still. The total absence of wood and brick, the loftiness of the houses, and the inequalities of the ground, render it striking to the eye beyond description. I am a fool to say as much as I do about it."

His visit to the house of Professor Lee, the late orientalist, should not be omitted. He was directed thither by the coach-porters.

"The situation is a very pleasant one—retired but not remote. A genteel servant lad opened the door, and carried up my name; he then returned and conducted me into the study. A moment after the Professor came in, dressed in cap and gown; he read Mr. Horne's* letter, asked me a few questions, and then invited me to walk with him to the Library, which he said would close very soon. On the way he talked about German theology, Professor Stuart, Gesenius, &c., &c. In the Library he showed me the Beza MS. While I was looking at it, a man came up and said: 'Professor Lee, will you please to step to the Vice-Chancellor's?' 'Bless me,' said he, 'I quite forgot it.' He then asked a librarian in attendance to show me the Burckhardt MSS., and went off, saying that he would return in a few minutes. I saw no more of him. We were soon after turned out, and the doors shut."

From England he passed over into France. He was much impressed with what he believed to be the genuine politeness

* Author of the "Introduction."

of the French. On the road from Calais to Paris they were surprised by an invasion of French beggars.

"On setting out," he says, "we were assaulted by a host of beggars. Such an assortment of cripples, dwarfs, 'malheureux' and 'affligés,' I never saw before. The French beggars, however, are nothing like the English. The former are so amusing that I laugh all the time they are addressing me; they look as if they were joking and ready to burst into a laugh. At last, we got off. As we drew nearer to Paris, our postillions became more and more grotesque. Once during every stage they stop before an inn, and a dram is brought them, of about a tablespoonful of brandy. Some took cider in preference, and one pure water. The conductor drank nothing but beer, except a little wine at dinner. In the night we passed through Clermont, where Massillon was bishop; soon after which I fell asleep."

Few things in his journal are more interesting than the following description of a call he made upon old Gen. Lafayette. He had learned from a Mr. Curtis that

"Gen. Lafayette intended to leave town to-morrow, for which cause he and Mr. Adams urged me to go and deliver my letter. I accordingly hired a cab by the hour, and drove first to Meurice's; where I paid my bill; the man refusing to take the fraction as a franc (five sous) I then went to No. 6 rue d'Anjou, St. Honoré, and held the following dialogue with the porteress: 'Est-ce l'hôtel du Général Lafayette?' 'Non, monsieur, il demeure ici, mais l'hôtel n'est pas à lui.' 'Mais est-il ici?' 'Oui, monsieur, montez au gauche.' I mounted au gauche accordingly, and rang a bell. The door was opened by a servant, who informed me that the General could not be seen; but the next moment, asked whether I was an American. On hearing that I was, he said: 'Entrez donc, monsieur, entrez,' and ushered me through a vacant apartment into another, where about a dozen people were seated. These, I found, were persons who had appointments with the General. They were mostly plain, common-looking people; one was a soldier, and one a woman. The rule, 'First come, first served,' was very rigidly observed. While one was in the 'presence,' the master of ceremonies would ask the next his name, and then announce it as he entered. I waited at least an hour; had I foreseen what happened I should not have gone at all, but when once there I was resolved to get something for my pains. Once, indeed, I did propose to leave the letter, saying that perhaps it was too late for the General to receive me, but the majordomo said: 'Non, non; c'est égal; vous allez entrez tout à l'heur.' At last my turn came, and he took Mr. Rives's letter in. A few minutes after he came out, and invited me to enter. I passed through another vacant room into the General's bedroom: as I entered, he was tottering towards an inner door, to shut it. When he turned round he advanced, took me by the hand, and placed me on the sofa where he sat himself, saying that he was very much pleased to see me. 'How long are you in Paris, Mr. Alexander?' I wish to preserve as much of his conversation as I can. 'Did you leave your father and other friends at Princeton well?' I then said that I supposed he remembered Princeton very well. 'Yes, indeed,' said he, 'many, many years before you were born. I don't know whether you remember, but when I came to Princton I found my diploma signed by Dr. Witherspoon: it had been waiting for me forty years; and it was publicly delivered to me.' 'Yes,' said I, 'and I was present; I was a boy at school.' He then made me many offers of service, and on my asking how I could get into the Chamber of Peers he wrote me a letter to the Count de Somerville, Grand Référendaire of the Chamber, requesting him to give me a ticket. When I rose to go he shook hands with me, and said he would be happy to do me any service when I came to Paris again. He also requested me, on my return to America, to give his respects to my father and his other *friends* at Princeton."

The General did not forget his promise to his Princeton visitor.

"I was just dressed when some one knocked at my door, and in came Mr. Dunscomb Bradford (Acting American Consul) with a letter from General Lafayette, who has been searching in vain for my address, which I did not give him, as I thought that he was going out of town: The letter was directed: 'A Monsieur Joseph Addison Alexander, á Paris.' It enclosed a note with these words in the General's own hand: 'Gen'l Lafayette's compliments to Mr. Alexander, and sends him a diplomatic ticket for the Chambre des Paris—friday evening." Within this note there was another in these words: 'Les huissiers et gardiens préposés à la Chambre des paris introduiront dans la tribune diplomatique jusqu'á la fin de la session Monsieur."

One day after visiting the flower garden of St. Denis, and other places of interest, he

"Repaired to the fountain of the Palais Royal, where I was soon after joined by Mr. Jenks, and we went together to the Ecole Royale des Langues Orientales Vivantes. There we sat and tattled, 'till Monsieur Caussin Percival came in, Mr. Jenks reciting to him in vulgar Arabic. The other two pupils did not come. I then went with Mr. Jenks to his lodgings in the rue la Pelletiére. There he showed me some Turkish firmans."

One Sunday in Paris he heard Mr. Wilkes preach from the words—

'The foxes have holes,' &c. "He arrived at 11 o'clock last night. His prayers were beautiful, and his discourse though rambling contained some noble passages. We were introduced to him after sermon. Mr. Stoddard and I now proceeded to the Palais Royal and dined at Périgord's. We then went to No. 9 rue de Cléry, where I sat with Mr. Stoddard until half past 7, when we went to the Oratoire, and heard M. Monod expound the preface and first petition of the Lord's Prayer. He is wonderfully brisk and rapid in all that he says and does; and I have no doubt that he is the most 'efficient' man among the evangelicals. He is also clear and earnest in discourse; but quite inferior to Audubez in unction, and to Grandpierre in eloquence."

Here is an account of a Church in Munich, and of the manners of the Roman Catholic worshippers:

"By the way, we went into the 'Students' Church,' or University chapel, and saw a part of the High Mass service. It is the only plain Catholic church that I ever saw. The music was grand. I never heard fiddles and trumpets used in worship before. The German Catholics enter into the imposture with more intensity of feeling than any others. The lower people whom I see in the churches here, seem to go through their performances with a sort of solemn enthusiasm. I saw, too, in one of the churches, a card suspended on which was painted an apostrophe to the worshippers. It was really affecting, and displayed a degree of earnestness and tenderness very unlike the hollow barrenness of Popish Christianity as I have seen it elsewhere. One sentence as far as I can recollect, ran thus: 'God have mercy upon you, poor, forsaken, unhappy souls. The merciful God have mercy upon you for the sake of the mortal anguish (Augst der Blutsch witzender Jesus.)' This last phrase cannot be translated."

What is next to be related took place on or near the terrace of the Cathedral Church at Berne.

"While I was looking at the edifice, a young man of intelligent countenance, but rather beggarly-dressed, accosted me in French and talked about the architecture of the church. As he proceeded to ask me questions about the town, I told him that I was a stranger—'You are a Frenchman, perhaps?' 'No.' 'A German?' 'No. I come further than that.' 'Further than that? Are you Prussian?' 'No, further than that.' 'From Russia?' 'Further than that.' He next guessed America, but could hardly believe that I was born there, as I seemed to him too white. He asked me a number of questions about America, and then informed me that he was a mechanicien, but was familiar with all branches of science. He drew from his pocket two drafts and explanations of inventions of his own. He is travelling through Switzerland on foot, he says, spending his father's money."

On Thursday the first of August he found a place in a coach going to Lausanne by the way of Freyburg. His own account is graphic:

"I had scarcely taken my seat when the Englishman arrived; and it was well that I knew him to be such, for I should never have guessed it. He was a tall, thin, sickly-looking young man with a large moustache and a complexion darker than that of Italy or Spain. I broke the ice at once. 'Do you speak English, sir?' 'Yes sir; are you English?' 'No, I am an American.' 'Oh, that is the same thing.' I was as much struck with the dignified mildness of his manners, as I had been with the color of his skin. But he soon explained both by saying, that he had served six years in the East Indies, had come home with the liver complaint, and was travelling for his health. I have never met with a military man since I came to Europe who was not a gentleman. It is a fact that even the common soldiers are particularly gentle and obliging in their manner when accosted. My new acquaintance pleased me particularly well. He talked some Hindostanee, and answered many questions which I put respecting India."

While in Geneva he wrote an immense sheet upon every sort of topic to his brother James, in a hand wonderfully minute and compact, which is one of the finest of the few extant specimens of his writing in the old-fashioned free and easy, colloquial, epistolary style. In the course of it he takes occasion to refer to his growing attachment to republican institutions and to Presbyterian government; and then descants upon the manners of John Bull, European music, an old Swiss beggar, the transcendental philosophy, the Munich library; and in artlessly pathetic terms, acknowledges his unabated love and frequent prayers for his correspondent. Some of Gray's letters when abroad are not wholly unlike this. There are remarkable revelations of character and disposition in this letter. I can give but a part of this interesting document, which bears date Geneva, August 14th, 1833.

"MY DEAR BROTHER:

Though I have just dispatched a sort of catholic epistle to the family at large, yourself included, you will not, methinks, object to a more specific personal address. Your letter, dated June 26, I have read repeatedly, and thank you kindly for the news and counsels which it furnishes. There is a vein of melancholy feeling running through it which at first affected me by sympathetic contagion; but I soon recovered. On some points where we once agreed, we agree no longer; and among the number there are two at least which have to do with your epistolary sadness. In the first place, I have got new feelings with respect to politics. I no longer look at the details of our democracy with shame or loathing. I have dismissed the habit of regarding our republic as the certain prey of premature destruction. The other point on which my feelings have experienced a change is Presbyterianism. Everything that I have seen in England, Scotland, France and Switzerland, gives a rational confirmation to my hereditary confidence, and thus converts a prejudice into a strong conviction. Look at the various systems of church polity, and inquire to what extremes they run, and you will find these various and opposite extremes, almost without exception, shunned and remedied by scriptural Presbyterianism. The extremes of clerical and popular power, the extremes of strict and loose communion, the extremes of pomp and meanness as to forms, the extremes of rigor and license as to doctrine, the extremes of superstition and irreverence as to sacred things, the extremes of learning without piety, and the converse, among ministers—all these are held at arm's length by the wise yet simple constitution of our church.

"Two nights after my arrival at Geneva, having spent the daylight in the public walks, I was sauntering homeward, or rather inn-ward, when a bell began to ring. Recollecting that it was the first Monday in the month, I imagined that some of the evangelicals might be observing the monthly concert. I accordingly followed the sound, till it brought me to the door of the Eglise de la Fusterie, one of the principal city churches. The house was lighted, and a number of persons were standing round the doors. 'Qu'est-ce que c'est!' said I to one of them. 'Monsieur, c'est un chant; vous pouvez bien entrer.' The door resisted my attempt, but a moment after it was opened from within. The doorkeeper asked whether monsieur was a foreigner, and invited him to ascend into the tribune. Monsieur ascended accordingly, and looking down, saw the body of the church filled with well dressed men and boys, while a great number of ladies were collected round the pulpit. Over the 'clerk's desk' was a large blackboard with a piece of music scored in chalk. Before it stood a man with a long stick in his hand, with which he touched every note as it was sung. I said to myself, 'This is noble—a congregational singing-school on a splendid scale. It was not in vain that Farel and Calvin insisted on the introduction of psalmody.' I was more and more delighted as I watched the skilful and efficient manner in which the leader managed the performance; he did not sing himself, but beat time for the whole, by occasional directions, by clapping his hands, stamping his feet, &c., regulated the forte and piano to perfection. When a mistake was made he stopped them and corrected it. Nothing that I ever read or heard went half so far towards making me believe that a whole congregation might be taught to sing. Here was the proof auricular and ocular before me, and as I listened to the majestic swell of that majestic instrument, the human voice, I asked myself why the paltry organ above the pulpit was not thrown out of the window. I even went so far as to premeditate an article for the *Presbyterian*, lauding the zeal with which the modern Genevese, from infancy to hoary hair, apply themselves to psalmody, and calling upon the Christians of America to follow their example.

"My illusion was dispelled by a young man who sat by me in the gallery, and politely offered me half of his music-book. This encouraged me to talk; so I asked him whether it was an ordinary thing. He said, 'yes, it took place every week.' 'It is for the service in the church?' said I interrogatively. 'Oh, non, monsieur,' said he, with a look of surprise. He then proceeded to inform me that about two months ago a society was formed here for the purpose of learning and practising the national songs of Switzerland; that the number of members was about twelve hundred, and that this was one of their weekly meetings. Though such an association would, in other circumstances, have interested me deeply, I was so disappointed on discovering my mistake, that I felt disposed to slight the whole affair. I might as well have felt disposed to walk on my head; for in a few minutes they dispatched their evening's task, and began to sing some airs which they had previously learned. The words of the songs, the wild pathos of the melodies, the richness of the harmony, the appearance of the people, the historical associations, mixed together, formed a compound that was really intoxicating. What shall I say? I will have the magnanimity to leave it undescribed. One of the choruses sank so deep into my ears and brains, that I can never forget it; and if ever we meet again I engage to sing it *con amore* for your benefit. It is a very good specimen of the qualities which distinguish the Swiss airs, and which I cannot otherwise describe than by saying that they are expressively monotonous. This is eminently true of the Ranz des Vaches which I heard upon Mount Rigi. It kept time precisely with the jingling of the cowbells, and sounded as if the minstrel had been making variations to the ding-dong. At the same time it was wild, plaintive, and unearthly. I believe I am talking about the Ranz des Vaches, though that is not the subject of my story. The words of the song, or rather chorus, which I have engaged to sing, were these: 'Serrez vos rangs, enfans de Helvetie! Les oppresseurs ne sauraient les ouvrir. S'il faut tomber tombons pour la patrie! Pour savoir vivre, il faut savoir mourir.' How can the poor fellows who have just gone off to Bâle sing this on the eve of battle? How can they talk about oppressors, when their business is to separate two bands of fighting brethren? Unhappy Switzerland! God grant her a good deliverance! As you are gifted with a good deal of musical imagination, I invite you to employ it in composing a tune or tunes to the above words, which shall be at once monotonous and expressive, for the purpose of comparing your invention with the real air (unless you know it already) when we meet again. I have attended a second meeting of the Societé du Chant National. They did not sing Serrez vos rangs, but they sang another air, wild and lively even to enthusiasm, containing a eulogy on Switzerland. 'Ses hautes montagnes, ses belles campagnes, sont tout notre amour.' This was sung with amazing spirit; as was another, a solemn fugue, perhaps a dirge, in which there was a solo by a female voice, alternating with a sepulchral bass by 150 voices, and terminating in a wild, musical shriek by all the parts together. This was the last piece, and was followed by a thunder of applause from the performers themselves, or as a man who sat by me explained it, 'une explosion patriotique.' I have since reflected that I was too hasty in abandoning my inchoate argument. Though this was not a school of psalmody, it is equally relevant and valid as a proof of possibilities. If twelve hundred respectable Genevese, little boys, old men, young girls, and ladies of a certain age, can be brought into the harness by a mere feeling of romantic patriotism, what might not—ought not to be done in the American churches from a sense of duty, joined with a desire of rich enjoyment. I have used the phrase 'romantic patriotism,' not without design. It is a very instructive fact, that in England and America the cradle and home of freedom, political advantages are things of real life, and are never associated with poetical imagery; while in France, the favourite country of mock freedom, triumphal arches, statues, pictures, music and declamatory fustian are the insignia of liberty. And in general throughout the continent of Europe, men seem to think more of the name of freedom than of the thing itself. The patriotism that evaporates in song is ill-adapted to contend with the inharmonious prose of tyranny or rebellion. The 'common sense' of liberty is only known to England and her offspring—the haughty mother and the alienated child. Are we not bound to pray for England's welfare? If she should go to destruction, what a stupendous shipwreck! But there are more than ten in Sodom. How impressive Wilberforce's funeral must have been! The great ones did themselves more honor than the dead.

"But to conclude the chapter on music, I proceed to state that the psalmody of the French churches is, to my ear, most monotonous and insipid. They retain the old recitatives which are bound up at the end of the French bibles. Perhaps they sing the same airs here as in the days of Farel.

"I suppose I mentioned, in some former letter, that M. Monod, of Paris, gave me a line of introduction to Professors Gaussen & Merlet. On applying at the house of M. G., I understood that he was staying in the country. M. M. lives in the Eaux Vives, a suburb of Geneva. * * M. Merle d'Aubigné left his card when I was out. Yesterday (August 13th) I called again at M. Gaussen's, and found that he was just gone back into the country. I then set out in search of M. Merle's abode, and after asking directions of two men and two women in succession, I arrived at his house, which is beautifully situated on the water's edge in full view of the city, lake, and mountains, and surrounded by some very pretty grounds. Professor Merle d'Aubigné is a large, fine-looking man, between thirty-five and forty, as I guess, perfectly French in his looks and manners, full of animation, and extremely courteous.

* * * * * * *

"When I know anything about Kant and his successors on the throne, you shall have it I assure you. Meantime I turn to another subject which is rather more congenial. I am studying the Greek Testament, with no other commentary than the skies and mountains." [Part of the letter is torn away here] " * * Alp is quite a useful aid in understanding scripture. I am chewing upon the second of Matthew with laborious rumination. My rule as to quantity is, as little as possible. This little I turn upside down till every latent implication has been shaken out and every meaning brought to light. I ask myself questions in Greek, and answer them in the words of the évangile. (This was the mode ——— used at Munich, more than once in conversation). * * The references to the O. T. strike me with peculiar force; and the Messiahship of Christ looms very large through the prophetic spy-glass.

"It is a fact which seems surprising to myself, that I have never once since the 10th of April felt the absence of my books. For once it seems a pleasure to be bookless. Or rather, I happen to have one which is an equivalent for all. The sight of the Munich Library made me sick of books. * * It was oppressive: it was a silent insult to the brevity of life. The mind cannot be steady amidst half a million magnets.

"But methinks your patience will be thoroughly exhausted. Forgive whatever seems fantastic, frivolous, or foolish. I affect nothing which I do not at the moment feel. I am cheerful and yet very serious. I have reason to be both. I thank you for remembering me daily before God. He may have seen us, when we could not see each other, both employed alike. Christianity cares little for localities as such, and superstition makes too much of them. Yet as the scriptures have allowed us to associate our Saviour's prayers with the brook Kedron and the Mount of Olives, why may I not be pleased with the reflection that I have borne my friends in mind upon the Thames and the Seine, the Rhine and the Rhone, the Iser and the Danube? Why may I not say that I have prayed for thee, my brother, under the shadow of the Alps? May we both go from strength to strength, till we appear at last together on Mt. Zion and drink of the water of the river of life which proceeds from the throne of God! Our way may lie through deep waters, but they shall not—they shall not overflow us! With the tenderest love to all,

"Yours truly,
"Jos. Addison Alexander."

He thought Turin inferior to Munich and Philadelphia. Even in his travels he must dip into a book now and then. Here, the book was Botta. He writes:

"I have been reading Botta with great satisfaction; I finished the first book to-day. It is a singular fact that I should read the Stamp Act for the first time in this howling wilderness (Pace tua Augusta Taurinorum!). I do not admire Italian. It is very feeble and mawkish; though, no doubt, good for music. How far below Latin! I begin to like Latin again."

The following record is pleasing:

"The verse which I have been studying to-day is Matthew ii. 10: am astonished at the 'new light' which shines from the lamp of life. Perhaps it looks brighter in consequence of the surrounding darkness. Since I wrote the last sentence I opened the Greek Testament and saw these words:—'Ὃ ἔχετε κρατήσατε ἄχρις οὗ ἄν ἥξω.' I must try to hold my little light fast. What a superlative language Greek is! Since I began it anew in the spring of 1829, and read the Cyropaedia and Anabasis through without stopping, I have regarded it as the first of earthly tongues.

"Soft and gentle is thy hand,
   Shepherd of the chosen flock;
On the ocean, on the strand,
   On the mountain and the rock.
Wandering in a foreign land
   In perils oft, in sadness much,
   I have felt it to be such,
   I, I have known its soothing touch.
      (Caetera desunt.)"

Here are more of his Italian verses, composed at Turin:

When with aching head and heart,
   I have laid me down to rest,
Melancholy's poison dart
   Deeply planted in my breast:
A voice has bid the fiend depart;
   A hand—what hand I need not say,
   Has sought my anguish to allay,
   And gently plucked that dart away.

Sometimes nature seems a waste;
   And to my deluded eyes
All signs of beauty are effaced,
   From the ocean, earth, and skies;
While I seem miserably placed,
   Like one upon a sea-washed deck,
   An undistinguishable speck
   Amidst the universal wreck.

But when that gentle hand is laid
   Upon my eyes to give them sight,
The world at once appears arrayed
   In living robes of liquid light;
As if my sadness to upbraid:
   Rebuked, amazed, delighted, awed,
   On land and sea I look abroad
   And bless the handiwork of God.

Oft when I have wandered long,
   Led by some deceitful star,
And pause for fear of going wrong;
   Suddenly I hear afar,
The echo of the shepherd's song:
   The welcome and familiar sound
   Turns my bewildered feet around,
   And guides them to the pasture ground.

And now at length before me lies
   A valley dark and unexplored;
But through the gloom my soul descries
   The stately steppings of her Lord;
I hasten on in glad surprise;
   Let life recede; let death draw near.
   I cannot, will not, dare not fear,
   His rod and staff are with me here!

The thought that he was nearing Rome seems to have proved inspiring to him; or perhaps it was only the unwonted cup of coffee. After conning over the stanzas given above, he says:

"I then proceeded to compose the following, on a theme which I selected before leaving home, viz:

"Be still and know that I am God."

As this has been thought one of his noblest productions in metre, I make no scruple to give it without abridgment. For solemn grandeur of meaning, and for nervous diction and sonorous music he has perhaps not written anything that exceeds it,

I.

When fortune smiles and friends abound;
When all thy fondest hopes are crowned;
When earth with her exhaustless store,
Seems still intent to give thee more;
When every wind and every tide
Contribute to exalt thy pride;
When all the elements conspire
To feed thy covetous desire;
When foes submit and envy stands
Pale and abashed with folded hands;
While fame's unnumbered tongues prolong
The swell of thy triumphal song;
When crowds admire and worlds applaud
"Be still and know that I am God."

II.

When crowns are sported with and thrones
Are rocked to their foundation stones;
When nations tremble and the earth
Seems big with some portentous birth;
When all the ties of social life
Are severed by intestine strife;
When human blood begins to drip
From tyranny's accursed whip;
When peace and order find their graves
In anarchy's tempestuous waves;
When every individual hand
Is steeped in crime, and every land
Is full of violence and fraud;
"Be still and know that I am God."

III.

When to the havoc man has made
The elements afford their aid;
When nature sickens, and disease
Rides on the wing of every breeze;
When the tornado in its flight
Blows the alarm and calls to fight;
When raging Fever leads the van,
In the fierce onset upon man;
When livid Plague and pale Decline
And bloated Dropsy, form the line;
While hideous Madness, shivering Fear
And grim Despair, bring up the rear;
When these thy judgments are abroad:
"Be still and know that I am God."

IV.

When messages of grace are sent,
And mercy calls thee to repent;
When through a cloud of doubts and fears
The Sun of Righteousness appears;
When thy reluctant heart delays
To leave it's old accustomed ways;
When pride excites a storm within,
And pleads and fights for every sin;
Be still, and let this tumult cease;
Say to thy raging passions, " Peace! "
By love subdued, by judgment awed:
" Be still and know that I am God."

"I began another poem in the night which I did not finish. Le voici!

I.

When by strong love and sorrow led,
　The women hasten to appear
Where their departed Master's head
　Was laid upon its rocky bier,
Desiring there once more to shed
　The sweet, but sweetly bitter tear;
　The joyful words which met their ear,
Though by the lips of angels said,

> Like idle tales to them appear:
> "He is arisen from the dead—
>   He is not here!"

II.

> Yet when they saw the cold, hard bed,
>   For his sake to their bosoms dear;
> And saw their Master's body fled,
>   And the cast grave-clothes lying near;
> They in their turn to others said,
>   With mingled wonder, joy, and fear:
> "He has arisen from the dead—
>   He is not here!"

This is without doubt the sweetest and most delicate of all his scriptural paraphrases.

On the way from Florence he had an adventure with an old priest, a young Franciscan friar, and some seculars, the account of which is very entertaining.

"After I had waited an hour or two the vettúra came to the door and I got in. On the back seat there was an elegant old gentleman, in ecclesiastical costume, with a red ribbon round his hat. I asked him whether he spoke French. He answered, in Italian, that he had never practised it. On the seat opposite to him there was a huge pile of bundles, bags, &c. He laughed and said he had taken two places, one for himself and one for his things. We drove along the street called Pórta Rossa; and stopped before a coffee-house, where a boy got in about fifteen years of age, dressed in velvet, which is very common here among the lower orders. We stopped again before a church, where a young Franciscan friar joined us and a young priest. The latter sat inside with the old priest and me. The Franciscan and the boy sat in the cabriolet. We did not get away till after 12 o'clock. I found, from the conversation in the coach, that the young priest was in some way dependant on the old one, whom he treated with obsequious servility. His name was Pádre Luigi (Father Louis). The Franciscan's name was Pádre Leonardo, and the boy's Bartolomeo Novara. The old man was called 'Monsignóre' by the others, so that I did not learn his name. The boy was going to a convent in Rome to try whether he would like to be a Franciscan. He was from Genoa, Pádre

Leonardo from Port Maurice in Piedmont, Pádre Luigi from Pistoja, and Monsignóre from Siena. We stopped for the night at Poggibousi. The old Priest and I had rooms to ourselves, the other three 'had one between them.' We all supped together. The two seculars were very polite to me—the young one officiously so. The old one was truly kind and fatherly. I am very certain that no Italian travelling in America, would have met with such treatment from any two Protestant ministers. The Franciscan was civil but unpolished. The little Genoese had all the native grace of an Italian peasant, with a great deal of intelligence, modesty, and wit. The language was like music in his mouth. The Pistoian spoke in a very affected manner and pronounced *c* hard like *k*; *c* soft, like *sh*; *cucíno* he pronounced *kushéeno*."

Wednesday, Sept. 4.—They were called at an early hour and proceeded on their journey. The ecclesiastics spent a large part of the time over their breviaries. Their manner of praying, however, was a little odd. In the course of the morning they passed through Siena, and stopped before a book-store while the old priest bought a poem lately published. All of us read it. It was a satirical performance, lashing the priests among others. The old man made great sport of the Franciscan during the ride to-day, asking him curious questions and laughing about the idleness and voracity of the monks. He also talked a great deal to Bartolomeo, in a humorous way, about his turning friar. His object seemed to be to disgust him with the project, and I therefore liked his raillery very well, though it was rather unmerciful to the poor Francsican, who bore it with great patience and good humor. He seemed to be an honest, sincere, ignorant man. Pádre Luigi was a prim, affected, sly, hypocritical sort of a body. His business seemed to be to echo every thing Monsignóre said, by adding, " véro,-veramente-sicúra-va bene-si-si-giá-giá." We stopped at noon to breakfast at a village inn. The old gentleman took great pains to ascertain what I would like, and ordered it for me. When it came upon the table, neither he nor the rest would touch it; and I found that they were fasting, for they ate nothing but milk broth. At night they were more complaisant, for when we stopped at San Quirico, a village of Tuscany, they ate meat very heartily for supper. A large fine-looking priest came in while we were at the table, to pay his respects to Monsignóre. The latter, who took all the carving to himself, being unable to divide a chicken, made the other priest, who was sitting near, perform the operation.

Thursday, Sept. 5.—They were up and off betimes again. At Radicofani, the last town of Tuscany, their passports were signed. "The officer was very polite and inquisitive. At an inn, some distance further, we stopped to breakfast. I ate a thrush, (tordélla), Pádre Leonardo and Bartolomeo ate another, which the old man paid for. He himself ate nothing but soup, and Pádre Luigi, of course, did likewise. The vettúrino told me that my goods would have to be examined on entering the Papal territories, and that it would be useless to fee the officers because they would examine none the less. He also told me that the old priest besides his trunk and chests outside, and his pile of bundles inside, had the boxes under the seats full of things which (the man said) he was taking to Rome to sell. None of these, however, could be touched, because he had a *lasciáte passáre* from the Roman government, which is a very hard thing to procure; and sure enough, when we crossed the line and reached the custom-house, the old gentleman produced a paper, seeing which the officer backed out. The vettúrino now came round and told me that if I would give something to the fellow, he thought I might escape too, under the old man's wing. I accordingly inserted 20 cents into the hands of the illustrious officer, who bowed, and we drove off. This was a happy riddance, for I dreaded the inspection very much, having heard that in Romagna they are very troublesome and captious in such cases. The old gentleman chuckled very merrily over the affair, and seemed to enjoy my escape as much as his own. The first considerable town that we passed through after crossing the line was Aquapendente; where my passport was sealed and I was charged one paul, i. e. 10 cents precisely. The old gentleman, besides continuing his gibes at the Franciscan, played a practical trick upon him toward the end of our day's journey, which was very amusing, but I must not tell it here. At supper he talked about the British and Foreign Bible Society, and informed me that he had been in England, at the time when the Emperor of Russia and the King of Prussia were there. He and the other priests talked about celibacy and scholastic theology. Bartolomeo was a favorite with us all. I became, indeed, very much interested in him, though we could not talk together. His speech was more musical than any that I have heard in Italy. The old man called him Fra Bartolomeo, and sometimes Padre Bartolomeo. His reverence seemed to know all the tavern-keepers and servants intimately. Last night and to-night, at supper, the landlady came in to kiss his hand. The one last night brought her daughter Amabile in, and made her say '*Buon appetito, Signori.*' I feel much obliged to the old gentleman for his kindness and real politeness to me; and, in return for it, I hereby certify that he is the handsomest old man that I ever saw. His face, which is truly Roman, would grace an antique medal; his hair is white, and his countenance one that indicates a long life of temperance and health. His complexion, strange to say, is very fair, and his skin smooth as a girl's. He wears a blue frock coat, black breeches and gaiters, and a looped hat of peculiar form with a red ribbon round it.

Friday, Sept. 6. It rained tremendously during the day with occasional intervals of sunshine. I like this, because it tends to abate the heat and purify the air, and when it does rain I would rather be in a carriage than a tavern. Our vettúra, however, began at length to leak; and on arriving at Viterbo, Monsignóre found a package of sugar which was under our bench, fairly soaked. He laughed very heartily and spoke of it twice, as a good joke. His equanimity seemed really imperturbable. At Viterbo he told the waiter that I would probably like some meat, but that they would take boiled eggs, as it was Friday. I ate a mutton chop at the same table. We arrived at night at Ronsiglione amidst a pouring rain and found the tavern nearly full. I got a room to myself, however, as did the old man. This has been the case throughout the journey. As the waiter was making my bed, I asked him whether he knew the old priest—' Oh, yes,' said he, 'he is a bishop.' 'A bishop!' said I, 'bishop of what?' 'Of some little town,' said he, 'near Rome.' So, I have been travelling with a bishop all this time! Ecco!"

On *Saturday, Sept.* 7, the American traveller began to perceive a change in the face of the country. First, the corn-fields disappeared, then the vineyards, then the trees, then the bushes, till at length the motley party in the coach was surrounded by a scene of desolation. No houses, no enclosures, no cultivation, no people for miles together. " We were now in the blighted regions of the *Maúlria*. There was a strong smell of sulphur during some parts of the journey, proceeding from stagnant pools. It was like passing through the vale of Siddim. Milestones began to make their appearance, and at length we came to one on which was written VIA CASSIA. I began to think of Viri Romae, and grew sentimental. The solemn dreariness of the surrounding scenery strengthened the impression. Nor was it diminished when the bishop opened the window on his side and pointing to a weather beaten altar of gray stone, said—" Behold the tomb of Nero !" (Ecco il sepoléro di Neronec). After a while, vines again made their appearance, and the road began to be skirted by elms. We ascended an eminence and saw a town. " Roma!" said the bishop. He pulled me toward the window " Ecco il duómo di San Pietro !" It did not strike me as very grand, and I was surprised to see it at one end of the town instead of being in the centre. We crossed the Tiber on the Pons Milvius. A scum of filth was floating on its surface. The colour of the water is a dirty yellow. We entered Rome about five o'clock, through the magnificent Pòrta del Pòpolo. I again escaped the custom-house by means of the kind, though unscrupulous old bishop; and thus I have got to Rome without having my trunk opened, a thing which rarely occurs to travellers in the public conveyances. I should, no doubt, have lost some of my books, as Frazer did. We drove to the 'Hotel del l'Europa, in the Piázza di Spagna, where I took up my abode. The bishop and priest shook hands with me very cordially, and the old man thanked me for my company. I had not Italian enough to thank him as I wished, but he understood my looks. He showed me to-day a copy of the British and Foreign Society's Italian bible which he bought in Florence. I wish that instead of selling it he would read it himself, and, Oh, that it might convert him! And why not? 'The Law of the Lord is perfect converting the soul.'"

In the coach he composed some very striking and suggestive blank verse. I give the lines exactly as he wrote them :*

    The wheels ran smoothly on the Italian road, and all within was silent. Stiffly braced or carelessly relaxed, each traveller sat, and as he sat he slept. All slept save one, whose thoughts were wandering far beyond the seas in sweet yet bitter musing. For a time the ocean dwindled to a drop; and home—his father's fire-side, and his mother's form—were with him in his exile. Even there he felt himself at home; and well he might. For the resplendent moon, which he had seen go down behind the Alps, was his own moon, the moon which he had loved in foolish childhood; and the few bright stars that still kept watch were his familiar friends. The busy sprite who had bewitched his eyes, now made his ears to tingle. Parting words, adieus, and benedictions crowded back like ghosts but not to scare him. And with these mingled the lasts sounds which had

met his ear as he forsook his country;
first the hum of streets and markets, then
the busy stir and bustle of the port and last
the voice of the impatient ocean, as he
chafed against the New World. For the
wanderer loved that wild mysterious
music, in its swell and in its dying fall. To
him it seemed as if the strings of nature
had been swept by an almighty hand
and forced to give their diapason forth.
These were his thoughts in days long past;
and now that he recalled those days, those
thoughts returned; and with them came that
* * * * the sound itself, that
old familiar sound. The coach stopped; and
Italy was forgotten and he seemed to stand once more upon
his native beach. The coach stopped and the thought
that he was still a stranger in a strange land, all
at once entered his soul like iron. The coach went
on; and still that sound, * * followed
* * hard after. Weary of a dream
which, like the drunkard's solace, only
soothed in order to torment; he rubbed his
eyes and strove to be awake. But still the voice
of Earth and Ocean meeting filled his ears. He
is awake and every other sense performs its
office. * * * * * *
* * Thanks be to God, our senses are
contrived to disabuse each other; and as
oft the ear reproves the eye, so now at
last, the stranger called his eyesight to
his aid; and looking forth saw what? I-
talian vines, hung in festoons between
the trees; or spread as a green curtain
over frames like that which Moses reared
at Horeb * * * forming cool
delicious arbours hung with clustering ——s
of gold and purple grapes. The scene was void

---

* Almost all the verses which he wrote while travelling are written like prose. Milton has written verses in the same way.

of foliage and of fruit; but in its barrenness
there was a charm for him who now
surveyed it. 'Twas the sea. Not a Swiss
lake or fish-pond, but a sea, with its
blue convex surface reaching up to the
well marked horizon. Not a lake nor yet
the mighty ocean in its wild immensity of compass; but a sea, whose waves
have language, and whose ragged coast from
every inlet and projecting point sends
back the echo of a thousand years. These
are the land-locked waters upon which
the old Phenician crept along the
coast with coward daring—these the
waves, on which Carthaginian
learned to conquer and be conquered.
It was here that the first plash of
Roman oars was heard, e'er yet Duillius
had become a god *   * and reared
his mortal column.*

Composed in the coach between Viterbo and Rome, Sept. 7, 1833."

On Tuesday, Sept. 24, they were called by the servant at 3 o'clock in the morning. The sunrise was beautiful, but they were soon enveloped in fog. They crossed the Po on a pont volant and entered the Austrian dominions.

Their baggage was examined at the custom-house near the river, and Dr. McDonnell, an English-speaking companion, had to leave a trunk behind him. In the course of the day, the fog subsided and they had delightful weather. They breakfasted at Rorego, and dined at Padua. I now quote again: "The road from Padua to the sea-side is delightful. It is one long street skirted with gardens, parks, neat and sometimes splendid houses. The moon rose clear and the night was most superb. At Fusina we left the diligence and got into a boat. We stopped at a military station in the midst of the water to show our passports. Our first view of Venice was rendered more impressive by

* An allusion to the columne nostrata. See Cicero Pro Cu. 25. Oxon. p. 455 and De Senect. 13. Planc. 455.

the magnificent moonlight. We entered the grand canal and passed under the Rialto. We landed at the diligence office and exchanged our passports for tickets. The Germans went to a German inn. The priest, Dr. McDonnell and I went in the same boat to the Hôtel de l'Europe, but did not land, as it was full. We then went to the Hotel de Grand Bretagne, where we found two vacant rooms—one with two beds, the other with one. The priest took the latter, and we were obliged to be contented with the former. It is a very handsome one, with a large closet and a recess for the beds. The floor is of marble. The adjoining room is a dining-hall of magnificent dimensions. The house appears to have been once a palace. I saw on a card to-day, which was attached to one of my companion's trunks, his address thus given: 'Rev. Dr. MacDonnell, Bagot street, Dublin.' "

I interrupt the journal for a moment to look at an event at home which was deeply interesting to the young traveller. On Thursday, the 26th of September, the Rev. James W. Alexander, who was at this time residing in Philadelphia, and editing the Presbyterian and Biblical Repertory, went for a few days to Princeton, where he was met and informed that he was elected to the new chair in Princeton College, of Belles Lettres. He found all comfortably well on his return home the next Monday. I copy the following from a detached slip marked "Private Journal," of date of October 1st. It is in the hand writing of the elder brother, and evidently refers to the event announced above. "I have never had an appointment which fell in more with my feelings. During some days since I had the first inkling of it. I have prayed that the Lord would not suffer me to be called unless it were right that I should go. To-day I have been in some pain, but blessed be God I had choice mercies." On the third he records the arrival of good news from home; "also a letter full of happiness from my dear brother, J. A. A., Geneva, August 1st. The Lord be with thee, my brother!"

The goal of the absent Professor was now attained, and he was soon to become familiar with the daily life of a German University. His first impression of Halle was not prepossessing.

"Thursday, Oct. 23.—Here, as elsewhere, my first proceeding has been to walk about the town by myself, and get a general notion of it. This I was the rather disposed to do because I may possibly spend the winter here. I am inclined to think not, however, for a dirtier, meaner, and more dismal town could scarcely have been selected for the seat of a University. I saw but one fine house, and on that was inscribed 'Frankens Stiptinger.' There are a great many idle children playing in the streets. I was assured at Leipzig that the lectures were going on here; but I find, to my great disappointment, that they are not to commence for a fortnight.

"Friday, Oct. 24.—After breakfast I went with a servant to Dr. Tholuck's. The woman of the house seemed as much rejoiced to hear that I was an American as if she had been one herself. I waited in a little side room till the Professor entered and read Mr. Hodge's letter. He thinks I ought to spend more time at Berlin than at Halle; but that Halle should come first. He informed me that there are two Americans here—theological students—a Mr. Haverstick, of Philadelphia, who has been here a year; and Professor Sears, a Baptist, who came a few weeks since. Dr. Tholuck sent his maid to show me Mr. Sears's house. The woman there seemed likewise overjoyed to see an American. Mr. S. was not in, but she told me to come at precisely 12. I did so but he was still out. I called again at 3, and found him with a lieutenant who speaks English. After the latter had gone Mr. Haverstick arrived. At 5 they went with me to Tholuck's door, as I had promised to walk with him. We took a long walk out of the town. He talked about the moon, about German wildness, about Rome, about Mr. Hodge, about England, about Lee, about Mr. Möller of South Carolina, about Professor Stuart, about his own book on the Bergpredigt, and another which he is writing. We returned to his door about 6 o'clock. Mr. Sears was to have been there to meet me. As we did not see him Tholuck went with me to his house. He was not there, but we met him in an open space behind the library, where he and Tholuck walked up and down talking about the studies which Sears ought to pursue. Tholuck invited me to dine with him to-morrow at 1 o'clock. I drank tea with Professor Sears and talked with him till 9 o'clock, when he walked home with me to the hotel. I am almost persuaded to take up my abode here and stay till I am tired.

"Friday, Oct. 25.—At 1 o'clock I went to dine at Dr. Tholuck's. His sister, his niece, a young man, and a little boy were at the table. He talked about the Christian Advocate, Hegel, Schelling, presbyterianism, monarchy, the crown-prince, and the Obertollhausüberschnappungsnarrenschiffe. He showed me Bagster's edition of the New Testament (Hebrew). I told him about the man who borrowed Walker's Dictionary to read. He laughed excessively and translated it to the youth. I then returned to the hotel and soon received a visit from Messrs. Sears and Haverstick. They were going to see Dr. Rödiger about studying Hebrew with him. On their return they took me with them to Mr. Sears's lodging-house where I think of taking rooms. They offer me a parlour and bed-room, now occupied by a captain, for five and a half Prussian dollars a month. The captain, however, does not move till November. Until that time I am to have another pair of rooms almost or quite as good. Mr. Haverstick left us, and Mr. Sears went with me to Herr von Gerlach's but found that he and his family had gone out walking. I returned with him to his room and drank tea with him again. Just as we began, Herr von Gerlack's servant came to say that he would be glad to see us. We went at 7, and saw the Herr, the frau, and her mother and two sisters. We drank tea and ate some nameless thing like hominy with vinegar in it. We also had some wine. A Judge of some sort came in to take leave before going to Berlin. Herr von Gerlach talked magnificently about slavery, royalty and other matters.

"Saturday, Oct. 26.—After breakfast I paid my bill and caused the porter to transport my baggage from the Crown Prince to No. 31 Grosse Ulrichsstrasse where I took possession of my *stube* and my *kammer*. The former contains portraits of Zwingle, Melancthon, two other pictures and a funny little clock. Mr. Sears and I dined together in his room at 12 o'clock. In the afternoon I read Hengstenberg's article on the Sabbath, and looked over Tholuck's commentary on the Bergpredigt. At half past four we walked in the environs of the town. We then returned and drank tea.

"Sunday, Oct. 27.—In the course of the morning Professor Tholuck sent a note requesting me to walk with him at 11. (It was signed 'Dr. A. Thk.') At 9 Mr. Haverstick called and we went with him to the Marktkirche, where we heard old Mr. Fulda preach an election sermon, and read a long list of deaths, births and intended marriages. At 11 we went to Tholuck's and walked with him. (We all three jumped over a fence).* He took us into his house on our return to lend Mr. Sears a Hebrew bible and me a Hebrew grammar. At 2 o'clock Mr. Haverstick called again and took us to the Ulrichskirche, where we heard an orthodox sermon from a youth on Phil. iv. 4. At 4

* See page 321.

o'clock Mr. Sears and I went to drink coffee with Mr. Haverstick in real 'student style.' He made the coffee himself and told us that his expenses are not more than 75 cents a week. He showed us some of his hefts and told us a ghost-story. We talked about German philosophy and animal magnetism.

"Monday, Oct. 28.—At 11 o'clock Mr. Sears and I went out. At a corner we met with Mr. Calman, a teacher of English here, who showed me where to buy gloves, and put a piece of court-plaster on my face where I cut it in shaving, and borrowed Tennemann's smaller History of Philosophy. This latter I read during the afternoon. Before dinner, Baron Welzien called to invite us to drink tea with him. After 6 we went accordingly and found there Mr. Haverstick and Mr. Beutschel, an old gentleman born at Halle, who has been absent forty years, eighteen of which have been spent in Philadelphia, where he now resides. He returns very soon. After tea we ate apples. A soldier came with a paper to the lieutenant and was sent back for his musket.

"Tuesday, Oct. 29.—I finished Tennemann's Hist. of Germ. Philos. After dinner, Mr. Sears and I took a walk returning by the Waisenhaus. I bought a quire of letter paper and a list of the lectures. I drank tea alone. Mr. Sears went to Director Schulze's. I was invited too, through Mr. Calman, who sat with me some time this afternoon.

"Thursday, Oct. 31.—I read DeWette's Introduction nearly all day. Before dinner Mr. S. and I took a walk to 'Lüdwig's etcetera.' On our way home we hired the Conversations Lexicon, and I put a letter into the Postoffice. At 5 o'clock Mr. Haverstick, Mr. Sears and I walked with Herr Professor Dr. Tholuck agreeably to an appointment which he made last night.

"Friday, Nov. 1.—Mr. Sears and I went to several bookstores to inquire for Hupffeld's Dissertation, Ewald's Arabic grammar, and Bopp's Sanscrit do. Mr. von Gerlach's servant came to invite us to drink tea there. We went an hour too soon. Tholuck called soon after but stayed not long. Then came Haverstick. Mr. von Gerlach talked about church and state.

"Saturday, Nov. 2.—I read Hebrew and Greek, and De Wette's Introduction. Mr. von Gerlach sent two volumes of the Ev. Kirch.-Zeitung. In the afternoon Mr. Beutschel called for Mr. Sears's letters. Afterwards Mr. Haverstick called and told us that Prof. Meekel was to be buried at 7 with a Fackelzug. We went to see it but saw it not.

"Sunday, Nov. 3.—In the morning we went to the Domkirche and heard Prof. Blanc on the first part of John xv. He reminded me of Dr. Carnahan. There were many soldiers present. In the afternoon we went to the Ulrichskirche and heard Candidat Valentin preach on the words, 'He that cometh to me,' &c.

"Monday, Nov 4.—At 10 o'clock Mr. Haverstick called and we all went to a room in the Gross Berlin and heard Tholuck lecture on 'Moral.' Our dinner came too late, so that we had to lock it up and hurry off to the Waage, where we heard Tholuck lecture on Galatians. We then went to see Professor Pott and inquire about his Sanscrit lectures, which do not begin till next Monday.

"Wednesday, Nov. 6.—I have heard Tholuck lecture thrice to-day. He invited us to drink tea with him Friday evening. I have been reading Numbers, Judges, Isaiah and Ecclesiastes in Hebrew; Matthew, 1 Corinthians, Acts and Revelation in Greek; DeWette's Introduction, Ewald's Grammar and Botta's America.

"Thursday, Nov. 7.—I heard Tholuck twice, and went to hear him a third time; but there was no light nor fire, and he postponed it until Monday.

"Friday, Nov. 8.—I heard Tholuck lecture twice. At night Mr. Sears and I went to his house and drank tea. Mr. Müller and Mr. Stier of Frankleben were present. He lent Mr. Sears a bundle of Anzeigers and me a book on Sin and Atonement.

"Saturday, Nov. 9.—We heard Rodiger lecture on Hebrew syntax. I went to the police-office for an aufenthaltskarte, but did not get it. Dr. Friedländer and Mr. Fulda were in Mr. Sears's room. Some Jews took possession of the room opposite to mine.

"Sunday, Nov. 10.—Luther's birthday (350 years old.) Tholuck preached in the Ulrichskirche to a great congregation. 'Ein feste burgist unser Gott'—was sung with a posaunenspiel. Mr. Sears was invited to dine to-day at Director Schulze's, but declined because it was the Sabbath. We walked with Tholuck in the afternoon. The quarterly fair has begun to-day.

"Monday, Nov. 11.—We attended Tholuck's lecture on ethics at 10. At 2 we went to hear Dr. Fuch, but the room was not open. At 4 we went to hear Dr. Pott, but he had begun before we got there.

"Tuesday, Nov. 12.—I have heard four lectures to-day; two by Tholuck; one by Fuch, on Genesis, and one by Pott, on Sanscrit. Tholuck had above a hundred hearers; Fuch, fifteen, and Pott four. Mr. Haverstick brought me a petition to the magistrates, for an aufenthaltskarte which Candidat Fulda had written for me. This I signed and delivered to the passport-shop keeper. Mr. Sears and I walked through the fair. Our landlady went out to buy me some stockings, and Mr. Sears some cake. I did not like the stockings, and the landlady's mother is to knit me some. We have joined a circle of newspaper readers and received two papers to-day.

"Wednesday, Nov. 13.—At 10, I heard Tholuck lecture on ethics. At 12, we dined on hare and apple-sauce. At 10, I heard Tholuck lecture on Galatians. At 11, Mr. Sears and I called again on Prof. Pott. At 3, we went to see Lieut. Welzien. At 5, we heard Tholuck lecture (for the third time) on the Psalms.

"Thursday, Nov. 14.—At 10 and 1, we heard Tholuck lecture. At 2, Mr. Haverstick went with me to the Orphanhouse, where I ordered some books. In the afternoon Mr. von Gerlach came to see us, in consequence of which, we did not hear Dr. Pott's lecture. He invited us to his house this evening; but we both had colds.

"Friday, Nov. 15.—I have heard four lectures to-day; two by Tholuck, on Galatians and Psalms; and two by Wegschneider, on 1 Corinthians and Dogmatik. For dinner to-day they sent us raw ham, gruel, and some stuff like salve. I received a written summons to appear before the magistrates.

"Saturday, Nov. 16. Mr. Sears and I went to the Waege after breakfast and heard Wegscheider lecture one hour, on 1 Corinthians, and another on the epistle of James—the latter in Latin. At 11, I went to the police-office and was questioned by the magistrate with respect to my profession, residence, and motives for stopping here. At 1, I heard Tholuck on Galatians."

Among the Americans he fell in with, was a young professor who was destined to high distinction in his own country, as the President of one of the colleges of the United States. This was Prof. Barnas Sears, afterwards the Rev. Dr. Sears of Brown University, and at present the respected Manager of the Peabody Fund in the South. The two young scholars at once became intimate, and long after these days Mr. Alexander delighted to refer to his intercourse in Europe with "Professor Sears." It gives me pleasure to present to the reader the following letter from Dr. Sears:

"In December, I think, of 1833, when I was residing in Halle, Germany, I was joined by Prof. J. Addison Alexander on his return from Italy. We lived in the same house, not only as Americans in Germany —a thing not very common in those days—but as ardent young men of kindred pursuits. We became as intimate as brothers. We were young professors who had taken a similar course of literary and theological studies, though under different auspices. What a range of intensely interesting topics was before us when we began to compare notes! Our college studies, the gaps of which we had just discovered, and were enthusiastically endeavouring to fill up; the value of classical studies, which we both defended against the attacks of Grimke and others; New England men, institutions, theology, literature, dictionaries, compared with those of a more Southern latitude, on which we agreed tolerably well, even theology and dictionaries not excepted; American and European scholarship; the relative position of England, France, and Germany in this respect; the different German schools of philology, philosophy, and theology; the men who represented them; Hebrew, Oriental, and Sanscrit literature. These and other kindred topics were discussed as earnestly as Reconstruction is now. What a chasm these thirty-five years have made! It is as if an age intervened between then and now. The first thing that struck me in my new friend was his somewhat voluble bookish German. My German was meagre but conversational; his was copious, but labored, being manufactured on the spot from the grammar and dictionary. Our German friends must have enjoyed the two specimens. I had been in Germany three months and he three weeks. I soon learned two traits in his character: a constant overflow (in private) of humour and drollery, and a shyness in respect to going into ladies' company. Once we were taking a long evening walk to Giebchenstein with Dr. Tholuck. The Doctor was small of stature, of imperfect sight, and timid and nervous as a woman. We came to a very high fence, running from a steep rock a few feet to the river. There was no getting round it; and it was already dark. We hoisted him up to the very top of the fence.* Prof. Alexander being also short, stood on tiptoe and tried to balance him; while I the taller one, was to spring over the fence and catch the Doctor before he should fall. It was too much for my American friend. The idea that we had 'such a body of evangelical divinity' in our keeping, and that, for a moment, it was so ludicrously poised in the air, made him almost burst with poorly suppressed laughter; and for a long time he would recur to that scene, making it appear like one in Gil Blas. We lived in Grosser-Ulrichs-Shasse, where the crowds passed when they poured out in going to the Pavilions. I shall never forget the fund of innocent humor with which he would stand at the window and make his comments upon

* See page 317.

individuals as they passed. It was a playful attempt to see how many amusing, yet pertinent, things he could say, without a moment's reflection, about hundreds of individuals, the moment they passed. I remember that when his store of wit seemed to be nearly exhausted, he said of the next one, 'there, that one ought to be spoken to,' and finally closed with a broad laugh, as he said the last thing he could think of, 'that one ought to be *slapped!*' We attended Prof. Pott's lectures on Sanscrit literature. The founder of that school of Philology, F. Bopp, was Prof. Pott's teacher. Mr. Alexander said, with his usual air of drollery, 'if the Prof. ever has a son, he ought to name him Bopp; we should then have Bopp Pott!' I should not have mentioned these little incidents but for the impression that many have that he was a sort of recluse who did not know how to unbend. Ludwig von Gerlach, since then at the head of the judiciary of Prussia—a nobleman of high rank, was an intimate friend of Tholuck's and was consequently our friend. Wishing to show us a special favour, he invited us to witness his family celebration of Christmas, which was to be magnificent for the splendor of the gifts bestowed upon the different members of the family, the two strangers not being forgotten. But there were two or three *female* Vons included in the arrangement; and not all that I could say could induce our inveterate bachelor to attend. This same von Gerlach was a devout monarchist, and looked with a superstitious veneration upon persons of royal birth. Hearing Mr. Alexander say that he had been presented to the young princess Victoria, then heiress to the throne, he listened with eagerness to the recital of the visit, and when the interest of the scene was at its height, and von Gerlach could resist his curiosity no longer, he broke out and said, 'and how did she appear?' The roguish reply was, 'rather silly!' The effect designed was complete. We heard no more about kings, and queens, and princes. Such instances of correcting an extravagant opinion were not uncommon with him.

"Professor Friedländer of Halle, was a great antiquary and lover of art. We were invited to tea at his bachelor's hall. So far everything was to my friend's taste; and we had a delightful social time. In the course of the evening, the Professor began on the antiquities of Rome, and had many questions to put on the subject. Whether from indifference or mere roguery we could scarcely tell, our young traveller remarked with great gravity that there was little to be seen in Rome 'but priests and beggars.' 'What a young man' said Freidländer, 'to go to Rome and come back with such a story!' That sort of running fire was kept on both sides for a good half hour.

"He made everything subservient to his studies. It was his custom when he went from one country to another, to go to a restaurant and there make a beginning in the use of the language, by calling for everything at hap-hazard that was on the bill of fare, and when it came in he would know what it was. But he told us he once got caught in that way. One morning at Rome, he gave one of those chance orders, and what should be brought him but a huge crab; which he paid for without eating.

"He was much amused at the custom among the Germans, of men kissing each other at meeting or parting. Pastor Stier, author of 'The Words of Jesus,' and other works on the New Testament, called on Tholuck while we were visiting him. They embraced each other, putting their hands around each other's necks, looking each other silently in the face, then kissing one cheek, and after a long pause kissing the other, till at length the good pastor broke out 'Herr Jesus! how long it is since I have seen you!' Tholuck admitted to us that such exclamations, common among Christians in Germany, are irreverent and therefore objectionable, although Luther apologizes for them. Professor Alexander told me afterwards of an amusing scene between Professor Hahn, editor of the Greek Testament, then visiting at Leipsic, and Professors E. Robinson and ——, who had been studying under Gesenius, Tholuck and others at Halle. Dr. Robinson was somewhat cold and phlegmatic in his temperament; Dr. —— (both of them young then, and neither of them doctors,) was, as Gesenius said of him, 'as affectionate as a woman.' When the two Americans were about to part in Hahn, he accompanied them to the Post-house; but while he was hugging and kissing the —— professor, the sturdy New Englander made off with himself to escape from the operation. I do not know how much my friend's humorous propensity led him to add to the original picture. His stories are always good, but had, I think, a little of himself in them—at least in their colouring. They were told for amusement.

"He was a great favourite of Tholuck's—more so than any other American or English visitor.* After he left Halle for Berlin, Tholuck often spoke to me of him in terms of the highest eulogy and admiration. 'He is the only man,' said he, 'who could *always* give me the right English word for one in German, apparently untranslatable.'

---

* Professor Tholuck has written a note to the editor of these memoirs, in which he expresses himself on this subject in terms of strong regard and warm encomium

Indeed these two men were in several respects, very much alike. They were both fond of the languages, classical, ancient and modern, and were adepts in them, being able to speak I know not how many of them. I have heard them both speak at least six. Both were great readers, and remembered everything they read. The studies of both had a wide range, especially in all that related to any one of the departments of theology. When they were together, conversation did not flag for want of topics.

"But after all, what most struck me in my daily companion and friend, was the earnestness with which he gave his whole soul to the *religious* interests of society. Everything in his mind centred in this subject. Most of our time was given to topics connected with the bearing of Christianity upon human society. Never did I with any man so completely go over the whole ground of all the branches of theology, the present state and prospects of the church in Europe and America, its struggles with foes and false friends, and the work yet to be accomplished by Christian scholars, as with him. The books which he published after his return to this country, are the best commentary upon the state of his mind at the time when he was laying in his stores of knowledge. To me the recollection of those golden days, is as pleasant, inspiring, and elevating as it is fresh and diverting."

Before leaving Halle, Mr. Alexander or one of the other Americans received his friends at a little entertainment, at which was present General von Gerlach. While they were sitting round the table, a grenadier came in with a despatch for the General, and whether overawed or not at the sight of the company, failed to give the customary military salute. The Prussian nobleman forthwith compelled the poor soldier to go all the way back (two miles) and return in proper form. Mr. Alexander was wont to relate this incident with lively pleasure, both as showing the character of Louis von Gerlach and as a sample of the continental punctilio.

At the beginning of the year he went from Halle to Berlin. I resume the extracts from his journals.

"Sunday, Jan. 5.—I went to the Domkirche at 11, and heard Strauss preach on the gospel of the day, (Matt. iii.) to a large and fashionable audience. In the afternoon I heard Lisco preach on the same subject to a house full of common people.

"Saturday, Jan. 7. I attended Hengstenberg's Exegetical Seminary. A passage in Hosea was read and discussed in Latin.

"Saturday, Feb. 1, 1834. Continued Mark and Jeremiah. At noon, heard Neander lecture on the monastic orders. At 6 o'clock, heard Bopp on Sanscrit grammar. Bopp had four hearers, and Neander four hundred. Hengstenberg held no seminary to-night. I read Maimonides on Forbidden Food, and Michaelis's Orientalische Bibliothek. Biesenthal brought me a very fine copy of Hinckelmann's Koran, to look at. I am afraid I shall buy it.

"January 20.—I began to read Rabbinical Hebrew with J. H. Biesenthal.

"February 4.—At 9 o'clock I went to the university and heard Schleiermacher lecture on the concluding words of the first epistle of Peter. He explains ὁ ἀντίδικος ὑμῶν διάβολος, of human slanderers, and paraphrases the latter part of the 9th verse, thus: 'Knowing that the Jews who have not embraced Christianity suffer as much as you do." Moreover, he says that the 8th verse cannot refer to demoniacal possessions, because in those, instead of the devil devouring men, men devoured the devil! The old gentleman is very fond of Lachmann's New Testament, and quotes its readings almost always with approbation. At 10, I went to No. 10 and heard Hengstenberg explain the 34th Psalm. This he thinks was composed by David, at a later period, in recollection of his escape from Gath. The 18th verse he applies to the righteous, not to those mentioned in the preceding verses. In both cases I think he was wrong.

"At noon, I went to the university and heard Neander on 1 Cor. xv. 48-54. He examined and rejected Lachmann's various reading in the 51st verse, viz., πάντες μὲν κοιμηθησόμεθα, οὐ πάντες δὲ ἀλλαγησόμεθα.

"Wednesday, Feb. 5.—From 8 to 9 I heard von Gerlach introduce the Epistle to the Hebrews. He lectures this winter on 'Introduction' only, and has a dozen hearers. His manner is lively and agreeable. I heard Hengstenberg on the 35th Ps., which he thinks is not *properly* Messianic. Tholuck says that H. has changed his mind of late with respect to the double sense, and now admits a sort of qualified duplicity. In the afternoon, Biesenthal came and we read a part of Maimonides's Letter on Astrology. At six o'clock I went to the university and heard Karl Ritter lecture on the geography of Palestine. He reads five themes in the week on geography in general, and delivers a public (i. e., gratuitous) lecture every Wednesday evening. He draws a map upon the blackboard as he goes along.

"Friday, Feb. 7.—I read the 22d chapter of 1 Samuel, and studied

Aben Ezra's preface to the Pentateuch. After dinner, I read the 37th Psalm, and tugged away at Aben Ezra. At 5 o'clock, I paid a visit to Professor Henstenberg, and found him, as I expected, writing and smoking. We talked about the Christologie, about Hitzig, Isaiah, Rosenmüller, Gesenius, DeWette, Hartmann, Tholuck, and the 'Hallische Angelegenheiten.' He says that he has an article from Halle, for the Kirchenzeitung, which will make as much noise as the one in 1830. It is to-day in the hands of the Censorship, and he is doubtful whether they will let it pass. If not, he will appeal to the King. On a former occasion, Tholuck thought that the publication of Gerlach's letter would ruin him: but it did him good. All that is good, says H., in Rosenmüller's Scholia on the Minor Prophets, is taken from the margin of Michaelis's Bible.

"Feb. 12.—Biesenthal and I read the preface to David Kimchi's Michlol, and part of his preface to the Psalms. He also showed me some remarkable passages in the Chaldee Paraphrases, and especially one at the end of Ruth. Moreover he told me that if I ever wished to study the Chaldee Paraphrases critically, I must have the אהב גר or φιλόξενος, published at Vienna in 1830. The author is a professor at Padua. At five o'clock went to see Von Gerlach, but found him in the entry talking to Hengstenberg. He promised to come and see me to-morrow, and informed me that Schleiermacher died to-day of an inflammation of the lungs. He had been ill five days.

"Thursday, Feb. 13.—Finished the song of Moses in the 32d chapter of Deut. Between nine and ten Mr. von Gerlach came to see me, and told me that Scheleirmacher would be buried on Saturday. He also stated that four men were spoken of as his successors; Nitzsch of Bonn, Twesten of Kiel, Lücke of Göttingen, and Olshausen of Königsberg. He says moreover that Hengstenberg lectures on the New Testament, in consequence of an injunction from ministry, designed, he thinks, to blast his influence. We then talked about the history of the American churches, and he proposed that I should collect and send him the principal authorities on that subject, receiving in return German books of equal value.

"Feb. 14.—I read the 42d Ps., and the 23d chapter of 1 Samuel in Hebrew. Then I continued the Michlol. At night I read Kimchi, Michaelis, and Guericke; Colossians and Acts. Biesenthal came in the evening to say that he would come at 12 to-morrow, as he wished to attend Schleiermacher's funeral in the afternoon. He brought a note to leave if he found me not at home. It was in Hebrew, and I have put it away among my autographs. He says that Neander cried when he mentioned Schleiermacher's death in his lecture, and the students cried too. Neander said, 'May it be allowed to him at the feet of the Lamb to see that clearly, which he struggled after here.' The last words of Schleiermacher's last lecture were 'Morgen wird dies klarer seyn.' S. is said to have been the real manufacturer of Lachmann's edition of the N. T. Lachmann himself lectures on Horace and on the history of German poetry.

"Feb. 18.—Read Deut. and Psalms in Hebrew; also Kimchi with Biesenthal. At night I went to see Focke, who invited me when I was there last to call and spend the evening without invitation. Soon after I arrived the Dean and Deaness of the Juridical Faculty arrived; and a little later the Dean and Deaness and Grand-Deaness of the Theological Faculty. Then came the Justizrath's brother and his wife. A good deal was said in conversation about Schleiermacher. They say that on the day of his death he partook of the communion and administered it to his family. He then repeated the Apostles' creed, and added, 'In this faith I die.' His last words were 'Die Barmherzigkeit Gottes!' *

"Feb. 21.—At half past four I went according to appointment to see Dr. Neander. He received me very graciously and was very talkative. He spoke German and I English, at his own suggestion. Part of the time, however, both spoke English and both German. We discoursed about America, England and Germany. He admires the Christian Observer very much and asked me who was the editor. He thinks we ought to have Universities with Theological faculties composed of representatives from the different sects. He laments the Einseitigkeit and Befangenheit of the German Christians, and says there is not a religious journal conducted in a Catholic spirit. When I came away he took a memorandum of my lodgings. I take this opportunity to say that I have been agreeably disappointed in Neander. When I first came, Ayerst told me there was no use in going to see him, unless I wished merely to see him, for he would stand still and look behind the table all the time. And Von Gerlach informed me that when Mr. Luttworth, of Paris, called upon Neander he did not speak one word. Another case of the same kind has been mentioned since. When I first went to his house, therefore, I expected to be in an awkward predicament, as I am the last man in the world to hold up both ends of the discourse. I now record it, however, as a fact, that Neander re-

---

* A few lines below this occurs the poetical tribute to Rezeau Brown.

ceived me at first with great cordiality and talked very freely. He has a canary bird in a cage.

"Sunday, Feb. 23.—At 9 o'clock I went to the French church, in the Gens-d'armes Market, and heard M. le Pasteur Henry, the biographer of Calvin, preach on the necessity of Christ's death. There were very few present, besides a number of children from the charity schools of the 'French Colony.' Henry looks at a distance like Hargous.

"February 25.—At 11 o'clock I went with Biesenthal to Professor Bopp's. There the Brahmin and I had a long discourse in English, about Sanscrit and all the Indo-Germanic tongues. I asked him questions about English, and he gave me a great deal of information. He was more polite and pleasant in his manners than any man whom I have seen in Germany. Most of his pupils study Sanscrit on account of its relations to classical philology; and he expects through some of them a great change in the aspect of Greek and Latin grammar. No particular grammar has yet appeared presenting the results of the Indo-Germanic researches. Pott will probably do something in this way. Bopp spoke very highly of Pott's recent publication.

"At 7 o'clock I went to Focke's. He asked me about a phrase in Rutherford's Letters. Soon after Mr. and Mrs. Ayerst came, and then another lady whom I have seen there before. The conversation was in English. We sang two of Watts's hymns. I read a chapter and Ayerst prayed."

On March the 3rd, he left Berlin.

"March 6.—In Göttingen we heard Ewald lecture on Biblical History. At 11 o'clock I went to see Ewald and introduced myself. I shall say no more of the interview at present than that I was delighted with the tout ensemble of the man."

On the 7th he left Göttingen, passing through Cassel, Marbury, Giessen, Frankfort on the Main, Weisbaden, Nassau, and Coblentz, and on the 11th I find him in Bonn. Here he called on Prof. Rheinwald, to whom he had a letter from Otto von Gerlach. On the 11th, Prof. Rheinwald took him to see Prof. Nitzsch, and then to the house of Augusti.

"They were drinking tea, and we drank tea, after which the folding doors were opened and we were taken in to supper. It was near

11 o'clock when we got away. Augusti was very funny. At parting he kissed me!"

On the 13th, he heard Nitzsch* lecture on *eschatology*, the last topic of dogmatik—Anti-Christ, the man of sin, and Christ's second appearing. Afterward, Rheinwald directed him to the works of Bleek and Sack, and gave him the last volume of his Repertory to take to Cousin in Paris, with a letter.

"At 2 o'clock, Rheinwald came up to my room and asked me to walk. Two others went along, a Professor in the Gymnasium here, and Simrock, a lecturer on the old German poets. We went to a garden and drank some coffee."

In the afternoon he was taken by Rheinwald to Freytag's, where he took tea with the Professor, his wife and daughter.

"He showed me several of his books, and talked a great deal. He asked me to take a copy of his Chrestomathy to De Sacy, and one to Renaud, the keeper of the MSS., at Paris; which I gladly agreed to do."

On the 14th of March he left Bonn,† and reached Paris on the 21st, where he remained in company of Mr. Patton and other friends, visiting interesting points until April 14, when he left for Havre, and sailed from thence in the ship Poland for New York.

Among the Americans on shipboard, who had known him also in France, and before, was Mr. Samuel Miller, now the Rev. Dr. Miller, of Mount Holly, N. J.

Dr. Miller has communicated the following sketches:

"From my earliest recollection, he was the wonder of Princeton for his linguistic learning on the one hand, and his semi-monastic life on

---

* While this work was going through the earlier stages of preparation, the imposing funeral of Nitzsch was occupying the attention of foreign journalists. Hengstenberg died while these pages were in the hands of the printer.

† Where he saw Cousin and De Sacy. The last-named "was very talkative, and when I came away ran through half a dozen rooms to bow me downstairs." Mr. Alexander never forgot or neglected an errand. He calls the Garden of the Luxembourg, "my favourite spot."

the other; and it seemed to be commonly imagined that nothing too wonderful could be told as to either of these particulars.

Though for almost a quarter of a century I lived in Princeton, and nearly all that time was nominally acquainted with Addison Alexander, it would hardly be right to say that I ever had an intimate acquaintance with him. I was a few years younger than he, and that, with his recluse habits, prevented any intimacy. He and I, in fact, had seldom if ever exchanged a word, beyond a passing salutation, until I met him as a preceptor, first at Professor Patton's Edgehill School, then in the College, then in the Theological Seminary.

At Edgehill, he struck me particularly as a very acute observer of all that was going on about him. It was difficult to elude his watchfulness. Of his learning I could form no competent judgment, but took for granted that it was prodigious, as I had always heard it was. Of my college acquaintance with him I have little definite recollection; a high estimate, formed at the time, of his scholastic qualifications as an instructor, chiefly lingers in my memory.

Some years before I met him as a professor in the Seminary, it had been my happiness—a real and very great happiness—to pass about a month with him on shipboard, returning from Europe. A day or two prior to our sailing, in the spring of 1834, he joined the party of which I was one, in Paris; where, only a few hours before our departure, I walked with him early in the morning through the streets, which the previous night had been the scene of a popular émeute, and were still partially obstructed by ruinous barricades, formed chiefly of the cubical paving stones. I found him a most entertaining and instructive guide, acquainted with everything I wanted to know, and quite determined to see whatever was to be seen.

The previous evening, I had met him at a sociable tea-drinking at the rooms of an American friend. Two or three ladies were of the party. Here he reversed all my notions formed in Princeton of his rigid self-exclusion from society, particularly female society, by proving remarkably unembarrassed and affable, in fact taking the lead in free, sprightly conversation with all around him. There can be no doubt, however, that his Princeton and Paris habits in this respect were as far apart at least as the two places.

On shipboard we had a month of something like intimacy. Most of the gentlemen were foreigners, or had wives to attend to; and we naturally attended somewhat to each other. We laughed ourselves through a preliminary sea-sickness, which perhaps served to get us together the more happily; and I found the association most entertaining and profitable. He was full of information, very communicative, wonderfully observant, versatile, and humorous. He had, I think, his Arabic* books with him; and whiled away part of the time in the study of them. Now and then he would extemporize a little Latin, having caught the infection perhaps from Dr. Samuel H. Cox, whom I, and probably he, had met in Europe some months before. A more interesting companion I could not well have found."

---

* One of his smaller diaries has a third of its space taken up with a catalogue of Chinese keys. It contains a numbered list of 210 vocables or word-signs There are also several consecutive pages of Hebrew.

CHAPTER X.

The time was now at hand for the absent scholar to return, and to enter on the most important business of his life. There was lively expectation in the little borough of Princeton, when it was known that one so well fitted by nature and grace, and who had made such unusual and extensive preparations to give new fame to the place of his adoption, was coming home refreshed by foreign travel and laden with the honeyed spoils of European learning. His father's family awaited the event with the keenest and most pleasurable emotions, and stood ready to welcome the wanderer with the warmest salutations of affection.

At the time anticipated, the happy voyager set his foot once more upon his father's threshold, the picture of health and delighted animation. While abroad he had been invited to accept the chair of Adjunct Professor of Oriental Literature in the Theological Seminary at Princeton. I have the authority of President Maclean, for saying that "The Trustees and Faculty of the College would most gladly have done anything in their power to secure his services permanently: yet no one questioned the propriety of his decision in this matter, as all knew that his studies and his tastes rendered him in an eminent degree a suitable person to be engaged in the direct work of preparing young men for the duties of the holy ministry."

As to Mr. Alexander himself, he does not seem to have hesitated for a moment in deciding in his own mind where the path of duty lay. He was not slow to see and feel that his life's work, for which he had been undergoing so wonderful a preparation, was to be at the Theological Seminary. It is undeniable that he was passionately fond of change; but he was also passionately fond of science and literature; a devotee to books and study; and the shadow of a great institution of learning was enough to keep him fixed in his place. He remained a teacher in the Theological Seminary, though he was not without alluring invitations to go elsewhere, from this time until the day of his death, a period embracing nearly twenty-five years. He had given himself to his Saviour, and he believed it to be the will of God as plainly indicated by the suggestions of Providence, that he should avail himself continuously of the best means of mental improvement which were at his disposal, with a single eye to thorough preparation for the task to which he felt himself to be called, viz. the exhaustive study and careful exposition of the sacred volume. To this grand end he now cheerfully bent all his faculties, and sacrificed some of his dearest inclinations.

He was strangely constituted. Much as he longed for variety, he was commonly contented to look for it in the perpetual re-distribution of his books, and the incessant re-arrangement of the furniture of his room. If this endless shifting of the scenery within his own study, did not suffice to please him, he would change his study by removing to some other apartment; and so on *ad libitum*. This was the case at least, in winter. It was hard for him to stay at home during the summer months. The long summer vacation which was now afforded him, was therefore the very thing to meet and satisfy his desire for travel and a totally different set of studies.

Mr. Alexander returned from Europe in May, and soon after entered upon the discharge of his duties in the Seminary, as the assistant of Dr. Hodge, in the department of Oriental Literature. His youth, robust health, powerful head, and his pleasing and at the same time commanding face, his quick motions, his mastery of the art of speech as well as silence, his precocious reputation for scholarship as well as for native ability, his rigid seclusion, his stern exacting discipline, and the contact of his fiery genius, from the first made a profound impression. The young men were fascinated. The new professor saw this at once and took advantage of it to carry out certain plans of his own which till then were novel in the recitation rooms at Princeton. Of course he immediately took the reins in his own hands, and, though he did not always ply the whip as he did at first, he never suffered them to slip from his fingers. It is true there were cases of insubordination; but with great force of character and with much play of satirical wit, as well as by a candid acknowledgment of error when he was at fault, he succeeded in putting down every émeute and making fast friends of some who threatened to be deadly foes.

The question has sometimes been raised, was Mr. Alexander's severe and unforbearing reproofs and sarcasms in the lecture-room consistent with the idea that he had a warm heart and a tone of humble piety? I desire earnestly to give the simple truth about this whole matter. If Mr. Alexander was cold, hard, cruel, truculent, and little under the habitual power of religion, as some seem to have supposed, the fact must have been known to the young men with whom he mingled daily, and to his colleagues in the Seminary. We shall find them taking a very different view of the case. Whatever may have been the promptings of his natural inclination, and I think it has been shown that his disposition was frank, simple and generous, he was a shining instance of the power of divine mercy. This has led Dr. Hodge to say:

"His religious character was very marked. He had as much of the humility and docility of a child under the teachings of the Word and spirit of God, as any man I have ever known. He seemed to have no difficulty in believing. Everything that he found taught in the scriptures he accepted without hesitation; and every portion of the received canon was to him part of the word of God. The strength and simplicity of his faith are so clearly impressed on all his commentaries and other writings, that they cannot escape the notice of any of his readers. He was conscientious, faithful, and punctual in the discharge of all his duties. He was never absent from the lecture-room or pulpit when called to be present, unless absolutely unable to attend. All his students were impressed by the tenderness of his conscience. If any manifestation of impatience escaped him in the recitation room, they were sure that the next prayer he made in their presence would show that he sought forgiveness of such lapses from his Father in Heaven."

Surely even in his natural disposition he was generous and amiable. One of his friends and colleagues* is satisfied that as a teacher he was not easily and well understood. The massive intellect, rich learning, and rhetorical power, could be always appreciated. But the rapid process, and apparent impatience of his manner, sometimes oppressed and discouraged the student. Often, he says, his quick and curt correction mortified the stranger, and sometimes left irritated feelings.

"It was only towards the end of the course, when his mind and heart had been measured out more fully, and some radiation of kindness had been sure to reach every one who was worthy, that many could attain to the just admiration and love with which his later pupils regarded him. Then it was solid. No patronizing air had won it; no flattery of self-love in the learner; but power, learning, eloquence, heart, and simple piety."

But even at the beginning, I may add to the words of this skilful judge of character, he was always comprehended by some, who united with fair talents and diligence in study a little boldness, an unsuspecting confidence in their superiors, a discerning generosity and sympathy, and a manner as far removed from obsequiousness on the one hand, as intrusive presumption on the other.

It will not fail to be noticed as we go on, that the men of the later classes were in the habit of repeating and exaggerating stories that had come down to them like ancient myths or legends from students of the earlier periods of Mr. Alexander's professorship, all of which went to show that the athletic and fiery Hebraist was terrible and even cruel to those who were so unfortunate as to attract his anger and thus bring down on themselves his witty repartee. I have been at no

---

* The Rev. Alexander T. McGill, D. D. Dr. McGill became associated with him long afterwards.

little pains to sift these stories to the bottom, and have embodied the results of my investigations in various forms, such as extracts from students' letters, descriptive sketches and anecdotes, running comments, and the like, which will be given to the reader in due order. The amount of what truth I have arrived at in the premises is this: Mr. Alexander made his first classes in Hebrew work like Trojans; and was often out of patience with gross negligence, vanity, or dulness, and sometimes treated the offenders without measure or mercy. But he was very peaceable after all was over; and gradually he became more and more tolerant and gentle, until towards the last, his steady meekness was more noticeable than the occasional flashes of his first or mistaken resentment. His detected errors he was always ready to acknowledge and repair. I now call attention to the words of one of his earliest pupils. Dr. James A. Lyon of Columbus, Mississippi, was a student at Princeton Seminary from 1832 to 1836, and thus spent some two or three years under the tuition of Mr. Alexander. He well recollects his first appearance in the lecture-room.

"He glided noiselessly and suddenly into the lecture room, and in a moment was *at* his chair, not in it; for he rarely took his seat before he commenced with a very short prayer, rapidly uttered, and before the class had all adjusted themselves in their seats, he had called on some student to begin the recitation. With a glance of the eye, quick as a twinkle, he seemed to comprehend the situation, and detected instantly who were present and who were absent. The recitations were invariably short, not exceeding three quarters of an hour. At the close of the recitation he darted out of the room, as his place was near the door, and gave no opportunity for parley with the students."

In Dr. Lyon's opinion, which it is but fair to state, he was not, in a social point of view, very accessible, especially if the visiting student manifested the slightest symptom of being too familiar, or of deviating from the exact subject of inquiry.

"He took a most unmistakable method of making a student of this kind feel, after he had answered his questions, or given the explanations sought for, that his absence would be very pleasant. This he did by remaining silent with his eyes fixed on the floor, at the same time playing with his fingers on his chair, or engaging in a loud whistle. If this did not speedily produce its desired effect, he would deliberately turn to his table and resume his studies."

Consequently, when the same writer visited him in his study, which he sometimes did, as he was a member of two or three of the professor's private and special classes in the study of Arabic, Chaldee, and the peculiar terminology of the Levitical ceremonial law, he rarely took his seat before he began his business; never asked a question which he did not regard as essential to the point; and the moment his business was accomplished, left the room. The result was that he was received without any very visible signs that he was unwelcome. Occasionally when he rose to leave, the professor would request him to sit longer; which, however, he but seldom did. "I dreaded" he says, "his finger-beat upon his chair, or his loud whistle, which was anything but music to my ear." This fear of him which so many had was unquestionably the source of much of the teacher's embarrassed restlessness.

Dr. Lyon was impressed with his exceeding avidity for study and work. Not satisfied with the ordinary daily recitations in the lecture room, Mr. Alexander proposed to such of the class as were so inclined, to form private classes with him in Arabic, Syriac, Chaldee, and other departments of oriental learning. At first, several students availed themselves of this opportunity of enlarging their fields of study. But most of them soon fell off, until at length the private class was reduced to three, Melancthon W. Jacobus, Joseph Owen, now a learned missionary in India, and Mr. Lyon himself.

"These private classes," says Dr. Lyon, "seemed to be formed as much for his own employment and improvement as for ours. He appeared restless and unhappy unless he had as much work as he could do. He was so thorough in everything he studied, that he needed not to review, and therefore seemed to have an aversion to travelling over the same ground twice. To him nothing was so tedious as 'a twice-told tale.' Hence he was constantly changing the field of study; and to some who were incapable of appreciating the magnificence of his mental powers, and the necessity there was for constant mental excitement he seemed *fickle*."

This impression was very general at all times, but as Dr. McGill, Professor Hepburn, and others will abundantly show, was not altogether just. He had not yet mellowed down into the tractable and sympathising teacher he afterwards became.

"He was not considered amiable during the first years of his service in the Seminary, but on the contrary rather severe and unforbearing. The students were afraid of him. How he became afterwards I am not able to say. Doubtless, however, he became more patient as he grew older. He was sometimes fearfully sarcastic, having no tolerance for the proud, impertinent, or self-conceited, whom indeed, he did not hesitate to cut in twain with a word, or a look, or a sneer."

Mr. Alexander was a terror to the idle, and often took pleasure in making such expose their own ignorance and reveal their own lazy devices.

"I recollect that on a certain occasion one of the idlers was called on to recite in Hebrew. As a substitute for studying the lesson word for word, so as to be able to give a correct translation, he simply memorized the English version. It so happened that he was called to read, when within three verses of the end of the chapter. He read one verse of the Hebrew, but instead of giving the rendering of the verse read, he gave that of the succeeding verse. The professor said nothing, but with a cruel smile on his face exclaimed, 'read the next verse'— which he did, still travelling ahead; 'now,' said he, blandly, 'read the last!' The poor fellow read the Hebrew, but looked up in utter dismay amidst the roars of the class, at his humiliating and ridiculous exposure."

If we now turn to the outer world, we shall find there was not much change in the situation of things in the village. Professor James Alexander was still occupied at the college. Every fortnight a literary club met in Princeton. On alternate weeks there was a sederunt of a strictly clerical association. The members of the literary club at this time were Drs. Alexander, Miller, Carnahan, Howell, Maclean and Rice; Professors

Dod, Henry,* Jaeger and Alexander; and Tutors Stephen Alexander,† Hart,‡ and Wilson. These were delightful reunions. The older brother of the two Alexanders especially enjoyed them, but the younger was not indifferent to their attractions. They were, strictly speaking, literary soirées, and were the means of putting in circulation a good deal of scientific and other useful knowledge. It was evidently this association with the savans of the college, that set Mr. Alexander about the perusal of such popular works as Herschel and Mudie. This is almost the last we shall hear of the exact sciences. He never pursued these studies far, but I am certain that they entertained him. The reading of Oriental books was still a great hobby with him. Hebrew was his atmosphere and his sunshine. It coloured him, as the leaf colours the silkworm. The Pentateuch and the Psalms, and Biblical archæology and antiquities, were his principal subjects in the Seminary. In the afternoon or evening, when his eyes began to grow a little heavy over Kimchi and Michaelis, he had many a lively chat with one of the old Romans, or with quaint, comical Thomas Fuller, or Spottiswode, or Chrysostom, or Jerome, or the marvellous romancers of the Thousand and one Nights.

Other and more informal gatherings offered their attractions to those who liked them. There was, of course, much to draw strangers to the fountains of learning at and near the college. On Sunday, August the 9th, the delegates from the Congregational Union of England visited Princeton, and doubtless visited Dr. Alexander, and could not fail to excite the interest of his son Addison, though it is more than probable that he sought no introduction to them. The foreign gentlemen were Mr. Andrew Reed, minister of Wickliffe chapel, Hackney, London, and Mr. James Matheson, of Durham, another dissent-

* Joseph Henry, LL. D., of the Smithsonian Institution.

† The present distinguished astronomer of that name—not related to the subject of these memoirs.

‡ John S. Hart, LL. D., now principal of the State Normal School situated at Trenton, N. J. See Forty Years' Fam. Letters for further particulars in regard to this club.

ing minister. Mr. Reed was known as the author of a work entitled "No Fiction." Mr. Matheson was the son of Greville Ewing, and was said to be a leader in Reform. It might be supposed that Mr. Alexander missed no chance of seeing such people and increasing his stock of ideas, which had just been enlarged so much by personal observation, as to the manners, events, and general state of things abroad. His habit in this respect, however, was somewhat singular; he kept his room, and saw only those who called; but he did not fail to inform himself. His acquaintance with the contents of the German periodicals, with the state of English parties, and with the genealogy of the crowned heads, to say nothing of the margraves, electors, archdukes, count palatines, and other titled nobility of Europe, exceeded anything I ever met with. He seemed to know these little minutiæ connected with high life beyond the Atlantic exactly as a first-form boy at Eton is expected to know his quantity. It was just the thing that suited him, to wind in and out through the whole length of a tangled historical succession, where the name of a given personage is often changed and concealed by the acquisition of his coronet, and to be able to tell you who was who. No one knew, or surmised, better than he did, who at any given moment was the Lord Chancellor of England, who the Lord Chief Justice, who the Lord Chief Baron, the Chancellor of the Exchequer, &c. &c. carrying the thing down, in some cases, to lists of ordinary knights and baronets, and their seats, and even untitled members of parliament.

Let us now turn once more to the Journal. In the absence of Dr. Hodge, Mr. Alexander now had the third class almost wholly to himself. He taught them Hebrew and archæology. They read the Psalms, which he studied himself very carefully in private, comparing the text with the different versions and commentators. He amused himself reading the Thousand and one Nights in Arabic, and learning Ethiopic grammar. He also wrote a little daily for the Repertory. Early in July he finished a massive article on the Antiquity of the Pentateuch, founded upon one by Hengstenberg. This should be read as an elaborate introduction to his work on the Psalms. He was busy, during the same month, at a review of the Life of Roger Williams by Professor Knowles. "History," he writes, July 25, "is still my amusement." He continued to be employed pretty much in this way throughout the summer. On Mondays, Tuesdays, Thursdays and Fridays, he heard the Third class in the seminary recite each day—in the morning on Hebrew, in the afternoon on Biblical antiquities. In Hebrew they were at this time reading the Prophetical Psalms. On Wednesdays and Saturdays he had no recitations. On the sixth of August he records:

"This afternoon I took up Cicero's Works, and read the introductory oration against Verres with a great deal of pleasure. I derive more satisfaction from the classics than when I had to teach them; then it was a task, now I feel it to be a pleasure. I was particularly interested with the allusions to the politics of Rome—electioneering, canvassing, intrigue, &c., &c. How much human nature is like itself!"

That evening the Literary Association met in Dr. Alexander's parlour; it is thus described by the junior professor:

"It is composed of the faculties of the college and seminary, with some other literary characters, and is held at the houses of the members in succession. Some subject is proposed at the meetings for conversation, and occasionally papers are read. At this meeting Prof. Henry gave a verbal account of a magnetic needle which he had invented for the purpose of determining the variation. After this there was a free conversation on the subject of lightning-rods; and it was agreed that Professor Henry should furnish something in writing on the subject at the next meeting. The other gentlemen present were Professors Torrey, Maclean, Dod, Alexander and Jæger, of the college; Professors Alexander and Miller, of the seminary; Tutors Hart, Alexander and Wilson, of Nassau Hall, and Principal Wines, of Edgehill."

The Journal is resumed:

"August 7th.—I am reading Genesis in Hebrew, with Bush's notes, for the purpose of fixing my attention. I am also reading Jay's Closet Exercises, morning and evening, with much delight."

The day previous he finished the revision of his article on Roger Williams. It was now ready for the press. The July number of the Repertory, which had just appeared, contained two articles from the pen of Mr. Alexander: one on German New Light, another on the Life of Rowland Hill. The former is learned and satirical, and the latter is in his happiest and sweetest vein, and might easily deceive most of the admirers of his brother. A third, on the Antiquity of the Art of Writing, was already in the printer's hands for the October number, and on this seventh day of August he began an article on Guericke's Manual of Church History.

"My method," he says, "is to write, between twelve o'clock and dinner, seldom more than one hour—often less. In this way I do not feel the labour, and keep something always ready. I am now ahead of the press, and if others do their part I shall not be hurried and dunned for my contributions."

He the same day lectured extempore on the twenty-second Psalm. These oral and unwritten discussions were among his most ingenious and masterly efforts. They were the free outpourings of a mind that was always full to the brim.

He had been reading Ethiopic grammar this summer, giving a few spare moments to it every day. He finished Otho's Compend on the 9th of August, and immediately framed a purpose to attempt the Psalms in Walton's Polyglot. He read, the same day, some chapters on Herschel's Discourse on Natural Philosophy, with the liveliest satisfaction. I find the following record for

"August 20.—Finished Herschel's Discourse on the Study of Natural Philosophy, from which I have derived much satisfaction. Many things that were once vague to me, are now distinct. I have derived a tolerably clear idea of the inductive method; have met with valuable hints as to the means of acquiring knowledge, and above all, have experienced an agreeable and salutary excitement. I have read the book chiefly in the afternoon, when my regular studies were concluded. The same time I shall now devote to Mudie's Popular Guide to the Observation of Nature, which I began to-day. My other studies proceed as usual."

It was commonly supposed that Mr. Alexander had not even the elementary knowledge in the natural sciences. The reader is now aware that this was an error. During the summer he had read a selection of the Psalms in Hebrew with the Third class. In private he had studied Sanscrit and Ethiopic grammar. In the evenings he had been reading history, and about the end of the summer had finished Fuller's Church History of Britain. He had then taken up Spottiswode's History of the Church of Scotland, and read about one half of it very closely. Finding, however, that a large proportion of the work was occupied with matters of mere civil interest, he had confined himself thenceforth to the part which was purely ecclesiastical. In this way he read the remainder of the work, and reached the end of it about the first of November. This is an exact *résumé* of his literary occupations for the season, with the exception of a few unimportant rambles among the English Classics and the Ancients. Minor details are of course excluded from this summary. He also wrote on different parts of Scripture for his private use, five articles in the Repertory, and one or two little books.

The winter session of the seminary opened on the sixth of November. In prospect of the duties of the new term, he records:

"My only regular public employment will be the instruction of the lower classes in Hebrew. I have a private class in Arabic; in private I read two chapters in Hebrew daily, making scholia on them as I go along, by way of preparation for minuter study afterward. This method I commenced on the 22d of September, when I made a calendar for the remainder of the year, assigning to every day a chapter in the historical, and one in the poetical books. When I chance to miss the lesson of a day, I pass it over and go on to the next. If at the end of the year I like the plan as well as I do now, I shall form a calendar for 1835, so as to finish the Bible in a twelvemonth. This, however, is not to exclude the more critical reading of other passages, and particularly those which are recited by the classes. My plan includes a chapter of the Greek New Testament for every day. This part of it, however, I have not so fully executed as the other. At this, as at other times, I leave some portions of my plan of study to be gradually formed according to events. The only additional items on which I have resolved are Sanscrit and history. In the former I must resume the grammar—in the latter I have not yet fixed upon a subject."

Little incidents of the time help to take us back to the scenes in which he moved. The Episcopal Church (Trinity) was consecrated in Princeton towards the close of September. Twenty clergymen in all were present, and among them three prelates, Bishops White, Ives, and Doane. The venerable and beloved Bishop of Pennsylvania preached a sermon of an hour's length, and was induced to stay and attend commencement, which was then the last Wednesday in September. That night the Rev. James W. Alexander drank tea with the three Bishops at Professor Dod's, and records his pleasure in a letter to his friend in Trenton. Alluding to Bishop White, he says, it was like being transported to a purer air to talk with him. About this time Tutors J. S. Hart and Stephen Alexander were made adjunct professors in the College. The Rev. Dr. Benjaman H. Rice, who married a sister of Dr. Archibald Alexander, the brother of the Rev. Dr. John H. Rice, of Union Theological Seminary, Virginia, was now pastor of the Presbyterian church in the village, and sometimes made very warm and powerful appeals from the pulpit. He had been for years the honoured pastor of the Tabb street Presbyterian church in Petersburg, and his memory is still precious in Virginia. From Petersburg he went to New York as pastor of the Pearl street church, and from New York to Princeton. Coleridge died this year; and the news created a stir in the literary circles of academic Princeton. Amidst these and other changes, the new professor in the Seminary moved on steadily in the prosecution of his enormous labours as linguist, exegete, lecturer, review-writer and miscellaneous reader.

Few teachers have had a greater fondness for keeping their eyes on their pupils after the days of tuition were over. The pleasant gentlemen, above all, and especially the earnest

Christians and creditable scholars were never lost sight of; and he was always ready to lend them a helping hand and give them brief but timely counsel. Though not fond of writing letters, he has written many to such persons and for such purposes. His old students, many of them, remember and speak of this trait in his character.

The recollections of one* who is himself reputed to be the master of many languages, and among them, a number of those with which Mr. Alexander was acquainted, can hardly fail to prove interesting. He writes:

"My personal acquaintance with Addison Alexander was short; altogether too short for my good. When I entered the Theological seminary at Princeton, he was absent in Europe. When he returned I was for some time in his classes. It became necessary, however, for me to leave the Seminary before I had finished the full course."

Mr. Scott entered upon missionary labors in Louisiana, but prosecuted his studies, till by the aid of notes which he obtained from the manuscripts of the Professor and from fellow students he completed the careful study of all the topics, themes, and authors usually embraced in the Greek course.

"Having, as you would suppose, some difficulties in the way, especially in prosecuting Syriac and Arabic in the cypress swamps of the Mississippi and Red rivers, I sought Professor Alexander's aid, and he was kind enough to write memoranda of books and suggestions, and remarks on the languages from time to time: but I think only two of the letters have escaped the ruins of removals and of time." †

The writer always admired him from the first time he ever saw him.

"His warm heart, his breadth, depth and originality of thinking, and his method of prosecuting thought, and his prodigious learning, always charmed me."

Sunday the 19th day of October was a day darkened by

---

* Rev. William A. Scott, D. D., of New York.
† These have perished or disappeared.

heavy clouds. Mr. Alexander read aloud to his brother James from Owen, and the whole of John Howe's sermon on "Why hast thou made all men in vain?" which both esteemed better than Robert Hall's on the same text. Their father was spending the day at Burlington, in company with Professor Dod. Monday was signalized by a cold north-wester, which however did not prevent Mr. Alexander from arranging his new chamber in the Seminary. Tuesday marks the date of a visit from Dr. Hilyer of New England. He remembered seeing Dr. Alexander in Philadelphia about 1800, just before the latter made his trip to the eastern States. Dr. Hilyer was at that time in great depression of spirits and did not expect to live. He heard the young Virginia clergyman preach from the text, "Why art thou cast down O my soul?" The announcement of the text, he said, was overwhelming to him. The troubles of the next month was known afterwards as "the dark day." Candle light continued till nine o'clock a. m. Dr. Archibald Alexander sat reading by a candle at this hour. Rain fell, and a yellowish fog obscured and choked the atmosphere. Henry Clay was in Princeton on the 25th. These rapid touches may serve to bring up the picture of the times.

A heavy affliction was now however, to darken the house of the elder brother. On Saturday, December 15, he had gone after tea to his brother's new study in the Seminary, and had there spent an hour or two in reading and conversation. On his return to his own house, where he had left his little son Archibald, he learned that he had been seized with a croupy hoarseness. The disease was rapid and fatal. When the daylight of Monday came, the father perceived with agony that one night had made him a mere wreck. He had been a blooming, fresh and hearty little boy; he was now become pallid, wan, and haggard. Not long before he was released from his sufferings he tried to sing. He also put up his hands and said, "I want to say my prayers." He passed away with but little pain. He was the third son of his father, and was a great favorite with his grandfather, and indeed with the whole house. He was a little over two years old. The father's comments on the event are recorded in his unpublished diary. It was he says, "a lapse into slumber. * * I feel a blessed consolation in the belief that this dear lamb is safely gathered into Christ's bosom."

This sad blow brought grief to the hearts of all the relations, and among them to one who was thought by many to be hard and unfeeling, but who was as soft and gentle as he was strong and at times imperious. His studies went on much as usual, though Mr. Alexander was always varying the particulars of his scheme.

Mr. James Alexander meanwhile was busy with his classes, and writing for the Repertory and the Presbyterian, of which newspaper he was still the editor, as well as working for the New Jersey Lyceum. Like his brother at the Seminary, he gave himself no rest, and made it a point to read all great and good books that reached his hands, besides many volumes which he could not fully commend. He was a most rapid reader. He was now upon Simeon's works, Guericke's History of the Church, Fichte, Hegel, Fuller, Wordsworth, Neander, Coleridge's Aids to Reflection, David Russell's Letters, Butler's Lives of the Saints, Hannah More's Life, besides many reviews and pamphlets and much in Hebrew, Latin, Greek, and German. He was buying up works on Hebrew, English, and Anglo Saxon. He was richly acquainted in the principal modern languages, and in several others that are not generally known. He was also full of schemes of literary usefulness and practical benevolence. He had the Juniors five times a week in the De Oratore of Tully. He also delivered occasional lectures to them. He filled a volume or more every year with diary accounts of the weather, descriptions of people and incidents, and of natural scenery, recorded conversations, plans of sermons, Latin prayers and marginalia, French epistles, elaborate quotations, comments and criticisms, abundant sketches of character, religious confessions, sportive effusions of fancy, and every species of agreeable and instructive reading; the whole done in a style of composition and penmanship that might excite the envy of many a famous littérateur. His sensibility to fine sights, sweet sounds, animating temperature, and the charms of art and literature, was of the most exquisite sort and the most tremulous acuteness. But we must return to the subject before us.

It is amusing to go back to the childish and youthful days of the restless commentator, and to his father's remark in one of his letters to Mrs. Graham that Addison had a repugnance to teaching. In after life, in addition to his regular classes in the Theological Seminary, Professor Addison Alexander was seldom without private pupils who came to his room, and hardly ever without a small class or two of enthusiastic orientalists, generally the pick of the Seminary, who also frequented his study at certain hours and had a larger and more genial experience of their preceptor's extraordinary mental vivacity and the bursting fulness of his animal spirits and social good humour than any others. His punctuality on these occasions often cut short these agreeable interviews in the very middle.

During the years 1834 and 1835, Messrs. Hugh N. Wilson (now the Rev. Dr. Wilson) and John S. Hart were associated in the tutorship of the College. Being of kindred tastes they employed all their spare hours together in linguistic studies. Having read together nearly the whole of Herodotus and about two-thirds of the Hebrew Bible, they determined to begin the study of Arabic, and applied to Mr. Alexander to teach them. Although the application involved a serious tax upon his time, he gave a most ready assent, and appointed the hour from nine to ten of every evening for the purpose. He was occupying at that time rooms in the basement of the Seminary Chapel, and hither every night (except Sunday) for nearly a whole year, the two young men resorted, no inclemency of the weather, even in one instance preventing their attendance. Knowing how precious was the privilege accorded to them, they felt disposed to avail themselves of the advantage to the utmost. During this course they went through the Arabic Grammar under his instruction, and read the whole of the Koran except the last two or three chapters. In this course of reading and study, besides the knowlege of Arabic, they received continually frequent hints and suggestions such as might be expected from a man of his ripe general scholarship.

"Nor were oriental learning and linguistics the only topics of that favoured hour. Never was teacher more genial or more freely communicative, and after the lesson of the evening was finished, other topics connected with literature and theology came up, and we drew at will from the exhaustless fountain open to us. Nor did we often go away with our buckets empty."

Before beginning this arrangement, he told them with some distinctness that he would give them *an hour*, and they understood from his manner that a moment beyond the hour would be counted as an encroachment. Knowing well his peculiarities, they were careful to leave precisely at the striking of the clock, no matter how interesting might be the topic under discussion. They were equally careful never to enter his room a minute before the time, even if they had to stand out in the cold for the clock to strike.

"This quiet and precise punctuality," writes one of them,[*] "seemed greatly to please him, and reconciled him evidently to bearing with us longer than perhaps he might else have done. For he always managed to make us feel perfectly welcome, and poured out the resources of his learning for us with unbroken profusion up to the sixtieth minute. But when that moment came, the stream of talk suddenly stopped. There was not a word to be said: he was ready to return once more to his silent studies."

He then goes on as follows:

"No hours of my life have been hours of greater intellectual activity and pleasure than those now described. There is something particularly quickening and stimulating in this kind of intercourse with a man of genius, and I felt my own mental energy taking fire from his."

The impression which he made upon them in this familiar encounter of mind with mind, was that of

[*] Dr. Hart.

"a man of prodigious intellectual strength united with prodigious intellectual activity. It was the power of the locomotive, and the speed of the telegraph united in one machine. Indeed the most noticeable thing about him was the general roundness and completeness of his powers. There are numerous instances on record of his prodigious power of memory. I have myself recorded one feat of this kind. But the mnemonic power is usually accompanied with a weakness in some of the other faculties. In him, on the contrary, every other intellectual power, reason, imagination, fancy, attention, judgment, and so forth, seemed to have an equal development. He excelled accordingly in everything which he undertook. He did not often indulge in personal reminiscences. One of these, which I remember, described the change of views he had undergone while in Europe in regard to the character of Napoleon I. He said that he had gone abroad with that view of Napoleon's character once nearly universal in this country, and derived from our familiarity with English literature. It was in fact Napoleon as seen by Englishmen who did him the greatest injustice. His remark was, that in every part of Europe which he visited he saw proofs of the constructive, regenerating, and beneficent power of Napoleon as a civil ruler. It is not impertinent, I suppose, in this familiar memorandum, for me to say just here that we college boys always used to see in Addison's head a remarkable likeness to Napoleon."

This fine tribute is confirmed by the language of the other pupils in this class. Dr. Wilson also mentions one or two things omitted by his friend, and gives a few recollections of an earlier date.

"My acquaintance with Dr. Alexander dates back to the time of his entrance upon public life. At that time Professor Patton had just opened Edgehill School—of which Addison Alexander was one of the first teachers; and there he prepared his edition of Donnegan's Lexicon. Prominent among the young men of Princeton, and in the circle of his friends at this time, were John C. Young, Albert Dod, Rezeau Brown, and Samuel Winchester; all of whom, alas! are now, like him, numbered with the dead.

Dr. Hart has probably mentioned our Arabic studies with him. I do not remember to have seen any notice of the long narrow notebook which always lay upon his study table, waiting, it would seem, for some inspiring thought or treasured sentiment, and waiting not in vain. Day after day we could see that new pages were turned, and that the numbers, (for each jotting was carefully numbered) rose continually higher."

The minute chronicle of Mr. Alexander's life which follows will be interesting to scholars and the lovers of personal detail. During the month of December he pursued the various subjects mentioned in his last entry and added new ones. The third class were now under his direction, and reading the history of the flood in Genesis. In the way of an expository lecture the instructor treated the class to an extemporaneous and lively commentary upon the history of Joseph. At each recitation, too, an essay was read upon a subject assigned by the teacher, and relating directly to the subjects upon which the class were engaged. With the second class he read Isaiah. On Dec. the 31st he records,

"We have to-day finished the sixth chapter. This employs me more or less during the week, though I meet the class only on Wednesday morning. Besides studying the text itself, I compare the ancient and modern versions, and the notes of Chrysostom, Jerome, Theodoret, Jarchi, Aben-Ezra, Kimchi, Calvin, Michaelis, Grotius, Vitringa, Gesenius and Hitzig."

In private he had continued the plan of reading Hebrew daily, and I find him at this date making out a calendar for 1835. His Arabic class had read the extracts appended to Rosenmüller's Grammar, and more than fifty verses in the Koran. It also appears from his diary that he was not without the stimulus of companionship in some of his private studies, and that he was thoroughly interested in the languages of Upper India. He writes,

"I am teaching —— Hebrew, and A. A. Hodge Greek. I read a little Sanscrit daily. I am now engaged upon 'Neal's History of the Puritans;' which I read at night. I have written two more articles for the Repertory which will appear in the forthcoming number. They are both reviews—the one of Charles Stewart's 'Travels in England,' the other of 'Bush's Commentary on the Psalms.'"

He had completed one of his books for the American Sunday School Union, and had abandoned the other. The subject was the Life of Elijah. Another on the same subject had just been purchased by the "Union," "and the execution of music," writes the modest author, is not satisfactory to myself or others. One has curiosity to know where the fault lay! This wish is not gratified. I again return to the Journal.

"I finished the first book of Eusebius's Ecclesiastical History last week. I read it alternately with Josephus."

One should have gathered from what comes next that Mr. Alexander had not always been the most exact and punctual of clock-work scholars.

"I have gradually fallen into a pretty systematic plan of study, which with the leave of Providence I shall retain in the coming year. The most that I ever read before family prayers in the morning, is a chapter of the New Testament in Greek. Between breakfast and prayers I read Sanscrit. After breakfast I prepare for the lecture or recitation of the day, and pursue my private studies in Hebrew. Two hours at noon are appropriated to exercise and dinner. In the afternoon I study Isaiah and intend to take half an hour for writing. An hour and a half is assigned to public and private devotion. Three evenings in the week I read Arabic with my private class. An hour at night I give to Eusebius and Josephus, alternately, another to Theology (Turretin at present), and another to writing. Before I go to bed I read the newspapers or Neal's History of the Puritans, as I feel inclined."

Then we have this solemn prayer and dedication of himself to God:

"May the next year be a happy one, intellectually and spiritually! May less time be wasted than in any former year! May my faculties be better employed than ever before! May I be more entirely devoted to my Master's service! May I daily grow in grace and in mastery over sin! May all my studies and employments be blessed to the sanctification of my soul! The Lord in mercy grant it for the Saviour's sake."

There is little to show what he was doing in the year 1835. At least outside of his study and his class-room. His correspondence, which was almost exclusively with Dr. Hall, is altogether barren of incident, and his diary as usual, is chiefly taken up with the record of his daily studies. The truth is he was now stretching himself like an athlete in preparation for the great tasks of his life. One day was as another and yet more abundant in the spoil of conquered languages and tributary literatures. He was learning every hour something new about the Bible and his own heart. He was in the springtide of early manhood. He was the picture of florid health. He was full of animal spirits, and was an enigma of muscular, nervous, and mental force. He was becoming accustomed to his post in the seminary, and began to find it delightfully congenial to his tastes and suited to his powers. There was only one drawback. He was growing more and more in love with Greek, with Europe, with the New Testament. His predominant inclination was no longer what it once was. He found himself perpetually lured away from his Oriental studies into what he regarded as forbidden paths. There was therefore a conflict of purposes or desires in his mind which he feared might be prejudicial to his highest success, but which in the wisdom of Providence was overruled and made a singular blessing to the Church.

The winter of 1835 in Princeton was cold. On Wednesday the 7th of January the thermometer went down five degrees below zero, and the snow was hard on the ground. On that day Mr. Alexander walked upon the crust to see his brother James, who was unwell; and found him enjoying the Olney Hymns. Princeton in those days seems to have been agog with rumors. For instance, it was said that an attempt had been made upon the life of the President of the United States; and then that Calhoun and Benton had fought a duel, in which the latter was killed and the former wounded. There was also much talk of a possible war with France. March came in like a lion; and though there were occasional vernal appearances, and blue birds were twittering in the warm sunshine, yet the snow soon returned with great violence. The rough gales seem to have blown good to Mr. Alexander, for it brought him a Danish manuscript which was in after years a source of considerable pleasure to him. On Wednesday the first of April, the clerical meeting was held at Dr. Miller's. The subjects of discussion were the establishment of lectures against Popery; the superficial cast of the age; the republication of Boyle's religious works; Dick's Theology; Moral Philosophy; &c.

But we turn back to the Journal. On the 14th of January, Mr. Alexander finished the seventh chapter of Isaiah with the second class.

"It is," he writes, "indeed a most difficult scripture."

What follows, relative to the great German Commentator and his theory, cannot fail to be of interest to the intelligent reader:

"Hengstenberg has convinced me that the Messianic interpretation is encumbered with fewer difficulties than any other. But the difficulties which it has are very serious. I am especially at a loss how to interpret the fifteenth and sixteenth verses in consistency with Hengstenberg's hypothesis. I am very far, however, from being willing to abandon it. It does not follow, because I cannot explain everything according to a theory, that the theory is false. There may be positive evidence sufficient to establish it beyond the reach of doubt, though a thousand difficulties still beset it."

He was, at this time, suddenly visited with another fervor on the subject of geography, and this time for geography viewed in its connections with history.

"I have been thinking," he says, "of a plan for geographico-historical research. It is to select some portion of the globe and make it the object of particular and long continued attention. I shall, probably, choose Africa at present, and my design is to go back as far as I can, and ascertain what the first intimations are which history affords respecting that vast continent. I had scarcely formed this plan when

I came upon a passage in Josephus exactly to my purpose. It is in his Archæology, Book I., chapter 16, page 24, D. E., Geneva edition, 1611, where he traces the name *Africa* to Epher, the second son of Michan (Genesis, xxv: 4) on the authority of Alexander Polyhistor.'

On January the 16th he expresses a strong contempt for Antony Theodor Hartmann. His own language is amusingly vigorous and racy:

"The preface to his book on the Pentateuch is very absurd. The cant of the Rationalists about love of truth, philosophy, *Kritisch* and *Unkritisch*, turns my stomach. Hengstenberg* has more sense in his little finger than these men in their loins. Hitzig on Isaiah is disgusting. He is far worse than Gesenius, more unblushing and malignant; his remarks on the offer of a sign to Ahaz (ch. 6) are worthy of Tom Paine."

And then he breaks out in his vehement way:

"John Pye Smith and Moses Stuart give up the prophecy in Isaiah. They may give up what they please for me. While the Germans are groping their way back from infidelity, we are slowly (?) moving towards it."

He continued his lectures on Isaiah.

"February 18.—To-night I have been reading Thomas Aquinas on Original Sin, and find it very entertaining. The method is so perfectly mechanical and uniform, that I lose sight of it completely, and think only of the thoughts presented.

"March 7.—I have been reading Vol. III of the Quarterly Review (Feb.-May, 1810). For some reason old periodicals please me more than new ones. Time seems to mellow them. I am very fond of reviews. The variety of topics is entertaining, the rather as there is no methodical arrangement; while the unity of form and spirit distinguish works of this sort from miscellaneous magazines. The articles in this volume are very unequal, but almost all bear the impress of classical scholarship and general refinement. Whether the subject be political economy,

---

* The Biblical Repertory fairly groaned under the burden of allusion to this writer, imposed upon it by Mr. Alexander.

politics or poetry, there is still an air of gentlemanly elegance that commands respect. There is great diversity in point of tact as well as taste throughout the volume."

In the entry which follows he gives his views of the comparative merits of two articles on the same subject, though under different covers. His mental ingenuity is always apparent when he begins to compare and analyze.

" March 9.—Walsh's letter on the Genesis of the French Government is revived in the Quarterly for Feb. 1810, and in the Edinburgh for April, 1810. I like to compare such articles. The one in the Edinburgh is written with far more vivacity and ease of style, and exhibits a high degree of stirring popular eloquence, but it is flippant and lawyer-like. The Quarterly article is careless and unequal, but dignified and serious, with an air of sincerity which is wanting in the other. Its style, though less pointed, is also less monotonous; and there are passages here and there, which in classical richness and depth of moral tone have no parallel in the Scotch review. It may be fancy, but I think I can mark the contrast between the scholar and the advocate, even when both are merged in the politician."

Mr. Alexander with all his passion for hard reading was always a great lover of miscellaneous literature, even in the more restricted and popular sense of these words; and used to hang with delight over the English Quarterlies, when those great journals were at their zenith, in the days of Jeffrey, Sydney Smith, Horner, Canning, Gifford, and their able confrères. One of his younger brothers informed me that Mr. Alexander's acquaintance with current literature, which was something that never ceased to excite the astonishment of those who knew him best and saw him most constantly, was due originally to the fact that he made it a point to read almost everything in the Quarterly and Edinburgh Reviews during nearly the whole period of the unchallenged supremacy of these great critical organs. This not only afforded continual refreshment to his mind, but enabled him to know with accuracy where to meet with what he wanted in volumes in which the information was to be obtained at first-hand. Mr.

Alexander was never satisfied with the gatherings of others he was not content unless he could gather for himself. His main end here, however, was pure recreation.

The month of April found him as busily engaged as ever. He was still interested in geography, especially the geography of the Bible. He was reading Greek and Hebrew in vast quantities. He was approving himself a workman that needed not to be ashamed.

"April 13.—I continued my collections for a Hebrew Reader, and read Genesis iii with the third class. I began to prepare for my lecture on Galilee, writing on the interleaved copy of my geography. Since the beginning of the year I have read the Pentateuch, Job, and Joshua in Hebrew; Matthew, Mark, Luke, Romans, 1st and 2nd Corinthians, Galatians, Philemon, and James in Greek."

CHAPTER XI.

FRIDAY, the 24th, was Mr. Alexander's 26th birthday, on which occasion his brother James writes, "Gratia, misericordia et pax, a deo triuno, semper super fratrem dilectissimum maneat!" The joys of this fraternal intercourse will never be fully comprehended by those who have been left behind them and who did not witness the occasions when the two scholars met. Recent memories of such meetings no doubt partly prompted these warm ejaculations of piety and brotherly love. The affections of the elder born were radiant and diffusive, and were fixed with a special and unalterable fondness upon "Addison." But he the younger, had small acquaintance of the kind that ripens into intimate friendship; and with his manly impulsive heart he spent his feelings with all the greater absence of restraint and with all the more intense devotion, on a few. Chief among these few were the members of his own family, and the dearest of his companions and friends was "James."

Let us now take a look out of the professor's window, and see what was going on around him in Princeton and a neighbouring city. The Linden trees were half out early in May. Lilachs were in full leaf, and ready to burst into flower. The grass was everywhere becoming green. The Seminary examination occurred on the 6th; Dr. Green presided. In the afternoon Dr. Green dismissed the students with the customary address.

This was the month of the Anniversaries in New York, and Mr. Alexander went on to hear the speakers. I find him on the 11th at the meeting of the Sunday School Union and of the Assemby's Board of Education. On the 12th he "stepped into the Anti-Slavery meeting" and heard Birney, and George Thompson of Liverpool make speeches; after which he went to the Anniversary of the Colonization Society, where he heard Dr. Bethune, Dr. Hewett and Dr. John Breckinridge; from thence he went to the Peace Society, and at night to the adjourned meeting of the Colonization Society. A Krooman and several Africans were on the stage.

He soon returned and began to crowd his great folio blank-book with entries relating chiefly to his studies.

What comes next will be attractive to those who retain an interest in the great battle between the Old and New Schools. The Assembly was at this time in session at Pittsburg.

"May 15.—We are all agape to hear something from the Convention and Assembly. The session of the latter has been, for several years, looked forward to with lively interest, but never with so much as now. There is this singularity about the present case,—that public expectation has reference, not to some one specific question, which is likely to come up, but to the whole tenour of the Assembly's proceedings; or, in other words, to the relative strength of parties. This may, or may not be indicated by the choice of Moderator. For several years this first step has been taken by mutual consent, without dispute."

In the next entry he returns for a moment to his quiet occupations at home; but is soon beguiled again to the topic of fascination.

"May 26.—I finished my inspection of Luther's letters, and the first draft of the first part of my Archaeological Catechism."

He hails with delight the first tidings from the Assembly.

"We hear to-day from Pittsburg, that Dr. Miller preached the opening sermon in the absence of the last Moderator, and that then a very curious, and I suppose unexpected trial of strength took place. Dr. Ely nominated Dr. Beman; on the ground that he was the latest Moderator present as a commissioner. He was voted into the chair; but not long after (I forget whether at the same or another session) he was excluded and Dr. W. McDowell substituted. Now, so far as I can discover from the book, it lay entirely with the Assembly to select any person as their temporary chairman. There was no rule requiring that he should have once been Moderator; much less that after he was appointed he should be thrown out to make room for another not a member of the body, simply because he had been Moderator since. I draw the conclusion, therefore, that the exclusion of Beman was a party act and a sufficient index of the prevailing power. This is confirmed by the fact that Dr. Phillips, who was nominated by Dr. Miller, was elected Moderator by a majority of 100 (I write from recollection), though not only an Old School man, but an Act and Testimony one. Though I can easily suppose that some of the New School men, according to custom, joined the majority to avoid defeat. I cannot help regarding this election as a proof that the Old School party is decidedly predominant. *Quod felix faustumque sit!*"

On the second of June he wrote several sheets towards a revise of Bush's Hebrew Grammar. Besides his daily lessons in Scripture, he read nine chapters in Hebrew with Vitringa's analysis. This was to be the subject of his readings with the second class this summer; and he wished to get it familiar to his mind in its general connection, instead of becoming familiar with it piecemeal, which he found the winter before to be "very disadvantageous." "The minute verbal study of these chapters," he writes, "I shall leave to be attended to from week to week."

The next record gives among other things, further statements concerning the Assembly and its doings.

"June 10.—I read Isaiah, xl.—xlviii. in Hitzig's German version, comparing it with that of Gesenius and with the original. I also read the chapters in Hengstenberg's Christologie, on the nature of prophetical inspiration. It is announced to-day in print that John Breckinridge has been elected Professor of Pastoral Theology, and J. A. Alexander, Adjunct-Professor of Oriental and Biblical Literature."

Professor James Alexander was now busy upon Tully and the Antonines, and amusing himself with the ranz des vaches. The father went on an early day in June to lay the cornerstone of a new Presbyterian Church in Freehold. Dr. Archibald Alexander was now one of the busiest of men, and yet though he almost never left his study, he lavished many hours daily on the students who repaired to him for counsel. His biographer thinks he gave up half his time to them. They would run in at all hours. The keen sidelong glance of that bright eye seemed to read them through and through; but the quick ear and apprehension of the great practical philosopher seized at once the point of difficulty or embarrassment, and his wisdom and benevolence seldom failed to relieve the student's doubts or to inform his ignorance.

In the month of May, Mr. Alexander, as we have seen, was elected by the General Assembly, Adjunct Professor of Oriental and Biblical Literature in the Theological Seminary. This compliment he modestly and firmly declined. The Board of Directors sat in September. This was his opportunity, and he availed himself of it to convey to them his sense of the honour that had been conferred upon him, and of his inflexible opposition to the proposed change. Here is his letter to the President of the Board:

"I beg leave to communicate through you, to the Board of Directors, my determination to decline the appointment with which I was honoured by the last General Assembly. Should the Board desire a continuance of my services, I am entirely willing to retain my present station as an Assistant to Professor Hodge."

This not proving altogether satisfactory to the learned gentlemen of the Board, they sent a committee to wait on him. But here are his own words:

"After a meeting of the Directors, I was visited by a committee of the Board. After conversing with them, I persisted in declining to accept the appointment of Professor, but consented to the postponement of the whole affair, if the Board thought fit, till the next meeting; which was done accordingly."

There is not one word on his side of this correspondence, of pretended unfitness for a post for which he must have known that he was probably better qualified on the score of preparation than any other man in the church. We have here a fine instance of real humility as distinguished from its counterfeit.

After a lapse of six years he now again became a teacher at Edgehill, which was at this time under the direction of Mr. E. C. Wines. This filled his hands to superfluity; since he was called upon to teach sixteen hours a week, besides his ordinary Seminary duties. He had also given lessons during the year to several youthful pupils, and regularly instructed a private class in Arabic. During the same time also amidst the multifarious labours of his study, he had read through the Old Testament once, and the New Testament twice, critically. He was becoming a master of new languages. He was daily fired with new zeal in the old ones. Zest, playfulness, chameleon volatility, directness, tremendous energy, unwearied diligence, unconquerable perseverance, absolute triumph over difficulties, marked him in all he attempted.

The allusion in the following extract to the Dean of St. Patrick's cannot be passed over without calling the attention of the reader to it specially.

"To night I finished the first volume of Dean Swift's correspondence, which has given me much amusement, for with all its folly and heartles-ness, there is a humour so unique, and a common sense so exquisite, that I feel even the nonsense to be the nonsense of a master. Besides, I am passionately fond of all familiar correspondence; the more minute the better; and in this case, the society in which the writer lived, gives the letters even a historical interest. After Swift changed his politics, he abused Addison often, but confesses now and then that he is the most agreeable man of his acquaintance."

Mr. Alexander had a vast liking and respect himself, for his namesake Joseph Addison. Swift, though, was in some respects the more congenial spirit. He loved these casual rambles among the hedge-rows of literature. The amount of his general reading alone was enormous. He is sharp upon Washington Irving. It is best to give his own words:

"Finished the Crayon Miscellany, No. 2, which contains a few good sentences and thoughts, but on the whole is a paltry catch-penny. The style lacks the merit which once gained Irving celebrity, though it exhibits a constant striving after beautiful expression. The sentimental feeling about Byron is contemptible; the style in which it is clothed is mawkish and nerveless; and the whole book is unworthy of the Sketch Book and even of Bracebridge Hall, and of course vastly lower than Knickerbocker."

It was Mr. Alexander's opinion that the first books both of Irving and Dickens were much their best; and in this opinion I think that a majority of sensible people concur.

About the middle of July, Mr. James Alexander went to Saratoga in search of health and recreation; and remained there, or in the vicinity, the greater part of the summer, drinking the waters and talking with such men as Mr. Pierpont the poet, Dr. Wayland, and Dr. McClelland, and feasting his ears with German and Italian music. He returned much invigorated. Soon after, on the last day of August, he was escorted one evening to see Chancellor Kent; of whom he writes to Mr. Hall, " spent a grand evening with Chancellor Kent," and whom he describes elsewhere, as " robust, loquacious, boyish, comical, and oddly snappish and pleasing. His manner is so singular as to baffle description." He ever continued to regard the Chancellor as one of the greatest and best of Americans.

The scene now changes again to Princeton. The Hebrew professor was meanwhile making progress in his studies and with his classes.

It appears that he kept up his communications with Germany, and now and then refreshed himself in the old paths of Oriental romance and poetry. His habits were healthful and regular, with the exception that his labours seemed excessive, and that he gave himself no sufficient bodily recreation.

"August 13.—I rose early and walked; studied and wrote notes on the fifteenth Psalm. Read the fortieth Psalm with the class. Dr. Hodge received a letter from James Clark in Boston, enclosing a note in German to me from Biersthal, my old acquaintance and Rabbinical instructor. He promises to send me his Manual Hebrew Lexicon which he began while I was there, and wants a situation in America.

I read a capital review of Sir John Sinclair on paper currency, in the London Quarterly for 1811."

"September 7.—Read Psalms xvi, xci, with my class. Added a codicil to my article on Prelacy. Resumed the perusal of the Thousand and One Nights in Arabic, which I suspended on the 13th of September last year. I am also rapidly revising Jaubert's Turkish Grammar, which I studied on my voyage to Europe, so that I am likely to become again quite Oriental."

Dr. Archibald Alexander on a Sunday in September preached in the Chapel a powerful extemporaneous discourse from the text "Consider your ways." It was very awakening and penetrated the heart and conscience of many. On such occasions there was often a return of Virginia warmth; and pictures addressed to the fancy were mingled with shrewd touches of human nature and profound and moving appeals to the springs of human action. There were times when Dr. Alexander could sway the passions at his will.

One may know the impression that would be produced on an audience by warm, lively appeals from such a man to the imagination and feelings; especially when we take into view the faultless taste of the style, and the indescribable accompaniments of voice and manner. There are people now living in Virginia who remember him perfectly as he appeared at the time that he preached at Briery, and who confirm all that has been said as to the exceeding sweetness and pathos of his intonations, and the imitimable naturalness, freedom, and cordiality of his delivery. There are some, indeed, whose recollections go back to a much earlier period. Most of those, however, who knew him in those days have passed away.

There is little in his printed sermons to put one in mind of the familiar and often unpremeditated but sparkling outpourings of his youth; they are elegant and not devoid of unction, but grave and severe, and almost wholly bare of ornament. His style became more and more Doric in its simplicity, as he grew older and advanced in experience. His friend Dr. Speece sportively compared his efforts in his earlier days to the gambols of a mettlesome colt in a broad pasture. It was not until Dr. Alexander's removal to Princeton that his manner underwent a marked and decided change. The characteristic to which I refer, was an extraordinary power of bringing the scene he was depicting before the very eye of his audience. He held in his hands the wand of a magician. He was undoubtedly one of the most natural and graphic speakers in America. He saw the thing himself, and made others see it. There was nothing theatrical about this; or approaching in the remotest degree to such a quality. He held his audience under precisely the same kind of spell that a good story-teller, who is interested in his subject and who draws inspiration from the open mouths and sparkling eyes of his little hearers, can throw around children. This was due to his own childlike simplicity. His expressions were as nearly colloquial as was consistent with an almost absolute purity and propriety of diction, and a singular felicity in the choice of words. His sentences, too, were neatly rounded, as if by a sort of happy chance or careless and unconscious grace, and were often very harmonious. But before one could well detect anything like cadence or rhythm, the tune would change, or rather would be broken up, just as in fireside talk. His tones even in his most spirited moments were those of animated conversation.

I am again indebted for important facts to Dr. Jones of Bridgeton. For the greater part of Mr. Jones's term of study in the Theological Seminary Mr. Alexander was Adjunct-Professor of Ancient Languages in the College of New Jersey. The new Professor was appointed during Mr. Jones's last year; and the pupil remembered to have heard at the time of his election that one distinguished minister had expressed the opinion, that "only one Addison Alexander was born in a century;" while the other felt sure that but one such man was allotted to a generation.

"One of these persons was the venerable Ashbel Green, formerly President of Princeton College; than whom few were better qualified to pronounce judgment on a scholar. It is not too much to say that those most competent to judge would be the last to pronounce such a eulogy extravagant."

All that this gentleman had ever heard of Mr. Alexander before he came under his instructions, was far more than realized by what he saw and learnt of him while his pupil. In addition to his ordinary and regular instructions in the Seminary, he proposed to form a volunteer class, to meet on Saturday afternoon "our only holiday" and to study the Book of Leviticus, in a more private and familiar way. Four of the young men gladly accepted his invitation, by meeting him for an hour each week; and the writer of the sketches which I am now using is persuaded that only those who then and there listened to these informal exercitations can form an idea of the interest with which the young professor contrived to invest his exposition of a book which under a less fascinating treatment might have seemed dry. He goes on as follows:

"During one session of my Seminary life, it was my rare privilege to reside under the same roof * with Professor Alexander; both of us occupying lodgings in a house near the Seminary."

Here it was that he became better acquainted with the man than he had, or otherwise could have been.

"His writings and his instructions in the recitation-room had excited my wonder and admiration at the vastness of his resources and his skilful management of them. His powers of mind, his acquisitions and the facility with which he gained all kinds of knowledge seemed to lift him above the level of mere mortals, and to place between him and me an impassable gulf. Brought nearer to him by residence in the same house, his mind became to me more a 'phenomenon' than before. There seemed to be no difference in his case between work and play. Study to other men is a toil; attended or followed by fatigue. In his case there seemed to be no greater tension of mind while engaged in his profoundest investigations than when he was reading for entertainment. All forms of mental employment seemed equally easy to him. I never heard him complain of weariness; and I never saw him when

---

* At Mrs. Henderson's, on the Trenton Turnpike, just at the foot of the hill north of Judge Field's.

he seemed weary. What would tax any other mind I ever knew seemed mere entertainment to him. The old proverb, 'no man is great to his own valet,' was not realized in the case of Addison Alexander."

The writer's private intercourse with him at this time, and at a subsequent period, when his duties called him at least once a year to Princeton, enhanced his estimate of

"His moral excellence and the prodigious intellectual powers of the man. The nearer I approached and the more closely I studied him, the more I saw to admire, and the more astonishing seemed his capacity. The glance of his mind was alike comprehensive, keen, and minute. The decisions of his judgment were rapid, beyond those of any man with whom I ever conversed; and they were as sound as they were rapid."

Among the personal traits which impressed themselves upon his notice, in private intercourse, were "transparent honesty and truthfulness, perfect simplicity of character, and the rarest union of simplicity and commanding dignity." A more thoroughly honest man he never knew; and he questioned whether such ever lived.

"I never knew him to utter, as his own sentiment, what I did not believe to be the actual exponent of his views. I never knew him to equivocate or prevaricate, or practise deceit in any form or shape."

He never knew a man who had a greater repugnance to anything approaching pompous pretension, or parade.

"In his manners and conversation, in his lecture-room and in the pulpit, in his great critical works and in his fugitive writings, there was an extraordinary absence of everything like an attempt to impress one with an idea of his greatness. You could not but *feel* it; but it was not because he made an effort to convince you of it. You felt his greatness just as you feel the greatness of a lofty mountain or a Gothic cathedral."

After speaking of his conscientious regard for truth and charity, Dr. Jones continues:

"This same tenderness of conscience and of feeling was often evinced in a way which elicited the admiration of his pupils, and greatly heightened their estimate of his piety. Like all other theological teachers, he was occasionally brought into contact with students who annoyed him by their indolence, heedlessness, mental sluggishness, or self-conceit; and such he would sometimes rasp with no little severity. Whenever this occurred, his students noticed that for some time after, his prayers before his class were marked by unusual humility of tone and tenderness of spirit; as if the recollection even of a merited castigation had cost him profound regret."

So habitual was this exhibition of a tender spirit under such circumstances, that students on their return to the class after a temporary absence from the recitation-room, frequently suspected that some one had been recently visited with one of these telling rebukes, from the peculiarly subdued and reverential tone of the Professor's opening exercise.

A pupil of some years' later date,[*] in referring to Mr. Alexander's bearing towards his classes, remarks that the only fault he could ever see in him as a teacher, was his impatience of dulness.

"He seemed to entertain towards the very dull or incorrigibly stupid youths, who are found in almost every academical class, a feeling akin to resentment or indignation; and he frequently showed them no mercy. There are, I believe, several traditions in the Seminary of his unsparing severity to some very pious, good brethren, or who were esteemed such, which (so run these traditions) aroused the feeling of the class against him."

There were traditions of this sort afloat when this writer was in the Seminary.

"I could not account for it until I had the opportunity of observing him in the class myself. I then ascertained, or fancied that he had no conception of the slowness and dulness of some minds. He thought therefore that the only hypothesis by which he could account for the manifest failure of some of his pupils to make any adequate progress, was that they were idle and neglectful of their duties. In his view,

[*] Dr. Rice, of Mobile.

for a Seminary student, a candidate for the ministry, to neglect the advantages furnished him by the church, to waste his time in idleness or frivolity, was a great sin and shame. In his eyes it was hateful hypocrisy; and he had the most profound scorn for everything like sham and pretence in religion."

It is true, too, that in so large a school as Princeton was then, there are always some who deserve sharp censure on the score of laziness:

"A sort of literary antinomians, concerning whom the Professor felt in a measure as the apostle Paul did concerning those who would turn the grace of God into lasciviousness, 'their damnation is just;' and he did condemn them without much compunction. I think that he was naturally of quick temper,* but I have no doubt that it was somewhat soured and rendered a little morbid by his earlier experiences as a teacher in the Seminary.

"He learned afterwards to make more allowance for want of capacity, and to feel more Christian charity towards real offenders, while he still condemned their conduct. After I entered the Seminary, I saw but little of the petulance, anger, and undue severity, for which he had a reputation among former classes. It must be said, however, that the students who made fair progress in his department knew nothing and could remember nothing of this nature. The severity of his reproof was often solely in the tone and quality of the voice."

He remembers a case in which he was himself the sufferer:

"He asked me why a certain form of a Hebrew word was not so and so, naming the normal condition of the word. I replied with, I believe, a somewhat flippant manner, 'It ought to be.' His answer came instantly flashing back, 'No it oughtn't!' and I felt a sort of thrill shoot through me like the electric shock." He could not tell, at first, what caused the sensation, but soon discovered that it was due entirely to *the tone of voice* in which the few syllables of reply had been uttered.* "It made me cautious ever after of the tone in which I an-

---

* This is doubtless true; and his other emotions were as quick and energetic as his "temper." His temper was certainly at times bitter. I do not imagine, however, that his temper was ever habitually or even for a length of time continuously sour. Dr. Rice, probably, does not mean this.

swered his questions. He then went on very pleasantly to say, 'You mean that it *would* be so, but for such and such circumstances.'"

"I have in the course of my life met with three teachers of pre eminent ability as teachers, and he was the foremost of them all, for pupils of intellect above the average. For dull boys he was not so good, for the reasons above stated. If a young man had anything in him, and was disposed to make use of his advantages, Mr. Alexander could draw it out better than any teacher I ever saw.

"His instructions were characterized by surpassing clearness. There was no mistaking his meaning; and there was no mixing of subjects, no confusion of thought."

The same writer also refers to his directness and brevity, and to the happy peculiarity of his diction.

Few persons of scholarlike habits and recluse disposition have had such talents for common talk, or more carefully concealed the gift from the vulgar. In allusion to Mr. Alexander's social qualities, and the unaffected charm of his manner when he was at leisure and among his friends, one of his warmest admirers† writes, that he never monopolized conversation as Coleridge did; and never like Johnson, attempted to bear you down by the weight of his greatness,‡ or the force of authority. "With intimate friends he would take his proper share in conversation; and in this, as in his writings, there was no redundancy of words, nor irrelevancy of ideas." His manner was that of perfect ease and unstudied simplicity; his language precise and elegant; and all his utterances were marked by point and condensation. So finished was his ordinary talk that so far as accuracy is concerned, it might have been committed to print without correction. And the same may be said of his oral interrogations in the recitation-room.

---

* It has been strongly impressed upon me that with his talent and love for personation, he sometimes may have copied after the Captain of the Samson, of whose manner of scolding the sailors without being angry he has expressed his warmest approval.

† Dr. Beach Jones.

‡ And the writer might have added, never, as Prescott says Macaulay did, oppressed you with the ponderous weight of his matter. He was always easy and colloquial.

"A competent judge who had never heard of Dr. Alexander's fame, would have pronounced him an extraordinary man simply from listening to his questions to his class. As to all the minute laws and elegancies of language, both written and spoken, he had no superior. In orthography, orthoepy, and syntax he was a model.

"With all his vast, various, and even curious learning; with all his addiction to study; with all his recluse habits; Mr. Alexander was one of the wisest practical judges of men and affairs whom I have ever known. He rarely erred in his estimate of men, and was one of the wisest of counsellors on almost any subject on which he was consulted."

That one so immersed in books should sometimes be abstracted when moving among men, or that he should be careless or oblivious of little things, would have excited no surprise, because such is usually the case. "Yet a keener observer of all that was passing in the busy world around him, it would have been hard if not impossible to find. Names and circumstances and peculiarities of manner indelibly impressed themselves on his mind. Little incidents were as accurately retained as great events and fundamental principles. He has reminded me of things I had said, many years after I had utterly forgotten them."

The friend to whose exact recollections I owe so much of the materials of this account, winds up a paragraph by saying, that

"When we consider the versatility of his powers and his love of change, and the fact that he rarely, if ever, carried two successive classes through precisely the same routine of studies, and constructed scarcely any two of his sermons on the same plan; it will furnish another proof of the healthiness of his mind and the solidity of his piety, that he should never have adopted theological whimsies nor darted off in heretical aberrations."

This is admirably said. With all his changes he ever swung back again like the agitated needle and pointed steadily to the pole of duty and right inclination. Like Wordsworth's lark, however he might ruffle his plumage and beat the air with his wings, it was only that he might soar the more easily into the bright skies; he never forgot his nest, and his little household cares upon the ground. In brief, with all his seeming and real vacillations, with all his inexplicable flights and descents, he always remained

"True to the kindred points of heaven and home."

There is little of positive value to be gathered from this part of Mr. Alexander's private correspondence. He seldom wrote letters except on matters of business, and these were commonly very short. He corresponded, however, at irregular intervals with a few intimate friends. The only one to whom he occasionally poured out all the feelings of his soul in his epistolary effusions, was his brother James. There were certain men nevertheless to whom he wrote with great freedom and with great satisfaction to himself and them. Among these the first place is due to Dr. Hall of Philadelphia, and afterwards Trenton, to whom he continued to write copiously. His neighborhood, his position at one of the great centres of polite information and of the operations of the Presbyterian Church, his intelligent congeniality of feeling, his tried friendship, and his incessant communications with the professor's elder brother, made this intercourse at once valuable and full of enjoyment. When he removed from Philadelphia to Trenton, the country scholar could not resist the temptation of keeping *au courant* of what was passing on the banks of the Delaware, and found or created many occasions of reminding his friend of his own fixed position at Princeton. Mr. Hall possessed one great advantage over the mass of Mr. Alexander's acquaintances, he had a perfect comprehension and an exquisite appreciation of his humour. This led to the most comical imaginary strife or mock-warfare between them. This will explain the fact that half that is contained in these letters must be regarded as pure irony. This statement is necessary to meet the case of those who have a sort of colour-blindness in this matter. Mr. Alexander was really modest and humble, yet it will be perceived that he often writes to Mr. Hall in a tone which if serious would be one of supercilious condescension, or arrogant presumption. Of course all this was the merest fun, and was so taken by his correspondent. Sometimes the letters are refined burlesques. They are frequently couched in the language of diplomacy. They are often signed with a succession of upright hair-strokes crossed with flourishes of the pen in the form of an hour-glass. Sometimes they are from a bishop, in due pomp of ritualistic precision, and breathe the most sacerdotal or even Prelatical spirit. Sometimes they are from a very testy and punctilious "star preacher" (a character whom Mr. Alexander abhorred most intensely) who is solicitous about the times and circumstances of his personal exhibition, and inquires anxiously, or gives directions, about the benches in the aisles. Some of the letters are made up almost wholly of the current ministerial slang or cant. Often the writer is half in earnest in what he says in a strain of ironical affectation, and chooses this mode of conveying real feelings. Sometimes he writes gravely on some subject requiring or inviting grave attention. In all cases he shows unlimited confidence in the discernment and fidelity of his Philadelphia agent, caterer, and friend. Not a few of the letters are on questions of ecclesiastical procedure, the General Assembly and the New School controversy, &c., and are full of references to the names and characters of living men. They are also remarkably and intentionally local in their allusions, and are some of them by this time quite unintelligible. Now and then I have fallen in with one which could be understood only by the man who wrote it, or possibly also the man to whom it was written. Restricted as the field of selection is thus made it yet presents a number of letters which however uninteresting they may seem to the superficial reader, will undoubtedly afford a vantage ground to those who wish to see the soul of the writer in its undress garb, and from a multitude of minute disclosures of character and feeling, to ascertain for themselves what manner of man he really was. These letters will be introduced from time to time according to their dates.

Princeton was at this time suffering greatly from the ravages of a disease resembling what is now known as the typhoid or enteric fever. Many deaths occurred sometimes in one family. Dr. Howell, the friend and physician of the Alexanders, whose family had been scourged and reduced in numbers by the fever, died himself on the second of November. Early in December the great fire was raging in New York, and the reflection in the heavens was distinctly seen at Princeton, and mistaken for an aurora. We have but few glimpses of Mr. Alexander in the midst of these occurrences, but such as they are they indicate the fervour and the brave energy with which he was holding on his way as a student.

Monday the 21st, like several of its predecessors, was a bad day; mizzling and slippery. During the whole of this dull day Mr. Alexander was closeted with Mr. John Porter Brown, U. S. Consul at Constantinople, decyphering under his eye an Arabic letter which was sent to Mr. Brown by the U. S. government as a test of his knowledge of the language. Mr. Brown was applying for the situation of interpreter at the Porte. The letter was found to relate to certain missionaries at Beirut.* Mr. Brown also gave Mr. Alexander a Ferinda, such as are used by the Hadjis. It was very beautiful, writes his brother James.

On Lord's day, the 27th, Dr. A. Alexander preached another remarkable sermon in the Seminary chapel. It was on Regeneration, and struck his eldest son as being as great an effort as he ever heard from him. It was astonishing how he would sometimes flame up and electrify the audiences that had grown accustomed to his colder and more didactic sermons. He certainly had the faculty of thinking and composing while on his feet, at times looking as if he were forgetful

---

* The prospective Consul had hunted all over the United States for some one to make out the MS. Among these he went to Peter S. Duponceau, President of the American Philosophical Society, who asked if he had seen Professor Addison Alexander, of Princeton? On his saying he had not, Professor D. said he had better proceed thither at once. My impression is that several other scholars had been baffled by that manuscript. They found out between them that it was written in the Morocco dialect.

of the presence of hearers, in a degree that has not often been equalled.

One thing in the pulpit ministrations of Mr. Alexander which specially arrested the notice of devout and reflective minds was his prayers. In these, as in his sermons, he spoke as at the time he felt. At times there was much more of fervour and unction than at others. But never were his prayers eloquent addresses to his audiences.

His reverence for the great Hearer of Prayer was profound and self-abasing. He seemed to forget everything but the presence of the Divine Majesty. If he had a fault in this exercise it was the condensation of too much in a brief compass. He poured forth his adoration, confession, supplication, and thanksgiving, with such rapidity that only by the closest attention could his fellow-worshippers accompany him. His prayers might sometimes be styled grand; but grand not because he sought to make a grand prayer, but because the themes were so grand, and because they were so simple, so free from everything like parade. It would not have been strange if a man of Mr. Alexander's scholastic habits had lacked simplicity and unction in prayer. That he was characterized by both of these excellences, was to his friend one evidence of the reality and depth of his piety. Like his venerable father, Dr. Addison Alexander was in conversation very reticent as to his own religious experience. But when he came to prostrate his soul before God, in public devotion, his piety unconsciously disclosed itself. " I remember attending a meeting of great interest, at which several foreign ministers addressed the Synod of New Jersey; and where Mr. A. was called upon to lead in prayer.

" At the close of the services one of the most spiritually-minded members of the body remarked to me that the prayer of Dr. Alexander had been to him by far the most impressive and profitable part of the evening's services; and in this opinion my own judgment fully acquiesced."

Mr. Alexander was not usually in the habit of writing out his prayers; but I find a little volume for this year which contains some specimens of his private devotions, and some liturgical forms which were used at the opening of his lectures and recitations in the Seminary. They are not at all like the petitions I have heard him offer extemporaneously, which were more abundant, particular and colloquial. Subjoined is a single specimen:

"Jan. 18, 1835.—Matt. xxv. Lord, may I be ready when Thou comest! May my lamp be burning! O, give me a watchful spirit and save me, O save me, from forgetfulness and sloth!

"Teach me, O Saviour, how to estimate my privileges; help me to resolve that every moment shall be spent for Thee! I renounce vain amusements, idle talking, slothful ease, useless reading and all mere literary, intellectual pleasures. If life is a span, how can I find time for mere diversion? I forego them all, not grudgingly, but with a willing heart. Thou, who hast made me willing, accept and bless the sacrifice! O, for the art of redeeming time! Wilt Thou not teach me, O my God? I ask of Thee, for Christ's sake, not to let me waste a moment hereafter! May I be burdened with the weight of my responsibility! May I feel, more and more, what work I have to do, as well as undo! The habits of five and twenty years are to be broken, and new ones to be formed. Mercy and help, O, Lord, my Sovereign Lord! Thou who lovest little children, make me a little child! Make me humble, simple-hearted, tender, guileless and confiding! Kill my selfish pride! Shiver my hard heart! Break my stubborn spirit! Make me love my kind by making me to love Thee! O soften me, my Saviour, by showing me Thy own tender, bleeding, melting heart! Purge envy from my heart by causing me to live and work for Thee! O, that this foul fiend were wholly dispossessed! I bless Thee for trials—may they do me good! Compel me to remember that I am not my own! Save me from being the object of envy or ill-will. Save me from the wickedness of trying to excite it! Lord, I would give the world for true humility. O, make me—make me humble!"

One of the prominent traits of his disposition in after-life, was rare freedom from the canker of jealousy or envy, and a very low opinion of his own powers and influence. This, indeed, had always been the case, as was best known to those of his immediate family; but from this time onward the trait became more marked and fixed.

The following resolutions are appended to the preceding prayer. They relate to the practical guidance of his life.

"RESOLUTIONS.

"1. I will try to perform every act of my life with conscious regard to religious motives. I will eat, drink, talk, study, teach, write suffer, not only as a Christian, but with Christian affections, with the love of Christ in my heart.

"2. I will try to live for a death-bed, and for eternal life. I will try to remember what it is I am living for, and to form the habit of remembering it always—not at certain seasons only.

"3. I will try to be tender-hearted and to love my fellow-creatures. I will deny myself, in order to cherish the affections. I will try to show that I am no misanthrope.

"4. I will try to maintain an humble spirit; I will try to live as though it matters not whether I be known or unknown—honoured or despised. I will try to rejoice in the eminence of others. It is hard, but I will try it in the strength of my Redeemer. But, O my Lord, Thou knowest I may try forever, yet in vain, without Thy grace!

"5. I will try to hate sin. I will think and think about my Saviour's sufferings, till my heart is broken. I shall fail a hundred and a hundred times; but I will still persist till my proud heart yields, and I become a little child. O, that my head were waters!"

"Feb. 26.—Hear me when I call, O God of my righteousness! Thou hast enlarged me when I was in distress; have mercy upon me and hear my prayer. Rebuke me not in thine anger, neither chasten me in Thy hot displeasure. Lighten my eyes lest I sleep the sleep of death. Remember not the sins of my youth, nor my transgressions. According to Thy mercy remember Thou me, for Thy goodness' sake. O Lord pardon mine iniquity, for it is great! Turn Thou unto me, and have mercy upon me; for I am desolate and afflicted. The troubles of my heart are enlarged. O bring Thou me out of my distresses! Look upon mine affliction and my pain, and forgive me all my sins. Mine eyes are ever toward the Lord, for He shall pluck my feet out of the net. O keep my soul and deliver me; let me not be ashamed, for I put my trust in Thee! Lord, I believe, help Thou my unbelief! Let the blood of Christ purge my conscience from dead works, to serve the living

God. Let me have grace whereby I may serve God acceptably! O, Jesus Christ, the same yesterday, to-day and forever, by Thee let me offer this sacrifice of praise to God: and O, Thou God of peace, who didst bring again from the dead our Lord Jesus, that great Shepherd of the sheep, through the blood of the everlasting covenant, make me perfect in every good work to do Thy will; work in me that which is well pleasing in Thy sight, through Jesus Christ, to whom be glory forever and ever! Amen."

The lamented Dr. Edward Yeomans, of Orange, N. J., has contributed the following sentences on this subject:

" The structure of his public prayers strikes me as a marked example of his ready aggregation, or setting things in array. And in this field his peculiar facility was another excellence. In extempore prayer it is as easy to develope a train of thought as to string together common-places and stereotyped phrases. Dr. Alexander did neither. The hardest thing to do, extemporaneously, is to enumerate particulars connected rather by a *real* than by a *logical* association; and this is the thing to do in prayer—set forth things connected more by a common root in the heart's want, than by abstract or mechanical relations. This came naturally to Dr. Alexander. I think I have never heard any other extempore prayers so characterized as his by this simple *collection of things* directly asked of the Lord, and at the same time so ready and orderly in the enumeration of the things. He asked for things instead of descanting on subjects."

Nothing was ever more truly or justly said. The prayers of this mighty man of God, were as simple as those of a little child; but they were also the prayers of one who sometimes found it natural to unburden his heart in sentences and phrases, which though familiar in his mouth as household words, were such as are not often met with in the language of formal and studied devotion.

There was a certain peculiarity about the prayer before lecture. Dr. Moore says that his petitions in the class-room always struck him much more forcibly than his recitations.

"They had that wonderful concentration and variety with an essential sameness, which you notice in Calvin's prayers at the close of his lectures on the Minor Prophets; which while they are always substantially the same in their leading outlines, yet gather up and concentrate in a few words the substance of a whole lecture. His prayers were remarkable for their suggestiveness. He would bring in a word, in some connection that would suggest its etymology, or some philological fact associated with it, which threw a new and rich light on the thought expressed; and although he never dwelt on the suggestion or carried it out in detail, or seemed to have thought of it before, it gave food for thinking long afterwards. His wonderful fluency showed itself in his prayers more than in any other exercise I ever heard him in; and I felt the power of his intellect in packing, condensing and arranging thought, without losing any of its perfect clearness, but rather giving new light by its angles of crystallization: in his prayers in the class-room more than anywhere else. His command of language then was very wonderful, indeed to my mind unsurpassed, especially in that scholarly collocation of words that showed meanings and relations of them in his own mind which this peculiar collocation indicated without exactly expressing, and suggested so much more than was said."

On Monday the 13th of December, Professor James Alexander made the acquaintance of Signor Borsieri, a friend of Silvio Pellico, who had been for fifteen years a political prisoner in the dungeons of Italy. Mr. Borsieri was before or afterwards presented to Mr. Addison Alexander, and became, if I mistake not, one of his numerous foreign teachers. One Captain Stuart, a British Army officer, on half-pay, who had been stationed many years in Persia and was thoroughly acquainted with the Persian language, was about this time introduced to Mr. Alexander. The Captain was a genuine John Bull, dressed in a smock-blouse. On being asked to give examples of the Persian pronunciation, he consented by uttering a number of harsh throat-splitting gutturals. Mistaking the smile of his listeners and the impression he had made upon them, he exclaimed in a tone of gratified bonhomie, as if he meant to echo their inmost feelings, "Pretty language!" There was no end to the fun the cloistered student had with these outlandish people, and with the mistakes and idiosyncrasies of the workmen in his employment.

CHAPTER XII.

The notable event of the year 1836 was the election of Mr. Alexander, in the month of February, to the chair of Oriental and Biblical Literature in the Union Theological Seminary, just established in the city of New York. The fact was never generally known; for like his father and brother before him, Mr. Alexander seldom spoke of such things; indeed, never without strong reason. This, however, he respectfully declined. Dr. Archibald Alexander on such points was almost absolutely dumb. His son Addison was not quite so reticent, but very much so.

In January I find him writing comments on Leviticus for the benefit of his private class. These records possess great exegetical value, but are not suited for extract.

"Jan. 16.—Finished my comments on the 5th chapter of Leviticus. The work becomes more and more interesting as I get along with it. The chaos of the ritual begins already to assume some shape. In the afternoon I read Leviticus v. 5-6, and afterwards wrote my notes on Chap. vi. 1-7."

At night he diverted his mind over Dyer's History of Cambridge, and Burnett's History of His Own Times. These nocturnal rambles in all good literature were of the utmost advantage to him in his subsequent labours as a commentator.

It was at this time usual with him to go through most of his heavy work before the twilight. With candles came the joys of discursive wanderings at the sweet will of fancy. Perhaps none in Princeton had more real, inward contentment.

"Feb. 13.—Finished the Edinburgh Review for October last. The first half of it is dull. The article on Bolingbroke is slight compared with that in the Quarterly. Its only value consists in its citations from Mackintosh's manuscripts. The article on political associations and on the House of Lords interested me, because they let me into the existing state of politics. I had no idea of the strength of the Tories, until I learned it from the concessions of this writer. But the leading article undoubtedly is the best. I cannot help feeling still that the estimate of Mackintosh's power is exaggerated; partly through the influence of party spirit: but the castigation of Coleridge pleases me much, not only by its truth and spirit, but by the vivacity and vigour of the style, which is worthy of the old days of the Review. The writer must be Jeffrey; there is not wit enough for Sydney Smith; the style is too correct and elegant for Brougham; too rapid, affluent and laboured for Macaulay. The concluding observations are original, ingenious, and to me consolatory."

The hints disclosed in these extracts of his knowledge of contemporary English politics, are not delusive. He kept abreast of the whole intellectual movement of the age. As in his youth he was mindful of the words of the oracle, and found no subject of uninspired knowledge more instructive or entertaining than *man*.

FROM MR. ALEXANDER TO MR. HALL.

"PRINCETON, April 4, 1836.

"*My Dear Sir:*

"I make bold to draw upon your kindness for a favour. The accompanying parcel is a Latin Dictionary, sent to me from Germany, in sheets. It is there already bound in one volume, and I am very unwilling to have it bound in two. I am afraid however, to trust a country binder with so thick a book. You will oblige me greatly by having it strongly, neatly and compactly bound in calf, and causing the binder's bill to be sent to me. The book itself may wait for a convenient opportunity. The inclosed letter has relation to the American Quarterly Review. As the bearer of my despatches is a minor, I put it inside for greater safety.

"Very truly, yours,
' J. ADDISON ALEXANDER.

"P. S.—As you may have some influence on the new régime of the Review, I beg that you will take some pains to free it from two evils, which have greatly hurt it: (1) The elementary or ABC character of many of its articles, particularly those on scientific subjects, some of which have resembled the prefatory chapter in a college text-book. (2) The want of that unity in principle and sentiment, both political and literary, which gives the Edinburgh and Quarterly their peculiar charm by investing them respectively with a personal identity of character and tone. In my (humble) opinion, the admission or exclusion of discussion and diversity of sentiment, on *leading questions*, is precisely that which constitutes the specific difference between a modern Magazine and a modern Review.

"I likewise hope that the new editors will abolish the distinction between *reviews* and *critical notices*, as a magazineish feature unworthy of the great guns of periodical literature.

"Excuse this excursus and likewise the binding-job, with which on second thoughts, I am ashamed of troubling you; but those who live in the centre of the world must expect to be plagued with commissions from the circumference!"

Tuesday, the 5th of April, was a cool, beautiful day, of the late winter species. The frogs had just began to sound their instruments in the meadows upon Stony Brook. The college examination was going on. In the evening Dr. Archibald Alexander preached powerfully to the students from the passage, "There is joy in heaven over one sinner that repenteth," &c. At the close he was seized with a deadly faintness, which however left him uninjured. On the 17th, which was Sabbath, Dr. Archibald Alexander completed his sixty-fourth year. The college vacation commenced about the middle of the month, and Professor James Alexander took a trip to Virginia. On the 19th of April his brother Addison writes to his Philadelphia friend for Richardson's Arabic and Persian Dictionary, which he afterwards reviewed in the Repertory; and on the 19th of May, to thank him for some books he had had bound and lettered for him, and to beg him to go in quest of an inkstand of peculiar shape. These commissions were always discharged with punctual fidelity, and this fact went far to cement a friendship which was already one of great strength. Mr. Alexander never forgot a kindness, and though he said little, was one of the most grateful beings I ever knew.

The Commencement this year was largely attended, and was dignified by the presence of General Harrison, who made a speech in the Campus.

It is now my privilege to spread before the reader some of the recollections of the Rev. James B. Ramsey of Lynchburg, Va., who was four years under the tuition of Mr. Alexander as a student in the Theological Seminary, viz: from 1836 to 1839. His reminiscences will be all the more prized when it is known that they were written in the chamber of suffering, and at much cost of strength and feeling. Dr. Ramsey entered the Seminary in the autumn of 1836, but does not think he ever spoke to Mr. Alexander except in recitation. He has, however, a very definite impression of him as he appeared in the class-room, and of the impatience he manifested and uttered, at the idleness of some of the students. The remarks were usually very brief but very keen; and made him very unpopular with a portion of the class.

"My own feelings," says Dr. Ramsey, "and that of others too, of all as I regarded it, who took the right view of the subject, was that he never uttered a sentence *too severe* for conduct so utterly unworthy of a student for the ministry.* I felt glad that conduct which it seemed to

---

* Dr. Hall writes, that his relations to Dr. Alexander, from the time when the former became a member of the first class he taught in the Seminary, to that of their last interview previous to the death of the latter, were of the most agreeable character. He has none but pleasant recollections of him. He admired him as a prodigy of learning and a most versatile genius: while he loved him for the kindly interest he manifested in all who wished to make progress in their studies. "He was never pleased with young men who neglected preparations for the class-room, or who attempted to recite when it was too evident that they had given little attention to study. His patience was sometimes sorely tried by students who seemed to lack conscientiousness, and a proper sense of their responsibility as candidates for the ministry." Dr. Hall never knew him to administer a rebuke to one of this class unless it was richly deserved, "and there can be no doubt that his keen satire in a few such cases has done immense good to many others besides the persons addressed."

me, would have incurred censure in a Freshman in college, and have placed him in the lowest grade at least of scholarship and diligence, should be held up to scorn and contempt.

"In the autumn of 1837 he volunteered to give a course of lectures to three or four of our class, on the book of Leviticus. Drs. Daniel Stewart and M. W. Jacobus were of that number as well as myself. The exercise was recitation and lecture intermingled, and was a rich treat." He was never more at his ease than on these occasions, or appeared to be more completely master of his theme. An abstract of these lectures is still preserved by this pupil. "He evidently took great delight in communicating knowledge, and before such as appreciated them he poured forth copiously his stores of learning with great childish simplicity of language and manner."

The intense abhorrence and disgust which the Professor ever showed for these Seminary drones, their culpable ignorance, and especially the attempt to cover it up, and to give an impression of knowledge where there was evident consciousness of neglect, and for everything like conceit, rather tended to make Mr. Ramsey take a strong liking to him; for it seemed to him that

"There were some there, who, had they been dealt with as faithfulness to the church required, would have been dismissed and ordered to betake themselves to some other calling in which laziness and vanity might better be tolerated."

The opening lecture one year while the writer was there was delivered by Mr. Alexander, from the passage "Let no man despise thy youth," and it was made to bear with tremendous severity upon those who were frivolous and negligent of their duty; and though some thought its spirit of caustic satire not altogether appropriate, it was heartily approved by the writer:

"I have no doubt," he says "that it was just the very thing needed, and that by the very keenness of its point it penetrated the blunted sensibilities of a few who could be made to believe in no other way, while it did good to the whole class, profiting even those who were tenderly conscientious and circumspect."

The pupil thought then and thinks now that the Professor showed, as he says, "not a little patience with our blunders and slowness in learning the Hebrew." And the impression always produced on his mind by his teaching was that of great kindness and magnanimity toward all who appeared anxious to do their duty. He was himself exceedingly timid, and whenever called upon in class during the first year, rose confused and often found it difficult to express himself without painful hesitation; yet he fails to remember having seen the first mark of restless anger in his teacher, or to have been treated with anything but the greatest gentleness; so that he often felt grateful for the forbearance shown, and to use his own words, "very much ashamed of myself for giving occasion for it."

The same writer was one of those who sought him out in his study, and like most others who did so was agreeably disappointed.

"My first visit to his room was, if I remember right, at the end of the first year, during vacation, and it was in consequence of his sending for me, to offer me a situation as teacher in a private family in town (Commodore Stockton's). I occasionally after this called upon him, but never without a *positive* cause; and I always found him perfectly accessible and ready to hear patiently, and attend to, anything I had to say: and there was no professor there to whom I went with more perfect freedom from undue constraint than to him." He had much more difficulty in feeling at his ease with some of the other professors. A "vast gulf" seemed to separate him from them. This, he imagines, may have been "all his own fault."

"On one occasion I remember calling on him (Addison)—it was during my last year—with a passage in Hebrew, in 1 Sam., chap. xx. which I could make nothing of. He looked at it, and not finding any solution of the difficulty, after looking at some commentaries, told me to call in again in a few days; and in the mean time he would see if he could find any more plausible attempt at a solution."

Before he called, the Professor sent for him and showed him, in some old German, commentary what seemed to be a very ingenious solution indeed, based of course upon the supposition that some slight error must have crept into the text.

"It was, however, the *interest* which he so promptly took in the matter, and the pains he was at to find out everything which could be found out in that little affair of minute criticism, that was so pleasing to a student, such as I then was, and that was so unlike what many have thought of him."

The minuteness and wide extent of his scholarship were constantly appearing in the allusions and illustrations to which the teacher continually had recourse, especially in his familiar and least elaborate lectures.

"No one" he says, "could help feeling the vast difference between the instructions of such a man, and those of one perhaps equally familiar with the immediate subject of instruction," but one who in his comparative ignorance of, or non-acquaintance with, matters which were but remotely connected with his chair, should be constantly betraying that he was a man of "far narrower range of thought and knowledge."

He seemed to be almost unconscious of his own large resources; and his pupils always believed him to be just as humble as he was learned and able. There was often exhibited a feeling of dissatisfaction with himself and his own methods and plans,

"And a way of speaking of others who were greatly his inferiors in every particular, that seemed strange to those who regarded him as so great a man." This feeling of dissatisfaction with his own arrangements, "led him very frequently to change his course and method. His ideal of everything seemed to be even further beyond his attainment, than his attainment was beyond that of almost all others."

The writer pays a just tribute to the value of his teacher's oral expositions:

"As an exegete, I hardly know how he could be excelled. His *analyses*, with which he introduced each exegetical lecture, so concise, so clear, so simple, were themselves far better than most commentaries." To their class he lectured only on part of Isaiah and the Messianic Psalms. "To his lectures on the first ten chapters of Isaiah I owe more than to all the other instructions received in the Seminary, as to the method of analyzing and expounding Scripture." Speaking of the valuable labours of certain other expositors, the writer goes on to say that he profited comparatively little by them in this respect. " I learned indeed the meaning of much I did not know before; I received a certain quantum of explanations; but I did not even *begin* to learn *how* to explain the Bible myself. But I had not got through with the first chapter of Isaiah with Dr. Alexander's lectures till I felt as if I had become conscious almost of a new power. Every passage he touched seemed to be suddenly lighted up with a new beauty and glory, and often a single remark would be so suggestive that it seemed at once to pour light all over the Bible, to bring up into new and striking association other truths and passages, and to stimulate the mind to the highest activity, and fill it with wonder at the amazing fulness of God's word."

The class of expounders to whom Dr. Ramsey had referred, were equal to no such mighty office as this. They

"Would give us the minute details of criticism—repeated over and over as they occurred, and leave us to generalize for ourselves. Dr. Alexander would bundle up a hundred of these at once, and give us the principles.

"Another striking trait of his exegetical lectures was that his faith in the simple statements of the Bible was so childlike and so perfect. This reverence for the sacred text was one of his noblest qualifications for an instructor in these times. This was abundantly manifest in his works, but the impression made by his lectures as we heard them, was still stronger.

"The comprehensiveness of mind, and the elevated point from which he looked on any topic of Biblical exposition or of ministerial duty enabled him often to compress into a remark some pregnant truth that no amount of details could ever have imparted. I got more good from a single remark of his, made to a few of us who met him the last year in a private class, than from all the lectures and books on Homiletics. It was in substance this: to collect the other passages of Scripture bearing on the same point as the text, and to let your heads and divisions be but the exposition, virtually at least, of these; and thus avoid the danger of substituting human reasonings for God's Word, and at the same time secure endless variety."

Dr. Ramsey regarded Mr. Alexander's as the most powerful intellect with which he ever came in contact.

"It was, to my apprehension best characterized as *massive*. But it was as beautiful, as well proportioned, as it was massive, and all its operations were as easy and exact as they were powerful. To use rather a rude comparison, it was like an elephant's trunk; it could pick up a pin, and pluck up a tree by the roots, with equal ease.

"And yet the meekness and teachableness of the man was just as manifest. He seemed to be ready to learn something from everybody. And the perfect docility of his great mind to the slightest whisper of God's Word was its crowning glory.

"It would be strange indeed if, so conversant as he was with God's word, and reverencing it as he did, he did not manifest it by his holiness and nearness to God. And especially during the latter part of my course in the Seminary were we impressed with this; and the remark was often made that Dr. Addison was a man that walked with God, and was evidently growing in grace. His preaching, his lectures, and his prayers gave proof of this. And on all proper occasions he would converse on the subject of experimental religion with a zest and interest, that showed how much he meditated upon it, and how he sought to have his own heart brought under its full power." While a student, Dr. Ramsey did not see him very often in private. "Of course my personal intercourse was very limited: the vast distance between us in every respect rendered it impossible for me to venture into his company except when necessary."

He often heard the students speak of the Professor's traditionary "peculiarities;" but if Mr. Alexander possessed traits which could be described by this term, he never became cognizant of them; he was never placed in circumstances in which he observed any special peculiarities.

This testimony is greatly strengthened by that of others. The dreaded Hebraist was of the sanguineo-choleric temperament; and though naturally patient and affectionate, he had a stern eye to duty; was inflexibly honest and just and if his anger was once kindled, it burnt like tinder. The spark, however, was extinct almost as soon as it was struck out. There were at these rare times a flash—a blaze—an explosion; and then all was over: but not before some one had been struck down and terribly shaken by the concussion.* After giving way to his impetuous feelings, none was more ready to acknowledge his failing than he was himself: but not so were some of his best and most pious pupils. There were some in nearly every class, who like Dr. Ramsey justified him with scarce an exception in everything he said and did while in the chair. This is as much as can be said for most thoroughgoing disciplinarians, and perhaps as much as need be said for any man.

But in the popular sense of the term, he was not very peculiar or eccentric. He was the roundest man I ever knew. It is a great though common mistake, to suppose that there was anything *outré* about him. He was certainly diffident, or rather shy, and sometimes bashful, and that to a very poignant degree, and some of his habits of mind as well as of body had possibly become a little morbid, and in both cases from the disuse or seclusion of certain of his powers. But he was not as compared with men generally, odd, droll, or queer. He was no Samuel Johnson, as that huge personage appears in the pages of Macaulay and Boswell. He was no mere *helluo librorum*, like Dr. Parr, with no acquaintance with the world and in a manner lost to the feelings and sympathies of his race. He was no Dominie Sampson to be annoyed because he could not give his friend Dandie Dinmont the praise of "erudition." He was, it is true, a man of extraordinary learning, and of great powers; he was to a great extent isolated from his fellow beings: but when one drew near to him one found him to be in other respects, like any other man of cultivated taste and refinement.

Many current stories about him are sheer lies, and some of them very malicious ones. A sufficient answer to all such idle tales is the unquestionable fact that Mr. Alexander, whatever else he was, was a pleasant Christian gentleman, and a

---

* As in the case of another, of whom he has written very amusingly, the sufferer smarting under the sting of his terrible repartee too often mistook "cool contempt" for "rabid rage."

man of exquisite common sense. It is true that for the most part he shunned promiscuous company. It was his fancy to do so. He had no time for society. Every hour was consecrated to hard work in his Master's service. Then, again, he had perhaps as much morbid consciousness of being observed, and as violent a repugnance to being stared at and commented upon, and patronized by his inferiors, as any man living. And to crown all, the habit of solitude had become to him a second nature.

As Byron did not like to be treated as a poet, but as a man of the world; so Mr. Alexander did not like to be treated as a prodigy, a book-worm, a dangerous person to approach, or in any sense an exceptional man; but as a gentleman of piety and good breeding, with the common manners and sympathies. He felt that he was *not* exceptional in the sense supposed, and with his acute observation and sensitively quick apprehension of the thoughts and designs of those who approached him, it hurt his nice sensibilities and touched his self respect, when he was regarded in a light that was so untrue and so obnoxious to his feelings. He was equally averse to being either browbeaten or flattered. If he was exceptional in anything, it was in the strength and honest expression in his case of this very natural state of mind. There were no anomalies in his psychological structure; every deviation, so to say, from the usual or regular inflection, was strictly subject to the law of the formation. Any one might know beforehand precisely how he would act in given circumstances, so far as one may ever know this in the case of a person of great talents and originality and quick emotional impulses.

If he was met boldly, frankly, unsuspectingly, and treated as any other man of high notions of propriety and nice feelings of delicacy; and he were not too much occupied to stop work: no one could be more agreeable, more conversible, more friendly, more free and easy; or if an opportunity arose, more full of sunshine and gaiety; in short, more perfectly delightful as a companion. But there were certain classes of men he could not always tolerate; there were certain moments when he could not, and would not put up with bores, idiots, sponges, and sycophants; or with curious visitors who were blown with self-conceit or bursting with arrogance. If such characters persisted in annoying him, he would sometimes administer a reprimand which even a fool case-hardened in his folly could never forget. He would now and then have recourse to the weapon of sarcasm; which in such cases would gleam for a twinkling in the air and then take off the head of the offender like the cymitar of Saladin. More generally in such situations he was simply silent, cool, impassive; answering in mild but expressive monosyllables; and soon turned his back upon the intruder. He also found it extremely hard to get along with very timid persons, or those who were too evidently afraid of him. It worried him and made him appear cold and taciturn. Often this was nothing but sheer sensibility. At times he had laid out a certain amount of work and did not wish to be disturbed. At such times, not caring to open the door and bow his visitor out, he would adopt such a manner as sufficiently to intimate that he was engaged and did not choose to be interrupted. Any man of real sense could tell when this was the case, and could see at once that no unkindness was meant. All these little individual traits which have been so much overdrawn in some quarters may be resolved, except so far as they sprung from physical causes, or from close application to his studies, into varying expressions of a certain sensitive shyness and fastidiousness of feeling, coupled with a wish to be thought like other men; an instinctive and refined knowledge of human nature; and the most transparent honesty.

It ought also to be said that like his father before him, he was to some degree under the influence of changes in the weather. He was shrewdly affected by the east wind. This was still more true of his brother James. A bright, clear day acted upon him like champagne. Dark and wet days operated as a damper on the spirits. In the case of Dr. Archibald Alexander, the effect of easterly weather was instantaneously felt, and exhibited by a drooping gait and air, and an absence of his wonted elasticity and buoyant cheerfulness. In the case of his son Addison, the same effect was produced, though not so invariably, and never in anything like so great a degree. The weather often occasioned him disagreeable bodily sensations, and sometimes made him silent, or gave him a touch of the "blues." He acknowledges his vulnerability on this point in several entries in his European Journals.

But after taking everything into the estimate, and looking at him in the broad, common way, it must be conceded that Mr. Alexander, though greater and better than most of them, was, on the whole, and especially in little things, surprisingly like the rest of mankind. He was not a monster, or a learned automaton; but aside from his gifts and attainments, a gentle, tractable, teachable, loveable, true-hearted man.

His pupils were not slow to find this out; and numbers of them, after becoming fairly acquainted with him, stood in greater fear of several of the other Professors than they did of him. They were, as a body, proud of him; and looked upon him as one of the noblest Christian scholars and brightest geniuses in the world. Whenever it was announced that he was to preach in the town of Princeton, the students would desert the Seminary chapel almost *en masse*. They knew that they had some reason to expect one of his brilliant flights of eloquence. These he would not often give them in the chapel. He would merely lecture in a close exegetical way. They called him by an amiable nickname, which however disagreeable it would have been to the feelings of the Professor, showed how much at home they felt in his presence, and the affection they had for his person.

The simple truth was that those who attended to their lessons, which were always made plain to the dullest comprehension, could not fail to be fascinated and at length carried away captive, not only by the teacher, but the man. There was at times something so childlike and *naif* about him; something so engaging about his looks, the tones of his voice, and his characteristic ways in the class-room, as well as about his patient, kind, forbearing, cordial disposition; mingled with, or rather in a subtle way succeeded by an indefinable something that was on occasion so startling, swift, magnetic, so impregnated with genius, so peremptorily commanding awe and obedience, so suggestive of slumbering or waking prowess, and so ominous of assured triumph; in a word, something so strangely Napoleonic; that, as on other accounts, his favorite pupils had for him much the same sort of vivid feeling that the Old Guard had for the First Consul and the Emperor; while the body of the class had the more quiet feeling of admiration that was generally prevalent in the French army.

He had, too, the "art Napoleon" as an instructor (which was possessed in so high a degree by Dr. Thomas Brown of Edinburgh, and by Sir William Hamilton and Professor Faraday) of inspiring his pupils with a lofty enthusiasm, which did not burn out when they left the halls of the recitation-room. What he was as a Professor may be inferred from the fact that with all his other gifts, he was apt to teach. Dr. Hodge testifies that he always secured the attention, admiration, and confidence of his classes. He never failed to interest them in the subject under discussion, and he never failed to instruct them. "His views were comprehensive, and so clearly exhibited that the minds of his pupils were expanded under his influence, at the same time that they were elevated. He made the Bible glorious to them. This remark I have heard from the lips of those who sat under his teachings."

Almost the only hint I have been able to obtain from the diaries in my possession as to Mr. Alexander's outward life at this time, is contained in the brief statement that on Monday, the 3d of October, after a night of rain, and while his father was in New York, and amidst tidings of more deaths from "the fever," he was engaged in "the removal of his effects into the ancient house on the Canal street."* It is hard to

---

* This was an old house that had been removed from another part of the town and occupied by a Mr. Noah Green, and was from this fact playfully called "Noah's Ark."

keep up with his various changes of geographical position and residence. His migrations were almost as short and quite as frequent as those of good Dr. Primrose from the blue bed to the brown. He hung over every new scene like a humming-bird, poised indeed, but ready to dart at any moment. The delight he experienced in these strange movements was that of a child in its fervour and intensity, and was just as transitory.

Among his principal companions this year were his two private pupils, Henry M. Alexander his youngest brother, and Samuel Harrison Howell, son of a skilful physician of Princeton. The boys used to meet him at his quarters on the Trenton Turnpike, and when out of school had much pleasure and fun with him. When the fever was raging in the neighborhood no family suffered more grievously than that of Dr. Howell, the faithful nurse and medical adviser of the sick. Several members of his family contracted the disease, and two of them died of it, as he did himself. Mr. Alexander was much affected to learn that his little pupil and playmate was also seized sometime afterward, and wrote him a long whimsical letter in the shape of machine poetry; portions of which are here given, not to show his genius or his learning but his simple kindness of heart. They vividly paint the scene presented to master and pupils in their leisure hours, as well as the rude furniture with which the memory of the teacher was associated in the minds of the pupils. They also greatly magnify the very questionable advantages and ornamental qualities of the quaint house on Canal street, into which the former was thinking of "flitting." I can only find room for the first part of this letter.

"I thank God for the favour, as I reckon it to be, not only to yourself and your relations, but to me; and I trust that he will give you, in exchange for pains and tears, entire restoration and a length of happy years. I have tried hard to forget you, Hal; but how can I succeed, when every chair I sit upon, and every book I read, recall to recollection in one way or another, my little playmate, room-mate, pupil-friend, and younger brother? When I look at the round table, or the broken arm-chair, I easily persuade myself that he is sitting there; and when gaizing from the window I can almost see him still, coming slowly with his books and his umbrella down the hill. Methinks I hear his light step upon the entry floor, and the sound of his umbrella as he sets it by the door. I hear him turn the lock; I see him enter with a smile, my solitude to sweeten and my languor to beguile. Methinks I see him offer me an apple or a peach, with a look that overpays me for the little I can teach. Methinks I see him put his cap upon the closet shelf—every motion, every attitude is that of Hal himself. But when I wish to speak to him the vision fades away. I miss the gentle voice that used to cheer me every day. I miss the real presence of my real little friend. I miss it in the evening when my toils are at an end. I miss it in my homeward walks; I miss it even more when I sit in my old elbow chair behind the chapel door. Whatever else I see or have, I find I must and shall continue to miss something and that something is my Hal. But when I recollect my boy that you are safe and sound, I feel that for repining I have no excuse or ground."

Even if he should not be allowed to see his face again, it will always be grateful to his heart to hear that his pupil is good and happy. He nevertheless indulges the hope of a pleasant re-union with his little friend, and in the meanwhile resolves to do his best to keep in good spirits.

But Mr. Alexander was not always to be found on Henderson Hill or at the "Ark." He was as fond of going about as ever. The modes of travel were at this time a little antiquated; though railways were in use, and the applications of steam well understood. A gentleman of Newark, for instance, wishing to go to Princeton, would perhaps ride in his stanhope or barouche to the Market-street stand, where he would find a horse car, in which he would be conveyed to the Brunswick dépôt. There he would enter a steam carriage, which would take him from the depot to East Brunswick. Thence he would be hauled in an omnibus to the wagon-coach running to Balser's tavern; which being at the juncture full, would have to be exchanged for an old fashioned stage-coach, that was sure to break down at or near the canal barge at Kingston, from which the jaded traveller was fain to emerge and deposit himself in the canal-hack plying betwixt the Princeton Basin and the collegiate groves and campus. There was much room for adventure on these trips, and the vicissitude suited the temper of a man who like Mr. Alexander loved to go through as many small external transformations as possible. The journey was notwithstanding very irksome and fatiguing.

On Thursday, the 20th of October, the arrival of a young Greek from Athens was reported, one of Dr. King's proteges, by the name of Luke Oeconomos. He was subsequently followed by another named Constantine Menaios, from whom Mr. Alexander learned the Romaic, and under whose guidance he became a proficient in writing and perhaps speaking it. Mr. Oeconomos was a young man of talents, amiability and virtue. He was graduated at the college of New Jersey in 1840, and died at Clarens, in Fairfax county, Virginia, the 7th of May, 1843. He was at the time a teacher of the Greek language in the Fairfax Institute. His disease was a galloping consumption. There is for many a mournful interest connected with his somewhat romantic history and untimely fate.

Early in March of the next year, Signor Borsieri had the pleasure of introducing his Princeton friends to the Count Confalonieri, an elderly man, a fellow prisoner of his, who had been in bonds fifteen years. These were golden opportunities to the two Alexanders of learning the spoken tongue of Italy. The elder brother's 33d birthday occurred on the 13th. Not long after this Mr. Borsieri made a profession of his faith. I think Mr. Alexander gave this gentleman lessons in English. He certainly played this part to several foreigners, receiving their instructions in return.

Soon after this, Professor James Alexander was invited to take the Presidency of Hanover College in Indiana. He however declined the honour.

Mr. Alexander, on the 26th, was in torture with a swollen face. He was very subject to this affection, which he styled a "jaw-swell." His relief on such occasions was an odd one. He would lecture immoderately, and on the most difficult parts of scripture. He used to say this was the only way he knew of diverting his mind from the pain. This remark is strictly applicable rather to the common dull tooth-ache than to a violent inflammation of the cheek and jaw such as this was. I have seen him sitting in his recitation-room with his hand thrust against his face, and swaying to and fro with rapid movements of his body, but pouring out his usual torrent of exquisitely chosen words and fascinating his class with some of his most remarkable lucubrations. Sometimes he would have to pause a moment from the sheer intensity of his sufferings.

The synod of Philadelphia convened this day. The great topic of interest before the body was the controversy between the Old and New School parties in the church. The Rev. W. L. McCalla made an attack on Princeton. His argument was an able one, but he was called to order for his strong language and personal allusions. He was, however, allowed to proceed with his invective, or rather his impassioned remonstrance. The theme is an inviting one, but the days of this heat are now over, and the subject of this memoir took no active part in these discussions. Indeed, I have no positive information as to what his precise views on the mooted questions were, except that he was a staunch old school man, with general sympathies with his colleagues at Princeton. Whether he went as far in the direction of moderate views as some of these, I do not know. He was editor of the Repertory during the flagrant outbreak of this quarrel, but took no further part in the engagement than to print the articles of others, and occasionally to launch witty sarcasms at the men who in his opinion were the chief troublers of Israel. His arguments were all of a purely incidental and unpremeditated character.

Mr. Alexander about this time undertook the teaching of two of the sons of Captain Stockton, U. S. N. The instruction of a younger member of the captain's family occurred at a later date. These gentlemen now speak in most grateful terms of the preceptor's kindness and assiduity, and love to tell of the odd humours of their master when books had been laid aside. He made the two eldest of these write letters to him in a large thick folio volume, using the same book himself for most of his own writing between times, and filling it, or inducing them to fill it with letters, compositions, poems, and critical comments. Some of the writings in these big books are well worthy of being kept carefully, as they have been by their owners.

I give the following remarkable letter to Mr. Hall, which sufficiently explains itself:

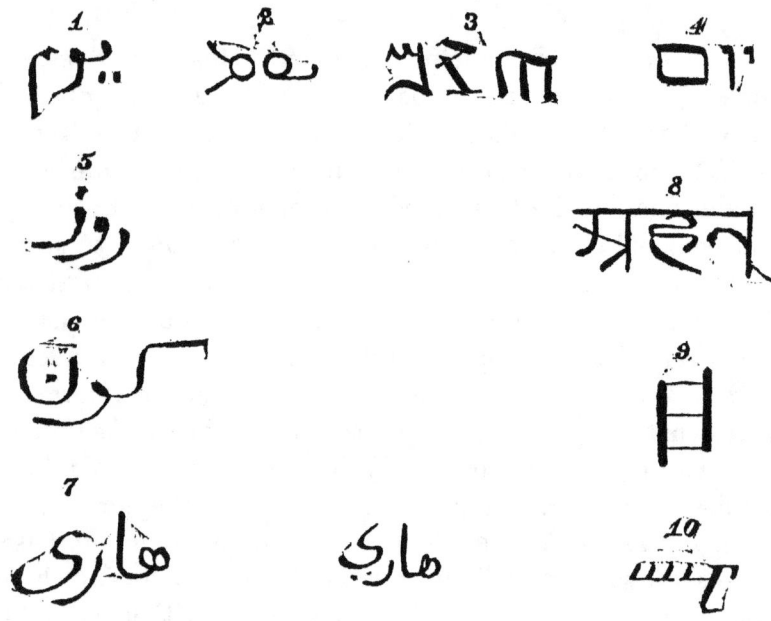

"PRINCETON, *January* 13, 1837.

"MY DEAR SIR:

"The number of alphabets, you know, bears no proportion to that of languages; and among those of which I have a smattering the variety of character is by no means great. I have selected the word "day" as being short and simple in all the languages exemplified above. The horizontal line (1, 2, 3, 4,) exhibits a four-fold diversity of character in the languages of the same family; and it so happens that the word which I have chosen is precisely the same (yōm or yūm) in all four. The vertical column (1, 5, 6, 7,) illustrates, on the other hand, the application of one alphabet to four languages of different stocks. The Arabic *yūm* (or rather *yaum*), the Persian *rōz*, the Turkish *gūn*, and the Malay *hárī* or *árī*, though wholly unlike in sound, are all in the

Arabic character. To these examples I have added the Sanscrit *ahan*, the Chinese *jĕ*, and the Armenian *ahr*, all likewise meaning *day*. It is a fact worth noticing that the Chinese character is used by the greatest number of men, and the Arabic over the largest surface; at least it is so said. The latter is employed (with additions and modifications to express peculiar sounds) not only by the Persians, Turks, and Mohammedan Africans, but by several of the Indian races. The Sanscrit is thought by philologists to be, on the whole, the most perfect form of alphabetical writing.

"I have two books begun which I have not touched for a year, perhaps for two. The one is a series of dramatic sketches almost entirely in the words of Scripture explanations, descriptions, &c., being introduced as stage-directions. My idea was, that each scene should be accompanied by a picture. The scenes are of course detached, and the only object was to attract attention to familiar subjects by a change of form. When I broke down I had written Scene 1. A well near the city of Nahor, ten camels kneeling by the well—two men sitting near—Eliezer by himself. Sc. 2.—Isaac's encampment near Beersheba—Rebecca's tent. Rebecca and Jacob (the deception of Isaac). Sc. 3. The plains of Moab; Naomi, Ruth, Orpah, in mourning garments. Sc. 4. The wine-press of Joash the Abiezrite, in a retired spot surrounded by oaks—Gideon, the son of Joash, threshing wheat—a stranger approaches and sits under one of the oaks. Sc. 5. The priests' chamber near the Tabernacle in Shiloh, containing two beds on which Eli the High Priest and Samuel, a child, are lying—a voice—"Samuel! Samuel!" &c., &c.—Sc. 6. A field near Ramah—Saul and a servant sitting beneath a tree—Saul, "Come, let us return, lest my father leave caring for the asses," &c. Sc. 7. A field near Gibea—Jonathan and David—David, "What have I done? what is my iniquity?" &c.

"My other book was a conversation on King David's nephews, intended to show how many not uninteresting facts may be overlooked even by the diligent straight-forward student, unless he takes the trouble to compare scripture with scripture.

"As usual, I became convinced before I had well begun, that the plan was not worth carrying out, and I abandoned it. I am not willing, however, that you should suppose I have never even attempted anything. Yours truly,

"Jos. Addison Alexander."

The next letter I shall give is also addressed to Mr. Hall.

In it he refers to the Asiatic languages, and inquires for a cheap American set of the Edinburgh or Quarterly :

"Princeton, *December* 21, 1836.
"My Dear Sir:
"My friend and room-mate Harrison Howell, who brings you this, will take charge of my Lexicon if it is in your hands or if you will direct him to the binder. I am sorry to trouble you with these small jobs, and by way of proving it I herewith send you my John Bunyan to be dressed *—fine but very plain. I feel that I have some claim on your time, in consequence of my prompt attention to your application made last summer for some scraps of language. Did my answer miscarry? or is it printed? Pray lay the blame on Amos Kendall † and let me know what I must do. My grammars and lexicons are at your service, especially the latter, as so many of them have enjoyed your protection. Seriously I have mislaid your letter and do not recollect precisely what you want.

"In some of your publications or perhaps in your private letters you have spoken of a plan devised by Trevelyan and others for reducing the Asiatic languages to the Roman orthography. Have you the details of the plan in any form? Again, in what form is your large map of Palestine put up, and what is the price thereof? James I believe on reflection has one; but I have not been in his study for eighteen months, as I live in Canal Street and he in Mercer. Once more, do you think that in any of the second-hand book stores it would be possible to find anything like a complete set of the Edinburgh or Quarterly Review, as republished in America, at a very reduced price? James thinks such an article cannot be in the market; but nobody knows what a man may sell to second-hand dealers. If you will answer these inquiries at your leisure, say before the end of 1837, and add any practical or other observations upon these or other subjects ; not forgetting to repeat your prescription for the dose of unknown tongues without delay —you will confer a favour upon   Yours, very truly,
"Mr. Hall,⎫   "J. Addison Alexander."
"E. S. S. J.⎭

"1. If the binder knows of my existence, and will trust me, please to give Harrison his address, instead of troubling yourself about old Bunyan.

---

* And lettered simply "Pilgrim's Progress." J. A. A.
† The Hon. Amos Kendall, who was Postmaster General under Jackson.

"2. I have just heard that my lexicon is come, and feel much indebted to you.

"3. Mr. John P. Brown, our diplomatic dragoman at Constantinople, told me last winter that reed pens or reeds for making oriental pens could be procured in Philadelphia. If you know where such an article is venal, I should like to have it priced by the bearer.

"(Finis.)"

CHAPTER XIII.

I now present the reader with some graphic reminiscences of Mr. Alexander as he appeared to the class of 1837. The writer of these memoranda* was himself a member of the class, though not an intimate acquaintance of Mr. Alexander; and in the admirable sketches which follow he is unable to conceal the traces of his own native humour and benevolence. He begins by saying that he does not belong to the variety of mankind who keep journals of their own lives and times; and therefore owing to the lapse of years, has now "rather dissolving views of the men and scenes amidst which" his earlier days were spent. He now wishes for some such record:

"For as one of the ancient Greeks thanked the gods that he lived in the days of Pericles, so the students of Princeton who lived in the days of Addison Alexander had reason also to be thankful. It was indeed a privilege to be trained under such a teacher; and the consciousness of that distinction does not diminish as time adds new honours to his name. The period of my acquaintance with Professor Alexander was the golden age of the Seminary. The venerable men who gave that institution such an elevated rank and position were then at its head, and in the prime of their usefulness; Dr. A. Alexander and Dr. Miller being the senior professors, and Dr. Hodge and J. Addison Alexander the junior professors. The last named was then a young man and yet had reached the full meridian of his fame and popularity. He had not only a high standing in his own peculiar department of Oriental literature, but also ranked very high for his attainments in ancient and modern languages. He was considered by the young men in the Seminary as a regular prodigy—a perfect polyglot; and they believed he was master of so many tongues that the tower of Babel need never have

* The Rev. David Teese, White Plains, N. Y.

suspended operations if he had only lived in those early ages, and been appointed superintendent of the building.* We had great pride in our Oriental Professor. He was an oracle, and an object of universal admiration, to the enthusiastic youth. They would follow his judgment on Jewish literature or antiquities in preference to any of the Rabbis either ancient or modern. We venerated the fathers of the institution; but with the natural partiality of youth we attached ourselves to the junior Professor, and worshipped him as the rising sun."

The young Professor was one of those rare men who realize to the eye of the beholder one's preconceptions of what the bodily presence of a person of great intellect ought to be. The description which follows of his *personne* will prove attractive, and is corroborated by innumerable voices. The freshness of his complexion, and his corpulent fulness, diminished gradually as he grew older, and had entirely left him before the termination of his last sickness.

"As the visible presence of great men is always a matter of curiosity and interest to the reader, I may offer a remark on that subject. At the time now spoken of, the personal appearance of the Professor was quite interesting and attractive. He was, as we said, in the dew of his youth, and its bloom was on his cheek. A remarkable high and polished forehead was the indication of his massive intellect; and the thin covering of hair was (in our judgment) the indication of exhausting mental labor. His face, however, was not 'sicklied o'er with the pale cast of thought.' By no means; it was round and plump; and his complexion was that of the full-blown red rose. His colour would come and go very easily, and he used to blush like a girl. It was a fancy with our class that in form and features he was an exact fac-simile of Napoleon; and that there never was so perfect a resemblance to that great man to be found in all the world. Each time I looked in his face I thought of 'The great Captain.'"

The likeness to Napoleon was very commonly noticed.

---

* Byron said that Mezzofanti ought to have been interpreter at the Tower of Babel. The idea seems to have been borrowed from Pope. See also Princeton Rep. on King James's Bible.

It was not a close similarity of features; Mr. Alexander's head and body were much broader than Napoleon's. It was his full person, his impressive front, the regularity of his countenance, the impetuous brevity of his speech, and the look of power in his face, which reminded so many people of the great Frenchman. In shape and size Mr. Alexander's head bore a wonderfully striking resemblance to the cast of Count Cavour's. His face and bust were not unlike the picture of Swift in one of the old Penny Magazines. His head was a grand one; that would have befitted Jupiter Tonans.

The same writer touches delicately upon the subject of his gifted teacher's shyness and humble opinion of his own powers. He was observed to avoid what the world calls company:

"He had a girlish modesty and diffidence at this period of his life which prevented him from going into society, or enjoying much pleasure in social intercourse. Many remarkable traditions were current among the students in regard to the difficulties and embarrassments which he met with in his necessary intercourse with men."

This, Mr. Teese thinks, might have proved in his case a bar to the most extensive usefulness as a pastor, and concludes that his preceptor was more adapted to a chair such as the one he then occupied, than to the charge of a promiscuous congregation. This opinion is given for what it is worth, and without comment. It is right to say, however, that Mr. Alexander's aversion from society, and lack of enjoyment when in company, were often much exaggerated; as was also his supposed inability under such circumstances to take his part in general conversation. He was sometimes, though rarely, a fascinating member of such promiscuous circles. There is evidence of this fact in the statements of several witnesses which are contained in this volume.

The class of '37 was pushed forward with the greatest vigour. The evidence of the Professor's diligence was unimpeachable. He laboured with a will and with a quenchless enthusiasm. The poor fellows were almost exhausted, and some of them completely overwhelmed, in the effort to keep up with him. The class was divided into two sections; each section recited two lessons a day, and each lesson occupied an hour. Says the good-natured writer to whom I am indebted for these particulars:

"You may be sure that neither the Professor nor the students had much time either to eat or sleep. For myself, I was as busy as a nailer; and to keep up with the demands of the teacher, and attain enough Hebrew to pass the Presbytery, I had to rise up early and sit up late and eat the bread of sorrows. To speak the plain truth, we did think the Professor was a little exacting; and that our condition was not much better than that of Israel in Egypt under the old task-masters. Our progress up the hill of science was like the upward progress of the unhappy Sisyphus—'with many a weary step and many a groan.' To our class, at this time, the ardent Professor devoted six hours each day, of arduous toil; and after we had passed our three years under his faithful eye, we thought we had learned enough of oriental literature to teach Hebrew anywhere, except, perhaps, in a German University. So severe was the labour that several of our class succumbed under the effort, and gave up their attendance on the class lectures; and to those that continued faithful and hopeful to the end, there remained days of weary toil and nights of arduous study. The school-boys in the 'Deserted Village' had learned to trace the day's disaster in their master's face; but we often had a premonition of our trouble before we saw his face. For as one division of our class came out, the other went into the class room; and mingled thus together we were admonished by those before us of danger ahead, in some such words as these, 'O you'll catch it to-day!' 'O 'tis dreadful!' and similar encouraging expressions indicating what we might expect."

Few teachers would have dared to attempt, and fewer still would have persevered in the attempt, to force onward a body of young scholars in this way, against their own inclinations and convictions; and fewest of all would have finally achieved the end desired. It was the privilege of Mr. Alexander to succeed in everything he set his heart on accomplishing. He knew quite accurately, or soon found out, the limits of his own capacity; and would not continue long in a course in which he did not feel sure of success. He had the knack of ascertaining also precisely what his pupils could do; and he had the art or the power of making them do it.

"It is but proper to say, however, that we were greatly encouraged by our progress under the Professor's admirable training; and by the knowledge that it was all for our own good that our present condition was not joyous but rather grievous. The enthusiasm of the teacher imparted itself to the students; and under every green tree, in the well-beaten garden walks, in the adjacent woods, as well as in the Seminary, in the study, and in the class-room, young men were seen walking, or lying down, or sitting; with their limbs stretched out on the grass, or over the mantel-piece, or on the backs of chairs; all intent on the perusal of one book—'Bush's Hebrew Grammar.' Memory loves to linger round those days of youth, gone never to return; and upon the pleasant employments and associations with which they were connected. Of all the great names we there venerated, not one now remains, except as an object of memory to which each passing year adds new lustre; for the memory of the just is blessed."

This whimsical, while yet genial and delightful picture, might be repeated again and again and accepted as true for every one of the succeeding years, were it not that as the years multiplied, the Professor became year by year more and more gentle and easy to be entreated, and more and more reasonable in his demands upon his students' time and brains. When he became a teacher of Church History, he had grown so wise in all these practical matters that a person more easy to be satisfied with a creditable recitation could not be found. He never was able altogether to suppress his contempt for Boeotian ignorance, or utter stupidity, or for the pert conceit often attendant upon laziness, which will sometimes elude all vigilance and find their way even into the Halls of sacred learning. Then his eye would flash, and his face glance fire. He would sharply reprove, or else would terribly confound with one of his annihilating sarcasms, which demonstrated at the same time the folly of pupil and the genius and authority of the master.

It however took a great deal to move him in those days. He was silent in presence of some of the most grievous exhibitions. In reply to the question, "What barbarous tribes invaded Europe at the close of the fifth century," a poor fellow who had stood the hot fire of Mr. Alexander's cross-examination without blenching or even so much as uttering a word, suddenly exclaimed, apparently very much to his own relief, "the Barbarians!" The Professor, who sat writhing under this rejoinder, showed in his face the traces of an inward conflict between mirth and anger; but merely said in a tone of contemptuous commiseration, "That'll do, sir! The next!" The stolidity of this man was almost incredible. On another occasion the Professor asked him, "What change took place in the orders of the clergy at such and such a period?" referring to the introduction of metropolitans. The response was startling, "They were reduced to the same footing with the laity, sir!" This of course produced an explosion of laughter among the lookers-on; but the Professor contented himself with saying, "Oh, no!" in a tone of utter disgust, and permitted the unfortunate blunderer to take his seat.

Early April was full of the usual vernal promise. The aspen at Dr. Alexander's Seminary-gate was in blossom, and the fields were beginning to change their winter raiment. Mr. Alexander was writing "Words of a Scribe," "Nails by the Masters of Assemblies," &c., in the Sunday School Journal. The Presbytery at Bound Brook appointed Dr. Archibald Alexander and Mr. Yeomans their clerical commissioners to the Assembly. The Hebrew Professor was not yet a licensed minister, and not yet editor of the Repertory; and of course performed no public acts in this stage of the difficulties. The weather continued exceedingly lovely, and the temperature gradually rose to a point of oppressive heat.

On the 30th, which was Sunday, I find that Mr. Alexander was lying sick. He had suffered from a high fever in the night, with delirium and severe pains in the head. Dr. Forman cupped him in the morning and afterwards bled him pretty freely. Whether from this cause or not, he swooned;

but soon began to exhibit symptoms of amendment. On May day he was better, though still gravely diseased, and after a bad night showed marked improvement.

Dr. Sprague* dismissed the students with a striking address on Ecclesiastical Ambition. If I were to continue this minute diary of Princeton matters, I should lay myself open to the charge of writing the memoirs not of one man, but of many. I shall, however, from time to time fill gaps in the narrative in this way. In general it will be sufficient to mention only those incidents which have a direct bearing on the life of Mr. Alexander. The great Assembly of 1837 of course occupied all eyes, but its events need not be touched upon here. Mr. Alexander was not called upon to take sides one way or the other until the division occurred, at which time he went heart and hand with the Old School. As soon as he was able, the enfeebled scholar took a jaunt as far as Baltimore, and returned about the 20th, somewhat recruited. He spent the night with his brother, and the two chatted over the scenes of travel.

The northerly winds of the next day prepared the heavens for a clear sunset. Fires were cheerful, and news came of the Old School majority. The foliage was exuberant before the Spring went out, and by the 31st, Summer was fairly enthroned in the latitude of Princeton. It appears that Mr. Alexander was again absent from home; and he must have gone somewhere in the immediate vicinity of the Assembly, probably to Philadelphia, for on June 8, Thursday, his brother records in his journal:

* The Rev. William B. Sprague, D. D., of Albany, writes that he remembers Mr. Alexander as quite a small boy, when he himself was in the Seminary, in 1816; but he knew nothing of his remarkable powers till after Mr. Alexander had passed through college. "Dr. Addison Alexander" he continues, "was a man of so much mark, and in some respects stood perhaps so entirely alone, that it was hardly possible to move in any intellectual circle without having a definite idea of him. So often as I met with a Princeton student during the period of his Professorship, I was sure to hear the highest possible testimony rendered to his great talents and learning, and to his almost matchless facility at communicating knowledge."

"Addison writes to me every day. His letters keeps me informed of Assembly matters. It is expected that the New-School men will go to law. Some say sooner or later there must be a new Church, and that it will be called the American Presbyterian Church. What will ours be called? Whatever may result, our descendants will look back on the doings of the Assembly of 1837 as among the most momentous in our history."

A wonderful revival was going on at New Brunswick. Nearly seventy souls were indulging a good hope through grace of eternal life. Among the preachers were the Rev. Messrs. Abeel, Jones, and the Rev. James W. Alexander. The work soon spread to Metuchen. In June, the Presbytery met at New Brunswick to take measures to extend the benefits of the awakening to other churches. The deep feeling continued for many weeks.

On the 24th of July Mr. Alexander writes amusingly to Mr. Hall, for Sir Thomas Browne, and makes fun of one of the Latin tenses.

PRINCETON, *July* 24, 1837.

"MY DEAR SIR:

"As I write in a hurry, I cannot do justice to your valuable letter, but must rush at once in *medias res*. If it is the new English edition of Sir Th. Browne that Whitham has, you would oblige me much by securing it for me. I am a little puzzled by your use of the praeterperfectum, when you say, "I have seen a copy of Lamartine." If this be not a melancholy reminiscence of some former vision gone forever, but a statement of what is still visible, I should be very glad to get, not the poems, but the travels.

"Yours sincerely,

"J. A. ALEXANDER."

The next letter contains a comical allusion to the Infant Library. The old manuscript was, like enough, something new and humorous.

PRINCETON, *August* 8, 1837

"MY DEAR SIR:

"I hope this will find you in recovered health. If any of the infinitesimal books are missing, they shall be forthcoming. I have just laid my hands upon an ancient MS., a fragment which I enclose without reading it over. If, by any process, you can render it available, in whole or in part, as material for your invaluable labours, no one will be more pleased or surprised than. Sir,

"Yours most, &c.,
"J. A. ALEXANDER."

The study fires were resumed in September; and the anticipations of Professor James Alexander were realized, when

"The crackling billets, flaming high
Shall send a gleam to every eye
Of happy inmates round the hearth,
Full of warm friendship and pure mirth.
Here let the hoary grandsire bask
And grandame ply the worsted task,
And hardy urchin frame his snare
And chubby girl her sports prepare,
While John with school-boy tone rehearse
The newest book in prose and verse."*

With the exception of the proper name, this is a true picture of one of the homes in Princeton. There were almost always young pupils in the house, and the daughters of friends or cousins often came in from abroad. These were happy days, days of sunshine and intellectual and religious improvement. The *aerugo animi* was unknown, and the hours flew like a shuttle.

The winter session of the college began on the ninth of November. There was a clerical meeting that day at Dr. Miller's. The topic before the Association was certain questions relating to the status of the coloured people.

This year Professor James Alexander brought out the essays of Charles Quill, which had a great run for a while. They were afterwards reprinted with the title of "The American Mechanic," and still later incorporated with a new series, under

---

* From an imaginative sketch by the Rev. J. W. Alexander, which was first printed in the Newark *Daily Advertiser*.

the style, "The American Mechanic and Working-Man." The author once told me that he knew most persons would set a higher value on his life of his father, but that he himself considered these essays the best thing he had ever done; though at that but a small contribution to our Presbyterian literature. The essays are terse and sprightly, and very instructive; with a fine flavour of the Bible and of the Latin and English classics.

The letter which is subjoined, asks an important question in the interests of the Repertory:

"PRINCETON, *December* 1, 1837.
" MY DEAR SIR:
"I write in haste, at the request of Dr. Hodge, to beg your aid in an important matter. As you are in the habit of reading many journals, can you state, for the benefit of an "Association of Gentlemen," whether the doctrine of the Oxford Tracts, the new form of Church of Englandism, has been distinctly endorsed or adopted by any of the Episcopal papers in this country. If you could refer to documents and vouchers, *tant mieux;* but even your ipse-dixit will be worth a great deal. Dr. H. is also anxious to obtain a sermon on Tradition, by Henry M. Mason. Perhaps you could procure it for him. I hope to let you hear from me soon in a less troublesome manner.
"With the highest consideration, &c., &c.,
"JOS. ADDISON ALEXANDER."

" MY DEAR SIR:
" I observe that my last contributions to the Journal were clothed in an editorial dress. This is more agreeable to my taste as well as flattering to my vanity. My only misgiving is, that many of the scraps I send you are repeated sometimes in my lectures to the students, and might perhaps be recognized, if rendered too conspicuous. I begin however to be sick of series; and to think that even scraps lose much of their intrinsic value by conglomeration. I send you a few paragraphs from a work of Baxter, which is very little read. I have no objection to your making any of them 'leaders,' if you wish.

"Mr. Whiting of Jerusalem writes to my father, that a number of American and English people are now in the Holy Land, waiting for the Second Advent; having been much encouraged by the earthquake of the first of January.

"Do you suppose it possible to get any Portuguese books in Philadelphia? I should like very much to obtain a Grammar, Dictionary, and Lusiad. Yours,

"J. A. A."

A few letters to one of his little pupils are now given to show how pleasant he was in his relations to them. The politeness of these communications is remarkable. It was not his nature to be intentionally rude. He was gracious and courteous to the smallest child. Sometimes indeed, like most other schoolmasters, he spoke short to them, but he did it for their good.

The first of these letters from which I take extracts is dated October 28. In it he says, in allusion to a playful discussion they had together as to comparative merits of the two great cities:

"October 28, 1837.
"Dear J. :
"I shall not try to defend poor New York any longer, but allow you to prefer Philadelphia henceforth and forever. You know, indeed, a little more about New York than I do; as I never visited the theatre, and hope I never shall. You forgot to mention which of the Museums you had seen; and I am quite surprised that you say nothing about Broadway, the Battery, or the City Hall. Perhaps you do not look upon the fine bay as belonging to the city; or you would hardly have omitted to express your admiration of that splendid sheet of water, which is said to be unrivalled in the world for beauty except by the Bay of Naples.
"Yours affectionately,
"J. A. Alexander."
"If you find any difficulty in reading my letter, please to let me know, and I will try to write a little better."

The next is an essay on the secret of true happiness, and though written for a boy, is richly worthy of perusal at the hands of grown up men and women.

"December 19, 1837.
"Dear J. :
"Your question is an interesting and important one. I must first tell you what does not constitute the happiness of man. I suppose you

know by your own experience that peevishness, and ill-humour, and angry passions do not constitute happiness. You must know too, that eating, drinking, or riding cannot make you happy; you would not be willing to eat, drink, play, or ride forever. I need not tell you that sleep and idleness would not make you happy. And do you think that money ever made a person happy? Some of the most miserable wretches in the world have been immensely rich. Perhaps you think that finery, fashion, and pleasure constitute the happiness of man. If you ever live to make the experiment (I pray that you may never make it) you will find to your sorrow that you were mistaken; and that none are more miserable in their hearts than some who seem most gay to others. The longer you live too, the more you will be convinced that people can be happy who have neither health, nor wealth, nor learning, nor amusements, nor distinctions. What makes these people happy? The only thing that can make *you* happy, even in the midst of all these pleasures in the world. I mean the favour of God. This, and nothing but this, constitutes the happiness of man. You may think it very far from pleasant to spend all your life in serving God; but if you think so, it is because you never tried it. A person born blind cannot understand how people should take pleasure in seeing sights; but if his eyes could be opened, he would understand it at once. That your eyes may be opened, my dear boy, to see and know what constitutes the happiness of man, is the desire and prayer of your affectionate friend,

"Jos. Addison Alexander."

The next is very kind and edifying:

" My Dear Boy :

"I have no right to scold you for doing what I do myself. I was about to begin my letter by finding fault with you for hastily writing 'I will try,' before 'Dear Sir'; but you see I have forgotten both the date and title. From this little circumstance we both may learn not to be too forward in condemning others, when we ourselves may be equally to blame. Much less, when we are more to blame. This is to quarrel with the mote in our brother's eye, when there is a beam in our own. 'Judge not that ye be not judged.' The question you propose gives me great pleasure. I trust you ask it not for form's sake merely, but because you really desire to know. The answer to it you must learn from the Bible; and I hope you will have grace to understand it rightly. Do you not know that you were born a sinner? That you need to be pardoned and cleansed, in order to be happy? You must feel this to be so; and you can never get what you thus need, but by God's favour. If you are pardoned and made holy and received into heaven, it will not be because you deserve it, or because you are so good; for by nature you are vile. It is a mere favour given to you by God, for the Saviour's sake; and if you are not willing to receive it as a favour you cannot receive it at all. Let the next question be—'Why did our Lord Jesus Christ live and die upon the earth?' Your last letter upon the whole, is as well written as the one before it; but I do not think it any better. Try to improve.

"I subscribe myself your faithful friend,

"J. A. ALEXANDER."

We now approach an epoch in the life of this quiet student. This was no less an event than the commencement of his *magnum opus*, at least if regard be had to its size, its fame, and its visible display of exact critical scholarship and almost incalculable stores of erudition. It was this book that gave him a name among the literati of Europe as well as America. At home it was spoken of everywhere. The world of letters rang with it. This never deprived the author of his masculine intrepidity of judgment, or one whit altered his serene modesty. He began the first actual writing upon his commentary on Isaiah on the 21st of June, 1836; as appears from the following extract from his day-book: "I began my notes on Isaiah and wrote on the first ten verses of chapter xlix." He commenced at this point because he had arrived at this place in the regular instructions to his class.

Even under the pressure of his gigantic exegetical labours he could not put aside the disposition to learn new languages. During this year he acquired the Polish; having an educated native as his instructor. It was always his custom to obtain what living guidance he could in his linguistic efforts. His principal studies during this year were connected with his commentary on Isaiah. Besides attending upon his regular classes in the Seminary, he was also engaged in instructing private classes in Arabic and Hebrew. These private classes were a great delight and refreshment to him. The men who composed them were never forgotten, and were some of them always greatly admired. One or two of them became professors and commentators themselves. Others, following just as strictly in the path marked out for them by the footsteps of their teacher, became themselves teachers of Hebrew and Oriental literature. This indirect influence of Mr. Alexander in moulding and giving purpose to the best minds in his various classes, can never be estimated.

His journals at this point consist chiefly of rough notes on Isaiah. He continued his Commentary, the study of the Polish; Malay and Chinese languages; and besides hearing the recitations of his private classes in Arabic, he gave instruction to several boys, whose habit it was to frequent his study, and after school hours to laugh and wonder at his stories. The multitude, difficulty, complexity and total mass of his studies at this period, will never cease to excite a surprise that borders upon unbelief. Nothing could be more utterly astonishing, unless it were the gaiety, the ease, the smiling unconsciousness of hardship with which the whole was accomplished.

He wrote some verses and sent them off this year to the Sunday School Journal, then edited by his friend Mr. Hall, which have since become widely and justly celebrated. They were the famous lines on the "Doomed Man." He wrote them very rapidly (one night, I think), put them in the post-box, and thought no more of them; indeed almost forgot them. He was afterwards inundated with letters asking for copies; making pertinent and impertinent inquiries; and crammed with undisguised compliments. One of these letters I once heard read aloud, and it was truly preposterous. The thing came to such a pass at length, that the distressed author one day remarked he had begun to think he was himself the doomed man. The stanzas which were so much admired, have been thought to be awfully solemn and impressive; and are certainly written with a terrible energy of diction.

The Saxon brevity of the words; and the terse antithetical point that is reached by the conception and arrangement of the successive clauses; and the wild, dirge-like cadence of the rhythm; it would no doubt be hard to equal. The lines had a great run. The papers got hold of them, and they have been circulating ever since. Many preachers have recited them at the close of sermons, and often with visible effect. They are included in at least one collection of hymns, a large volume put forth by the Baptists; and it is believed have been the means of awakening many souls. They have sometimes been attributed to Dr. James W. Alexander. They have often been reproduced in a mutilated form. Some time after their original appearance in the Sunday School Journal, they were handsomely reprinted on large square sheets of paper with broad margins. Dr. Rice, of Mobile, is my voucher for the averment that this was done by the New York minister. They were certainly reprinted by him in his little volume entitled Revival Tracts, in which he says erroneously that this was the first time they had been published with the author's consent. Dr. Rice, however, speaks of a conversation he had with the elder brother in New York, when the latter lived in White street, at the time of the appearance of the sheets before spoken of, in which the city clergyman told him that he had taken the verses from a drawer in his brother's table and had them struck off without the author's knowledge or express approval; and the Mobile editor points to a passage in the Familiar Letters of Dr. James Alexander, where the writer says that if Dr. Hall had not asserted and proved the fact of an earlier publication, viz., in the S. S. Journal, he could not have been easily persuaded that the lines had not had a quite different introduction to the public. It is obviously possible, (aside from Dr. Rice's evidence,) that Dr. James Alexander may have stated to Dr. Rice, through some lapse of memory, what Dr. Rice has affirmed to be his recollection of his words. It is equally possible that the memory of Dr. Rice himself may have swerved a little from the exact truth. The piece as originally written contained an additional verse, which is given with the editor's note of explanation in the Familiar Letters.

* See Fam. Let., vol. ii, p. 285, foot-note to letter of March 4, 1859.

I have been favoured by Dr. Hall with a sight of the proof-sheet for the Journal containing this stanza crossed out in red pencil marks, with the printer's well-known *theta* in the margin, also in red pencil. The stanza was omitted without any hesitation, upon the editor's saying that in his opinion it was "too horrible." The prevailing reason for striking it out may have been the simple fact that objection had been taken to it. Whether "too horrible" or not, the stanza would unquestionably have detracted a little from the singular merit of the poem. These lines are so well-known that it is not necessary to insert them here.

On the 29th of December, he wrote to his Trenton friend, advocating the printing of bibles giving the exact words of all the parallel passages, instead of mere references.* I make a single extract:

"It has been said already, that one principal objection to the usual method, is the number of irrelevant and mere verbal parallels by which the learner is perplexed without the possibility of choice among them, until after an actual reference to all. And one main end of the proposed reform, is to save time and labour by winnowing the margins of our bibles and commentaries; a process which will certainly reduce the bulk of matter to a much more reasonable compass. In short, the plan which I propose is this, that parallel texts which are really illustrative of any given passage be selected by an experienced hand, and printed at length. To perfect the arrangement, there might be a class of less important parallels (but none irrelevant) printed apart, for the benefit of those who are willing to pursue the matter further. None but those who have spent much time in the study of commentaries, knows to what extent the multitude of references would be thus reduced, and how much time and trouble would be saved to the poor learner. To others, the true state of the case can be made evident in no way but by specimens."

The next letter shows that he was at this time pursuing four distinct courses of exegetical study, and lecturing on

---

* The thing here proposed, as is well known, has since been carried out at the suggestion and by the labours of others.

each topic to the class. He excuses himself from writing in the S. S. Journal, thanks his correspondent for civilities, asks for more writing paper, and threatens a visit to Philadelphia.

"PRINCETON, *Dec.* 15, 1837.

"MY DEAR SIR

"I have, rather imprudently perhaps, undertaken four distinct courses of exegetical instruction in the Seminary, all of which require attention, and two of them laborious study. I hope this will induce you to excuse my repeated breach of promise as to journalizing for you. Please to consider yourself thanked by the anonyme for your late communication. I send the stray pamphlets and regret the error. I shall count it a privilege to obtain letter paper at all similar to this. My excuses above are not designed to blast all hopes of aid, but only to prevent impatience at the delay of my precious contributions. I hope to do something yet before February, in which month I anticipate the pleasure of a personal interview ; and in the meantime,

"Am yours,

"JOS. ADDISON ALEXANDER."

In the undated communication given below, he begs in his usual serio-comic strain for Wettenhall's Greek Grammar and the Family Cabinet Atlas.

"MY DEAR SIR:

"Do you think it would be possible to find in Philadelphia, two copies of Wettenhall's Greek Grammar (in Latin), either the English or American edition ? If you should learn the existence of such phenomena, whether at first or second hand, I would thank you to secure them for my benefit. I likewise wish to get two copies of the Family Cabinet Atlas. By picking them up and sending them by the first occasion, with a memorandum of the price, you will much oblige

"Your most obedient servant,

"J. A. ALEXANDER."

"Mr. J. HALL."

The letters of this period to Dr. Hall would be enough of themselves to convince the sourest skeptic that the writer of them was a man of versatility, kindliness, humour, true politeness of heart, and heavy intellectual labours. It would add to this impression if I could recover reams of paper now burnt up. The recollections of survivors are now my only resource.

The studies in Isaiah, and those bearing upon collateral subjects, were carried on again in 1838. His private class in Hebrew was resumed and continued. His class duties in the Seminary were performed with exemplary zeal and patience. The year is marked by his entrance on the distinctive work of a preacher. He was received as a candidate under the care of the Presbytery of New Brunswick, in February, and during the month of April was licensed as a probationer for the Gospel ministry. His first efforts in the pulpit were anxiously expected, and were accepted with applause, as tokens of a noble career as an expounder of Scripture, and as an orator apt to teach, and to win souls. The most intellectual were charmed, the most frivolous were awed and arrested, the most simple were instructed in the mysteries of the kingdom. This year is also signalized by his connection with the Princeton Review, of which he now became an associate editor. The light now broadens for a while upon his path, owing to the comparative fulness of the journal.

He was visited on the morning of January the 1st, by a Mr. Burgess, who was then supplying the place of Dr. Robinson, in the Union Seminary of New York. At 11 o'clock he heard Dr. Rice preach on the duty of praying for a reign of righteousness. In the evening he attended the monthly concert of prayer in the Seminary. As a sample of his method of preparation and instruction at this time, I insert what follows. No one can fail to be struck with the conscientious thoroughness and diligence such statements imply, and the power of rapid and consecutive reading which they betray.

"January 2d.—I examined my private class on the book of Nahum. In preparing for my lectures to this class, I have read every word of the Septuagint, Targum, Peschito and Vulgate; a great part of Jerome's commentary; every word of Jarchi, Kimchi, and Aben-Ezra;

every word of Grotius, and in Pool's synopsis, J. D. Michaelis, Rosenmüller, and the Comprehensive Commentary. This course of reading, though laborious, has been highly satisfactory; the rather as I have secured, in black and white, the results for future use."

It is somewhat amusing to consider the force of the word "laborious" in such a connection. The thing so described would probably have broken the back of any other man on this side of Germany.

Here is something about the Princeton savans:

"January 3d.—Attended the conversazione at Professor Henry's. Mr. Stephen Alexander gave an account of the solar eclipse which is to take place in September, illustrated by drawings, and a map of the United States, drawn by Professor Henry on a very large scale. I wish very much to have such a map or maps, for the illustration of my lectures on Biblical Geography; and Mr. Henry has kindly offered to superintend the preparation of one for me."

It appears from a record in another volume, that he was now making some bold and singular experiments with his class in the Seminary. Among others was the plan of giving out Hebrew words and phrases to be taken down at his dictation. The results of these trials are given in the subjoined extract from his journal. He got his cue from Germany.

As this entry lets us into the secret of much of his thinking on the whole subject of lecturing and questioning a class, I may as well bring in just here a few words by one of his pupils Professor Andrew D. Hepburn of Miami University, in reference to this matter: though belonging to a much later period they come in properly at this point. After many pages of unqualified, though discriminating eulogy, he goes on as follows:

"While superior to any man I ever heard as a lecturer, I think Dr. A. failed in another part of the work of the class-room; in his questioning on the lectures. The questions were always clear and sharp; it was impossible to misunderstand them, but they were rigidly confined to what had been said in the lecture. He allowed no digression; he demanded only what had been said. He never made, so far as I recollect, any explanations in the hour devoted to questioning. He never allowed another to put questions to him in the class-room. He once told us, that those who had questions to ask could write them and place them on the desk, and he would answer them at the next meeting; but that he could not answer extempore. I do not know why he adopted this method of requiring the bare repetition of what he had communicated. That he had some definite principle I do not doubt; for more than most of our professors, had he made the subject of methods of education a matter of study."

It will be seen from the record now to be given, that Mr. Alexander's methods were indeed a matter of deep and sagacious study with him, and that at one time he permitted extemporaneous questions to be put to him by members of the class.

The opinion expressed as to the failure of the teacher as a catechist will not be concurred in by all his pupils. Of course I shall not presume to decide such a point The account given of his manner of questioning is undoubtedly correct. In addition it may be said that a series of questions, having almost precisely the same purport would be fairly hailed at a silent student. The object of these questions which were all as simple as possible, was to draw out from the lips of the embarrassed student a single sentence giving part of the substance of the lecture he had heard at the previous recitation.

"January 6.—I adopted a new method in my Hebrew recitations. Instead of making the class read the whole of the lesson, which is very tedious to them and to me, I merely ask questions on the different parts. I am pleased with the experiment. I had previously adopted the European method of lecturing at one recitation on the part to be recited at the next; and am convinced, now, that it is the true method of imparting the most knowledge in a given time. I was formerly, prejudiced against it, as a plan adopted merely to save labour and make superficial scholars. In this I was first shaken by my visit to the German Universities, which made me ask myself, how is it that this method of instruction is adhered to in a country principally noted for its love of change? If anything could have been gained by innovation the Germans would have tried it. I have now removed my doubts by fair experiment, and am persuaded that, even in elementary instruction this plan is the best. As for the usual objection to it, that it enables the indolent to dispense with study, and deprives the studious of the advantages which flow from independent intellectual effort; it is founded on a mere mistake. The only effect of this sort, is, to elevate the standard of acquisition by sparing the necessity of hunting after some things, and thus leaving time for the mastering of others. But the great argument in favor of the method is to my mind, this: that it enables the teacher to direct the student's mind as to what he ought to study. The student of the Bible, for example, needs to be informed by one who knows what are the real difficulties of a passage; not one in ten of which might possibly suggest themselves. When there are different opinions to be weighed, he needs a brief, clear statement of them, and at least an outline of the reasons pro and con. These he can digest and compare in private study; and his intellectual acts will thus become more elevated and salutary in proportion to the variety and complexity of their objects: always provided that the latter are not too various and complex for his time or strength; which of course must be left to the discretion of the teacher, and is one of his most interesting and important duties. These statements might, indeed, be made after the student has prepared his lesson; but the result of my experience is that they are then too late. After toiling through a task in which he feels no interest, because he does not know the interesting points of it, he is apt to regard all further illustration as surplusage; as something added to a thing of which he has already had enough. When, on the other hand, explanatory statements are made before he enters on the careful study of the lesson, his attention is awakened by the hope of valuable aid, and the fear of losing something which he ought to get keeps his attention steady. Then when he retires to private study, what he studies has at least some interest made from having been, the subject of public remark; and when he comes to recite, he comes with at least a curiosity to know how others have succeeded; and however negligent in private, what he has already heard in public renders him competent in some degree to judge his fellows. All this tends to make the exercises interesting, which if not a *causa quâ*, is a *causa sine qua non* of all improvement. The effects which I have described, are not suggested by imagination. They are rather at variance with my former fancies, and are the products of my own experiment. I began the new method at the opening of the session, with the 2nd class in studying Isaiah. My plan with former classes has been to assign a lesson and to hear the whole of it read, translated, and grammatically analyzed. The effect has been that while a few men, who would make progress under any method, have pursued the study both with pleasure and advantage, the greater number have been listless, and learned nothing in the lecture-room beyond what they acquired in their rooms. Under the new method things are wholly changed. The class, by no means a superior one in intellect or zeal for knowledge, seem now, with scarcely an exception, to be deeply interested in the study; and the most of them take copious notes, spontaneously of course, at each lecture. At the same time, those who would have done well in the other case, appear to make still greater progress; so that I am greatly encouraged in my labours."

"The next step was to introduce the method in my private classes, and with like success. I had no thought of trying the experiment with those who are beginning to read Hebrew, until very lately. I had, indeed, determined long ago, to introduce the practice of writing more; and with that view had the lecture-room refitted with conveniences for writing, and required the new class from the beginning to write at my dictation the first outlines of the grammar. For this purpose they learned to form the characters as soon as they learned to read them; and a number of the class can now write Hebrew words with great facility—all, I believe, except some one or two, with tolerable correctness. In order to maintain this habit, I continue to propound short sentences once a week to be translated into Hebrew; and have been surprised not only with the execution, but also with the interest taken in the exercise, which is wholly voluntary. I had supposed, however, that the old plan of reading Hebrew would be necessary, at least for the present session; but the contrast between these dull recitations and my exercises with the other classes, led me to another experiment, viz.: that of explaining beforehand the more difficult points in the passage to be read, and directing attention not only to grammatical, but also to exegetical questions connected with the lesson. In order to gain time for this, I mean to catechise the class on those points which are really difficult, and let the others go, except so far as they are brought up by the questions which the students are allowed to ask. To-day, after examining several on the first eight verses of the 8th chapter of Genesis, I lectured colloquially on the eight which follow. Besides mere grammatical phenomena, I touched upon the two words rendered *generations*, in v. 9, and the difference in their meaning; the true sense of *righteous* and *perfect*, as applied to Noah; the use of the words *flesh* and *way*, in v. 12; the meaning of *the end of all flesh is come before me;* the materials of the ark and its dimensions; and the meaning of the word translated *window*, in v. 16."

The next lets the reader still more fully into his plans, and enables him to comprehend the scale on which the young professor was projecting the future.

"January 9.—At 10 o'clock I met my private class. Having finished Nahum, I began to-day to lecture on the twelve Psalms of Asaph. These Psalms I propose to study no less thoroughly than Nahum. The books which I expect to read upon the subject are: the four chief ancient versions; the three Rabbins, Jarchi, Kimchi and Aben-Ezra; Calvin, Cocceius, Pool's Synopsis, Grotius, J. H. Michaelis, De Wette, Rosenmüller, Klauss, Stier, Ewald. I devote much time to these private classes, not for their sakes merely, but for my own improvement, which is sensibly promoted by the stimulus of teaching. What I learn in this way will be also available in teaching future classes, whether in public or private."

The next day he made this entry:

"January 10.—Read Genesis xxv. xxvi. xxvii. and Matthew xiii. in course. I have for several years read the Old Testament once, and the New Testament twice in twelve months; according to a calendar of my own invention. My rule is to read four chapters of the New Testament every Sunday, and one of the New Testament with three of the old every other day, besides Sunday. To bring the numbers out exactly even, I divide the 119th Psalm into eleven portions."

The next entry has reference to his studies in modern Greek.

"I read to-day a number of colloquial Greek phrases with my friend Constantine Menaios, an Athenian and a member of our college, with whom I have read, talked and written Greek since the beginning of the session. Besides the assistance which he gives me in the language, he is highly intelligent and well-informed in everything relating to his country. The January number of the Princeton Review is through the press at last. Since it was put to press, Mr. Dod has consented to become the editor, conjointly with myself. To this condition I have agreed for the purpose of obtaining his services for the work. I have written for the present number a desultory article on Melanchthon's Letters, and a few short notices of books and pamphlets, one or two of which will be thought ungracious, and perhaps they are."

The following record shows what he was doing with his private class:

"January 12.—Lectured on the eighth and ninth chapters of Leviticus to my private class, consisting of George Hale, Melancthon W. Jacobus, Jacob W. E. Ker, and Daniel Stewart. These men are the flower of our senior class in relation to Biblical Philology. I meet them every Friday morning. I am at present reading what I wrote upon Leviticus when teaching a private class two years ago."

The secluded student did not forget to think of the poor and houseless, and few were more liberal even to the most worthless beggars. On January the 13th he wrote these words:

"A most enchanting day: while the ground is frozen hard and the walking therefore good, the sky is clear, the sun bright, and the air like that of May—an Italian winter. What a mercy to the poor in these hard times!"

He sometimes thought of writing again in metre; but soon abandoned the idea. The most beautiful of Mr. Alexander's verses are on themes connected with or immediately drawn from the Bible. His favourite themes were those which combined a sacred, a biographical, and a dramatic interest. Such a theme he had found in "Esau," and such a theme he now thought he saw in Judas.

"January 13.—I have some thought of trying my hand at a dramatic poem to be called 'Iscariot,' correcting some popular mistakes as to the character of Judas, and presenting it, poetically, in a juster light. I have little time for such employments, but it might do good, and by printing the thing in the Literary Messenger I might pay my debt to the conductor for the last two volumes, which he wishes to be paid for not in money but in writing."

The diary of home events is then resumed.

"Mr. Dod brought from New York several books for our review.

Into my hands he put Roberts' Visit to Muscat, &c.; for J. W. A. he brought Gardiner's Music of Nature; for Dr. Miller, Henry's Christian Antiquities; for himself, something on Phrenology.

Here is a specimen of the exegetical writings that crowd his journals of almost every year.

"January 14, (Lord's day.)—I have always been accustomed to suppose that vs. 6 and 10 of Matthew xviii. related literally to children. On reading the chapter to-day I am inclined to think that *little ones* in these two verses means humble Christians, in reference to the expression παιδίον τοιοῦτον which is again to be explained by the comparison in v. 3 and 4. 2nd, A true Christian must in this respect be a little child: whoever receives such a little child as a true Christian receiveth me: whoso shall offend such a *child* is a child in this sense, i. e. an humble Christian."

Here is his account of a sermon:

"Heard my father preach from Isaiah xlii. 16. His design was to show that actual conversion is a very different thing from what the subjects of it previously expect. He mentioned among other particulars, that a soul when under true conviction seems to itself to be growing worse and worse; which is graciously so ordered to preserve it from self-complacency: which is also true with respect to pungent feelings, which the awakened soul desires without obtaining. In like manner men expect their exercises after conversion to be something supernatural, and wholly unlike what they had before; whereas they find them to arise as naturally as their former thoughts. He related in the sermon two cases illustrative of the slight occasions of conversion; one was that of a person who being disappointed in his expectation of going to a distant church, walked out with Doddridge's Rise and Progress in his hand, to read alone. During that walk, as he ever afterwards believed, he underwent a saving change; the reality of which was attested by the piety of fifty or sixty years. The other case was that of an Irishman (Jno. Ross, I believe) who had been brought up strictly a Roman Catholic, and never heard Protestant preaching till he made his escape from a British man-of-war, into which he was impressed during the blockade of New London, and passing through the town went into a place of worship, was awakened and converted, and became a student in the Seminary here. Looked at a little book just published proposing a new order of missionaries: viz. intinerant preaching physicians—and a peculiar course of education for them, and substituting medicine for the dead languages. The substance of the volume might have been put into a dozen pages; but the thoughts are good. We are too much disposed to overlook the fact that the way of the gospel was prepared at first by miracles of healing, which opened the people's hearts and made them willing to hear the truth. The same effect in kind has followed from the exercise of medical skill among the heathen."

The brothers sometimes hit upon the same solution of a difficulty. Here is an example, "The same interpretation of Matthew xviii. 10, which I have suggested on page 20, occurred to James in reading the chapter two days ago, but I find to-night that it is given by Beza and other old writers." The journal of the day proceeds as follows:

"Received the 28th Annual Report of the American Board of Commissioners for Foreign Missions. The January number of the Princeton *Review* has at length appeared. A great improvement in appearance on the former volumes. The paper is large and white, and the cover much more sightly. This last change is owing in a great measure to the decision and industry of the new editor, who plagued the printer till the object was accomplished, after much experiment. I think the number a fair, readable number. It contains an article on Melancthon's early Letters, by myself; one on Pastoral attention to Children, by Dr. Miller; one on Expository Preaching, by James W. Alexander; one on Incidents of Travel, by Dr. Alexander; one on the Oxford Tracts, by Dr. Hodge; one on The Physical Theory of Another Life, by Mr. Yeomans of Trenton; and one on the South Sea Islands, by Mr. Dod. I also wrote the notices inserted in the quarterly list of books and pamphlets at the end of the number; as many more were excluded for want of room. We were anxious to begin the list in this number, even on a contracted scale, to show that it would hereafter form a regular part of the work. I have now to commence my preparations for reviewing Roberts on Cochin China and Muscat. I have never been kept so busy within my recollection. I have reason to be thankful that my business is at once so agreeable and useful, whether in public or private."

The following letter to Dr. Hall is undated, but certainly belongs to this year. The same cover embraces a translation of a Greek prayer, and extracts from Rutherford and Leighton, of whom the latter especially was a favourite writer with him. He criticized his behaviour in ecclesiastical matters with impartial severity. I have heard him say of the former that he did not please him as a writer half so much as old Boston. This was one of the points on which Mr. Alexander differed from his brother James, who hung over Rutherford's letters with an unfading delight. The brothers agreed in admiring the great learning and singular piety of both. The exegetical remark next made is worthy of attention. The letter itself contains an interesting fact with regard to Makemic.

"My Dear Sir:

"As my day-book is still in your hands, I believe I will trouble you to get a third bound to match it. I am making extensive inroads on the first already. I will thank you to buy Millington* when it appears. I learn from James that Mr. Packard had said something to him as to our not noticing the Dictionary. Did, or did I not explain to you that I had actually written a short notice—nay, that it was in type and had been read in proof, but was excluded in consequence of my co-editor, who knew nothing of it, having given the printer something to be put before it? I knew nothing of the error till the sheet was printed off. I have been reading Spencer's Letters. He says Makemie, the first Presbyterian minister in America, left his library to your church. Have they it now, and does it include the pamphlet on Lord Cornbury's persecution? I would come to Philadelphia to see it.

"William hastens me.

"Yours truly,

"J. A. A."

He drank tea on the 17th at his brother's, where he met the Rev. Oscar Harris, originally of Goshen, N. Y., a pupil of Dr. Fisk's, and a graduate of Williams college. They went together to Dr. Miller's to attend the Philosophical. There they fell in with the Rev. David Magie, of Elizabethtown, and Wm. B. Kinney, Esq., of Newark, and Dr. Carnahan, Dr. Rice, Prof. Dod, Prof. S. Alexander, Principal Hart, Tutor Cooley, Dr. George M. Maclean, and their venerable host, Dr. Miller him-

* Millington on Engineering.

self. Messrs. Maclean, Dod, Kinney, and Magie had just come from the Common School Convention; " which " writes the enemy of all conventions, in his " Day-Book," " seems to have been a very interesting meeting. It was resolved to petition the Legislature for the existing School Law, and the appointment of a minister of public instruction. Speeches were made last night by Mr. Frelinghuysen, Mr. Aaron of Burlington and others."

It is evident that the free and easy conversation at these re-unions pleased him; and though he may have been often a silent member of the club, he never failed to pick up and carry off with him something in the way of knowledge or mental stimulus. In his regular journal I find the following record of this meeting

"January 17.—Went to the Literary and Philosophical meeting at Dr. Miller's. After prayer by Dr. Carnahan, Mr. Dod suggested as a theme for conversation, the expediency of forming a New Jersey Historical Society. Several facts were stated in illustration of the fact that what is done must be done quickly. Mr. Kinney said that certain ancient records of the town of Newark, which he had examined some years ago, had now disappeared. Dr. Miller stated that a chest full of Gen. Morgan's papers had been found in Mr. Teneyke's barn, some years ago, broke open and the papers scattered. J. W. Alexander referred to the case of Dr. Minto's papers, which he and I had examined some years since, and out of which I formed a sketch of his biography and printed it in some petty Philadelphia paper. [Afterwards reprinted in the Princeton Magazine.] To show that original documents may yet be recovered, Mr. Kinney stated that the original grant of West Jersey to Wm. Penn and others, had been recently recovered by the State, through Mr. John R. Brown, to whom it was forwarded from Harrisburg, among some ancient papers relating to a suit in chancery; and that the original deed for the land on which Newark stands was lately brought to light from some obscure place in the country. Mr. Hart observed that in the Morford family there is the history of an ancient Princeton family, called Fitz Randolph, who owned the ground on which the College stands. Dr. Maclean stated that the two old ladies who nursed Gen. Mercer are still living in this neighborhood. Vice President Maclean informed us that Gen. Mercer was not buried here; that he died in Philadelphia. Mr. Magie also gave an entertaining account of an old woman whom he travelled with from Somerville to Elizabethtown, in whose father's house Gen. Washington lived, at Morristown. This old gentlewoman bore witness to the General's communing in the Presbyterian church there, and to his habit of daily prayer. This led to a discussion as to Washington's character, Dr. Miller doubting his piety, and J. W. A. and Mr. Magie suggesting that the way in which he died might be explained from his habitual reserve, and Mr. Dod affirming that the general opinion as to Washington's virtues, even if erroneous, was better than the truth. Dr. Miller related an interesting anecdote received from Dr. Barton, the amount of which was, that when Washington left home to take command of the Continental Army, he charged his nephew, Lund, to be hospitable, kind, and take care of his affairs. but not to trust any man, for no man can be trusted."

Afterwards he had some conversation with Dr. Carnahan about Aaron Burr, and the life of him by Davis, " which we wish him to review." He adds, " Mr. Hart has Tyndale's New Testament in his hands for the same purpose."

" A curious incident: four or five years ago, John Hart imported from Europe Baxter's works, in twenty-odd volumes. One volume was missing, and he replaced it by another [order], but with a volume which did not match the rest in binding. To-day the missing volume has appeared; brought by Mr. Harris from Mr. Jones in Brunswick, who found it in the hands of one of his parishioners, by whom (or some one else) it had been picked up in the streets of Princeton, soaked with rain; I bought the set from Hart last year."

I think it must have been at night after getting home from the Philosophical, that he penned what follows. It will be perceived that his mind was still excogitatiny plans of Bible study and instruction.

" January 17.—I have conceived a new plan for my biblical instructions, if the Lord should spare my life and keep me here. It is briefly this: to abandon the practice of reading scraps with the classes; and, in lieu thereof, lecture continuously on the whole Old Testament. The beginning class are now studying Genesis. After finishing that book, I propose to take up Exodus, and go as far as I can during the first year; after which I can pursue the course, in a more private way, with such of the class as may choose to attend. In this way I think I could expound the Pentateuch at least, and perhaps Joshua and Judges, before the class leave the Seminary. My object in this method would be, chiefly to compel myself to study the whole Bible critically in course, and to record the result of my researches. In order to attain this end as soon as possible, I might make the next new class begin with Ruth instead of Genesis, and the following class with Esther; and carry each forward, without any omission, to the end of the year. On this plan, with God's blessing, I believe that I might finish the historical books (Genesis—Esther) in three years, and possibly the whole in five. I shall never feel at home in Scripture till I have accomplished such a course, in the Old Testament at least, and possibly not till I despatch the New. *Quod felix faustumque sit!*

"January 21.—Read the Missionary Herald for 1822. I began to read the journals of our American Missionaries in order from the beginning several months ago, and have continued so to do at intervals. The connected view thus presented of a history so full of incident is deeply interesting. I wish I had time to read more regularly and constantly."

This course he continued till he had read and mastered the whole series. No one took more delight in missionary news, or complained more bitterly when the intelligence was meagre. He thought that with whole boundless continents their own, our gifted missionary writers might oftener get beyond the horn-book of the Sunday-schools.

"January 19.—Mr. Boyd asked my opinion of Roy's Hebrew Lexicon. I told him that the specimens which I had seen before the work was published were exceedingly absurd, but that I had not examined the book since." He continued the reading of Baxter's Christian Directory, which he had begun long before, and resumed at very irregular intervals. "His fervour, plainness, and directness," he records, "are inimitable." On the 21st, (Lord's Day) he drank tea with his brother James, who read him some passages from "Essays, Sermons, &c.," by Henry Woodward, a clergyman from Ireland, "characterized," as he testifies, "by piety, originality, sober wit, independence, and a charming style of vigorous simplicity." He hoped his brother would review it, for the sake of giving extracts. "One of the most important duties of the religious press, it seems to me, is that of bringing to the knowledge of our public truly valuable matter *ab extra*." He heard Dr. Rice preach from "They that are whole need not a physician, but they that are sick." "First letter from Malta (Missionary Herald, 1822, page 179) says, 'I write you in much haste, and you will not forget that I am only giving you a prima facie view of things here.' Would that he and other missionaries would continue to give prima facie views, instead of abridging road-books and geographies.

"January 22.—The Watchman of the South to-day contained an extract from Dr. Chalmers, addressed to his own students and advising them how to conduct their own studies. I was much pleased with the whole of it, but most with what he says about the critical study of the English Bible. I have myself been thinking of a lecture, speech, or article on that same subject, and may hatch it before long.*

"January 25.—One of the chief pleasures of exegetical study, when rightly conducted, is the gradual reduction of confusion into order, and the gradual dawn of day upon the darkness of the text."

"January 26.—Received a letter from Rev. John C. Brown, a grandson of Brown of Haddington, and now a missionary at St. Petersburg, who was here a few years since, and was then requested by my father to enquire whether Persian manuscripts could be procured there. He writes that the Rev. Mr. Glenn, Missionary in Persia, would gladly aid us in procuring anything of that kind, but requests me to send a list of what I want, and what I am willing to give, promising to submit it, if I choose, before he forwards it to Mr. Glenn, to Mirra Carim Bey, Adjunct Professor of languages (oriental) at St. Petersburg, and considered the most learned Persian in Europe. Such commissions have frequently been given, but seldom recollected after such a lapse of time, even by missionaries of our own church and country. I am therefore the more indebted to Mr. Brown's kindness. Received the Foreign Missionary Chronicle for February. It is now conducted on an excellent plan (that of the Church Missionary Register), giving a general view of Protestant Missions. The *Herald* has kept all missions but its own too much in the dark.

"January 27.—I have been reading lately a file of the 'Friend of India,' edited by John C. Marshman, son of the Baptist Missionary. He was educated in England; and was evidently connected with the public press there, probably as a reporter. This appears from that peculiar tact and style for which the regular English editors are so distinguished.

---

* Here we have the germ of the inaugural address.

The paper is a general one, not exclusively religious, and is not only conducted in an admirable spirit, but affords the best views of East India affairs that I have ever been able to obtain. I have read it with special reference to the controversy respecting the expediency of printing oriental books in Roman letters, on which subject I have some idea of writing a review.* The papers were lent to me by the Rev. John C. Lowrie." His notion of Dickens is given below:

"I read to-day some parts of the last volume of the Pickwick Club. The author I have long regarded as possessed of an original vein of humour, and an unrivalled talent for describing personal habits and appearance. He has ruined himself here by undertaking a continuous story. I think his original sketches by Boz equal to all the Pickwick Club together. Mr. Dod returned to-day from Philadelphia, bringing a new edition of Bentley's works, Upham's Mental Philosophy, and John Aug. Smith's Discourse against Materialism."

"January 29, Lord's day.—Heard Dr. Rice preach from Rev. ii, 25—against antinomianism. (1) What have Christians already? (2) How must they hold it fast? He suggested two interpretations which were new to me: one was, that when our Lord says that Abraham desired to see his day, and saw it, and was glad, he referred to the trial of Abraham's faith, (Gen. xxii); where the doctrine of vicarious atonement was taught by the substitution of the ram for Isaac. This thought suggested one to me, entirely different, viz. that this trial was intended to give some idea of God's love in sending his own Son to die for sinners. I must pursue both ideas at some other time. The other interpretation new to me, was that by our Lord's being glorified in his saints, and admired in his believers, we are to understand that the angels who attend him at his coming, unable to look upon the brightness of his glory, will admire it as reflected in his people. I have read the survey of Protestant Missions in the last two numbers of the Missionary Chronicle: it puts a new face upon the whole matter. Our American Missionaries, instead of being every thing, are but a fraction of this glorious unit. I am surprised at the accumulation of missionary effort in South Africa. There are representatives of the United Brethren, the London M. S., the Glasgow M. S., the Rhenish M. S., the French Protestant M. S., the American Board, the American Baptist Board, the Church Missionary Society, and the Wesleyan M. S. What a brilliant

---

* He afterwards wrote copiously on this subject. See article in the Princeton Repertory on Robinson's & Smith's Palestine.

constellation! There are three missionary families in as many ships, sent by our Presbyterian Board, now on the ocean and in need of prayer.

His method of exegetical study is thus recorded:

"Jan. 27. I have been studying Ps. lxxiii to-day, with the commentaries of De Wette, Rosenmüller, Klaus, and Ewald. This, I think has been the most delightful exegetical investigation I have made (I do not mean to-day's work only). I am now persuaded that I greatly erred in making it a rule to read a number of commentaries through consecutively; in consequence of which I felt no special interest in any part, and was scarcely able to distinguish the hard parts from the easy; and although I was glad to finish my task, the doing of it was more irksome than agreeable. In studying this Psalm I have pursued another method. I first read it carefully in English to obtain an impression of its import and arrangement, and observe what passages appeared obscure. I then compared the English with the Hebrew to determine how far the former seemed to need correction. By this time, one or two verses had begun to stand out from the rest as specially difficult and interesting (e. g. vv. 10 and 25), while others appeared so in a less degree, and the remainder seemed entirely plain. I then compared the four ancient versions—Greek, Latin, Chaldee, Syriac: first on the more, then on the less, perplexing passages; during which process several new modes of explication started into view. I then read Calvin and Cocceius on the same parts; then De Wette and Rosenmüller; then Klaus and Ewald. Before I finished this course, I felt a curiosity and interest almost intense with respect to the meaning of the obscure parts, which feeling effectually precluded that of weariness. I believe that I have also been too much in the habit of writing while actually studying a passage. This not only broke the train of thought, but kept me uneasy through the fear of losing something which I ought to note down. On the other hand, I find that my memory commonly retains every suggestion worth remembering, and when I have to look back for something I forget, the repeated reference is really an advantage."

The Presbytery of New Brunswick met on Tuesday, the 7th of February. The Rev. Mr. Comfort, of Kingston, preached the sermon. There was a large attendance. The event of interest was the reception of Mr. Alexander under the care of Presbytery, after an examination *pro formâ*. The adjournment was to the second Tuesday in August; the meeting to be at New

Brunswick. The tidings from every quarter were of awakenings and revivals. Philadelphia, New-York, Pennington, and other places, were much stirred. The *conversazione* on the 14th was at Professor Stephen Alexander's. The sound of sleighbells might be heard late at night, and the merry ring of laughter from the young people who were pleasure-taking.

Mr. Alexander thus refers to his own connection with the Presbytery:

"February 7. This day I was received under the care of the New Brunswick Presbytery as a candidate for license. Quod felix faustumque sit! Sine te, Domine, nil possum! This is the first step toward the execution of a purpose which I formed eight years ago." *

The same day Dr. Yeomans called upon him to borrow a number of the Christian Baptist Review, intending to write on the Bible translation controversy, about which he and Mr. Alexander had some talk.

Here is a continuation of the journal:

"Feb. 11. Dr. Miller brought me an article which he has written for the Review, on Henry's Christian Antiquities, which I am to revise and complete in some way.

"Feb. 15. The exercises of the Seminary recommenced. I have been busy all day preparing articles for the Review. Finished the article on Christian Antiquities, and continued my own on Nordheimer's Grammar.

"Feb. 17. I finished a review of the first part of Nordheimer's Hebrew Grammar and laid it aside until I get the rest.

"Feb. 22. This being the day set apart for prayer in behalf of Colleges, Dr. Miller preached a sermon in the church from Job ii, 4, 5. Chiefly remarkable for a severe denunciation of those persons in the neighbourhood of Colleges, and particularly here, who for the sake of gain encourage the students in vice, and even tempt them to it. Attended a prayer-meeting in the church at night; Dr. Rice made an address.

"Feb. 24. Received an article from Mr. Dod on India as a missionary field, by John C. Lowrie, lately a missionary to Lodiana. I sent

---

* And consequently while he was tutorial professor in the college, and not long after the time of his conversion.

some time ago for the remainder of Nordheimer's Hebrew Grammar, and yesterday it arrived by mail charged with four dollars postage. Finished my article 'On Naming Places,' and sent it to the Southern Literary Messenger. The first article of ten for the Princeton Review (next number) is in type; it is on Henry's Christian Antiquities: the second (on Roberts's Embassy) is also in the printer's hands: a third was received to-day (on India): and a fourth on Nordheimer's Hebrew Grammar; a fifth on Tyndall's New Testament; a sixth on Phrenology; a seventh on the Baptist Bible-translation controversy; and an eighth on the State of the Church, are nearly ready.

"Feb. 25. Heard my father preach from Psalm ii, 12. 'Blessed are all they that put their trust in him.' God oftentimes leaves his children to conflict with doubts and temptations all their lives, because spiritual comfort would betray them into self-complacency and spiritual pride. The reason we are unhappy even under a sense of sin is because we cannot trust. Finished the Missionary Herald for 1827. There is a pleasing alternation in the interest of the different missions. As the Sandwich Island Mission becomes settled and established, the Palestine Mission becomes highly interesting.

"Feb. 26. Received the remainder of Nordheimer's Grammar and completed my review."

Wednesday, the 28th of February, the Club met at Dr. George Maclean's. Mr. Alexander this day received a charming letter from the grammarian Nordheimer.

On the 4th of March, four English beggars were on the tramp through Princeton. If strollers called at the door of Mr. Addison Alexander, they were either eagerly admitted or else abruptly dismissed. Sometimes he invited them in of his own accord, and picked up much useful and amusing information from the wretched vagabonds. He was especially pleased if they were from continental Europe and spoke a foreign language. He was amused at their contradictory stories, and often imitated their incredible relations in his tales to children.* He kept at

* He used to tell a story about a wifeless and childless beggarman (whom he would personate) that had, together with his consort and offspring, passed through some surprising adventures; having been blown up in an earthquake, shipwrecked in a volcano, etc., etc. Compare this with Charles Lamb's closing words in his "Complaint of the Decay of Beggars."

one time a large volume in which he recorded their histories and imaginary escapes, and which he styled the "Book of Beggars." * At another time he kept a boy posted at the door with directions to slam it in their faces after giving them a few cents. In Ireland and among the Alps these creatures only tormented him, and he could hardly rid himself of their filthy company by talking Persian and Arabic at them and making impassive gestures which seemed to show that he was a traveller from some strange country and unacquainted with the tongues of the Continent or of Great Britain. A single extract from his journal will illustrate the way in which he derived information from wandering mendicants.

'Talked French to a Spanish priest from Mexico and gave him an alms. He gave me an account of the way in which he preached. He says that it is customary in Catholic countries to preach sermons out of printed books, and that another priest usually sits below the preacher and prompts him. Very few, he says, make sermons *de la tête*.'

The next record he makes seems to show plainly that he was making advances in the Divine life.

"March 11. I have experienced to-day a new religious impulse leading me to take delight in the reading of the Scriptures, in prayer, and in the ordinances of God's house, and dispelling the guilty gloom which has, for some time, brooded over me. The Lord preserve me from delusion! I have renewed my vows and here record the fact."

His studies went on pretty much in the usual way.

A few days after this, he finished Deuteronomy again, having read it in Hebrew, comparing the English version and De Wette's German. He has now, *i. e.* by the 14th, read the Pentateuch again in Hebrew since the beginning of the year.

The entries which follow may serve as examples of all.

"March 14, 1838. Attended the conversazione at Dr. Rice's; Present Drs. Miller, Rice, and Torrey; Professors Maclean, Dod, J. W. Alex-

* Doubtless with remembrance of the eccentric volume to which Luther condescended to write a preface or introduction.

ander, Henry, J. A. Alexander, S. Alexander; Tutor Cooley. Dr. Torrey exhibited some specimens of the metal magnesium, which he converted into magnesia by burning. The next meeting is to be at Professor Maclean's.

"March 20, 1838. Received as a present from the American Sunday School Union a copy of their new Bible Dictionary, elegantly bound. Received at the same time a number of English papers of December and January; saw a letter to my father from our former pupil, Professor S. B. Jones of Oakland College. Another old pupil of ours is now in Princeton, the Reverend Geo. Burrowes, of Port Deposit, Maryland, who graduated here in 1832, and was afterward a tutor in the College and a student in the Seminary. Received to-day a copy of a new book on the Limits of Human Responsibility, by Dr. Wayland.

"March 23. Finished the Book of Joshua again."

He then announces another change of programme:

"I have reluctantly determined to suspend my rule of scriptural reading by a calendar, and to adopt another method. I find that it is too much of a task at present, and that it does not answer any useful purpose, to read just so much without regard to the difficulty or importance of the passage. I propose to begin Romans and Judges, on the plan of reading everything attentively and more than once; the quantity to be determined by the time. If I do not like the method, I can return at any time to my calendar, which is made out to the end of the year.

"March 24. Drank tea and spent the evening with my brother. Looked at the new Nova Scotian *jeu d'esprit*—Sam Slick. It is much superior to Jack Downing; less exaggerated, and constructed for a definite moral purpose. It must be a great treat to John Bull. I have formed two new plans to-day. One is, to reduce my diet, both in quantity and quality; with a view to intellectual and moral effect. The other is, to suspend my commentary on Isaiah and write a popular analysis instead. This might excite an interest in the prophet and prepare the way for detailed exposition; though, in my opinion, analysis is three-fourths of the exposition wanted."

CHAPTER XIV

THE beginning of the career of such a preacher as the subject of this memoir is commonly admitted to have been, is an event that will be approached with a quickened interest on the part of the reader who is inquisitive as to the sources of the young minister's power. Great attention was of course paid to the rumour that Mr. Alexander, who though he had so long occupied one of the chairs of a school of theology had not yet entered the pulpit, was to be carried through the usual course of interrogations and formally authorized to preach that good news with his lips which he already published by his example. His diaries disclose the fact, that his own spiritual exercises in prospect of this crisis were profound and humble. The church court before which he expected to appear was holding its sessions but a few miles off, at Lawrenceville. He accordingly made no delay, but accepted the offer of Dr. Benjamin H. Rice and rode over to the little village where, after the preliminary trials, he was, on the 25th of April, duly licensed by the Presbytery of New Brunswick as a probationer for the Gospel Ministry. The following account of the proceedings is from his journal. It will be perused with gratification by such as desire to be minutely informed as to all the particulars relating to the affair, as it were from the lips of the person himself most deeply interested in the issue of the business.

On the 25th of April he records:

"Dr. Rice called for me with his carriage at 8 o'clock, and I went with him to Lawrence,* where we found the Presbytery sitting in Mr.

* A familiar abbreviation.

Hammill's schoolhouse. I then read my exegesis *De Sacrificiis*, my cri.ical exercise on Gen. xlix, 8-12, and my lecture on Micah iv, 1-5; and was examined on Theology by Mr. Perkins, on Church History by Dr. Rice, and on Church Government and the Sacraments by Dr. Miller. We then repaired to the church where I delivered my sermon on John iii, 36. Dr. Miller and Mr. Dod were in the pulpit with me. The latter read the hymns and made both prayers. We then descended from the pulpit. I answered the constitutional questions and was licensed."

This is the whole of the simple narrative. He has preserved his "Latin exegesis" (as it is absurdly called) in one of his manuscript books. There is nothing specially noticeable about it, except that it is short, and in a very different style from Turretin's.

The advent of the young preacher created a decided sensation among the ministers as well as the mass of ordinary hearers. The venerable President Green heartily said that he was "orthodox." Other dignified and famous clergymen, men who were not easily driven from their self-possession, were heard to echo this sentiment and to express themselves in the language of unbounded eulogy. In the midst of this commotion there was one at least who, though deeply interested in what was going on, was not at all excited and was as simple as a child in the expression of such feelings as he had. This was Dr. Archibald Alexander.

A member of the senior class of 1838, gives the following account of the manner in which the happy father received the news that his son had preached his first sermon.

"It was while I was at the Seminary that he was licensed to preach. The interest excited by his first sermon was very great, as you know, both in Princeton and in the cities. I happened to be in Dr. Alexander's parlour one Monday evening, after Addison had preached the day before for the first time in New-York, when a lady from New-York who had just arrived came into the room. She began at once to tell of Addison's preaching, and the great interest it had excited." The venerable Dr. Archibald Alexander was present, and was greatly animated by what he heard. These were tidings he had long wished and expected to hear about his son. No one had ever better gauged the young man's capacity. But he had doubts on one point: and that was his voice. He feared he could not be heard in a large church. How natural and affecting the picture that is brought before us by Dr. Ramsey!

"I well remember," he says, "how eagerly the good old man listened and enquired, and how delighted he seemed. 'Did he speak loud enough?' he asked, 'I was afraid Addison would not speak loud enough.'"

Dr. Ramsey continues that he himself always loved to hear him, and never heard him without profit.

"You know that everybody rejoiced to listen to him, that could appreciate God's truth declared, illustrated and enforced, by all that genius, learning, and simple, forcible, transparent diction, which in him were so remarkably combined. It seems to me you will not find it a very easy task to characterize his preaching. I could not do it. It was so endlessly varied. At one time, brilliant, dazzling, overwhelming; at another so plain as to be almost without an illustration, except of the simplest kind, yet deeply interesting; at another, severely exegetical so as to be, in the estimation of many, dry. Did he ever, do you suppose, compose two sermons on any one plan? It seems to me that his two volumes of sermons are enough to show how the church has suffered by Procrustean rules for sermonizing, by making the sermon a thing so different from every other kind of composition, except in its being an exposition of God's word.

"The power of perfectly natural intonations in delivery was shown very fully by his preaching. Reading, as he did generally when I heard him, quite closely and with scarcely a gesture, he thus always managed to secure attention, and to hold it to the end without weariness either to himself or his auditor. His tones, almost as much as his words, contributed to the strange art by which he was wont to cause his thoughts to be immediately apprehended by the hearer."

Among those who listened to his first discourse after licensure was one who has never ceased to cherish a glowing sentiment of admiration for the genius and piety of Mr. Alexander, and who has associated his own name with Christian authorship.*

"It was my good fortune," he writes, " to hear the first sermon he preached on being licensed by the Presbytery. It was in the Princeton Church, before a crowded auditory composed of the faculty and students of the Seminary and College, with all the principal families of the village, who were attracted to hear the first effort of the learned Professor in what had been to him, till then, the untried art of public speaking. His success was perfect. He went through the whole service with an ease, self-possession, propriety, and solemnity which would seem to have marked a preacher of many years. That first sermon established his reputation as an attractive popular preacher, and from that time forward it needed only to be known that he would preach to fill any house of worship in Princeton with the élite of the place." †

---

* The Rev. Professor L. I. Halsey, D.D., of the Seminary of the Northwest, the biographer of Lindsley, and the author of " Literary Attractions of the Bible."

† In a series of letters to the Northwestern Presbyterian, on the great preachers of the last quarter of the century, the same writer thus refers to this peculiarity of Mr. Alexander's modes of preaching:

"As a preacher he possessed endowments of the highest order, and he was equally successful in whatever style he chose to deliver the sermon. He could enchain the attention of an audience when he read his discourse closely from a manuscript, with scarcely more gesture than was necessary to turn the pages; and he could thrill and electrify the same audience, when without a line before him, he poured out a swelling and magnificent stream of thought with all the fervid animation of the most impassioned delivery. From the time he was licensed, he took his position, as it were by a single bound, among the most admired and powerful preachers of the times; and his services were in constant demand, not only in the pulpit at Princeton and its vicinity, but in the largest and most intelligent congregations of New-York and Philadelphia."

It is in connection with his account of this sermon, that Dr. Halsey introduces the following passage into his "Distinguished Preachers of the Last Forty Years:"

"Nothing could exceed the rapidity, energy, force and fire of his impassioned delivery. At times it was like a rising flood; it was a sweeping, onrushing, impetuous torrent. And yet it was always free from any approach to extravagance or verbiage. It was the lightning of thought. It was the heavy artillery of truth. It was the eloquence which combined the four elements of original, stirring thought, brilliant diction, magnificent imagery, and a soul in

It was no doubt painfully embarrassing to the young Professor to deliver that sermon. It was an experiment even to himself. He had always low views of his fitness and calling as a preacher. He thought his proper place was in the chair. In this he resembled his old preceptor Lindsley, and like him was strangely ignorant that perhaps " his forte was his magnificent preaching."

One of the first things about his pulpit efforts that attracted general notice, was the diversity of his methods. The unexampled variety in the plans of his sermons and the modes of his delivery of them, struck everybody who heard them. There was, however, a rich peculiarity of thought and diction in all of them. The gentleman just quoted, who heard him constantly at this period, testifies:

"From the first his style of preaching was unique and original—I should rather say his styles of preaching; for I have never heard any one preach in so many different ways as marked his manner during these first years of his ministry. His services were in great demand, and he preached often, both in the Church and the Seminary Chapel, besides being frequently called to New-York and Philadelphia. At times he appeared in the pulpit without a line of manuscript, and delivered what seemed an unwritten discourse, teeming with profound and striking thought and brilliant imagery, with a precision and wealth of diction which nothing could exceed, and with all the impassioned animation and ardor of an extemporaneous orator. At other times he would place his manuscript of large size paper on the pulpit desk and read it without indeed appearing to read it, turning the pages as he advanced, but no more trammelled or constrained as to gesture, look, or voice by the paper than if he had been preaching without notes. Then again I have seen him stand in the pulpit and preach, reading from a little sermon-book which he held up in both hands, going through the entire discourse without a gesture, or a look at the audience, while every eye was fixed upon him, and the attention of every hearer riveted by

earnest. Without any thing of what would be called the graces of manner, or the attitudes of oratory, he had the very essentials of true and powerful pulpit eloquence in the truth he uttered, in the words and images with which he clothed it, and in the ardour of his delivery."

the perfect articulation and emphasis of his voice, and the exceeding richness and originality of his matter."

The effect was the same under all these various methods.

"It mattered not in which of these methods he preached. He was always interesting, and at times sublime and thrilling. I could scarcely say in which of the styles I admired him most. I never heard any preacher who seemed to me so completely independent of all the aids of external method. In every method alike he poured out the richest treasures of Gospel truth. With him the form seemed to be nothing. In every style it was the eloquence of brilliant imagery, of powerful thought, of rich and choice diction, of impassioned feeling. I never heard any preacher who seemed so little indebted to the rules of rhetorical art, or rather so fully the creator and master of his own art. In this respect he was a law unto himself. It would be difficult to say which was the most remarkable characteristic of his preaching: the fervor of his own spiritual emotion, the grand movement of his thought, his magnificent imagery, or masterly command of language. His diction was at once simple, chaste, ornate, copious, and forcible. It was perfectly radiant with thought, luminous with flashes of imagination, and surcharged with feeling. Though he always spoke with clear and distinct articulation, his words flowed with great rapidity, indicating the quick and powerful movement of his mind. I cannot recall a single instance in which he ever, either in the pulpit or lecture-room, hesitated a moment for a word, or failed to get the right one; although his utterance on all occasions was remarkable for its rapidity. His reading of the Scriptures was also marked by the same rapid and yet distinct articulation. This power of expression, both by the tongue and the pen, was but the natural exponent of the clear and powerful intellect with which the Almighty had endowed him."

He was now, of course, busier than ever as, in addition to his usual engagements, he immediately took to writing sermons, and was continually in request as a preacher. His valuable aid was greatly sought after, especially by churches in New-Jersey and Philadelphia; and the eloquent licentiate was not at all unwilling to oblige his friends and serve his Master by speaking to sinners of the joys and wonders and dangers connected with redemption.

On the 3d of May, 1838, the cautious scholar wrote a letter to the President of the Board of Directors of the Seminary, accepting the Professorship to which he had been appointed by the assembly of 1835. The Directors on receiving his acceptance resolved, that he should be inaugurated at their next meeting, which would occur in September, and that he should pronounce an inaugural address. Dr. Spring was appointed to deliver the charge to the Professor.

During parts of April, May, June, August, and September, he was travelling; chiefly to and from points between Princeton and Washington. He took several extensive tours and many short rambles. He was at various times at Philadelphia, Wilmington, Baltimore, and the Federal Capital. Sometimes he was alone, and sometimes accompanied by one of his brothers. His longest sojourns were at Philadelphia. I have found among his papers minute accounts of the little humdrum incidents of these excursions, stating the events of each day with a precision and uniformity that would exhaust the patience of the reader. The truth was, his pleasure lay mainly in the substitution of other scenes and associations for those to which he was daily accustomed, the rapid transit from city to city, and the agreeable alternation of travel by water and travel by land.* Nothing of lively interest occurred to vary the essential monotony of these ever shifting and never changing diversions. But few extracts from this narrative need be given here. In the intervals he was as busy as at any other time.

When in Philadelphia, where he was thoroughly at home, he commonly put up at the public house known as Sanderson's; walked hither and thither in search of small adventures (that would have been adventures to nobody else) on the streets, and made necessary or trivial purchases at the

---

* " He unconscious whence the bliss,—
  Feels . . .
That all the circling joys are his,
  Of dear vicissitude."
        Gray. (Little, Brown & Co., 1853, p. 128.)

shops. On Sunday, when he was not engaged to preach himself, he went to hear some one or other of the city pastors, or strangers who were advertised in the newspapers. Now and then he fell in with an acquaintance; and though avoiding observation and recognition as much as possible, indulged in a good deal of casual intercourse with old and new friends, and appeared at times to enjoy these wayside encounters with no little zest.

Dr. Joseph H. Jones has told me that he could scarcely ever get a glimpse of the ubiquitous linguist; of whose society he was very fond and whose memory he holds in exalted estimation. The same is true, without doubt, of the majority of his Philadelphia confrères.

In addition to these journeys taken commonly without definite object and, as it were, with malice prepense, he was constantly going off somewhere to preach. He was invited hither and thither; had his bag full of fresh sermons (the best in a popular point of view that he ever wrote); was in the luxuriant bloom of his bodily, mental, and emotional powers; and was ready and even eager, on all fit occasions, to make full proof of his ministry and to preach "the glorious Gospel of the blessed God." He astonished and enraptured the best minds and the warmest hearts of every assembly over which he threw the spell of his glittering eye and thrilling accents; and many a hardened sinner was made to feel his guilt and danger, and to see the ample provision that had been made for his salvation. His own soul often took fire under these awakening influences, and his voice rang out as sweet and passionate as the note of a bugle.

He was in Washington on the 9th of May, with one of his brothers. He records:

"After tea we walked through Pennsylvania Avenue, and found the village (city) very dismal. It is a mere collection of suburbs without any urbs, or as James describes it, a moderate town pulled out like India-rubber to make it big. It has all the discomforts of a city, with few of its comforts. What a mistake it was to leave Philadelphia for the purpose of creating a central city which is now far less central to the twenty-six States than Philadelphia then was to the old thirteen—a great city without commerce or government munificence! What a chimera.

"Wednesday, May 16. I had intended to go to-day, but as I hear I can reach Philadelphia to-morrow before 2 o'clock, and as Hoffman has the floor in the House of Representatives, I have determined to remain one day longer. I did remain accordingly, and heard Ogden Hoffman, who was interrupted or answered by Rhett, Legare, and Waddy Thompson. I also heard J. W. Jones of Virginia, and Henry A. Wise in reply."

The spring had been very tardy in its advances. May was more like one of the earlier vernal months. The weather, however, was soft and balmy, after a period of unseasonable cold. From Philadelphia came the important tidings on the 18th, that the General Assembly was divided, and that the new-school party had seceded. Dr. Plumer was moderator of the old assembly, and Dr. Fisher of the new. These were exciting times, and Mr. Alexander took a deep and lively interest in them, and kept himself informed of all the ecclesiastical movements; but it does not appear that he entered actively into the controversy. His ecclesiastical life dates from the disruption of the church. He sided heartily with the old-school incumbents. The article condemning the Exodus of the new school men came out during his editorship of the Repertory, but was not written by him. No man was more strictly old fashioned on all points of doctrine, and on most points of policy. Whatever were his views, none could call in question his honesty or independence, or his courage. Assured in his own conscience, he was indifferent to censure, and laughed at intimidation. It had been as easy to govern John Knox or Martin Luther.

On Lord's Day, May 20th, Dr. Archibald Alexander preached one of the most eloquent sermons ever heard in Princeton, on the text, *Sin no more*. He awakened the cold and somewhat academic audience as he had done the warm assemblies in his youth. His hearers were deeply impressed. Not long after this, his old teacher Mr. Baird was in town, and received a pleasant greeting from one or more of his former pupils. He was becoming a great traveller, and frequently showed his face in Princeton on returning from one of his tours abroad. He liked nothing better than to recount the incidents of these journeys. I find that Mr. Alexander was at this time absent, having gone to Philadelphia with his father. He seems to have proceeded to Boston and other places in New-England, and then returned to the Pennsylvania Capital. He wrote home almost daily; an unusual thing with him. Saturday, the 26th, he had diverged as far as Elizabethtown; where he was to preach on Sunday.

I give below the only record he has left of this journey. It seems to have been penned in Boston:

"Lord's Day, May 20. Waterbury's Church. Beecher, 'Have I any pleasure in the death of the wicked.' Beecher again, 'Seek first the kingdom of God.'"

It is hard to clothe a skeleton journal with flesh and blood. The days were not alike, but it is scarcely possible to revive them in their distinct individuality. The materials at my disposal are not such as to enable me to hit off the physiognomy of each transient period; a few touches here and there must suffice. Professor James Alexander could not be induced to give a favourable answer to a solicitation from the church in Petersburg, which he received about this time. The younger brother was still in motion upon various neighbouring railways. On the 18th of September he came home from New-Brunswick, bringing with him clouds and signs of bad weather. He dined with his brother, and was, I doubt not, very communicative and entertaining about his journey. He was never more agreeable than after such returns. His eyes would fairly sparkle with fun and pleasure, and the little ones would laugh louder than ever at his amusing inventions.

On November the 11th, he records:

"To-night I heard Dr. Rice preach from Acts xvii. 30, on the duty of repentance. Anniversary of my last awakening. Thanks be to God for his unspeakable gift! I have lately finished Lockhart's Life of Scott, which I read with much interest.

"Nov. 17. Within a few days I have read the trial of Warren Hastings."

On Sunday the 8th of December, he arose for the first time in the Seminary Chapel; and there can be no doubt that he was listened to with the greatest attention.

Among those who watched with interest his dawning reputation as a preacher, was Dr. Charles Hodge, the friend of his boyhood and his colleague in the Seminary; a man who above almost all other men, had opportunity and ability to know and rightly estimate the greatness and variety of the gifts with which God had endowed him, and the breadth of the charmed circle that limited his attainments and means of influence. Mr. Alexander's intellectual wealth was like treasure hid in a field. One had to resort thither for it; it was not exposed in the market-place. Dr. Hodge had seen the treasure buried, and, of course, knew what it was. He writes as follows as to his mode of preaching:

"As a preacher, he had, for an intelligent audience at least, few equals. His mode of constructing his sermons was various. Sometimes his preaching was exegetical. He would take a passage of greater or less extent, and so expound it that his hearers would be astonished at the treasures of truth which it contained beyond what before they had apprehended. Sometimes his discourses were graphic; abounding in the highest kind of description; filling the mind with æsthetic and devotional feelings so mingled as to be hardly distinguishable; and diffusing through it a purifying delight.

"He generally wrote his sermons and used his manuscript in the pulpit; but never slavishly, as though he needed it. He always appeared to be master of himself and of his subject. I have heard him in the Seminary Chapel (if the solecism be intelligible), read extempore. That is, he has gone into the pulpit with blank paper, and in a level tone of voice, and without the slightest hesitancy, deliver a discourse as though he were reading from a book; not addressing his hearers, but reading to them. This was not an exhibition of a power of committing to memory without writing, but was done apparently off-hand, with little or no premeditation. This, of course, was not done for display, for he did not expect to be detected; but if, when called on to preach, he could not lay his hand on a sermon which suited his purpose, he would adopt this method. Preaching to theological students was not so agreeable to him as addressing a promiscuous audience, and he seldom spoke in the Chapel with the animation which characterized his manner under other circumstances."

This year, Mr. Alexander became one of the editors of the Biblical Repertory; to which he had already contributed a series of remarkable essays upon exegetical, critical, biographical, historical, and miscellaneous subjects. Associated with this change was that of the title of the periodical, which now acquired new fame in connection with the additional description, " and Princeton Review." He loved to call it so himself; but the old title is still the more popular one.

Some letters written to one of his young pupils at this time, will give us some idea of the kind of influence which he exercised upon them.

"JULY 7, 1838.

"MY DEAR BOY:

"As you are improving in your mathematical studies, I propose to reward you with a letter of unusual length. It is sometimes said that people of quick tempers are more affectionate than others; and this may be partly true. But that can be no reason for neglecting to restrain your temper. Why may you not be both good-tempered and affectionate? If you had a dog which was extremely fond of you for six days in the week, but on the seventh would go mad and bite you, do you think that his good habits and behaviour in general would reconcile you to his bites at other times? I am the more disposed to urge you to improve in this respect, because you have improved so much already since I first became acquainted with you. Go on, my dear lad! and with Divine help you may conquer this and every other evil disposition.

'῞Αυτη ἐστὶν ἡ νίκη ἡ νικήσασα τὸν κόσμον, ἡ πίστις ἡμῶν.'

"And now let us change the subject of discourse. I am sorry for the accident which befel your hat on the fourth of July, and hear that you are somewhat extravagant in your expressions of delight and gratitude for national independence. Do you not think that many people celebrate the day without remembering why it is kept? And can you tell me what is the connection between liberty and rockets—independence and turpentine? The accidents which happen on the fourth of July throughout the country, are very numerous and often very lamentable. But the worst of all is the intemperance and riot which prevail, under the pretext of rejoicing in our freedom. Many prove in this way, that although they boast of freedom they are utterly unfit for it. And now as this may be the last letter which I shall address to you, I wish before I close to beg that you will lose no time in gaining all the knowledge that may be within your reach; as life is short and you have much to do. With this advice and my best wishes, I bid you adieu. Yours sincerely,

"ADDISON ALEXANDER."

In another letter to the same, of Sept. 21, 1838, he tells him he must keep a journal.

"To-morrow you will please to commence a journal of your own adventures, studies, and employments, which I wish you to keep for my information and your own improvement until you can resume your correspondence, either with me or with another teacher. In writing this journal, you must be particular and put down everything which is at all important on the one hand, or amusing on the other. Write very often and little at a time, putting down things as they happen, before you have had time to forget them. As this will be your principal employment for some time, I hope you will take pains to tell me a great deal and to improve in writing. Your affectionate friend,

"JOS. ADDISON ALEXANDER."

During the summer of 1838 and the winter of 1838–1839, Mr. Alexander wrote most of his best sermons, and was continually called from home to preach. The record of his studies and reflections for the earlier part of this period is preserved in a volume of singular but eccentric interest. It is, regarded outwardly, a square thick quarto bound in sheep and made of unsized white paper, and is labelled on the back, "Day Book No. I." In this volume he not only kept as usual a copious journal of thoughts on different parts of the Old Testament, especially Isaiah and Nahum, and the earlier historical books, as well as plans of sermons, bare skeletons, random hints, and sermons in extenso; but wrote doggerel verses, and scribbled letters in every sort of hand-writing and in every style of courtly periphrasis. Scraps of unintelligible nonsense are here and there scrawled right across a profound comment on Isaiah. Sometimes there is nothing but the signature, and the sugared compliments that were then, and are still, somewhat fashionable among foreign ambassadors; or the assurances of chilling politeness which we look for from persons who, though inimical to one another, are yet not quite at dagger's draw. The book also contains amusing epistles to Constantine Menæus in modern Greek. It is one of the finest specimens of his calligraphy.

Here are a few more records from his journal:

"Sunday, July 1. Sermon by my father; communion administered by Dr. Rice. Monthly concert in the afternoon. Sermon at night by Dr. Rice, on the First Commandment. [Opened] Bryan Owen's treatise on the Mortification of Sin, and read several chapters with a deeper effect upon my heart and conscience than I have experienced for years from any book. Recommenced the reading of the Bible by my calendar; began with Job xxxiii, and Matthew vii. With the former I used Rosenmüller's Scholia in a cursory manner. Began to write a sermon on Romans x. 4.

"July 3. Abandoned the writing of my sermon, and concluded to prepare without writing.

"July 7. Resumed and finished the writing of my sermon on Romans x. 4. This is the second sermon I have written. I have preached ten; two of these twice, and one three times. Dr. Rice has invited me to preach to-morrow evening.

"July 8. I heard Dr. Miller preach in the Chapel from Rom. viii. 33. I read the Missionary Herald for July, and Owen on Temptation. At night I preached in the Church my sermon on Rom. xx. 14. Every experiment brings me nearer to the conclusion that I can preach more acceptably and profitably 'without notes' than with them. My present purpose is to write most of my sermons and to read none of them. I wish, as early as possible, to form such a habit as will tend most to increase my ministerial usefulness. Lord guide me! On this occasion I read my sermon. It is the second that I have written.

"July 9. Wrote six pages of a sermon on Ephesians iii. 14. Received a letter from the Rev. J. H. Jones, requesting me to supply his pulpit on the 22d instant: 'agreed.'

"July 15. Preached in the first Presbyterian Church, New-York, an expository sermon (John iii. 36), without the manuscript. At night I went to John Macauley's Church, and heard him preach from the text, 'I remembered God and was troubled.'

"July 17. Received a letter from Dr. Pennington, inviting me to preach before the Young Men's Society of Newark, on the evening of the last Sabbath in August.

"July 22. Expounded the 6th of Isaiah in the Spruce-street Church, Philadelphia. Dined at Mrs. Hall's, and in the afternoon read my sermon on Hebrews xi. 10. Drank tea at John Hall's again, and went with him to hear Bascomb preach in Dr. Skinner's Church.

"July 23. 'No peace to the wicked.' Wrote a full analysis of a sermon on the above text, with one or two paragraphs written out at length. I propose to try this method of preaching, as compared with the reading and the pure extempore method.

"July 25. Wrote a similar analysis of a sermon on Psalm xvii. 15. My method is to write the leading ideas under every head, on the right-hand page, having the left for any passages that I may choose to write at length. I propose to try this method in Philadelphia next Lord's Day. This evening, several of us met at Dr. Hodge's to take leave of Dr. Breckinridge; after some conversation we joined in prayer with Dr. Hodge, and bade Dr. Breckinridge farewell.

"July 26. My brother began to remove his effects to Dr. Breckinridge's house. His wife and I dined there, and I lodged there at night, as I expect to do hereafter.*

"July 29. Preached in Dr. Boardman's Church, Philadelphia, from full notes on the text, 'There is no peace, saith my God, to the wicked.' In the afternoon, I read my sermon from the text, 'Awake thou that sleepest and arise from the dead, and Christ shall give thee light.'"

The journal is filled with statements of this nature. The few extracts given may serve as samples.

One of the most intelligent of his Princeton hearers † thus refers to his power over his congregation:

"I only knew him by his sermons and his writings. Judging of

---

* The house he had occupied since April of the last year, was at Mr. Voorhees's, corner of Nassau street and John's Alley; and in the very centre of the village hubbub.

† The Hon. Richard S. Field.

him by them, I would say, he was a man of great learning, great eloquence, and great intellectual power. I frequently heard him preach; and embraced every opportunity of doing so. He was by far the greatest preacher I have ever heard. I have never known any one to compare with him. He possessed every quality for a great pulpit orator, physical as well as intellectual. His face and forehead were massive, large, and round; his voice combined the highest degree of melody and the greatest compass and volume; and when he chose to be eloquent, his eloquence was of the very highest order. I say, when he chose to be eloquent; for what always struck me more than any thing else was this—that he never seemed to put forth all his power, but, on the contrary, impressed you with the idea that he had a fund in reserve upon which he might have drawn to any extent. What he did, never seemed to cost him the slightest effort. I always felt that there was nothing in the way of eloquence which he might not have done."

By the 30th of July, the family of the elder brother were well settled in their new house, and could give thanks for a profusion of comforts; though during all this period they were passing through a sore trial. Mr. Alexander, at their warm entreaty, took up his lodgings under the same roof. At one time or another, he had nearly every room in the building.

The advent of a teacher of elocution set the brothers about the business of guarding and strengthening their voices. They both took lessons, but afterward concurred in very contemptuous views of this branch of instruction. Perhaps they carried this prejudice too far. The older brother used to say that the great pulpit orators, such as Bourdaloue, Massillon, Hall, and Chalmers, were not made by the elocutionists but in despite of all their artificial rules. The subjoined record shows what progress they were making under Mr. Bronson:

"Addison and I are taking lessons in barking and howling, and ventriloquism, from an elocutionist named Bronson, and who with much stuff, has also certain discoveries on which I thought I myself had hit; *

---

* He refers to his own review of Gardiner's Music of Nature, in the July number of the Repertory, p. 268.

but which he carries so far as to convince me that the Laryngitis (erroneously called Bronchitis) is preventable."

It is worthy of remark that in his last journey to Philadelphia, shortly before his death, the younger brother jotted down in a copy of the History of Methodism by Dr. Abel Stevens, the word "excellent," in approval of a long passage in that admirable work on this subject of "elocution" as related to true eloquence and as illustrated by Whitefield. His notion and that of Dr. Stevens was, that if a man had the soul of oratory, he would be very apt to have the form; and that ardent and melting sympathy have more to do with the highest effects of eloquence than terror.

This was the secret of Mr. Alexander's own power in the pulpit. He had not the tricks and graces of the mere histrionic performer. His influence was that of a man thoroughly in earnest and in loving sympathy with his hearers, importunately pleading with them to be saved through the great sacrifice for sinners. I am glad to refer in this connection to the words of a thoughtful admirer of Mr. Alexander's preaching, who brings out his character in this respect very forcibly. The writer I am about to quote is a physician living in the West, far in the interior.

He knew Dr. Addison Alexander well, and in all his phases. He says:

"Mr. Alexander was one of the most attractive preachers to me that I ever listened to. He was no orator in the ordinary acceptation of the word. His sermons were generally written and closely read, or if not written, delivered without raising his eyes from the Bible before him; his utterance rapid beyond that of any other speaker I ever listened to except Dr. Robley Dunglison, of Jefferson Medical College, Philadelphia; making no gestures, only an occasional emphasizing fall of his right hand, with the fingers closed, standing firmly and squarely on his feet, without motion, there were yet but few men I ever heard preach to whom I would sooner give the palm for *eloquence*. I remember hearing him deliver a sermon on the text, 'Remember Lot's wife,' which I shall never forget while I live, if I forget it ever. The effect upon the audience was visible and audible: all present seemed drawn forward in their seats, and holding their breath ; and when he paused to breathe, you could hear the inhalation of the mass of his hearers over the whole church. It always seemed to me that if there ever was a man whose sermons would read as well as they sounded, it was Addison Alexander: but many years after. I read this very sermon, printed among others in the volume of his sermons, and I must say that I felt as if a portion surely had been left out. I missed something—which something I now feel must have been the intense biotic force, magnetism, brain-power of the *man*. This sermon was one which no one but himself could have produced, or have delivered with the same effect. You know that Dr. Archibald Alexander was considered unapproachable in his own peculiar style of preaching, and yet I have heard his son Addison fully equal him in that very style; except that the glance of the eye, and the individualizing dart of the forefinger with which the 'old man eloquent' was accustomed to launch the truth into the very heart of some particular person before him, were always wanting. And so also I have heard him preach in the styles that were thought peculiar to Dr. Miller and to Dr. Hodge, and, *me judice*, equalling if not surpassing them in their very best efforts."

He cannot say that these efforts of his were predetermined adoptions of the peculiar modes of thought of these other ministers. He rather thinks not: but only that the coincidences or resemblance of styles resulted from the "exuberance of his mental activity that led him to try every mode by which it was possible for thought to be communicated from one mind to another."

One of his pupils, the Rev. B. T. Lacy, D.D., of St. Louis, gives the following account of the matter:

"His preaching was to mee xceedingly attractive and impressive. The style was so fine, and the order so lucid. The truth was so clearly and boldly stated, and the fervour so genuine and so animating. Although he seldom touched the chords of pathos, at times I have heard him when he was scarcely surpassed, either in tenderness of emotion or depth of solemnity. All the varied powers of his mind seemed to work together, and to move in perfect harmony with each other. Hence his discourses were ordinarily distinguished as much for one quality of excellence as for another. He was always logical and argumentative ; always rhetorical and imaginative; always fervent and solemn. And these different and dissimilar elements were not separated and disposed into different parts of the discourse: they interpenetrated each other, and were beautifully and naturally blended into every portion of the sermon. His *manner* was peculiar, and consisted chiefly in the distinct and very rapid reading of his manuscripts, with great stress of voice and force of emphasis, which impressed you with the earnestness of the speaker and the importance of the message, and which invariably carried you on with him. He always secured the undivided attention of his audience. No preacher ever impressed me so much with the sense of his *power*—a power both intellectual and spiritual—both in the man and in the message. If such a comparison may be tolerated, or will serve to illustrate the idea, the impression of *power* which he made as he swept right on through his manuscript, in the earnest rapidity of his utterance, was not unlike that produced by a train of cars, propelled by a mighty engine, with great speed and irresistible force right on upon the iron track. And the resemblance did not end here: the hearer felt that if he did not attend closely to every sentence, he should be left behind and should not again be able to recover his lost position."

I now return to the narrative. August the 8th was the centennial anniversary of the Presbytery of New-Brunswick. On the morning of the 12th Dr. Archibald Alexander and his two sons were all preaching in Princeton, and without previous concert: the former at the Seminary Chapel, and the others respectively at the Church and the African meeting. Mr. Alexander preached again at night. His services in the pulpit were called into constant requisition. He was now everywhere recognized as a powerful and persuasive minister of the Word. Towards the close of the month he went to New-York on one of his little summer jaunts, returning after a few days' absence. He preached in the city, and had some religious conversation with an aged serving-woman who was at the point of death. A few extracts from his diary during this month may not be unacceptable:

"Tuesday, August 21. Dr. Nordheimer lectured on the Hebrew alphabet. Took a lesson from Bronson, the elocutionist. Nordheimer and James dined with us.

"August 23. Second lesson from Bronson; learned to hold my breath; second lecture from Nordheimer on syllabication; finished my sermon for the young men of Newark.

"Sunday, August 26. Preached in the First Church at Newark on Romans x. 4, in the Second Church on Ephesians v. 14. At five o'clock heard Dr. Nott preach on temperance. At night preached to the young men on Matthew vi. 33.

"Sunday, Sept. 2. Finished the Gospel of John and continued Owen on Indwelling Sin. Remember, from this time forth, to set apart a certain time in the morning and at night for spiritual exercises. Remember also, to be slow and temperate in eating; to join, *ex animo*, in the prayer at table; and to think at every meal of the Giver of your mercies. Remember thirdly, that from this time forth your time must be more conscientiously redeemed; and, O thou holy and long-suffering God! help me to keep these resolutions.

"Partook of [my] the Lord's Supper with some degree of pleasure and profit. My father preached from the words, 'It is finished.' Resolutions, 1st, To avoid temptations, especially those which do so easily beset me. 2d, To redeem time. 3d, To give set times to private devotions. 4th, To cultivate an habitual spirit of prayer, and for this purpose to practise ejaculatory prayer. 5th, To cultivate expansive and benevolent feelings. 6th, To avoid the extremes of moroseness and frivolity, sanctimony and worldliness. Give me grace, O Lord! to keep these resolutions.

"September 14. Presented Nordheimer with Passou's Greek and Freytag's Arabic Lexicon. He took leave. I finished my article on Hengstenberg in a hurry, with the printers at my heels."

He was, shortly after this, installed in his chair as Professor of Oriental languages and literature; as we learn from the following record:

"September 24. Heard Dr. McElroy dismiss the students. At night I was inaugurated. After singing, Dr. Green prayed; I read and subscribed the formula, and delivered my inaugural discourse, and Dr. Spring his charge.

"Sept. 25. My inaugural address was requested by the Board for publication. Heard Warren Scott's annual oration."

The inaugural address of the young professor must have been listened to with rapt attention and delight; for it is one of the best things he ever uttered. It will be found entire in the Repertory for April 1839, where it forms the larger part of a review of his brother's little volume entitled, " The Scripture Guide. A Familiar Introduction to the Study of the Bible." As in his first essay before the Philological Society, he had amazed and charmed his youthful compeers by leaving the tomes of antiquity and going to the neglected pages of our own literature; so when every eye was turned upon the travelled Hebraist, and every mind was probably in expectation of a wide and accurate display of Oriental learning, the modest scholar uses all his genius in an effort to exalt the English Bible. The discourse is marked by novelty and originality of substance; by great force and cogency of statement; by those traces of erudition which he was not able, or did not care, to hide; by felicity of illustration and diction; by wit, sarcasm, keen excoriation, playful innuendo, sweet and wholesome humour; by admirable common-sense—of the kind that was once loved in old England: and has an aroma of the old practical writers, and of his own closest devotions, and (towards the close) a kind of rushing eloquence that reminds one of a stream that chafes its bed and threatens to burst from its embankment. It is a comprehensive plea for the study of the English version *pari passu* with the original. The main discussion is laid off under seven heads. The image that is contained in the concluding sentence of the address, was one of those grand and happy conceptions of which his mind seemed to be full, and which came from him spontaneously whenever his reason and feeling were strongly excited by the proper stimulus. With him, to *think* at all was to *express* in his choicest language. He seemed to be as automatic in this respect as Mozart or Coleridge.

The 26th was Commencement; and on that day the Hon. James McDowell, of Virginia, pronounced an address of fervid rhetoric and rare sagacity before the two literary societies. The weather was stormy. It should seem from the annexed entry in his journal that Mr. Alexander, who was perfectly acquainted with the fame of the orator, had purposed to hear him, but was prevented by the incessant pouring showers.

"Sept. 26. Confined to the house with rain. Missed McDowell's speech." The traditions of this speech still linger among the Princeton students; and I have heard that there are gestures and turns of expression there now which are clearly traceable to its influence.

There is no other record until October the 2d. From his diary it appears that Mr. Alexander now preached his first sermon memoriter, and was not displeased with the experiment:

"Having breakfasted with Mr. Dod, I set off with him in my carriage for Freehold, where we arrived at noon, and found the Rev. L. O. Brown preaching on the history of David and Nabal. After sermon, the Presbytery met, Mr. Dod in the chair. They were chiefly taken up in the examination of candidates. I preached at night from Mark xiv. 41. My first attempt to preach from memory."

Here is another entry touching sermon-making:

"Dec. 23. Preached in College, Matt. vi. 33; read closely; disliked the sermon more than ever; written on a bad plan; skeleton made first; no spontaneous flow of thought. The best part was half a dozen pages which I wrote last night; declamation at the end very frigid. *Requiescat in pace.*

"Sermon at night by ———; genuine Yankee sermon; metaphysical, not scriptural; clear, logical, acute, ingenious, heartless, orthodox: moral and natural inability; when they talk of this I never know what they believe. Thankful I do not 'sit'—as they say— 'under' the best of such preaching; I should starve."

"Professor Alexander's peculiar repugnance to every thing like ostentatious parade," writes one who heard much about him at this period, "was evinced in various ways, after his entrance upon his career as a preacher. The extraordinary character of his sermons at once arrested public attention, and drew crowds of hearers; especially from among the most intelligent classes. It was impossible but that so acute an observer of all that passed around him, as was Mr. Alexander, must have been aware of his popularity; when preaching in the same pulpit for successive weeks and months, he saw the pews of our largest churches densely packed, and the aisles filled with supplementary benches. Yet so far from seeming elated by these evidences of his acceptableness, or assuming those airs of consequence, which popular preachers are apt to acquire; he was at times not a little dismayed by such demonstrations. I have no doubt that his feelings were akin to those of Robert Hall, whom in very many traits he resembled, who in the later years of his life could scarcely be induced to preach in London, because of the throngs who pressed to hear him. Both of these great men felt the sanctity of their work, and the fearful responsibility of God's ambassadors to perishing men. Both were aware that when men are drawn to listen to the preacher for the sake of his talents as a preacher, there is little likelihood of their being benefited by the Divine ambassador."

At one time he preached in the afternoons in a school-house in the neighbourhood of the little town in which he lived. Referring to these efforts, one of his students says:

"His sermons at Queenston were always preached without notes, and were generally plain, instructive discourses, delivered with great rapidity of utterance, perfect fluency, and intense earnestness. Though his speech was so rapid, such was the clearness of the thought, and the distinctness of the enunciation, that there was nothing lost by the ear of the audience."

His more elaborate sermons were generally read. Conversing with this gentleman one day on this subject of reading sermons, Mr. Alexander expressed the opinion that every preacher ought to try every method, and finally settle down upon that which he can make most effective. He then asked his companion if he did not think that reading was his most effective mode of preaching, intimating that in his own opinion it was. His acquaintance very readily agreed with him.

The Rev. James W. Alexander once remarked to me (what has since been published as his opinion) that he and his brother Addison were differently constituted as to this matter; for that in his own case the imagination was never more stimulated than in extemporary preaching; whereas in the case of Addison the reverse was true: the embarrassment of appearing before an audience without notes of any kind, or some other cause, hindered the movement of his imagination, though the excitement of speaking greatly encouraged and excited other powers, such as the memory, the reason, and the faculty of rapid, exact, fluent, and felicitous expression. Writing was, on the whole, a greater stimulant than speaking, in the case of the younger brother. He reasoned out his propositions with equal force and facility at one time as at another, and always with the most admirable novelty and cogency. He expressed himself under all circumstances, whether pen in hand or in the presence of an auditory, with nearly the same ease and conciseness, and with a vigour and precision that have put many persons in mind of the complex, fine, quick, yet invariable movement of powerful machinery. But when he spoke extemporaneously, he seemed to be darting to and fro very swiftly upon the surface of the ground; whereas when he wrote, he often seemed to be plunging through yawning chasms into the bowels of the earth, or hovering over the abyss of waterfalls, or climbing dizzy mountains, or rioting among the clouds and colours of sunset, or soaring like some bird of strong pinion into depths of distant azure, as if he were making for the very zenith.

When he wrote, he sometimes seemed to exult in the opulence of his own vocabulary, and to experience a kind of exuberant joy in marshalling in skilful order the images of glory that peopled his brain, and threw an iridescent splendour over his exciting meditations. This was seldom the case when he discarded verbal recollection, together with the assistance of manuscript in the pulpit. He then commonly stuck to his text considered as a proposition to be merely analyzed, expounded, and energetically pressed upon the conscience and religious feelings of his hearers. His mode of procedure in such cases was by profound, suggestive remarks upon the *nexus* of particular inspired utterances, or upon the general principles of Scripture exegesis; by admirable processes of deductive logic; interspersed with pithy, homely observations drawn from his large acquaintance with the ordinary character of his fellow-beings; and by simple and direct appeals to the heart.

His genius, under such conditions, seemed to be some "creature of the elements," rather than merely the ordinary powers of his mind harnessed to nobler work. It would be wrong to think that all his written efforts were of this lofty or aerial description. His sermons on paper sometimes differed scarcely at all from the sermons which in a manner sprung from the occasion. There was infinite diversity, moreover, if not between the two principal classes of sermons, yet among his individual discourses. It is not rigidly true, either, that he was never imaginative except when he was in the chains of manuscript. He would sometimes break away into splendid imagery and vehement appeals, when he had written nothing. But this was an exceptional experience with him, and probably happened most frequently when he had a blank book before him, or one virtually so, (as he occasionally did) and could employ his eyes and his fingers in turning over the leaves. Whether this was a mechanical necessity, like that which is observed often in absent-minded people, or whether it arose from mere caprice or whim, or from excess of morbid consciousness, it would be hard to determine. I have myself seen him turn his leaves alternately in opposite directions.

It is certain that he was in no way dependent on his paper, either for his thoughts or his language; and that his verbal memory was fully equal to his invention. It seems most likely, on the whole, that he distrusted his powers as an extemporaneous orator; and that his fancy,* and to some extent also his feelings, did not often take fire except in the atmosphere of his study, or in the pulpit after he had written out every word.

Every one of such discourses would be concatenated link by link, and made as bright and invulnerable as a suit of chain armor. In his later years, he changed his whole theory of

---

* I here use the words imagination and fancy in their popular sense, and not in the sense accepted by psychologists *après* Coleridge.

sermonizing, and wrote his discourses almost exclusively in this style. His taste had become bare and severe like that of the Greeks; and his preaching, though comprehensible as ever, and more deeply instructive than at any former period, lost in great measure the pomp, the magnificence, the martial tread, the plaintive music, the terrific power, the strange captivating charm, that had characterized it at an earlier day. He also became much less impassioned. This was owing in part to the gradual exhaustion of his physical energies. As years rolled on, he became much more calm in his manner, as he was also much less hot and impetuous in his temper.

The following hint of Mr. Alexander's employments at this time is from his brother's diary for the 23d of December:

"We might accomplish more if we were not foolishly asking ourselves so often, how long such and such a great work would take us. Mr. Robert B. Patton used to engage in most laborious lexicographical works. When Addison asked him how he had patience to go on, he said, that he never thought of asking how long it would take him, but went on as if it were to be his work for life.

"Addison tells me he finds the same thing good in his Commentary on Isaiah. Our Lord's maxim about taking thought for the morrow seems to have very wide applications."

I find this entry for Dec. 9th, in his own diary:

"Began a new method of studying the Scriptures in course. In order to keep up my attention, I have determined to read with a view to exposition."

There was a bright frost on the morning of the 12th. It was Wednesday, and the clerical meeting was at Dr. Rice's. The topic was the abridged creeds and communion covenants of the New England Congregationalists. The Rev. James W. Alexander made remarks in opposition to the new modes, and his little speech was requested for publication.

The younger brother records on Monday, Dec. the 17th:

"I resumed my labours on Isaiah, beginning with the thirteenth chapter."

This work now went on pretty steadily for a while; but was soon again interrupted. In a letter to Mr. Hall, which he wrote during this month, he makes an odd reference to Cicero. Here is the letter itself:

"Princeton, Dec. 19th, 1838.
My Dear Sir:
After reading Secretary Burrowes's manifesto about sealed returns, unsealed returns, &c. I came upon the following in Cic. Orat. 3 in Cat.*
"Cum vero summis ac clarissimis hujus civitatis viris, qui, audita re, frequentes ad me, convenerant, literas a me prius aperiri mane quam ad senatum deferri, placeret; ne, si nihil esset inventum, temere a me tantus tumultus injectus civitati videretur; negavi me esse facturum, ut de periculo publico non ad consilium publicum rem integram deferrem." The above you are at liberty to publish (but not in your "valuable journal") as your own discovery, and this douceur, I trust, will make you lend a willing ear to two petitions which I have to offer. The first is, that you would have the goodness to inform Sam where he can procure some Congress paper, or *quocunque nomine*. The other is that you would "aid and assist" him in procuring a sermon-case (*horresco re ferens*) made on a plan of my own invention—black morocco covers, but stiff with pasteboard, and adapted to letter-paper folded once—or say the largest pocketable size.
Hastily and truly yours,
Jos. Addison Alexander.

The narrative is now once more resumed. On Monday, April the 15th, if we could have had a peep at them, we should have seen Mr. Alexander reading Croker's Boswell to his brother James. How the talk must have flowed, with such a theme to tempt to every species of discursive remark! Both the brothers were hearty friends of Samuel Johnson, and neither of them ever tired of his foolish but incomparable biographer. They regarded Johnson's table-talk as the strongest and best in print. They both loved to read about Dr. Goldsmith and his peach-blossom coat and his silly conversational explosions. They concurred in the opinion that Irving made a mistake in not dwelling more on the oddities and amusing

---

* M. Tull Cic. Orat. in L. Catilinam Tertia, iii. 10.

weaknesses of "Goldy." The elder brother once said to me, that Macaulay had damned Irving with faint praise in his celebrated article in the Encyclopædia Britannica, where after speaking highly of Forster's life, he adds of the American writer, "Mr. Irving's style is always pleasing."

The talk of the two brothers was much on sermonizing, and they both loved to quote their venerable father as authority. One day, one of them tells the other that he had heard his father say a man ought not to begin with making a plan. Neither should he wait till he is in the vein. "Begin, however you feel, and write till you get into the vein, however long it be! 'Tis thus men do in mining. You may throw away all the beginning. Men who write with ease, can think best pen in hand. This applies to sermons, and also to books." These are the thoughts of Dr. Archibald Alexander modified by the mind of one of his sons. It will be seen that he coincides with Dr. Johnson on this point. The prevalent view of his eldest son was different from that of Dr. Alexander as here expressed, and the younger of the two seminary professors could certainly never do anything unless he was in the vein. The majority of literary men have opposed the dictum of Johnson. Macaulay told Prescott in London that he had moods* for writing, and seldom put pen to paper at other times.

Tuesday, the 23d, was a delightful day, and Mr. Alexander and his brother occupied the same carriage to Lambertville, in company with Dr. Carnahan, Dr. Rice, Dr. Maclean, and a young lady by the name of Brown. The budding loveliness of spring lay all around them, as they wended their way in full view of the Blawenburg vale and the Sourland mountain. They arrived a little late at Lambertville, for Mr. Yeomans had announced his text; though he broke off as soon as he caught a glimpse of Dr. Rice, who was appointed to preach. Mr. Alexander preached at night. The next day was equally fine, and was taken up with the Presbyterial proceedings. Professor Alexander, of the College, moved certain resolutions

---

* See Life of Prescott, by Ticknor.

touching the independence of the Church on the State. The occasion was a memorable one for the subject of these sketches, for on this day he was exactly thirty years old, and on this day he was solemnly ordained as a minister of the Gospel. The moderator of Presbytery was Mr. Perkins. Several young men were licensed. The meeting was harmonious and agreeable.

CHAPTER XV.

Mr. Alexander was still a licentiate at the time the writer * I am about to quote entered the Seminary, and he has a distinct recollection of the period of his ordination. It was an occasion of much interest and pleasure to all the students. Mr. Alexander was already somewhat renowned as a pulpit orator, and still more as a precociously-gifted sermonizer.

"Though but a probationer for the Gospel ministry, he had, even at this early day, obtained an enviable popularity as a preacher, and was greatly sought after by the most intelligent and fashionable congregations. They were attracted by the high fame of his learning, and edified by the variety and extent of Gospel truth in which his sermons abounded; for he fed the people with knowledge and understanding."

The following remarks are literally exact, as well as highly amusing:

"For the encouragement of such as read their sermons closely, and pay but little attention to their audience, I may say that if they read more closely than he, it is a pity! He took no pains to conceal his notes, nor to 'cheat the eyes of gallery critics' by any 'underhand' measures, such as shading his notes from public view, taking stolen glances at them as it were, and then launching out like an indèpendent swimmer. He scorned all concealment, and proclaimed to all his faith in the pen. He evidently had a great contempt of the opinion that reading sermons spoiled their effect, and was not slow to express it; for on one or more occasions that I heard him he took up his note-book in his hand, held it up between himself and the people, turned page after

---

* Rev. Mr. Teese, of White Plains.

page, and read leisurely through the discourse without once casting his eyes on the congregation. And yet there was earnestness and enthusiasm, both in his composition and delivery."

It was natural that the young men should have much curiosity as to the manner in which this terrible inquisitor would himself stand inquisition. The result was surprising. He sometimes confessed ignorance: Dr. Alexander never pretended to know what he did not know. He thus often confounded sciolists who put questions to him which no one living or dead could answer with certainty. He was as honest in this respect as Socrates and Dr. Johnson. When the latter was asked by a lady why he should have made such a mistake in his Dictionary about the pastern of a horse, he replied: "It was from pure ignorance, madam." It is said that Mr. Alexander was once invited by the President of a college to dine at his house with a number of the clergy and literary people of the place, and that the host put the same question all round the table about a vexed context in Isaiah, wishing to draw out his guest the commentator. Of course various decided opinions were elicited. When it came to the turn of Mr. Alexander, in reply to the question, "And what do *you* say is the meaning of this passage?" he answered, with expressive brevity: "*I* do not know."

But to return to the narrative. When he was about to be ordained, he must of course be examined, according to the Form of Government, in regard to his literary and scientific attainments; and especially his knowledge of the Greek and Hebrew languages. Nothing could have been more agreeable to the young men of the Seminary, who exulted in the prowess of their young leader and wanted to see him fairly tried; not doubting for a moment that the event would shed *éclat* on the reputation of their teacher, and in spite of his excessive modesty and the sensitiveness of a genius which " blushed so to be admired," would make him as widely famous they knew as he deserved to be. There was doubtless mixed with this feeling a half-malicious and half-mirthful pleasure, such as from the beginning of the world has animated the breasts of students under similar circumstances. The teacher was to be taught! The Hebraist was to be quizzed in Hebrew! There was the flavour of a jest here that could not be resisted. The tidings ran everywhere that Mr. Alexander was to be examined at such and such a time in the ancient tongues.

"This excited great amusement among the students, and we attended in order to see one who had puzzled so many of us by his own examinations himself questioned and examined, and made to suffer some of the misery which he had so often occasioned us. We thought of the old story of 'The engineer hoist by his own petard.'* However, we did not anticipate any 'fizzle,' such as we had often seen in the class-room; on the contrary, we had entire faith in the all-sufficiency of our young Professor, and entertained rather a feeling of wonder at the presumption of men who undertook such a work as his examination. The service indeed was one of much difficulty to the Presbytery; for very few of the members cared to examine the candidate, especially on Hebrew, of which they probably never knew a great deal and had forgotten much of that. However, the candidate made no great ostentation of his learning, for his reply to several of the questions was, very much to our surprise, 'I do not know.'" †

On the 29th, Joseph John Gurney was in Princeton, and attracted much attention by his noble presence. He preached twice in Quaker meeting. The elder brother describes him, in his journal, as a large, portly, heavy-looking, red and white Englishman. He made the impression of a strong intellect

---

* " For 'tis sport to have the engineer
    Hoist with his own petard."

† He gave the same answer to a single question at his licensure, unless my informant's memory is at fault. Dr. A. A. Rice, of Wyoming, Kentucky, was present when Mr. Alexander was examined before the Presbytery of New Brunswick, as he thinks, for licensure. "I remember," he says, "nothing of his examination but one question and its answer. It was during the examination upon his literary course. The question was put to him, 'What is taste?' and his answer was very prompt, 'I don't know.' You may imagine my astonishment at this answer; for I thought that if there ever was a man who knew everything, it was Addison Alexander."

and an accomplished man. There was great charm about his manner when he was a little excited. His devout love for the Saviour and the Bible was obvious.

On the 9th, Thursday, the important news came by letter from Philadelphia, that Judge Gibson had declared for the Old School on every point. "Laus Deo!" writes Professor J. W. Alexander in his Every-Day Book. "Judge Gibson's opinion gives the Old School everything which they can desire. "Laus Deo per Christum! Sit nobis gratia ut simus ab omnibus superbiæ malitiæque remoti!"

How faint are the echoes now of the din and turmoil of that day! The matters which interest us of the year 1868, will presently fade out of memory as did those of 1839. The waves of time wash everything to oblivion.

The house of the elder brother was now again thrown into mourning, and this time the anguish was for the first-born. Little George was born in 1831, and was therefore eight years old when he died. He had met with an accident in his infancy, and had long been a blind and helpless invalid. He had an astonishing memory, and a marvellous genius for music; though his other faculties were not equal to those of other children of the same age. George was a radiant little fellow; always full of joy and sunshine. He was, even above most other children, devoted to his uncle Addison, and would scream with delight when he heard his foot upon the first step of the outer porch. His uncle was never happier than when he was at his side singing to him and telling him stories. "He was," says his father, "a very small and feeble child at his birth, but afterwards improved so much as to be very lovely. But before he reached the age of two years, he was seized with hydrocephalus, and his surviving it seemed all but miraculous. From that time, his head began to enlarge, and this disproportion continued more or less, as long as he lived; so that for one or two years he was always in a lying posture." Within the last few years, he had improved greatly in health, and with a slight exception was never better than the year before his death occurred. The event shed grief into the hearts of all his kinsfolk, and every accustomed scene was for a time enveloped in gloom. This affliction was, without doubt, deeply and tenderly felt by Mr. Alexander; for he unfeignedly loved the little boy.

Mr. Alexander was now thirty years old, and his mind and character were by this time stamped with the impress which they bore through life. There are abundant accounts of the impression which he himself made on his pupils.

The recollections of one who is himself a professor and a commentator will be read with pleasure. Says one of his favourite and most admired students:

"He was thirty years of age, when, after I had been his pupil during the Seminary course of three years, I was brought into a closer association with him as an assistant for introducing the Junior class to the Hebrew language."

The writer noticed the resemblance to Bonaparte. He looked and felt his power, but was modest, shy, and affectionate.

"With a Napoleonic face and form, he bore himself like a man conscious of power; yet he was shrinking as a child from publicity. He was notoriously shy of social gatherings, yet he loved to play with children, and spent much time in ingenious efforts to amuse and instruct them. These were his favourite recreations. It was comparatively seldom that he was seen in the streets of Princeton. All his living savoured of study; and this was his element, in which like a leviathan he disported."

The testimony of this writer to Mr. Alexander's abilities as a learned commentator is just as clear and emphatic. He was now scattering leaves of his Isaiah over the Repertory, and by this and other means drawing to him minds like those of Nordheimer, the philosophic Hebrew grammarian. The fact that this able man received the benefit of Mr. Alexander's suggestions while adding finish to his work is not generallo known. On these points Dr. Jacobus writes:

"The great attainments which he was known to have made in Oriental and European languages and his enthusiasm in Biblical learning, gave him a well-deserved fame at home and abroad, even before he had issued any of his commentaries. He attracted to himself that singular scholar, Nordheimer, who brought out his Hebrew Grammar under his eye, while lecturing at the same time to a select class of students at the Seminary. It was known that he was at work upon his Isaiah, and from the morsels of it dispensed to the students in the lecture-room, as well as from the hints and foretastes of it given through the Princeton Review, it was awaited with high interest. Other articles from his pen evinced his fertility of mind and his rare genius for grasping great points of controversy in various fields, and dealing with them in masterly style."

The writer adds that

"His imagination was glowing but chaste, and his logical acumen singularly keen and effective."

He was also a good judge of human hearts.

"He had an intuitive insight into character, and very promptly weighed and measured the incoming classes, man by man. Though habitually reticent in his intercourse with the students, and evidently not encouraging any familiarity, he was most genial in his temper and most agreeable as a guest away from his books, or as a friend in his own study."

Over the class he reigned as king.

"His power with the students was that which belonged to his lordship in the domain of truth. His whole aspect and air in the class-room commanded respect. They showed he demanded it, and could enforce it. Often a few sharp words would thoroughly dissect the folly or stupidity of a blunderer; or would lay bare the shallow impertinence of a questioner; until of the rest no man durst venture in that direction unless well fortified."

The testimony of Dr. Jacobus as to his traits of person and character need not be continued here, for it does not vary from the statements of others which are spread before the reader in this volume.

The following letter broaches the scheme of his Isaiah to one whom he often consulted on such points. Like Sir Walter Scott, he says, he needs the stimulus of a pursuing press:

"PRINCETON, Jan. 8, 1839.
"MY DEAR SIR:
"The persuasions of some friends and the assent of others have brought me to believe that I might do some service by putting forth a small work on Isaiah. The state of the case is as follows: I have a critical commentary written out for the press on the first six chapters and a part of the seventh. I have condensed notes (the fruit of much laborious study) on fifty chapters. The latter are so written that they might, with little change, be published as a popular commentary. They were, in fact, prepared with that intention. If I conclude to publish, I shall begin to print at once, for a double reason: 1st, Because I cannot write steadily without Walter Scott's favourite stimulus, a pursuing press. 2d, Because I should wish to announce the work *at once* as in the press. This method I could, of course, pursue with ease; as I should only have to abridge and transcribe; till the middle of the seventh chapter. Your judgment as to the whole matter will be welcome and a great assistance."

Here is another letter to the same person, and on the same subject:

"PRINCETON, January 8th, 1839.
"SIR:
"You will consider this letter as addressed to you in your official capacity, as *Chargé d'affaires* at Philadelphia, and as such give answers to the following queries: 1. Is there any present demand for a popular book on Isaiah? 2. Is Barnes's book forthcoming? 3. Ought the text to accompany the notes in such a book; and if so, ought it to be given verse by verse, or in slabs, *à la* Hodge, or at the top of the page *à la* Barnes and Bush? 4. Ought practical remarks to be incorporated with the explanations, or collected at the end of chapters *à la* Hodge on Romans? 5. Should any Hebrew or other foreign words be introduced into the text? 5½. Is duodecimo the best form for the book in question? 6. Should it be printed in Philadelphia, Princeton, or Boston? 7. What publisher would undertake it on reasonable terms? A speedy answer is requested. I am, sir, with sentiments, &c. &c.
"Your most humble, &c. &c.
"J. A. ALEXANDER."

Here is still another of these early disclosures of his purpose:

To the same.

"PRINCETON, Jan. 14, 1839.

"MY DEAR SIR:

"The friendly interest you have taken in my project induces me to lay the case before you still more fully. In studying Isaiah with a view to publication, I have been compelled to keep my eyes on two distinct classes of readers—those who can read the English version only, and those who can read the original along with it. In considering how I might most effectually benefit both classes, I have entertained successively a number of different plans; which, however, at the present juncture, reduce themselves to two; the alternative being this: Shall I write a popular note-book on the English version, à la Barnes, and on this foundation afterwards construct a critical commentary for the learned reader? Or shall I write a critical commentary; adapted to the wants of the Hebrew scholar, but legible and intelligible to all educated persons; leaving the expediency of subsequent abridgment for the use of Sunday-schools to be determined by the current of events? After some vacillation I have come to this conclusion; inasmuch as the production of a popular book would contribute little to the making of a learned one, whereas the latter would afford all the materials of the former; as there is little demand for anything at all on Isaiah just at present, and that which exists is chiefly among clergymen and biblical students; as the *indirect* influence of a critical work upon the unlearned public would be greater than that of a popular work on the more learned public; as those who know me would expect something critical; I am inclined to think that a book which should be critical, without being pedantic, would do me more credit and the world more good (in the end, if not immediately) than anything else I could bring before it. In this conclusion, right or wrong, I am confirmed by the deliberative judgment of my best advisers; and have now the honour to announce, that I propose to begin the loading of my great gun as soon as I can find a man to fire it off.

"This is of course a very different affair from that which I first mentioned, and which you proposed to Perkins. If you are still disposed to help me through the agonies of publication, you are fully authorized to state the case to any publisher you choose. The maximum extent of the book will be two volumes, like Stuart on Romans (say

1,200 pp. 8vo). It will have to be printed at New Haven for the sake of the unknown tongues, and very much in the style of Nordheimer's Hebrew Grammar, but on better paper.

"In addition to the reasons given over the leaf, I am more and more convinced that at least two thirds of the exposition requisite to make Isaiah intelligible, must consist of an analysis* and retranslation; both of which require space, and the latter justification too. There are numerous passages which no sagacity or strength of intellect could ever understand aright with an exclusive use of the English version."

The letter which follows, of the 24th, enters more fully into the same subject. He will not give the Hebrew text, except to avoid circumlocution. He will imitate the page of Stuart's Romans. He praises the printing of Nordheimer's books. He wishes to bring out his own work under the eye of Mr. Turner, and compliments his taste and judgment. He speaks of some picture-books and a volume of the Princeton Review which he desires bound. He begs for an American Latin-Greek grammar. He winds up with a sincere expression of thanks.

"Princeton, January 24, 1839.
"My Dear Sir:
"I have no idea of giving the Hebrew text, but merely intend to insert the Hebrew word, which is the subject of remark, where it is necessary in order to avoid awkward circumlocution. E. g. in commenting on chapter vii. 14, I should introduce the word עַלְמָה instead of saying 'the word translated virgin.'' It is impossible to say with certainty how much Hebrew there would be; but I think half a dozen words per page would be a large average. As to style, Stuart's Romans might be taken as a sample; especially those pages on which Hebrew occurs. I have insuperable objections, however, to its being printed there. Besides, Andover is no longer preëminent in that way. Nordheimer's books, and especially his Chrestomathy, are the best specimens of Hebrew printing in America. As to Zeever's type, it looks well *en masse*, but would not match with Roman type of the proper size; and his own book is, in some parts at least, incorrect. What I should de-

---

* This was a favourite but singular opinion of his as to the sacred books in general.

cidedly prefer would be to print it in New-York; under the eye of Nordheimer and Turner; the latter of whom has more typographical taste and judgment than any man in this country, out of Boston. I have written to them to know whether, in their opinion, the book could be well executed in New-York. This will cause some delay. As to terms, I do not mean to sell the copyright, but the edition. Further than this I can as yet say nothing.

"The picture-books are intended for a parlour table, and may be bound καλῶς κἀγαθῶς at your discretion; the 'Princeton Review,' &c. half bound in calf, with comely backs, also at your discretion.

"I sent you a note by Mr. Murray, bespeaking your kind offices in getting me two copies of the same edition of any Latin-Greek grammar ever published in America. I have heard of several, but no two alike. If you should light upon such articles, you will much oblige me by impressing Mr. Baird at the earliest opportunity.

"With many thanks for your assistance,
"Yours very truly,
"Jos. Addison Alexander."

The Rev. Asahel Nettleton, I find, was in Princeton at this time; having previously visited Elizabethtown. He was a great friend of Mr. James Alexander, who was always powerfully struck with his shrewd and solemn genius, his peculiarity, and his piety. His criticisms on certain passages of Scripture were eminently profound and pungent; and his grave, colloquial eloquence was based on the most sagacious experience and common sense. One evening, he preached to a crowded house upon the text: "In that day I will pour on the house of David," &c. It was a sermon of rare excellence and force, and singularly Scriptural. The day had invited to outof-door recreation. Grass was coming up in tufts along the unfrequented paths. The robin and the blue-bird were hailed as glad messengers. The conversation of the brothers ran much upon the use of the press. At one time, "Addison" quotes his father, as strongly and repeatedly giving it as his judgment, that "no one ought needlessly to write very much *below* his own abilities." This the younger brother seems to have urged as an argument with the elder why he should try his hand upon a higher class of books than he had yet essayed.

The view presented made a deep impression on him; but he never did himself anything like full justice even in his best books. It required the revelations of his posthumous correspondence to acquaint the world with the fact of his extensive learning in nearly every department of ancient and modern belles lettres, and his affection for the severer sciences. Much yet remains untold; but his copious ephemerides and journals attest his extraordinary industry and high attainments in various fields hardly touched upon in his familiar letters. Above all they show with what fluency and almost classic beauty he could write in Latin, and how easily his thoughts flowed into voluble French.

Sunday night, Sept. 29, the Princeton congregation had the satisfaction of listening to Mr. Alexander; a privilege which they always prized. He was now in the flood-tide of animal health; and he had only to leave the chapel and the audience of students, to ensure an overcrowded house. He loved a large promiscuous assembly; where he had a wide field of human experience to appeal to, and where he met with the minimum of local peculiarity; but even in a village he exerted great power over masses of men and women. He spoke best, undoubtedly, before a body of educated hearers; where, however, there was no predominance of any one element, such as preachers or theological classes.

There is a throng of testimonies as to Mr. Alexander's appearance and traits of mind and character in those days. I am glad to be able to present here the recollections of the Rev. T. V. Moore, D.D. of Richmond, Va. his pupil and friend:

"I entered Princeton Seminary in the fall of 1839, when the faculty consisted of Drs. A. Alexander, Miller, Hodge, and J. A. Alexander. My first sight of the latter was in the oratory, where the four professors were seated in a row; and having never seen any of them before, I studied their faces with curious interest. The head and face of Professor Addison Alexander struck me as very much like Napoleon's in some respects—in its massive breadth, in a suggestion of prodigious strength in reserve, and a certain indication of fiery energy ready to blaze out at a moment's notice. He was then very recluse in his habits and reserved in his manners; and was regarded by the students generally as a prodigy of learning, and possessing a power of sarcasm that it was very dangerous to provoke: and hence was held in more admiration and fear than love. It was with these feelings that I looked upon his face, and perhaps they gave it that Napoleonic impression which it had in my eyes, as I am not aware that any one else was struck with the likeness.* My first relations to him as a pupil, were in Hebrew; and as time wore on, I was brought into closer personal relations to him: and although I never could wholly divest myself of a certain fear in my intercourse with him, I found him much more accessible and kind than I expected.

"As a teacher he was remarkable for his minute accuracy and thoroughness. He never was satisfied with a recitation that did not go to the bottom of the matter in question; and although he sometimes flashed out into something like impatience, yet it was always when it seemed to him that the student was wilfully negligent. He was often wonderfully patient with mere dulness, but whenever anything like laziness was exhibited, and especially when self-conceit cropped out, they were sure to elicit a flash of sarcasm that was not soon forgotten. His power of repartee was so wonderful that every student stood in awe of it, and many a good Hebraist owes more to his dread of it than he is aware.

"On one occasion, after a very lame recitation in Genesis, which tried his patience no little, he abruptly brought it to a close, and announced that he would give a lesson for the next day adapted to the capacities of the class, and they would therefore take the *next verse!* The usual lesson being from twelve to twenty verses, the rebuke was keenly felt, and he had no more such recitations. Sometimes he used his satire severely, though I do not think unjustly. On one occasion a young gentleman gave a discourse in the oratory on the destruction of Sodom, that was very pretentious; and Dr. A. being in the chair, thought it needful to perforate his mental cuticle somewhat, and remarked when it came his turn to criticise, that Mr. D.'s discourse consisted of two parts; that which everybody knew, and that which nobody knew; and that he did not think that under either head Mr. D. had added to the stock of our knowledge."

The remarks of so good a judge, as to the effects produced

---

* The likeness was remarked by many others.

by his preaching at this time, will be accepted as evidence of positions I have ventured to take on other authority:

"His powers as a preacher were then in full development, and many of the striking sermons published in the volumes issued since his death were prepared and preached then, besides others which I wish could also be put in print. He had a wondrous fascination to me as a preacher at that time, and had a nameless power of delivery which he lost in later years, as I knew from hearing the same sermon in my own church which I heard in the Seminary (preached at my request), and yet with a diminution in the impressive power which I could not refer entirely to any change in myself. The impression one felt as soon as he commenced the exercises was that of immense mental power coupled with an intense emotive nature, which grasped you as if with the hand of a giant, and would not allow you to escape. He usually laid the Bible aside from the cushion, laid his manuscript on the cushion, and read with but little motion of any kind, or even raising his eyes from the paper. And yet in spite of these disadvantages he seemed to rivet the attention of the audience by a spell which only broke when he ceased to speak, and the long pent-up feeling gave way in the rustling noise of a crowd seeking relief from long and breathless stillness by changing their position. There was a strange charm in his voice then, a wild, wailing melody when he touched on the more solemn thoughts that he marshalled with such matchless elegance which had an Eolian sweetness, and which I can feel thrilling in my memory now after an interval of nearly thirty years. And there were times when he would bring out suddenly some of those grand or terrible conceptions which are scattered through his sermons, with an effect on my mind precisely like a flash of lightning. I felt actually blinded for an instant by the blaze, and would look unconsciously around to see where the lightning had struck. I have never had any speaker to produce these stunning, dizzy, and burning impressions on me as did Dr. A. at that time. It always has seemed to me that he had then a concentrated energy of emotive power which he gradually lost; and which was expended in those electric discharges from the pulpit, such as I never felt from any other man, and did not feel from him nearer the close of his life. I know a part of this was owing to the fresh enthusiasm of my own nature, but I also think that another and larger part of it was owing to the same fact in his nature. He was then in the peerless maturity of his powers; with all the burning energy of youth, and all the ripe development of later years."

www.ingramcontent.com/pod-product-compliance
Lightning Source LLC
Chambersburg PA
CBHW071620230426
43669CB00012B/2014